The Rise and Fall
of the
Kansas City Prophets

The Rise and Fall
of the
Kansas City Prophets

SAM STORMS

▲ CASCADE *Books* • Eugene, Oregon

THE RISE AND FALL OF THE KANSAS CITY PROPHETS

Copyright © 2026 Sam Storms. All rights reserved. Except for brief quotations in critical publications or reviews, no part of this book may be reproduced in any manner without prior written permission from the publisher. Write: Permissions, Wipf and Stock Publishers, 199 W. 8th Ave., Suite 3, Eugene, OR 97401.

Cascade Books
An Imprint of Wipf and Stock Publishers
199 W. 8th Ave., Suite 3
Eugene, OR 97401

www.wipfandstock.com

PAPERBACK ISBN: 979-8-3852-5859-8
HARDCOVER ISBN: 979-8-3852-5860-4
EBOOK ISBN: 979-8-3852-5861-1

Cataloguing-in-Publication data:

Names: Storms, Sam [author].

Title: The rise and fall of the Kansas City Prophets / by Sam Storms.

Description: Eugene, OR: Cascade Books, 2026 | Includes bibliographical references.

Identifiers: ISBN 979-8-3852-5859-8 (paperback) | ISBN 979-8-3852-5860-4 (hardcover) | ISBN 979-8-3852-5861-1 (ebook)

Subjects: LCSH: Prophets—Missouri—Kansas City. | Prophecy—Christianity. | Kansas City (Mo.)—Religious life and customs. | Bible—Prophesies. | Pentecostal churches—United States—History. | Toronto blessing.

Classification: BR115.8 S767 2026 (paperback) | BR115.8 (ebook)

VERSION NUMBER 012826

Unless otherwise indicated, all Scripture quotations are from The ESV® Bible (The Holy Bible, English Standard Version®), © 2001 by Crossway, a publishing ministry of Good News Publishers. Used by permission. All rights reserved.

Contents

Introduction: A Disorienting Cacophony of Emotions | 1

CHAPTER ONE
My Personal Journey with Mike Bickle | 19

CHAPTER TWO
Who Were the Kansas City Prophets? | 39

CHAPTER THREE
Who Is Mike Bickle? | 52

CHAPTER FOUR
Who Is Bob Jones? | 80

CHAPTER FIVE
Who Is Paul Cain? | 101

CHAPTER SIX
The Solemn Assembly and Signs in the Heavens | 131

CHAPTER SEVEN
The Blueprints and the Black Horse | 144

CHAPTER EIGHT
The New Wine of the Spirit and the Toronto Blessing | 160

CHAPTER NINE
A Third-Heaven Experience (?) and Controversy over Restoration of the Apostolic | 180

CHAPTER TEN
The Promise of Healing | 196

CHAPTER ELEVEN
"Noel Is Coming!" | 207

CHAPTER TWELVE
The Search for a Home | 216

CHAPTER THIRTEEN
The Great Prophetic Controversy | 227

Conclusion | 252

APPENDIX A
The Letter from Metro Vineyard Fellowship to the Executive Council of the AVC: July 4, 1996 | 257

APPENDIX B
The Grooming and Sexual Abuse of a Fourteen-Year-Old Girl | 281

APPENDIX C
William Branham and the Latter Rain of the Holy Spirit | 296

Bibliography | 299

Introduction
A Disorienting Cacophony of Emotions

THE TAINTED LEGACY OF the Kansas City prophets, combined with the implosion of the International House of Prayer, Kansas City (hereafter IHOPKC) and the sexual scandal in Mike Bickle's life, have together made for an explosive array of emotions in my own life. As I continue to process the reality of what happened, I struggle to identify which of many emotions is the most prominent and impactful.

My initial response upon hearing of Bickle's past life was one of utter disbelief. Experts often refer to this as cognitive dissonance. This has been defined in various ways, but in my case, it is the deeply disturbing phenomenon of holding two mutually exclusive beliefs, two contrary perspectives, neither of which is easily dismissed. On the one hand, few people have had so great a positive influence on me as Mike Bickle. On the other hand, there is no denying the fact that he is also a sexually broken man who abused multiple women, at least one of whom was fourteen years old at the time. To this day I find it virtually impossible to reconcile these two versions of Bickle. I suspect I never will.

Quickly on the heels of my cognitive dissonance came waves of overwhelming grief and sadness. Anyone reading this who has watched a former close friend and ministry companion be revealed as a fraud knows of what I speak. My heart was (and is) broken. As horrific as Bickle's sins have been (and perhaps still are), I struggle not to think of him with affection. I suspect that as time passes this will fade, and rightly so.

My grief soon turned to intense anger. As I contemplated the impact of his sin on the tens of thousands of young people whom he influenced over the years, my anger slowly became righteous rage. It is almost impossible to bear thinking of how many individuals have walked away from their faith because of Bickle's betrayal. And to think that, at least at the time of the writing and publication of this book, he has said nothing to them in terms of apology or repentance or sadness for having contributed to their spiritual deconstruction only casts gasoline on the burning fire in my soul.

And then there is profound embarrassment. As Bickle's most ardent defender over the past thirty-five years, my own lack of discernment weighs heavily on my heart. I have no explanation for why I (and so many others) failed to see beyond the surface spirituality of his life. Perhaps all of us were simply so captivated by his charisma and the aura of power that surrounded him that we were blind to what anyone else might more readily have seen. My failure to discern Bickle's true character will undoubtedly haunt me for the remainder of my life.

I suppose I should add one more painful emotion with which I grapple each day. It is fear. My fear is that the man I once thought I knew and whose friendship and influence I so greatly enjoyed may not be a born-again Christian after all. Many are quick to pull the trigger in denouncing Bickle as a wolf in sheep's clothing, a false prophet who never knew anything of the saving grace of Jesus Christ. That is a very real possibility. But I am ever so reluctant to reach that conclusion until Bickle openly denies the faith. Some may insist that his sinful lifestyle and refusal to repent betray any claim he might make to genuine saving faith. And they may well be right. But I choose to leave that in the hands of the Lord as I continue to pray for Bickle's complete, sincere, heartfelt repentance.

A Warning and an Appeal

Before you read another word of this book, please pay heed to both a warning and an appeal. The warning is designed to guard you from building your life and ministry on the basis of the many purported supernatural and prophetic events described in what follows. My greatest fear in writing this book is that some may be so enthralled with the stories of what allegedly occurred in Kansas City that they will attempt to mimic the conduct and approach to prophetic ministry of those who have come to be known as the Kansas City prophets. The sad and tragic fact is that the four most notable prophetic figures in the early years of the church in Kansas City were all sexually broken men. There were, as you will soon discover, several individuals of unimpeachable character who served alongside these men. But I digress. The concern I have that shapes this warning is that some may be tempted to reproduce in their own local expressions of the body of Christ the structures, philosophy, values, and ministry style of the "prophets." Please resist that temptation. By all means, learn the important lessons of both their success and failures, but do so with extreme caution.

There will also be a powerful temptation to minimize the sinful behavior of the "prophets" because of the profoundly supernatural nature of their experiences (on the assumption, of course, that these experiences were genuine, something yet to be determined). On more than one occasion, during the writing of this book, some who are quite familiar with the stories I tell have said, "But Sam, surely God would not have blessed the 'prophets' with such astounding and miraculous events if their sins were as grievous as you describe. Shouldn't we extend grace to them in view of the spiritual power so evident in their lives?" The simple answer to that is, No. More on this later.

The appeal is that everyone should read this book with a heightened sense of discernment. You will be repeatedly called upon to determine for yourself the legitimacy of the claims these men make. I am the first to admit that, as a former long-term proponent of the many supernatural events in Kansas City, I have become increasingly skeptical of several (most?) of them. Where I believe the Holy Spirit was truly at work will soon be evident. But this book is neither an unqualified endorsement nor a comprehensive repudiation of the individual "prophets" or of the biblical validity of what they said and did. With that warning and request, it's time to begin.

A Crisis in Christian Leadership

It almost goes without saying that there is today an ever-increasing *crisis of integrity and morality* among Christian leaders. It grieves me to say that, especially in light of what the author of Hebrews says about the accountability of pastors and elders. We read in Hebrews 13:17 that leaders in the church of Jesus Christ "are keeping watch over your souls, as *those who will have to give an account*." I'm not exaggerating or trying to be melodramatic when I say that every time I read those words I tremble. And so should every pastor or elder or leader in the body of Christ.

And yet, in spite of that text and the warning it issues, we continue to hear on a daily basis of moral failures and ethical lapses and bullying and deception among those who have been entrusted with the souls of God's people. Let me give you an example. The following is a report from only one day, July 13, 2024, found on The Roys Report (www.julieroys.com):

- Robert Morris resigns from Gateway Church; victim says church knew details of her abuse years ago
- Longtime pastor at Chuck Swindoll's Dallas-area megachurch fired for "moral failure"

- S.C. church parts ways with pastor who had child sex criminal conviction
- Convicted sex offender serving as "prison ministries campus pastor" at embattled Gateway Church
- Gateway settled lawsuit alleging sexual harassment, hostility at church Robert Morris founded
- Filing: Request to dismiss disgraced former SBC president's defamation case due to his "now-admitted lies"
- Christian billionaire convicted of fraud, could spend decades in prison
- Pastor to "rest" as church acknowledges it knew of his child sex criminal conviction
- Christian schoolteacher caught with child sex abuse material faces prison time
- Sixth woman joins group alleging Kansas City pastor abused them

Although that was the report on only one day, it is sadly representative of what is happening everywhere in the church of Jesus Christ.

Virtually every year a poll is taken among average Americans to determine what are the *most and least trusted* professions. Among the most trusted in almost every poll taken are doctors, scientists, and teachers. Among the least trusted are journalists, advertising executives, and at the bottom of every list in every poll taken are politicians. No great surprise there.

But what I find most disconcerting is where pastors or ministers rank. It is usually somewhere in the middle, just below TV news anchors, lawyers, and the police. The Roys Report of July 13, 2024, suggests that pastors and ministers might actually be lower than that.

Most polls indicate that there are at least ten other professions that rank higher in terms of their trustworthiness than do pastors. I don't like pointing a finger at pastors and ministers as ranking very low in this sort of public opinion poll. After all, I have been in one form of Christian ministry or another for half a century. But recent scandals in the professing Christian world might actually push pastors even farther down the list in the ranking of most trusted professions, or conversely, up the list in the least trusted professions.

I rarely have a day in which I don't read or hear of yet another pastor, whether in a megachurch or a mini church, having fallen into some sin: be it sexual immorality, or child abuse, or embezzlement of church funds, or bullying, or those many instances where a pastor has lied on his resume in order to get a job, or is caught plagiarizing his sermons. Then there are those who get caught reshaping the gospel, smoothing off the rough edges of biblical truth, or in some cases outright denial of explicit biblical teaching, all to enhance their status in the eyes of people.

If you think this is an entirely recent phenomenon, you would be mistaken. It has been present in the professing church for centuries. It is simply that in our day it has reached epidemic proportions. The apostle Paul speaks of it often in his letters. For example, in 2 Corinthians 4:2, he writes: "But we have renounced disgraceful, underhanded ways. We refuse to practice cunning or to tamper with God's word, but by the open statement of the truth we would commend ourselves to everyone's conscience in the sight of God."

Later in 2 Corinthians 12 he says that "such men are false apostles, deceitful workmen, disguising themselves as apostles of Christ. And no wonder, for even Satan disguises himself as an angel of light. So it is no surprise if his servants, also, disguise themselves as servants of righteousness. Their end will correspond to their deeds" (2 Cor 11:13–15). Does it surprise you to hear that Satan himself has "servants" in local churches?

After he had concluded his ministry in Ephesus, Paul addressed the elders in that city by saying, "I know that after my departure fierce wolves will come in among you [i.e. among the elders of that church] not sparing the flock; and *from among your own selves* will arise men speaking twisted things, to draw away the disciples after them" (Acts 20:29–30; italics mine). This is one reason why Paul laid down such strict and demanding requirements for any man who would aspire to be an elder (see 1 Tim 3:1–7).

The apostle gets even more explicit in 1 Timothy 6:3–5 where he talks of those who are "puffed up with conceit and understand nothing." Such a person "has an unhealthy craving for controversy and for quarrels about words, which produce envy, dissension, slander, evil suspicions, and constant friction among people who are depraved in mind and deprived of the truth, imagining that godliness is a means of gain." Such people, says Paul, "must be silenced, since they are upsetting whole families by teaching for shameful gain what they ought not to teach" (Titus 1:11). My point, in case you haven't picked up on it, is that the corruption, immorality, and greediness of so many pastors today is hardly a new thing. It's been around from the start.

With regard, once again, to The Roys Report, for several weeks in late 2023 and into the early days of 2024, there was one headline that appeared repeatedly in a variety of forms. I don't recall ever seeing or hearing of a scandal that received as much attention and notoriety as did the events relating to Mike Bickle and IHOPKC. To prove that this is no exaggeration, here is a list of stories that appeared at www.julieroys.com, dating from October of 2023 through April of 2025.

- "International House of Prayer Founder Mike Bickle Accused of Clergy Sexual Abuse 'Spanning Several Decades,'" by Julie Roys. October 28, 2023, 6:47 p.m.
- "International House of Prayer Leaders Admit Allegations Against Mike Bickle Include 'Sexual Immorality,'" by Julie Roys. October 29, 2023, 6:45 p.m.
- "International House of Prayer Announces Independent Investigation, but Victims & Advocates Remain Wary," by Rebecca Hopkins. November 6, 2023, 8:10 p.m.
- "International House of Prayer Hires New, Unnamed Law Firm to Investigate Alleged Abuse," by Julie Roys. November 13, 2023, 2:30 p.m.
- "IHOPKC Report Discounts Mike Bickle Abuse Allegations; Whistleblower Fires Back," by Julie Roys. November 16, 2023, 6:40 p.m.
- "Report: IHOPKC Hired Man Who Admitted 'Inappropriate Touch' of 16-Year-Old; Fails to 'Prioritize the Wounded,'" by Rebecca Hopkins. November 21, 2023, 12:50 p.m.
- "Former International House of Prayer Staff Lead Silent Protest to Highlight Abuse Allegations," by Rebecca Hopkins. November 29, 2023, 11:00 a.m.
- "EXCLUSIVE: Woman Says IHOPKC Founder Mike Bickle Used Prophecy to Sexually Abuse Her," by Rebecca Hopkins. November 30, 2023, 7:45 p.m.
- "IHOPKC Founder Mike Bickle Confessed to 'Bad Judgments and Bad Mistakes' with 'Jane Doe,' Ministry Leader Says," by Julie Roys. December 7, 2023, 8:56 p.m.
- "International House of Prayer Founder Mike Bickle Confesses to 'Inappropriate Behavior' 20 Years Ago," By Julie Roys. December 12, 2023, 11:10 a.m.
- "Main Alleged Victim of Mike Bickle Won't Participate in IHOPKC's Investigation," by Julie Roys. December 12, 2023, 6:30 p.m.
- "Mike Bickle Refused to Meet with Francis Chan to Discuss Allegations of Sexual Abuse," by Julie Roys. December 18, 2023, 5:55 p.m.
- "IHOPKC Disputes Allegation Its Director Covered Up Rape," by Rebecca Hopkins. December 21, 2023, 5:30 p.m.
- "IHOPKC Separates from Mike Bickle Due to 'Level of Inappropriate Behavior,'" by Julie Roys. December 22, 2023, 10:23 p.m.

Introduction

- "Executive Leader of IHOPKC Resigns in Wake of Mike Bickle Scandal," by Rebecca Hopkins. January 5, 2024, 11:30 a.m.
- "IHOPKC Admits 'Likely' Past Mishandling of Misconduct Reports, Asks for Community Buy-In," by Rebecca Hopkins. January 15, 2024, 6:54 p.m.
- "IHOPKC Bans 'Prophet' with Ties to Mike Bickle Due to Sexual Misconduct Allegations," by Rebecca Hopkins. January 18, 2024, 6:35 p.m.
- "Who Abused Whom?—Allegations Go Both Ways in Ongoing Sex Abuse Scandal at IHOPKC," by Julie Roys. January 24, 2024, 7:05 p.m.
- "Advocate Group: IHOPKC Founder Mike Bickle Covered Up Son's Affair, Threatened Whistleblower," by Rebecca Hopkins. January 24, 2024, 8:54 p.m.
- "Dr. Michael Brown Calls for 'New Direction' to Resolve IHOPKC Sex Abuse Scandal, Following 'Impasse,'" by Julie Roys. January 25, 2024, 4:22 p.m.
- "Charisma CEO Calls Exposure of Mike Bickle's Alleged Sex Abuse a 'Spiritual Attack,'" by Julie Roys. January 27, 2024, 10:22 a.m.
- "Report: Mike Bickle Had 'Inappropriate' Sexual Contact with 2nd 'Jane Doe,' Likely Abused Power," by Julie Roys. February 1, 2024, 12:46 p.m.
- "Woman Claims Mike Bickle Sexually Abused Her When She Was 14," by Julie Roys. February 8, 2024, 11:50 a.m.
- "Opinion: Mirror of Misconduct: How IHOPKC Crisis Manager Embodied Image He Was Hired to Fix," by Stephen Deere. February 8, 2024, 7:07 p.m.
- "EXCLUSIVE: 3rd Woman Says Mike Bickle Groomed and Sexually Abused Her, Beginning at Age 15," by Rebecca Hopkins. February 10, 2024, 8:25 a.m.
- "EXCLUSIVE: Open Letter to Mike Bickle from Alleged Victim, Tammy Woods," by Julie Roys. February 15, 2024, 6:42 p.m.
- "Analysis: New Reporting System Challenges IHOPKC's Culture of Silence," by Stephen Deere. February 19, 2024, 2:15 p.m.
- "Mike Bickle Contacted Accuser for Advice About Video Defending Himself and 'Prophetic History,'" by Rebecca Hopkins. February 21, 2024, 3:20 p.m.

- "Prominent Worship Leaders Kevin Prosch and Misty Edwards Confessed a Years-Long Affair, Sources Say," by Julie Roys. March 6, 2024, 7:54 p.m.
- "Charismatic Christian Leaders Declare Mike Bickle 'Unfit' and 'Disqualified' from Ministry," by Julie Roys. March 7, 2024, 5:45 p.m.
- "Opinion: Jack Deere Reevaluates Legacy of Mike Bickle & KC Prophets, Calls for Investigation," by Jack Deere. March 11, 2024, 2:50 p.m.
- "Opinion: Evangelical Leaders Should Criminalize Adult Clergy Sex Abuse, Not 'Restore' Offenders," by Julie Roys. March 18, 2024, 6:20 p.m.
- "Embattled IHOPKC to Close, Start New Organization to Limit Liability," by Rebecca Hopkins. April 16, 2024, 8:15 a.m.
- "Embattled IHOPKC Still Asking for Donations and Denies Plans to Close," by Rebecca Hopkins. April 18, 2024, 7:30 a.m.
- "Kansas City Ministry with Ties to Mike Bickle Celebrates 25th Anniversary of IHOPKC, Despite Sex Abuse Scandal," by Rebecca Hopkins. May 8, 2024, 7:45 p.m.
- "Investigative Report Debunks Mike Bickle's Often-Told '4:18 Prophecy' as False," by Josh Shepherd. May 16, 2024, 4:45 p.m.
- "IHOPKC's Forerunner Church Officially Closes: 'Sorry for the Pain,'" by Rebecca Hopkins. May 20, 2024, 4:45 p.m.
- "Former International House of Prayer Leaders Incorporate 'Sanctuary Church,'" by Julie Roys. July 2, 2024, 12:31 p.m.
- "IHOPKC Cancels Plan for New Church, but Says Prayer Room Will Continue," by Rebecca Hopkins. July 24, 2024.
- "Former IHOPKC Leader Launches, Raises Funds for New Kid Ministry," by Rebecca Hopkins. August 1, 2024.
- "IHOPKC Founder Mike Bickle Sexually Abused 17 Women, Investigation Finds," by Rebecca Hopkins. February 3, 2025.
- "Mike Bickle Groomed Me So He Could Abuse My Friends." April 2, 2025. Podcast at www.julieroys.com.

And this doesn't even take into account the reports in local newspapers or the thousands of podcasts and blog articles that focused on this crisis. The foregoing list may lead you to think that this book is about the International House of Prayer. It isn't. But had this crisis in Kansas City not occurred, I seriously doubt if I would have felt compelled to write about the

Introduction

rise and fall of the Kansas City prophets. The so-called "prophetic history" of Kansas City has for years served as the foundation for the prayer movement led by Mike Bickle. The events surrounding IHOPKC and the stories of sexual misconduct, abuse, and deception have led many to look upon the oft-told prophetic history with suspicious eyes. I include myself among them. Perhaps one day someone else will write the story of IHOPKC's implosion, but my concern is with the many alleged prophetic and supernatural events, dating from 1982 to 2000, that ultimately gave rise to the birth of the prayer movement in Kansas City. You will read more about the connection between the events of 1982 to 2000 and those of 2000 to 2024 in the pages to come.

Revelation or Ruse? And How Might We Know?

I fully expect that this book will be frustrating to many readers. That's not a very positive note on which to begin, but the frustration is due to the nature of our subject matter. A good many of my close friends who were to one degree or another connected with Mike Bickle, either because of their participation in IHOPKC or their presence at the church that Bickle led for eighteen years, are expecting something that I likely will not be able to provide.

I've spoken with quite a few who, because of Bickle's sexual misconduct and duplicity, have lost all confidence in the integrity of the Kansas City prophets. They simply cannot bring themselves to believe that someone who has been exposed as a liar and a sexual predator could possibly be telling the truth about the many alleged supernatural events that took place in Kansas City. Some have gone so far as to question the legitimacy of Bickle's salvation altogether. Or, if they're not rejecting everything as a ruse, they are so highly suspicious of the intent of people like Mike Bickle, Bob Jones, and Paul Cain that they think the so-called prophetic history in Kansas City should, at minimum, be kept at arm's length. The most they are prepared to concede is that certain prophetic events that have been verified by empirical observation, multiple eyewitnesses, and scientific analysis should be acknowledged as having actually occurred. But the vast majority of the claims of those three men (and a few additional individuals that we'll meet later on) should be rejected. Their testimony simply cannot be trusted.

That position is entirely within the range of reason, and I do not dismiss it out of hand. What makes it even more difficult for certain people to grant the prophets any wiggle room at all is that they are often the very ones who suffered under Bickle's leadership. To admit even a modicum of legitimacy to the stories about which you are to read is extremely, and understandably, painful to them. Added to this is the undeniable fact that thousands of people, mostly between the ages of eighteen and thirty, who were once energetic participants and staff members at IHOPKC are now disillusioned not merely about the authenticity of a particular spiritual gift but about Christianity as a whole. Painful stories of their deconstruction of faith, together with the bitterness of having been deceived by someone they loved and trusted, are increasing by the day.

Of course, there is another reaction to all that has happened with Bickle, Jones, and Cain. There are numerous folk who were greatly blessed by their ministries. These are men and women who perhaps knew the prophets quite well and have walked with them for many years. What they believe were undeniable expressions of divine revelation and supernatural activity make it almost impossible for them to admit that some, if not all of it, might have been fraudulent. They remain loyal to Bickle and the vision that gave birth to the 24–7 prayer movement. Or perhaps they were longtime members of Bickle's church from day one up to the time when he stepped aside to launch the International House of Prayer.

Recently I had lunch with a lady and her husband who was raised and educated as a confirmed cessationist. She told me her story and the event that opened her eyes to the work of the Holy Spirit and her eventual embrace of the gift of prophecy. It was in 1997 that I organized and led a conference in Kansas City that we called "Women and the Prophetic." It was attended by close to two thousand women from all over the country. This one lady spoke of the night when she received a prophetic word at the conference, which revolutionized her life and her relationship with the Lord. She struggled to hold back tears as she spoke of it. Her entire approach to Christ and the Scriptures has never been the same since. I mention this incident because it is a necessary reminder of the thousands of people, men and women, who benefited immensely because of what God did through the ministry of then Metro Christian Fellowship and its lead pastor Mike Bickle. As heartbreaking as it is that so many today are reeling spiritually because of his failures, numerous others are forever grateful for the way God used his ministry and that of the church to transform their lives for good.

Introduction

How Do We Judge the Validity of Prophetic Utterances?

So, where does that leave us? Are the examples that I will cite at length in this book instances of divine revelation, or are they all a ruse, and how might we know? I'll be honest and say that we might never know.[1] But I do believe we need to try. If that is the case, what are the standards of judgment in discerning what is true and what is false, what is a legitimate revelation from God as over against a humanly contrived ruse? Are there, in fact, reliable criteria that will help us in making such a crucial decision? The answer is yes, at least to some degree. I should explain.

We know from what the apostle Paul wrote in 1 Corinthians 14:29 and 1 Thessalonians 5:19–22 that we have a responsibility to evaluate any and all alleged prophetic words. The language Paul uses differs depending on which English translation one prefers. But they all amount to the same thing. We must never believe every utterance that comes to us in the name of the prophetic, but instead judge them, weigh them, assess them, evaluate them, sifting the good and true from the bad and false. The options are not that we either gullibly swallow everything that comes our way or that we automatically reject every prophetic word. The only viable and biblical response is to "test everything" (1 Thess 5:21), and having done so to "hold fast what is good" (v. 21) but "abstain from every form of evil" (v. 22).

How do we do this? Many, including myself,[2] have written extensively on this issue. Briefly, we must first ask the question: Does any particular prophetic utterance serve to encourage other believers? Does it edify or build them up in their faith? Does it bring consolation to their souls? This is based on what Paul says in 1 Corinthians 14:3 about the primary purpose of prophetic ministry. However, we mustn't conclude from this one verse that this is the only purpose of prophecy in the local church. The stinging prophetic rebukes of the churches in Revelation 2–3 as well as the way in which prophecy served to expose the secret sins of an unbeliever in 1 Corinthians 14:24–25 argue that prophecy has a wide variety of functions and fruit.

A second question to ask is whether the utterance comes from a heart of love and gives expression to the prophet's affection for those to whom his/her word is intended. Paul was clear in 1 Corinthians 13 that if someone

---

1. You will note in what follows that when I describe what transpired in Kansas City, I do not use terms such as "assuredly," "certainly," or "definitely." Instead, I say "perhaps," "supposedly," "allegedly," and other such terms that reflect my doubt concerning the truth of some claims made by the prophets.

2. See my treatment of the subject in my books, *Understanding Spiritual Gifts*, 188–98; and *Beginner's Guide to Spiritual Gifts*, 135–50.

prophesies but does not love, their words are worse than useless, they are destructive. Always ask the question: Does this prophetic utterance seem to be motivated by selfishness and a grab for power and prestige on the part of the speaker, or does it come across as selfless and designed to bless and encourage the one to whom it is addressed? I should add that the way in which prophecy may expose the secret sins of an individual is itself an act of love.

A third principle in judging the legitimacy of prophetic utterances is whether the statement is consistent with what is clearly asserted in Scripture. If any alleged "word from God" runs counter to the final, all-sufficient, authoritative written "Word" of the Bible, it must be rejected. Again, citing Paul, he said quite clearly that "if anyone thinks that he is a prophet, or spiritual, he should acknowledge that the things I am writing to you are a command of the Lord" (1 Cor 14:37). That doesn't mean we are to resist prophetic ministry or ignore his earlier command to "earnestly desire" to "prophesy" (1 Cor 14:1). It simply means that no word that claims to have come from God should be tolerated if it does not comport with the inspired written Word of God. It is also important to remember that simply because a prophetic declaration is consistent with Scripture does not mean that it is necessarily from God.

A fourth rule to follow is to evaluate prophetic utterances in the light of the apostolic traditions (2 Thess 2:15) handed down by Paul. The reference to what they were "taught . . . by word of mouth" obviously alludes to the oral instruction received from Paul during his stay in Thessalonica. The "letter" he mentions is likely a reference either to 1 Thessalonians or 2 Thessalonians.

A fifth guideline relates to prophetic declarations that are predictive in nature. Does the prophecy actually come to pass? Can it be verified by multiple witnesses? If not, reject it.

Sixth, the test of community is also of critical importance. Wisdom demands that we always run the "word" by others who have discernment and experience in evaluating prophetic revelation.

Seventh, there is also the test of personal experience. When Paul was given a "word" about the danger that awaited him in Jerusalem (Acts 21:3–4 and 21:10–14), he evaluated and then responded in the light of what God had already told and shown him (20:22–23). In effect, Paul says: "Yes, we all got the same revelation and interpretation, that suffering awaits me in Jerusalem, but we differ on its application." This means there is a vast difference between prophesying falsely and being a false prophet. All of us have at one time or another—some more, some less—prophesied falsely. We have spoken words we thought were from God that, in fact, were not. But that doesn't make us false prophets. It just makes us human! False prophets

Introduction

in the New Testament were non-Christian enemies of the gospel (cf. Matt 7:15–23; 24:10–11, 24; 2 Pet 2:1–3; 1 John 4:1–6).

The eighth criterion may feel a bit too subjective, but that does not mean it isn't essential. Always ask: Does this prophetic word sound like something the God of the Bible would say or do? Is it consistent with the way I see God relating to people in Scripture? Does it correspond to the attributes of God that are clearly taught in his Word?

The ninth principle to which I would appeal is whether or not you experience an immediate check or hesitation in your heart regarding the authenticity of an utterance that purports to be from God. Although this, too, is highly subjective, it shouldn't be ignored. It doesn't stand alone, as if to say that because you "feel" either inclined or disinclined toward a prophetic utterance that this is sufficient to make a final decision. But God has granted us the gift of "common sense" and we neglect it to our peril.

Yet another, tenth, helpful criterion to aid us is if an alleged prophetic utterance concerns such matters as marriages, babies, moves, or job changes, or other intensely personal issues. It seems reasonable that if God desires to make known something of this nature to a person, he will communicate it in some manner directly to the individual him- or herself. We should also be cautious in "prophesying" public, political, and natural disasters. Personally speaking, I'm highly suspicious of prophetic predictions about who is going to win the next presidential election or when the next earthquake may strike California. It doesn't take prophetic gifting to declare that my home state of Oklahoma is going to endure a devastating tornado at some time in the future!

Eleventh, I am also disinclined to embrace a prophetic utterance if it is used to establish doctrines, practices, or ethical principles that lack explicit biblical support. The purpose of prophecy isn't to provide others with guidance on what they should wear, which movies they should or shouldn't watch, or whether they should drink alcohol in moderation. And one doesn't need prophetic revelation to know that drunkenness is forbidden to the Christian!

The twelfth and final standard of judgment is the one that is perhaps most often found in those who are skeptical of the Kansas City prophets. We should evaluate the legitimacy of any word that purports to be the fruit of a divine revelation in the light of the character and ethical track record of the person who is speaking. This is what weighs heavily on the hearts of many reading this book. They are instinctively hesitant about those men and women whose moral rectitude is in doubt. A history of proven prevarication casts a long shadow on people who later insist they've heard from God.

A Sobering Disclaimer

I want to be clear from the start that my purpose is not to pass judgment on every event or supernatural phenomenon or alleged prophetic revelation that transpired in Kansas City in the years between 1982 and 2000. On certain occasions, my own opinion will be clear. But in many cases my aim is simply to describe the prophetic activity as it was communicated by those who experienced it first-hand and then leave to you, the reader, judgment as to its validity. I realize this may be frustrating to some, as you picked up this book hoping that I would settle this debate once and for all. If that is why you purchased this volume, I apologize to you on the front end.

To put it in the simplest terms possible, *never assume that I endorse as legitimate every alleged supernatural experience that I describe*. On several occasions I will simply narrate the story without offering a critical response. You may be tempted to conclude from my silence that "Sam obviously believes in the validity of this encounter." Please do not yield to that temptation. At other times I will call into serious question whether or not the event in question ever actually occurred. My appeal to every reader is not to assume that I always endorse the legitimacy of every story I tell.

As you will soon discover, my approach is neither to endorse without qualification the many supernatural incidents asserted by the prophets nor to dismiss them entirely. My aim is to do what Paul commanded in 1 Thessalonians 5:19–22: I will embrace what I find to be true, and I will abstain and utterly reject what is bad, errant, and unbiblical in the claims that are made. I'm quite certain that many will take issue with the decisions I reach. Some will go so far as to conclude that I have glossed over Mike Bickle's sinful shortcomings in order to preserve his reputation and my former endorsement of him. Others will insist that I have been far too hard and demanding on him and that Christian grace and love call for a more delicate response. I can't please everyone. I can only be faithful to my own conclusions that I pray are based on solid biblical reasoning and consistent with how prophetic ministry should operate.

My point is that there will be times along the way when you will grow angry with me for seeming to be excessively lenient with Bickle and the other prophets. You will conclude that I've been duped by them and that I've failed to consider the scope of their sinful and duplicitous conduct. Others will bristle with indignation at what strikes them as heavy-handed, excessive, and unjustifiable criticism of men who at one time powerfully impacted their life for good and for godliness. As stated, I understand both responses, and I am resolved to endure pushback from both sides of this issue.

I hope it is clear by now that this book is not an endorsement or unqualified defense of the Kansas City prophets. Neither is it an utter and angry repudiation of them. Please do not appeal to what I write to justify holding tightly to the stories the prophets have told, as if they might serve as the foundation for your confidence in Christ and the authority of the Scriptures. It is entirely permissible to be encouraged by those events that can be empirically verified, but simply because *some* may be true does not mean that *all* of them are.

One more comment is needed before we proceed. In speaking of the "rise and fall" of the Kansas City prophets, the reader may anticipate that the story I tell is linear, moving from the rise and global notoriety of the prophets to the ultimate fall or demise of those individuals and institutions associated with them. But that is not the case. My aim is to weave into a seamless narrative both the rise and fall of these individuals. Thus, you will find in each chapter a portrayal of both the spiritual success and fame of the prophets together with the reasons why they ultimately fell. I trust this will make the entire story more intelligible. That being said, let's begin.

An Important Clarification

My purpose in this book is simply to evaluate the legitimacy of the many so-called "prophetic" stories that came out of the church in Kansas City, of which Mike Bickle was the senior pastor.

I am not a trauma-informed or trained counselor. I am not a psychologist. I am a pastor and theologian. This will largely account for why there is little to no presence in the book of correct terminology to describe the traumatic impact on Bickle's victims. The language that I use (such as "sexual relationship," "sexual misconduct," or "sexual interaction" to describe Bickle's behavior) should never be interpreted as if I'm suggesting any degree of complicity on the part of his victims. They were the innocent targets of his sexual predation. I apologize in advance if my lack of training in addressing the dynamics of sexual abuse strikes some as a diminishing of the indescribably egregious and sinful behavior of Bickle or the devastating spiritual, emotional, physical, and psychological consequences experienced by his victims.

Addendum

"My Heartfelt Apology to the Body of Christ," by Sam Storms

February 7, 2025

[I posted the following article on my blog, www.samstorms.org, on February 7, 2025. I was moved to do so after watching the interview of Deborah Perkins by Julie Roys on February 3, 2025, a podcast that you can access at www.julieroys.com. It is titled, "Mike Bickle's Primary 'Jane Doe' Comes Forward."]

Most of you are undoubtedly aware of the horrible events that have been revealed concerning the predatory sexual misconduct of Mike Bickle. Numerous other sinful actions took place at the International House of Prayer in Kansas City that implicate former staff members and leaders. If you are hearing this for the first time, I encourage you to visit www.julieroys.com and read the many articles that have been posted since the Fall of 2023. You can also watch two videos where Roys interviews the first of several so-called "Jane Doe's" who were victims of Bickle. Her name is Deborah Perkins, a truly courageous and godly woman that I have known for close to thirty years.

It isn't my purpose to rehearse or describe the sordid events that took place at IHOPKC and in the many years preceding its establishment. My purpose here is to express my deeply sincere and profound apologies to those who suffered under Bickle's leadership or abuse because of my former endorsement of him.

Ever since I first met Bickle in January of 1991, through the years when I served as one of his associate pastors at the church he led, up through the present day, I have been his most vocal defender and advocate. I've written articles praising the ministry of IHOPKC and have responded to the many criticisms that were launched against Bickle. I must confess that I thought I knew the man. I regarded him as one of my closest friends. When I first heard of his indiscretions (that word is far too lenient for what he has done) on August 2, 2023, I couldn't believe what I was told. That is, until I had a long zoom call with Deborah and her husband, Murray, followed by several telephone conversations. The evidence began to mount with each passing day that the man I so passionately defended and admired was a wicked, two-faced abuser of women, most of whom were much younger than he.

Introduction

I'm heartbroken beyond words. When people ask me why I didn't discern anything during my thirty-five-year relationship with Bickle, I have no good answer. My only solace is that no one else detected anything amiss in the man. I'm not trying to excuse my blindness and lack of discernment. I simply don't know why God waited as long as he did to uncover Bickle and his sins. I am truly deserving of whatever ridicule or criticism comes my way for being blind to this man's true character. It forces me to ask, why would anyone ever trust my judgment again. I can't undo the past or gloss over my mistakes, but I can speak honestly and sincerely to many of you who are deeply wounded by my vocal support of Bickle through the years. It grieves me beyond words that some of you have walked away from the Lord and from his church because of Bickle's betrayal of all of us.

However, I also want to acknowledge the spiritual blessings and growth that many of you experienced during your time at IHOPKC and at Forerunner Church. In spite of what has been revealed of Bickle's behavior, I'm sure that there are people who look back on their time in Kansas City with fond memories and gratitude for what God did in their lives. That being said, I now proceed with the main reason why I'm writing this.

I apologize, repent, and ask forgiveness from my immediate family members (my two daughters, six grandchildren, my sister and her husband, and all their extended family) for the way I influenced them through my misguided endorsement of Mike Bickle.

I apologize, repent, and ask forgiveness from those of you who may have moved to Kansas City and joined IHOPKC on the strength of my endorsement of Bickle. Please forgive me.

I apologize, repent, and ask forgiveness from those of you who suffered under his abusive leadership because of words that I spoke in public in support of him. Please forgive me.

I apologize, repent, and ask forgiveness from anyone who was sexually victimized by Bickle, having put yourself in a position to endure such sin because you trusted my words of affirmation. Please forgive me.

I apologize, repent, and ask forgiveness from those of you who invested considerable sums of money into the "ministry" of IHOPKC and into Bickle personally, based on what you may have heard or read from me saying that he was trustworthy. Please forgive me.

I apologize, repent, and ask forgiveness from those of you who suspended your critical judgment of Bickle simply because I did. Please forgive me.

I apologize, repent, and ask forgiveness from those of you who have lost confidence in the truth of the Bible because of Bickle's sinful conduct and my failure to warn you about it. Please forgive me.

I apologize, repent, and ask forgiveness from those of you who have grown cynical or suspicious about the work of the Holy Spirit and the charismatic gifts because of your trust in my misguided belief that Bickle was a good and godly representative of what being a biblical charismatic should look like. Please forgive me.

I apologize, repent, and ask forgiveness from those of you who have walked away from your faith or from the church or are in process of deconstructing because of Bickle's transgressions, having put your confidence in him because you heard my endorsement. Please forgive me.

I apologize, repent, and ask forgiveness from those of you who suspended your pursuit of higher education or a career or even delayed getting married and having children because of the teaching of Bickle concerning the urgency to be prepared as "forerunners" of the imminent appearing of Jesus. Some of you may have embraced this approach because you knew that I had spoken highly of the "ministry" IHOPKC. Please forgive me.

I am certain that there are others to whom I owe this apology and request for forgiveness. I will continue to search my soul for insight on this, and whenever I discover other ways in which I misled you concerning Bickle and IHOPKC and caused you to suffer spiritually, emotionally, physically, financially, sexually, or theologically, I will quickly and sincerely repent and ask your forgiveness.

Until then, may God bless you and keep you and make his face to shine upon you.

CHAPTER ONE

My Personal Journey with Mike Bickle

MY WIFE AND I were in Kansas City in May of 2023 to attend the high school graduation ceremony of one of our grandsons. I didn't have much time but decided to drop by the International House of Prayer, Kansas City (hereafter cited as IHOPKC) to speak briefly with Mike Bickle.[1] Toward the close of our conversation, I suggested something to him that I had brought up on several occasions in years past. I didn't anticipate getting a different answer this time around, but such was precisely what happened.

"Mike," I said, "I think the time has come for me to write the prophetic history of Kansas City and publish it in book form." Up until that time, Mike had resisted my undertaking of this project, but on this occasion he surprised me by saying, "Yes! And you are the only one who can do it." I left our meeting energized and excited to undertake this project. Mike had his assistant send me all the material from his files and everything saved on his computer. I added this to my own collection of data and dates and launched a plan to write what I hoped would be an opportunity to clarify the events from 1982 to 2000 and to provide a defense of the work of the Spirit specifically in the context of the church in Kansas City.[2]

---

1. A recent book that dives deeply into the life, personality, and ministry of Mike Bickle is written by Bob Scott, who was an early friend and associate of Bickle in the foundational years of what was then known as Kansas City Fellowship. Scott, who was formerly married to Bickle's sister Tracey, also addresses the life and ministries of Bob Jones and Paul Cain. See Scott, *Some Said They Blundered*. Scott believes that Bickle's "personality traits suggest there are possibly three prominent things in play: Narcissism, Sociopathic tendencies, and high functioning Autism, also known as Asperger's Syndrome" (31). It should be noted that Scott is not a trained psychologist.

2. This book is almost exclusively concerned with events that transpired in the years between 1982 and 2000. The history of IHOPKC, which was founded in 1999, is yet

When I first moved to Kansas City in 1993 to join Bickle's pastoral staff, I immediately immersed myself in the videos, tapes, and a variety of other sources that spoke of the supernatural. I interviewed countless individuals who were present during the early years of the church and spent considerable time with those typically identified as the so-called Kansas City prophets. The time eventually came when I asked Bickle if I could write the story in book form. I was surprised when he said yes. The two of us sat down over the span of several days, devoting at least eight hours each day to put everything in writing. Mike would recount the events to the best of his memory, and I would type. I would frequently interrupt him and ask for clarification or elaboration on some specific event. But when we had concluded, he changed his mind and asked that I not write the book, as he believed there was much more to come in terms of supernatural activity that he wanted to include in such a volume. All of this transpired in 1997.

The numerous accounts of alleged supernatural activity sat silently on my computer for over twenty-eight years. I would occasionally revisit the stories and read them over again, sharing with others when asked as a way of encouraging us all about the marvelous things that God has done and still can do. There were numerous instances through the years when I shared these stories on platforms and in churches all across the country. Mike Bickle retold the prophetic history multiple times, beginning in 1986 and on several occasions from the inauguration of the house of prayer in 1999–2000 up to the present day. It was in 2021 that I launched a podcast through which I narrated the history of life in Kansas City in sixteen episodes. I also recorded each of these in videos with Remnant Radio. In the wake of the scandal that erupted in Kansas City in late 2023, those episodes have been removed, at my request. Only now do I feel the urgency of making available in book form what had been written over two and a half decades earlier.

It's important that those reading this book understand that I believed Mike Bickle to be an honest, godly, Bible-believing, Christ-exalting man whose love for the Lord and passion for his glory were genuine and heartfelt. I never had any reason to doubt his sincerity. He was, to all of us who thought we knew him well, a model of humility and holiness. That is what makes writing this book so indescribably painful. Like so many others, I had learned considerably from Bickle. Although he is five years younger than I am, his influence on me is impossible to calculate. He was not only one of my closest friends but a partner in ministry for several years.

---

another topic to be addressed by someone other than myself. That being said, as noted in the introduction, the scandal and eventual implosion of IHOPKC has stirred many to question either in part or whole the legitimacy of the prophetic history.

Mike and I, together with others on our staff, traveled around the country speaking at churches and conferences. We traveled to England, Scotland, Germany, and Norway, especially during our time in the Vineyard. While at home in Kansas City, I often drove Mike home at the end of each day. I say "home," although Mike and Diane have always lived in a duplex, first in the Troost area of Kansas City, then in Belton, Missouri, and now in Grandview, Missouri, a few short blocks from the International House of Prayer. His lifestyle was noticeably modest.

When I was first invited to join his pastoral staff in 1993 at what was then Metro Vineyard Fellowship, Mike couldn't answer me when I finally found the courage to ask what my salary would be. "I have no idea what I make," he said. "Diane handles our finances." He directed me to Don Steadman, the executive pastor of the church. Don explained that everyone on staff, from the youth pastor to the worship leader to Mike, all made the same base salary. It was about one half of what I was currently making as the senior pastor at my church in Ardmore, Oklahoma. Don explained that an additional amount was paid depending on the number of children in your home. I won't go into any detail at this point, other than to say that I panicked, fearful that I wouldn't be able to support my family on such a modest sum.[3] But we firmly believed that God had called us to Kansas City, so we made the adjustments to our lifestyle necessary to survive. Bickle had always contended that God instructed him to live a comparatively simple lifestyle and that if a person wished to join him in the work in Kansas City, he or she must commit to doing likewise. He never insisted that other churches follow his example. It was a personal calling and conviction that he believed was from the Lord. The purpose was to release more financial support to the poor and the missionaries around the world.

One example of Bickle's apparent naivete concerning financial matters occurred one morning as we were driving to work together. "Sam," he said. "Pull over into that gas station. I want to try something." He said that Diane had given him this card, which he proudly held up for me to see, together with a number, and that I could insert it into a machine and it would give me money. He was genuinely excited, as he had never heard of or seen a debit card or an ATM machine! I waited in the car for his return. He jumped in, gleeful, smiling from ear to ear, waving several $20 bills in the air, shouting, "Look! It worked! Money!"

I had never met anyone up to that point in time who appeared to be so indifferent toward the typical luxuries that most of us take for granted. He

---

3. I have written of the emotionally devastating impact this initially had on me in my book, *Understanding Spiritual Warfare*, 306–8.

was determined, by God's grace, to avoid even a semblance of the prosperity gospel, believing the latter to be a demonic lie that had sadly ensnared so many in the charismatic movement. At that time, Ann and I were thrilled to join him and the rest of the staff at Metro in our commitment to a lifestyle that would make available more funding for those around the world who were suffering in their service for Christ.

During my time in Kansas City there wasn't so much as a scent or hint of sexual sin in Bickle's life. I never saw him interact with another woman in what might be deemed an inappropriate manner. He was always respectful and seemed genuinely devoted to honoring Diane, his wife. There were never any rumors about Bickle, at least none that reached my ears. I was genuinely inspired by his example of single-minded commitment to purity and the centrality of Jesus Christ in all areas of his life. Quite honestly, if you had asked me then, "Who is the most godly, humble, and committed Christian you know?," I would have said, "Mike Bickle." Although many have argued that Bickle's theological orientation ought to have alerted me and others to his moral shortcomings, I must disagree. More about this later.

For six of the seven years we spent in Kansas City, my wife and I would spend two to three hours, every other week, in a small group that included Mike and Diane, as well as Michael and Terri Sullivant and Don and Julie Steadman. We all became incredibly close friends as we shared our lives, both the struggles and triumphs of our children, and countless other issues related to our common commitment to living for the glory of Jesus Christ. None of us at any time suspected that anything was amiss in Mike. His devotion to Diane seemed authentic, and his love for Christ was always evident. Or so we thought. In the wake of the recent scandal at IHOPKC, many have accused me of being naïve and undiscerning. They are, to some degree, correct in their assessment. On countless blogs and in personal conversation I've heard the same charge repeatedly leveled, "Surely you should have seen something, even a slight indication, that all was not well." Again, I suspect they are right. If there is any small consolation, it is that the Sullivants and Steadmans and every other staff member at the church, together with thousands who knew Mike well, were equally blind to what we would later discover was going on behind closed doors.

As I came to wrestle with my failure to discern anything amiss in Bickle's life, someone reminded me of the twelve apostles. Judas Iscariot lived with the eleven, and with Jesus, for at least three years. Night and day he walked with them, talked with them, and participated in numerous signs and wonders that included healing the sick, casting out demons, cleansing lepers, and raising the dead (see Matt 10:5–8). I can well imagine the late-night conversations around a fire as they processed together the events of a typical day. And yet through it all not one of them ever discerned that Judas was a thief who had planned on betraying Jesus. In the Upper Room, at the Last Supper and institution of the first Lord's Supper, Jesus said to the twelve, "Truly, truly, I say to you, one of you will betray me" (John 13:21). That no one suspected Judas is evident from their response: "The disciples looked around at one another, uncertain of whom he spoke" (John 13:22). The remaining narrative in John 13:23–30 reinforces their confusion about who Jesus had in mind. I'm not excusing my own lack of discernment by pointing a finger at the eleven. But it does keep me mindful of the fact that if someone wants to remain hidden and avoid true accountability, it is always possible. Although we don't read about it in Scripture, I can well imagine that the eleven tormented themselves for not recognizing the true character of Judas even as I have tormented myself in the wake of Bickle's disclosure. I'm not suggesting that Mike is like Judas or that his sin is anywhere near as heinous as the betrayal of Jesus perpetrated by Judas, but he was just as successful as the latter in concealing his sin from all of us.

In the wake of the scandal that erupted at IHOPKC in October of 2023, many have asked me and others why we didn't take action in the late 1990s and call Mike to account for his behavior, perhaps even imposing church discipline. This prompted me and Michael Sullivant to release a statement in early December, the text of which you can read in the Addendum at the close of this chapter.

Others have launched their attack by insisting that if our church was truly operating in the prophetic, surely God would have revealed to someone that Bickle was ethically compromised.[4] These critics insist that if the spiritual gift of prophecy were still operative, someone, somewhere along the line of the staff and congregation at the church would have known what was going on behind the scenes. This indicates a massive misconception of how the prophetic gift actually works. *No one can prophesy at will.* The revelation on which all prophetic ministry is based is not in the back pocket, so to speak, of any individual, no matter how gifted they may appear to be. If no one in the church (and especially in our small group) had divinely disclosed information about what was happening, it is solely because God chose not to reveal it to us. Prophetic ministry does not occur whenever we want it, but only when God wants it. For some reason, of which I'm largely ignorant, God chose not to reveal anything to anyone about Bickle's behavior. Any attempt to account for God's decision in this matter is pure speculation and of little help in our investigation of this issue. Having said

---

4. It is entirely possible that some in the church had suspicions, or perhaps even concrete evidence, of Bickle's misconduct. But if they did, no one ever said a word to me about it.

that, perhaps the Lord was giving Bickle an extended period of time in which to repent (see Rom 2:4). We may never know.

I remained in Kansas City until August of 2000 when Mike chose to step down as lead pastor of the church to establish the International House of Prayer, on the board of which I served as a director in its early stages. I was also a board member of Mike's ministry, Friends of the Bridegroom (commonly referred to as FOTB).[5] I had moved to Kansas City in 1993 specifically to work alongside Bickle and the prospect of remaining there in his absence had no appeal to me. It was then that I accepted the offer from Wheaton College, in Wheaton, Illinois, to join the faculty in the department of Biblical and Theological Studies. I served on the faculty at Wheaton from 2000 to 2004. When I decided I didn't want to spend my remaining years of ministry in a classroom, we moved back to Kansas City and lived there until 2008. During those four years my wife and I were often found in the prayer room at IHOP, although we never joined the staff. I spent most of my time traveling, speaking, and writing books in conjunction with my ministry, Enjoying God Ministries.[6]

My relationship with Bickle picked up where we left off in 2000 and we grew to be even closer friends and ministry companions. I can't begin to describe the many important lessons I learned from him in terms of prayer ministry and the work of the Holy Spirit. This lasted until 2008 when I accepted the call from Bridgeway Church in Oklahoma City to become their next senior pastor. My interaction with Mike diminished somewhat from 2008 to the present, although each time we traveled to Kansas City we had lunch or dinner with Mike and Diane. I knew nothing of anything happening at IHOPKC during those years that would arouse suspicion.

I was especially blessed at the time of my retirement from Bridgeway Church (August of 2022) when, much to my surprise, Mike and Diane, together with Jack and Leesa Deere, Daniel Brymer, and John Piper, all came to Oklahoma City to speak at the celebration service the church had orchestrated to honor my tenure as senior pastor of the church. Even then, I had no idea of what had transpired in previous years or what was about to be disclosed.

---

5. I resigned from both boards not long after we made the move to Wheaton College in 2000.

6. See www.samstorms.org.

A Deeply Disturbing Phone Call

Then I received a phone call on August 2, 2023. On the other end of the line was Dwayne Roberts, a man whom I had known from his days in Kansas City in the 1990s. Dwayne had been a part of IHOPKC from the beginning and was now, once again, living in Kansas City.

"Sam," his voice noticeably trembling with a sense of foreboding, "there's real trouble in the leadership at IHOPKC and I need to share something with you." He told me of a lady he referred to as "Jane Doe" and an encounter she claimed to have had with Mike in Paris in 1997. At the time, I had only vague recollection of Mike's trip to Paris and the five ladies and one man who accompanied him. Or if I knew about it back in 1997, I had long since forgotten about any of the details. Neither did I know who "Jane Doe" was, but it didn't take long for me to narrow down the possibilities. My sense was spot on, and ten days later I spent two hours on a zoom call with "Jane" and her husband. I had known her ever since she had moved to Kansas City in 1996, together with her brother and sister. She had always impressed me as a godly and sincere young lady, and the story she told me was shattering. It must have taken a considerable depth of courage for her to share with me the details of her physical interactions with Mike, not simply in Paris but in the subsequent four years up until her marriage to her husband. Of course, we now know that "Jane Doe" was Deborah Perkins, who courageously came forward to share her story.

I initially told Dwayne that there was simply no way on God's green earth that the Mike Bickle I knew could be capable of the things he described. But in speaking with Deborah (we knew her as Dee), I found no reason to doubt her story. To say that I was heartbroken is a massive understatement. My wife held out much longer. "It has to be a scam," she said. "Mike would never do any such thing." I wanted to agree with her, but the evidence began to mount beyond what Deborah shared, and I simply couldn't draw any other conclusion.[7]

The so-called Advocate Group (AG), which was supporting Deborah, was comprised of several individuals whom I had known quite well during and after my time in Kansas City.[8] I kept telling myself that these were not

---

7. The official investigation into allegations against Bickle can be read at Firefly, *Investigation of Mike Bickle*. The report concluded that Bickle had engaged in sexual misconduct with at least seventeen females.

8. Allen and Rachel Hood; Dwayne and Jennifer Roberts; Peter and Elizabeth Herder; Wes and Amanda Martin; Jono and Shari Hall; Samuel (and Maddie) Hood; John and Fran Chisholm; Dean and Jeanie Briggs. See their website, www.theadvocategroup.org.

the sort of people who would fabricate such lurid stories, especially since they had nothing to gain by them being true. They were all godly and highly respected individuals who repeatedly pleaded with me to join them in the investigation, ostensibly because I was a much closer friend to Mike than any of them. They were his spiritual sons and daughters, whereas I was his peer. I resisted. "I don't have any authority at IHOP," I protested. "This is the responsibility of the Executive Leadership Team (ELT). Let them address the issue with Mike." I was then told why the AG didn't have confidence that the ELT would act. More bad news. The now well-known story of Luke Bickle, Mike and Diane's son, as well as the presence on staff at IHOPKC of Brad Tebbutt, confirmed in their minds that little, if any, action would be taken when the ELT were made aware of Mike's misconduct.[9]

I won't go into additional detail about the troubles at IHOPKC, as the story has been repeatedly told on numerous blogsites, podcasts, and in several investigative reports. I share this information to establish a framework for why I decided to heed the call of countless individuals to tell this story. Of all those involved over the years, no one has been a more vocal advocate and defender of Mike Bickle than I have. In print, on platforms, and in numerous podcasts, I spoke of him in glowing terms, for that had been my consistent experience of the man. Mike actually wrote the foreword to one of my books and happily endorsed several others. I was now faced with the revelation that I may have been horribly deceived and lied to.

Everything came to a head in October of 2023. Deborah's husband, Murray, together with several individuals from the Advocate Group, called for a meeting with the ELT of IHOPKC and the lead pastor at Forerunner Church. A few days later, Murray met one-on-one with Bickle to confront him about what his wife had told him about the incident in Paris. Murray forwarded to me Bickle's email responses, and soon thereafter they were found circulating throughout the internet. I see no reason to cite them in detail here. Suffice it to say that they did not strike me as having been written by an innocent man.

On Friday night, October 27, 2023, representatives of the ELT addressed the staff of IHOPKC and told them that certain allegations had been brought against Bickle. They did not elaborate on the nature of these charges, an omission that greatly agitated several other leaders and staff members of the ministry, principal among whom was Dean Briggs. In view of what they regarded as evasive tactics on the part of the ELT, the AG released a statement the next day with considerably more details about Bickle's alleged

---

9. You can read about these incidents and others by going to the list of articles found in the introduction.

transgressions. Fearing that still nothing would be done, members of the AG appealed to me to drive to Kansas City to confront Mike personally. I contacted my good friend Francis Chan and encouraged him to join me in what I anticipated would be an extremely difficult encounter. Francis and his wife flew into Kansas City from San Francisco on Monday, October 30, 2023. He and I, together with most representatives of the AG, held a lengthy Zoom call on that Monday night, determined to figure out what should happen next.

I should briefly mention that during my drive to Kansas City on that Monday, Mike Bickle called me on the phone. He was agitated, to say the least. In all my years of ministry and friendship with Mike, I had never heard him speak to me in this particular tone of voice. He told me in no uncertain terms to turn around and drive back home to Oklahoma City. "What makes you think that I would meet with you," he angrily shouted. He proceeded to accuse me of conspiring with the AG to seek out alleged victims who would testify against him concerning sexual improprieties. I explained to him that I had done no such thing, that in point of fact, up until that very day, I had resisted the appeals of the AG that I get involved. Upon realizing that he had been misinformed about my alleged involvement, Mike calmed down and we soon concluded our conversation.

On Tuesday morning, October 31, 2023 (Halloween), I sent Bickle an email asking if he would meet with me and Francis. He agreed, but on one condition. He insisted that we not "interrogate" him but only allow him to share his story. I was understandably bothered by his response. To my way of thinking, an innocent man would have said, "Ask me anything. I'm an open book. I have nothing to hide." In any case, he invited us to his home at 4:00 p.m. that afternoon. Francis and I knocked on his door at the appointed time, only to be greeted by Chris Reed, formerly of Morningstar Ministries. He informed us that Mike couldn't meet with us, as he was engaged in an extremely important conversation. We didn't know who was in the house with Mike, but later learned that it was Stuart Greaves, a member of the ELT, and Eric Volz, who had been retained by IHOPKC leadership to serve as a public relations spokesman.

Some two hours later I received an email from Bickle, explaining quite briefly that he had been instructed not to speak with anyone. He then wrote, "Don't email me again." To say that I was shocked is an understatement. I honored his request for a week until I could no longer restrain myself. I wrote an intensely personal email to Mike explaining that he had one chance to restore his name and revive his public ministry.[10] He had to ascend the

---

10. You can read my email to Bickle in Addendum B at the conclusion of this chapter.

platform at Forerunner Church and at the prayer room of IHOPKC and openly, honestly, and thoroughly confess whatever sexual sins he had committed, repent for them, seek the forgiveness of his victims, and submit to whatever discipline the church leaders would then impose. I heard nothing in response, and as of the writing of this book I have had no contact with Bickle in any form.

Had no scandal erupted at IHOPKC, I seriously doubt if this book would ever have been written. But the collapse of that ministry has served to raise the question of the truthfulness and accuracy of what is commonly known in Kansas City as "the prophetic history." So, this book is about the Kansas City prophets. It isn't the book that I originally intended to write. I never dreamed that I would write about the "fall" of the Kansas City prophets. It was their "rise" that excited me. And yet now I find myself, like so many others, questioning the truth and authenticity of the many supernatural events that make up their story.

I should point out that many will consider this book as altogether unnecessary. Their belief is that the revelation of Bickle's sexual misconduct instantly and irrefutably discredits everything in the prophetic history. Some of them will be quite surprised that I have chosen to write this history, while others will undoubtedly regard it as a waste of time. In quite a few blog posts and podcasts I have heard it said over and over again that Bickle's transgressions automatically undermine every alleged prophetic event that he has communicated. If he lied to his wife, family, and ministry colleagues about his involvement with the women who have come forward, why would anyone trust anything else he has to say? It is quite inconceivable to many that God would ever supply such a man or the church he leads with genuinely supernatural stories or events that are undeniably miraculous. In short, their snap conclusion is that everything is a fabrication.

In speaking with numerous individuals who either sat under Bickle's ministry during his time as senior pastor of the church or who served with him at IHOPKC, I have heard a common refrain. The prophetic history in its entirety, they insisted, was weaponized to groom young women and to intensify the loyalty that people felt toward Bickle. Stories that ought to display the power of God were intentionally manipulated and used to expand Mike's control over his adoring followers. To this day, I find it incredibly painful even to write those words. But they may well be true. More people than I would like to count repeatedly told me that what should have been a testimony of God's love and supernatural provision was twisted to cover up sin. "He hoodwinked us," said one individual.

Trust me when I say that I completely understand that reaction. At the same time, I cannot endorse it without qualification. More investigation is needed beyond the simplistic (but possibly true) declaration that a man caught up in sexual sin would never be blessed by God to operate in truly Christ-exalting and spiritually edifying miraculous deeds and events. Why, they ask, would God choose to entrust to such an individual the precious and supernatural work of the Holy Spirit? That is a question that will appear repeatedly in the pages to come. Whether or not I have adequately answered it, or even if there is a cogent answer to what is obviously a profound mystery, is left up to each individual who chooses to wade through the stories that follow and the alleged evidence I cite in support of them.

When news of Bickle's misbehavior became public, I was inundated with snarky comments and self-righteous questions about what I *now* thought of Mike and all the things I had said about him in public. I understand why people did this. Of course, I deserved whatever criticism came my way for not having the discernment to see beyond the surface and into Bickle's true character. My only consolation, if it can be called that, is that this was the experience of countless others who like me believed a version of Mike Bickle that we now painfully realize was misguided. I don't take any pleasure in that fact, as if it might exonerate me from having misjudged the man. But the bottom line, as far as I can tell, is that no one saw or knew or heard anything in Mike that would cause us to question his Christian commitment.

This book, then, is only indirectly about Mike Bickle. It is, instead, an examination of the many *alleged* supernatural events that make up the prophetic history of Kansas City and what we might learn from them today. I say *alleged* because, to repeat a point already made, I have been asked hundreds of times if the scandal at IHOPKC undermines the totality of the prophetic history that has served as its foundation. As one person put it, should we *sift* it (differentiating between the good and the bad) or *scrap* it altogether?[11] You will shortly discover that I have chosen to sift and not to scrap. I cannot categorically dismiss things that I myself and other reputable sources have witnessed. I hope to determine in the pages that follow which events warrant our confidence and which remain suspect, if not entirely false.

My approach will be to tell the stories as told to me by Bickle and others in the church, as well as those that I was personally involved with or an eyewitness to, leaving it to you, the reader, to determine if they hold up under scrutiny. More than a few of the many supernatural encounters simply

11. Tammy Woods (about whom more later) states that the prophetic history "has been proven repeatedly to be founded upon falsehood, deception, manipulation, abuse, and exploitation. Exactly what is there to sift through for the sake of salvaging?" (Shepherd, "Investigative Report").

cannot be denied. They have been empirically verified and confirmed by people who were there and who witnessed them firsthand. But there are just as many incidents that rely almost entirely on Bickle's personal testimony (or that of Bob Jones and Paul Cain). One is left to conclude that in the case of these latter experiences the final verdict will depend on one's confidence in Bickle's integrity. As noted, until recently I had no reason to question the truthfulness of the stories he told. Has the recent scandal that has rocked IHOPKC called into question the accuracy of some, or perhaps all, of them? That is yet to be determined.

The Paradox of the Sinning Saint

One of the greatest challenges that all of us face is what I call the paradox of the sinning saint. What are we to conclude when people we've known and were persuaded were truly born again, justified-by-faith believers in Jesus, fall into sexual sin, and then refuse to publicly repent?[12] Of course, the sin may be something other than sexual in nature, but in chronicling the history of the Kansas City prophets there seems to be something of a pattern in the way these people morally deviated from the faith. In the wake of the scandal at IHOPKC, I was repeatedly asked (in person, by email, and through countless YouTube podcasts): "Sam, how could you insist these men are born again and on their way to heaven when they appear to remain unrepentant about their sexual failures?"

Let me be perfectly clear about one thing up front. I do *not* "insist" they are saved. They may not be. But it is not my prerogative to judge the state of someone's soul while they consistently affirm belief in the sinless life, substitutionary death, and bodily resurrection of Jesus. The "prophets"—to a man and woman, at least to my knowledge—never denied a single foundational truth of orthodox Christianity. Sadly, though, their ethical conduct often appears to conflict with their verbal confession. There is no shortage of those who believe they can discern the state of a person's soul and in self-righteous, condescending confidence they declare that the "prophets" and others like them are destined for eternal damnation. Again, they may be right. But there always remains the possibility that we are dealing with

---

12. As of the publication of this book, Bickle has remained silent. Numerous appeals for a public repentance have been sent to him by former friends and staff members, all to no avail. However, Bickle did release a formal apology of sorts that most, including myself, found to be entirely inadequate. It can be found at Roys, "International House of Prayer Founder."

people whose faith is sincere and saving but who, for whatever reason, have wandered from the path of Christian holiness.

At the same time, we must acknowledge that *for an individual to claim to know Christ while living in unrepentant sexual sin is profoundly unbiblical*. Their ungodly conduct may well be indicative of an unregenerate heart, all other things being equal, despite their professions of faith. Many will be frustrated to learn that my aim in this book is not to draw definitive conclusions about the salvation or damnation of any individual, be they gifted prophetically or not. Do I have suspicions about some of them? Undoubtedly so, but I will refrain from putting them in print until such time as any of them verbally and visibly abandon faith in Christ Jesus as Lord and Savior. Needless to say, at least four of the more prominent "prophets," having died, cannot be questioned about their doctrinal convictions. I have in mind Augustine Alcala, John Paul Jackson, Bob Jones, and Paul Cain.[13]

All that being said, we are still faced with a troubling conundrum. If the "prophets" (e.g., Bob Jones, Augustine Alcala, Paul Cain, Mike Bickle) are saved, how could they commit such heinous acts of sexual misconduct? If the "prophets" are not saved, how could they be the recipients of God's supernatural power as seen in spiritual gifts, angelic visitations, revelatory dreams, stunningly accurate words of knowledge, and other signs and wonders?

When I am asked these questions, I instinctively point people to the first-century church in Corinth. I must say that the Corinthians have all too often been given a bad rap. We've beaten up on them and cited their misconduct every time something similar takes place in people today whom we know. Paul's description of them is quite laudatory, to say the least:

> I give thanks to my God always for you because of the grace of God that was given you in Christ Jesus, that *in every way you were enriched in him in all speech and knowledge*—even as the testimony about Christ was confirmed among you—so that *you are not lacking in any gift*, as you wait for the revealing of our Lord Jesus Christ. (1 Cor 1:4–7; italics mine)

The italicized words are to be noted. Here was a church given to divisive factions and spiritual cliques (1 Cor 1:10–17), who had barely progressed beyond infancy in Christ (1 Cor 3:1). They had permitted "jealousy and strife" to flourish among them (1 Cor 3:3). Some were given to an over-realized eschatology (1 Cor 4:8), and the church in that ancient city had tolerated

---

13. By including John Paul Jackson alongside Cain, Alcala, and Jones, I'm not suggesting that he too was guilty of sexual sin. I am confident that John Paul was a good and godly man who remained faithful to his wife until the day he died.

"sexual immorality" among its members "of a kind that is not tolerated even among pagans" (1 Cor 5:1). They apparently had turned a blind eye, if not an approving nod, to a man who was sleeping with his stepmother (1 Cor 5:2).

The deeper we dive into Paul's first epistle to the Corinthians we discover that circumstances don't improve much. Fellow church members were taking their grievances to pagan courts to be judged by unbelievers (1 Cor 6:1–8). Some were depriving their spouse of sexual intimacy (1 Cor 7:1–5) while others were spending time in pagan temples, ostensibly celebrating a meal alongside overt unbelievers (1 Cor 8:1–13; 10:14–22). The conduct of many at the Lord's Supper was especially grievous, as Paul declared that their selfish, self-indulgent behavior had resulted in divine discipline, even premature death (1 Cor 11:17–32). And we can hardly overlook the way they had abused spiritual gifts, elevating some supernatural expressions above others and arrogantly thinking that tongues and prophecy were markers of a special class of believers to the exclusion of those whose giftings were less sensational (1 Cor 12–14). It staggers one's imagination to think that there may well have been a few who denied, or at least questioned, the bodily resurrection of Jesus (1 Cor 15:12–19).

And *these* are the very people whom Paul commends and comments that they are not lacking in any spiritual gift! Perhaps some of them were never saved in the first place, but Paul's effusive praise of them in 1:4–7 suggests that the majority were truly born again. I can imagine that others in the first century were asking Paul and Peter and John the same question I asked earlier: How can people who conduct themselves in this ungodly manner be saved? Let there be no mistake about Paul's theology in this regard. He pulled no spiritual punches in declaring that "the unrighteous will not inherit the kingdom of God" (1 Cor 6:9). This would include "the sexually immoral," "idolaters," "adulterers," practicing homosexuals, "thieves," "the greedy," "drunkards," "revilers," and "swindlers" (1 Cor 6:9–10). Paul's confidence is buoyed when he is reminded that "such were some" of the Corinthians who had since been "washed" and "sanctified" and "justified in the name of the Lord Jesus Christ" (1 Cor 6:11).

I must confess that prior to the exposure of sexual misconduct at IHOPKC I believed without question in the truth of what Bickle claimed. At the time, I had no reason to doubt the testimonies shared with me. Some of the stories were entirely dependent on Bickle's personal recollection while others involved numerous individuals who confirmed the reality of what happened. In addition, my wife and I were the recipients of several prophetic words from these men, words that proved to be profoundly accurate and a blessing to our walk with Christ.

This latter point raises another interesting question. Could it be that other prophetically gifted men and women in the Kansas City church who avoided scandalous sin and walked and ministered in humility and holiness of life were instruments of the Holy Spirit in the accurate and effective exercise of supernatural gifts? In other words, if we set aside Bickle, Alcala, Cain, and Jones and look only to others whose reputations are generally spotless (such as John Paul Jackson, Michael Sullivant, Noel Alexander, and James Goll), could the activities of these lesser known folk have been authentically supernatural and Christ-exalting? My answer is yes.

My aim in this book will be to rehearse each episode once again to discern, if possible, which stories are rooted in reality and empirical confirmation, and which ones are entirely dependent on Bickle's credibility as a professing Christian man. Where such a distinction cannot be made, I will leave it to you, the reader, to decide for yourself whether these remarkable events actually occurred or were, perhaps, fabricated to enhance the reputation of Bickle and his ministry.

I trust that by now you can see the dilemma I face. Does the moral failure of Mike Bickle cast some measure of doubt on the integrity of the numerous alleged prophetic scenarios that he has shared and that I will document in this book? Does his duplicity cast shade on the trustworthiness of his testimony? The reader will soon see where I land on the issue. I can tell you in advance that my evaluation will be something of a mixture, neither endorsing the credibility of all Bickle's claims nor rejecting them as the product of a fanciful imagination or, worse still, the deliberate, manipulative lies of a hypocrite. We must also reckon with the fact that even those events which rely almost entirely on Bickle's testimony may still be true, notwithstanding the shadow cast on his character by recent events in his life and at IHOPKC.[14]

Others will undoubtedly conclude that I have a vested interest in defending the truth of these events, hoping that I might in this way preserve my own reputation. I understand why some may think in this fashion. My only response is to be as candid and forthright in my evaluation as I possibly can and trust the Lord to bring to light any way in which I might still be deceived by a man who, sadly, did not turn out to be the person I thought he was.

---

14. Bob Scott, Bickle's former brother-in-law, who helped him plant the church in Kansas City, draws this conclusion: "After having lived it and watched it unfold for nearly 45 years, I believe that while some aspects of the prophetic history are true, other aspects have been conveniently deleted, edited, and repackaged to serve a personal agenda. It's been used as a means of validation as well as a marketing tool and fundraiser" (*Some Said They Blundered*, 158).

Addendum A:

A Response to the Allegations Against Mike Bickle from Two Former Colleagues

December 18, 2023, by Sam Storms and Michael Sullivant

Dear Friends,

We write to you today with sorrowful hearts. As many of you know, we both served on the senior leadership team at Metro Christian Fellowship (MCF) alongside Mike Bickle—Michael from 1987–2000 and Sam from 1993–2000. During those years, we were in (what we felt was) close fellowship with Mike and Diane—meeting as couples multiple times every month. This camaraderie continued until such time as Mike stepped down as lead pastor at MCF to form IHOPKC as an independent ministry.

    We were unaware of Mike meeting with or traveling in the company of young women during this time. Mike was able to successfully hide from us this dimension of his life. He never came to us with a request for prayer or with some confession of weakness and an appeal to hold him accountable. If he had, we would have faithfully stepped in to help our friend in whatever way we could.

    We were made aware of the allegations of clergy sexual abuse at different times over the past several months. We have now both spoken extensively with one of the primary Jane Does and her husband and believe what she has said about the sexual nature of their interaction. In her own words, it involved everything short of sexual intercourse. There is no reason to doubt the accuracy of her testimony. Our hearts break for what she suffered and for the ongoing grief this horrific injustice has caused her and her family.

    Sam and Francis Chan attempted to visit Mike at his home on October 31 where Chris Reed turned them away at the door. He said that Mike had been instructed not to meet or speak with anyone, which Mike later confirmed in a brief email to Sam. We were subsequently informed that Mike was following the counsel of Eric Volz.

    As a matter of conscience, we write now to publicly state that we believe Jane Doe. We deeply regret not being aware of her situation at the time it occurred. We have now been made aware of additional allegations directed at Mike for behavior subsequent to his relationship with Jane Doe. These are grievous and weighty. However, it is not our intent to address the legitimacy of those charges. That is the responsibility of whatever third party is secured to conduct a thorough investigation of what may or may not have happened in the context of IHOPKC for the past twenty-three years.

It is our opinion that Mike's most recent statement, while potentially a step in the right direction, is woefully inadequate. What is most lacking in it is explicitly owning the sin he committed against Jane Doe(s), repenting, and asking for forgiveness. Regrettably, Jane Doe is nowhere mentioned in the written statement he released.

We appeal to Mike, as long-standing friends and colleagues who have loved him and Diane, to search his heart and plead with the Holy Spirit to disclose any other sins committed. We pray that by God's grace he will find the spiritual courage to confess such sins, wholeheartedly repent, face the consequences, and humbly pursue the restoration and healing of anyone he has wounded. It is our love for Mike that constrains us to write this letter and call him to more open and vulnerable official examination for his confessed duplicity and moral failures as a Christian and a ministry leader.

Our sincere and heartfelt appeal is that the ELT at IHOPKC and the Advocate Group will together pursue an acceptable independent, third-party investigation. There is little hope that the truth will come to light, leading to a resolution of this matter, until such time as everyone involved cooperates fully with the investigative body.

Mature and compassionate spiritual leadership requires that we do not hurt those entrusted to our care. Lying when confronted with the truth, creating division in the body of Christ by intentionally preaching about betrayal and false accusation after being informed that allegations were forthcoming, lawyering up, making minimal concessions in lieu of true confession, and indiscriminately managing an image of oneself is the opposite of what a spiritually mature response should be to a crisis of this nature.

Christian leaders steward a holy calling and are held to a higher standard by God for living above reproach. By this, a leader embraces the risk that any undealt with and/or unconfessed sin patterns may be publicly exposed if they are disqualifying in nature and scope. Beyond this, leaders ought to welcome a lifestyle of transparency before family, friends, governing boards, and constituents. We believe Mike has had every opportunity to vulnerably share any temptations or struggles with sin with fellow leaders in order to find God's mercy and pathway to wholeness. Sadly, we believe he has not remained faithful to this commitment, but rather engaged in deceptive and manipulative actions to exploit the vulnerability of a godly young woman. As such, we are in firm agreement with Mike stepping down from Christian ministry.

The painful ripple effects of this sin have been felt far and wide. We grieve hearing the voices of hurt, angry, confused, and disillusioned current and former members of IHOPKC, and its related ministries. We urge you all to find safe people in your life to pray for you and support you as you process your experience. We pray for the peace and grace of God to be with you and upon you all.

Bearing with you in spirit,

Sam Storms
Michael Sullivant

Addendum B:

Email from Sam Storms to Mike Bickle, November 9, 2023

Dear Mike,

I know you said not to email you again regarding this matter, but I feel compelled by my conscience and my love for you and Diane. You may choose to stop reading and discard this email entirely, but I pray you will give your long-time friend a few minutes to speak his mind.

This situation has caused me more grief and pain and confusion than anything I've ever experienced. I do not exaggerate. I weep constantly. So does Ann. We both love you and Diane so very much and so greatly appreciate your ministry and that of IHOP. The last thing in the world we want to see is your name and reputation destroyed and the ministry of IHOP suffer. So please know my heart in what I'm writing.

From the beginning, I have refused to let my heart believe that you are guilty of the allegations brought against you. You have always been my spiritual hero, an example of humility and godliness beyond any other. As you know, over the years I have defended you at every turn, standing with you in the face of opposition and criticism. And I want it to stay that way.

My continual hope is that you are entirely innocent of all charges. But if you are guilty of even a small portion of what has been alleged, please hear what I have to say.

Again, while holding on to the hope that you are not guilty, let me say one thing in case you are. There is, as best I can tell, only one way to preserve your name and ministry. I know you have often said you won't defend yourself and that your reputation is of little to no concern to you. Praise God for that. But it is more than your name and reputation at stake. That of the Lord Jesus himself is on the line. I am confident that notwithstanding all that has occurred, your highest goal and value is to honor and exalt the name of Jesus. You have done this for decades and it is the reason why I've stood in your defense so faithfully.

I find it hard even to say, "if you are guilty," as the thought of that being a reality is devastating to me. But if you are, will you at least listen to and pray about the humble advice of one who loves you and honors you and is so deeply indebted to your influence?

There is one and only one way to turn this course of events into a redemptive moment that will bless not only you and Diane but the ministry of IHOP and the calling that God has on your life.

Will you consider standing before the people of IHOP and Forerunner and the world at large and humbly, honestly, and wholeheartedly confess your sin and repent of it all? Will you seek out those who you are alleged to have hurt and ask for their forgiveness? Will you then publicly state that you are willing to submit to whatever discipline the leadership of IHOP/Forerunner seek to impose?

And when I say "confess" I mean confess to 100% of what you have done. Nothing half-hearted or in part or only what you think you need to say to get by. If there is the slightest hint of insincerity this would prove to be a disaster.

I am convinced that if you would do this, on the assumption, again, that you are in fact guilty of what has been alleged, you will win over the affection and support of the people at IHOP and of the Christian world. Rarely do we see today in the church the kind of brokenness and heartfelt sorrow that I'm asking you to display. But you have the opportunity to shine a glorious redemptive light on the many truths of the gospel and the glory of God that you have stood for and preached all these many years.

I am certainly not asking you to confess and repent for sins you haven't committed. How ever many of the allegations are misguided and untrue, you have every right to deny. But if you will own your sin (like your hero David, in Psalm 51), then again, like David, your ministry and life can continue to flourish to the glory of God.

I hope you have read this far in the email. If you have, and find my counsel to be helpful, please know that I will do anything you ask of me to help you through the process. I would be happy and honored to stand beside you on the platform at Forerunner and urge everyone to hear your confession and to embrace you as a repentant brother in Christ whose primary desire is to honor and glorify Jesus.

But Mike, and this is so very hard for me to say, if you are guilty of some or all of the allegations, and you choose to deny and defend yourself, not only will you cost IHOP tens of thousands of dollars in attorney's fees, but more important still you will forever have lost the trust of so many people around the world whom you have touched and influenced for the good of the gospel.

Of course, if you are entirely innocent of all charges, then by all means stand firmly and do not capitulate to pressure, and provide whatever evidence you can of your innocence.

Well, I've gone on long enough. I know how heavily and hurtful all this must weigh on your heart and on Diane's heart. It weighs me down every second of every day. I hope at least you will receive this email and my counsel knowing that I do not write it as a sanctimonious, self-righteous man who has never sinned. My sin, like David's, is ever before me. I have failed the Lord in so many ways. I simply write as one hungry man telling another hungry man where he can find bread.

Blessings and love,

Sam

PS I know you as well as anyone and I'm aware of how you evaluate people and circumstances with unusual insight. I say that because I'm sure you will respond to this by telling me there are issues and nuances and forces at play of which I have no knowledge. And you are probably right. But I hope and pray that such factors will not blunt the truth of what I've written.

CHAPTER TWO

Who Were the Kansas City Prophets?

THE PAST TWO THOUSAND years of church history have been marked on several occasions by an undeniable outpouring of the Holy Spirit, an extraordinary manifestation of his presence and power. We typically call these *revivals*. Several of these revivals have been carefully documented. One thinks of the First Great Awakening, during the ministry of Jonathan Edwards (1703–58), and the Welsh Revival that began in February of 1904. Whereas some (but not me) question the authenticity of what became known as the Toronto Blessing (1994) and the Brownsville Revival (1995), the events associated with these outpourings of spiritual power have been well documented.

I am persuaded that the years 1980 to 2000 witnessed several expressions of the Holy Spirit's power that may well qualify as heaven-sent revivals,[1] some of which were in consequence of the Jesus movement that broke out in 1969–70 (here I reference *The Jesus Revolution*, a film that told the story of Lonnie Frisbee,[2] Chuck Smith, and Greg Laurie). The development of Calvary Chapel and its many congregations, together with the Vineyard and the ministry of John Wimber, led to the spiritual transformation of countless thousands across the country and even around the world. The Toronto Blessing and the Brownsville Revival (noted above) were two highly controversial expressions of revival power in the 1990s. This book is about yet another apparent extraordinary outpouring of the Holy Spirit on a more limited scale, dating from 1982 to 2000. Although based in Kansas City, Missouri, its influence was felt globally.

1. John Wimber, leader of the Association of Vineyard Churches until his death in 1997, preferred that they be called "renewals" and not "revivals."

2. Frisbee died of AIDS on March 12, 1993.

Some of the stories concerning the early years of Kansas City Fellowship (KCF) have already been told. In 1990 David Pytches (1931–2023), formerly a bishop in the Church of England and vicar of St. Andrews Church in Chorleywood, wrote a book entitled *Some Said It Thundered* that soon became an international bestseller. Pytches compiled his information largely from the many audio tapes of sermons he obtained from KCF. In addition to describing several of the profound prophetic events that supposedly occurred, he wrote about the lives and ministries of Paul Cain, Mike Bickle, and Bob Jones, among others. Although his book was fairly accurate, Pytches's account was unavoidably brief and sketchy. Its primary shortcoming is that it failed to describe the numerous supernatural events that allegedly occurred in the life of Mike Bickle and the church that he pastored.[3]

The church Bickle planted in late 1982 was initially known as South Kansas City Fellowship. It later became Kansas City Fellowship, until it was adopted into the Association of Vineyard Churches (AVC) in 1990 and changed its name to Metro Vineyard Fellowship. In a story that we'll explore later in this book, the church withdrew from the Vineyard in 1996 and took the name Metro Christian Fellowship.

Others have retold a number of the events of those days, some quite critically and with considerable prejudice. Mike Bickle himself described a few of the prophetic incidents in his book *Growing in the Prophetic*. Wesley Campbell has also retold selected portions of the story in brief, but pointed, fashion in his book *Welcoming a Visitation of the Holy Spirit*. So, the question may rightly be asked, "Why write about these events yet again?" And more to the point, was what happened in Kansas City—and, to a degree, is still happening—a genuine revival?[4]

One reason for undertaking the task of describing the events in Kansas City is that none of the accounts yet given is anywhere near complete. They are all selective narratives that omit much. There are a considerable number of highly significant prophetic stories that were never even mentioned in these works. My purpose in this book is to be as exhaustive as possible in the hope of edifying and encouraging the body of Christ and better equipping us to differentiate between what actually occurred and what may have been a fabrication. The fact is, several of the more profound prophetic scenarios were never shared publicly. They were certainly known by a number of people within the church and were carefully recorded and chronicled

---

3. The existence of the Kansas City prophets was first made known to the American evangelical world by Michael G. Maudlin in his article, "Seers in the Heartland." In the UK, David Pytches introduced them in *Some Said It Thundered*.

4. One of the more critical reviews of the Kansas City prophets is found in Keith Gibson's book *Wandering Stars*.

by Mike Bickle and others on staff at that time. Bickle, founder and former leader of the International House of Prayer in Kansas City, has also shared in more recent days much of what happened (largely in conjunction with the twentieth anniversary of the founding of IHOPKC).

But there are still certain supernatural events that purportedly occurred that I will describe in this volume, events that are made public in a more exhaustive way for the first time.

This narrative is also important because it is the first prophetic history of South Kansas City Fellowship/Kansas City Fellowship/Metro Vineyard Fellowship/Metro Christian Fellowship/International House of Prayer Kansas City, in addition to what Bickle has already published, written by an insider. Although David Pytches and Wesley Campbell were both friends of Mike Bickle, neither served on staff at the church nor had the opportunity to devote the needed time to investigate and research the vast number of audio and video tapes that were, for several years, stored away in the archives of the church.

Furthermore, they have not had access, as I have, to those individuals involved in the life of the church and IHOPKC who are able to provide data and insight into what occurred in those early days. I was on staff with Bickle for seven years (1993–2000) and spent countless hours watching video recordings and listening to audio tapes as well as interviewing the people involved. I was also present in Kansas City from 2004 to 2008 and, although not on staff at IHOPKC, spent considerable time participating in its many ministries. Most important of all, I have spent even more time in personal conversation with Mike Bickle, who provided me with the most intimate and intricate details possible of each prophetic word and event. Given these and other facts, I believe this book will meet a need in the body of Christ as yet unfulfilled.

Some Said We Blundered![5]

One additional comment is in order before we get down to business. A vitally important chapter in the story of the Kansas City prophets is the attack launched in 1990 against Bickle and his church by another pastor in the Kansas City area, Ernie Gruen. Most have heard only the broad outlines of this controversy and are not aware of how it ultimately was resolved. My aim is to bring light to bear on the entire story and what we can learn from it. It all began in January of 1990 when Gruen and his staff pastors

---

5. This is a sarcastic allusion to David Pytches's book *Some Said It Thundered*.

charged Mike Bickle with numerous theological and pastoral errors relating to prophetic ministry in the church.

Extensive investigation of these charges was immediately undertaken by John Wimber and others in the Association of Vineyard Churches, the results of which were published in *Equipping the Saints* magazine (Fall 1990). After conducting detailed personal interviews and reviewing all available documentation (largely under the direct oversight of Jack Deere and Jeff Grisamore), Wimber drew this conclusion:

> After reading every line of Pastor Gruen's document, listening to his tape, and interviewing as many people involved as possible, my staff and I are convinced that the accusations against the Metro Vineyard of Kansas City and Paul Cain are untrue. I find no evidence that they [Metro Vineyard of Kansas City and Paul Cain] teach heresy; have an occultic spirit; have unethical practices; promote bizarre, unscriptural experiences; have cultlike tendencies or teachings; or use prophetic gifting to take over churches. I do not believe that the Metro Vineyard Fellowship of Kansas City is a fully mature church; nor do I believe that their prophetic ministry is perfect. However, they have brought great blessing to me, and I welcome them into the Vineyard family.[6]

In chapter thirteen I will unpack the issues in considerable detail, as I have personal access not only to the lengthy document released by Gruen but also the exhaustive notes and information compiled by Jack Deere, who led the investigation. I am the first to admit that some mistakes were made, and people were hurt in the process. However, at every stage of this controversy Mike Bickle and the staff at the church were quick to acknowledge those errors and to repent when shown to have been at fault. Bickle has written extensively of the pitfalls of prophetic ministry and how to avoid them in his book *Growing in the Prophetic* (see especially chapter 6). All of us still have much to learn about hearing God's voice and are, I hope, always open to correction.

I also need to bring clarification to the label used to describe those in Kansas City who are the subject of so much discussion. Although the label "Kansas City prophets" is used frequently and is probably here to stay, there never was a cohesive group of prophetically gifted men and women who all lived in Kansas City and referred to themselves in this way. As for Bickle, he has often said that he "hated that name." There were undoubtedly a number of gifted people who either lived in Kansas City or spoke at

---

6. Wimber, "Response to Ernie Gruen."

the conferences hosted by the church that Bickle led. Bob Jones and Paul Cain are most often mentioned, although Cain didn't move to Kansas City until 1997. Others who ministered in the church and at conferences include Augustine Alcala, Michael Sullivant, John Paul Jackson,[7] David Parker, Noel Alexander, David Ravenhill, Greg Mira, James Goll, and to a lesser degree, Jill Austin. In addition, there are a few who are often included in the label of Kansas City prophets who never lived in the city and were never members of Bickle's church: Rick Joyner, Larry Randolph, Jack Deere, and Francis Frangipane among the more prominent.

One more important point needs to be made. In what follows you will read of the claims of many of these aforementioned individuals, claims that may strike some readers as outlandish, unproveable, and extreme. Perhaps some of them are. After all, in many instances we have no corroborating testimony beyond that of the individuals themselves. The early experiences in the life of Bob Jones and Paul Cain are especially noted in this regard. None of us can know with certainty whether what they claim to have experienced actually happened. No one was present to verify their story of angelic visitations or an audible voice from heaven. In telling their life stories I am not making any claim as to the veracity of what they say they experienced. I will simply provide a narrative on the basis of their testimony and leave it to you to decide whether or not they are telling the truth.

That being said, several of the supernatural and prophetic encounters that involved Bickle are confirmed by others who witnessed them or can be corroborated by means that cannot be fabricated. For example, it is one thing to claim that you have had a powerful dream in which the Lord spoke to you, or an angel appeared, but when another, without ever hearing of your experience, finds you the next day and says, "I saw what you dreamed last night. Here is what happened," and it matches perfectly the content of the dream, it is hard to remain skeptical. There will be in what follows numerous instances in which a supernatural experience is confirmed by revelation to another. Some cessationist critics, on the other hand, would attribute this sort of experience to Satan and his demons. In any case, once again I will have to leave it to you, the reader, to judge the authenticity of the many stories you are about to hear.

The question may be asked, why have I not responded to the numerous critiques and responses to the ministry of the prophets? That such negative assessments of the Kansas City prophets exist is beyond dispute. They are simply too many to list, although I have cited a few for those who wish

---

7. John Paul ministered powerfully to me and my wife. He died at the age of sixty-five and I joined Mike Bickle and Jack Deere at his memorial service at Gateway Church in the Dallas–Fort Worth, Texas, area.

to examine the other side of this controversy.[8] And of course the most detailed critique was that provided by Gruen, which is the subject of chapter thirteen. But my purpose in this book is to provide a careful chronicle of the events as they are claimed to have unfolded in the life and ministry of Mike Bickle and those who served alongside him, together with a critical analysis of their validity (where possible). Needless to say, I think I've closely read virtually all books, articles, and internet postings that insist the prophets are impostors and their stories fabricated. To delve into those would simply not serve my goals in writing this narrative.

What Sort of Biblical Glasses Are You Wearing?

As noted earlier, I anticipate a wide variety of responses to this book, everything from the gullible embrace of every story to a guarded hesitancy to an "I'll believe it when I see it" approach to mild-to-heavy criticism to mocking disdain, and somewhere along the way a few will rejoice when they encounter truth while remaining reluctant to endorse every jot and tittle of the many prophetic scenarios I describe. It is the latter that I hope for.

The apostle Paul never encourages naivete or blind affirmation of every word that purports to be prophetic. His consistent advice is that when we hear a statement or are told of an experience that we should "weigh" what is said (1 Cor 14:29). A similar exhortation is found in 1 Thessalonians 5:19–22. There the apostle encourages us all: "Do not quench the Spirit. Do not despise prophecies, but test everything; hold fast what is good. Abstain from every form of evil."

People often ask me how they should respond to someone who claims to be sharing a revelation received from God. I always tell them, "Don't be naïve. Don't be gullible. Don't believe every word you hear, even if it comes from someone you know to be reliable and godly. But neither should you be cynical and refuse to listen. The alternative to swallowing every purported prophetic word like mother's milk isn't to reject it out of hand. Rather, you should 'test everything' (1 Thess 5:21). When you have determined that

---

8. Numerous books and articles have been highly critical of Bickle and the prophets who ministered in Kansas City. For a representative sampling of some, see Cannon, "Old Wine in Old Wineskins," 8; Alnor and Lyle, "Controversial Prophetic Movement"; Alnor, "Kansas City Prophets"; Alnor, "Part Twelve"; Tillin, "Kansas City Prophets Exposed"; Hill, "Blessing the Church?";Tillin, "Harp and Bowl"; Danielsen, *Perfect Storm of Apostasy*; Wright, "Kansas City Prophets"; Hill, *Blessing the Church?* Among the dozens of articles critical of the prophetic movement, here I mention only a handful. See Dean, "Don't Be Caught"; Armstrong, "New Generation of Prophets?"; and Beverley, "John Wimber, the Vineyard, and the Prophets."

what someone has stated is 'good,' 'hold fast' to it. If you detect anything unbiblical or damaging, 'abstain' from it (v. 22)."

In all this, one thing is quite clear: It is a sin to "despise prophecies" (v. 20). It is one example of quenching the Holy Spirit (v. 19). So, on the one hand, don't be fearful of exercising biblically informed wisdom in the evaluation of claims to a revelatory word. On the other hand, don't despise or reject out of hand the possibility that God may truly have disclosed something to someone that is designed to build you up, encourage you, and console you (1 Cor 14:3).

This is precisely what I hope all of you will bring to bear on what you are about to read. I'm not asking you to decide up front that whatever is portrayed must be of God. To be bluntly honest, there are a couple of stories I'll share that I'm not entirely persuaded are of God. They may be. But then again, they may not. But neither do I want you to read further with a snide attitude toward all things supernatural. Which brings me to what I meant above when I spoke of "biblical glasses."

After more than a half century of public Christian ministry, I've grown somewhat accustomed to the variety of ways in which people read (or should I say, misread) the Scriptures. Some are so captivated by supernatural stories that they consider it a sin ever to employ their minds to evaluate what others tell them. At the other end of the spectrum are those who think it especially virtuous never to believe anything. Both attitudes are dangerous and unbiblical. I've known people, godly, Bible-believing people, who are happy to affirm the reality of the supernatural as long as it is kept tucked away neatly between the two covers of their leather-bound study Bible.

I'm not suggesting that people who embrace the doctrine of cessationism deny all miraculous activity in the present day. They don't, praise God. But they are exceedingly reluctant to put their stamp of approval on it should it come their way. Stories in Scripture of miraculous healing and deliverance from demonic bondage and resurrections from the dead and hearing God speak make for good bedtime tales to share with one's children. But they don't typically expect such phenomena to occur today, notwithstanding their repeated affirmations that they do indeed believe such might occur.

Those who identify as continuationists (the belief that all spiritual gifts are still imparted by the Spirit and are designed to build up the body of Christ) feel no qualms about declaring that what God did in biblical times he continues to do today. They view the world through glasses that are decidedly tinted to acknowledge that angels interact with us, that the Spirit still speaks not only through Scripture but also by means of prophetic gifts, that healing and tongues and discerning of spirits are valid expressions of the Spirit's work in our day no less than they were in Paul's.[9]

The interpretive spectacles worn by cessationists are often tinted by the fanatical and manipulative excesses of certain TV evangelists or internet/YouTube personalities whose primary motive is monetary gain. They often conclude that because some continuationists say stupid and self-serving things that spiritual gifts of a certain nature are no longer in operation.

On April 1, 2023, I sat down for a four-hour roundtable dialogue with two committed cessationists whose only argument against the validity of spiritual gifts today were video and audio clips of continuationists saying silly things that serve only to bring reproach on the name of Christ. They never once cited a single biblical text to support their view. My response to each of them was, "Yes, I agree with you. That is bad, and those individuals have no business being in Christian ministry. But what does that have to do with what the Bible says about spiritual gifts? Surely you're not suggesting that because these individuals do things badly that we shouldn't do them at all. Their behavior and misguided beliefs have no influence whatsoever on what Scripture says. I'm in your corner when it comes to the call for such people to withdraw from ministry and repent for the manipulative and God-dishonoring antics displayed. But again, *what does that have to do with what Scripture says?*" The answer is, nothing!

So, before you turn the page to read about the Kansas City prophets and their friends, ask yourself: With what sort of theological spectacles am I going to view and evaluate the claims being made? Will I reject them out of hand because certain people butcher the King's English, wear goofy clothes, and struggle to string together a theologically coherent sentence? I'm not endorsing any of the latter, but neither will I dismiss out of hand what they claim to have experienced simply because of their awkward public demeanor or lack of sophistication or strange accent or failure to enunciate clearly or their difference in belief from what I know to be true on secondary and tertiary doctrines.

So, in the absence of explicit biblical instruction otherwise, I urge you to read this book with an open mind, carefully weighing all things in the light of God's written word, and on the assumption that what the Holy Spirit did as described in Scripture he is still doing today, unless you have good biblical warrant for concluding otherwise.

---

9. In this regard I highly encourage you to explore the findings of Craig Keener in his magisterial two-volume work *Miracles*, as well as his shorter, more accessible volume *Miracles Today*.

Prophecy, Providence, and the Supernatural

A brief explanation is in order for those not familiar with the sort of phenomena that are described in what follows. Prophecy in the New Testament is speaking forth in merely human words something the Holy Spirit has revealed to you. It is often a mixture of infallible divine revelation and fallible human interpretation and application. It is no threat to the finality and sufficiency of the biblical canon and is always subject to the final authority of Scripture. If you are new to the prophetic, I suggest you read the relevant chapters in my book *Understanding Spiritual Gifts*.

The revelation from God may come in the form of a dream, a vision, a trance, an inward impression in your heart, an image, an audible voice, an internal audible voice, and numerous other ways in which the Spirit communicates with us. When Peter on the Day of Pentecost quoted the prophecy of the Old Testament prophet Joel he described what would occur in the "last days," a clear reference to the entire church age in which we live, spanning the years from the exaltation of Christ to the right hand of the Father all the way up to and including the time of the second coming. And the characteristic feature of this present era is the Spirit indwelling and empowering "all flesh," both Jewish believers and gentile believers, enabling them to "prophesy" (Acts 2:17). There are no restrictions as to gender, as both "sons and daughters" shall prophesy (v. 17). Again, "young men" will see "visions" and "old men" will "dream dreams" (v. 17). The Spirit has been poured out without regard to social or economic accomplishments, as "male servants" and "female servants" together will prophesy (v. 18).

But not everything in the experience of the Kansas City prophets is strictly what we call prophecy. In numerous cases, it was more an expression of divine providence in which God orchestrated events in ways that couldn't possibly be contrived or created by humans. What an unbeliever might call serendipitous turns out on close inspection to be a providential turn of events that can only be explained by appeal to the sovereign work of the Spirit. Certain experiences were self-evidently supernatural because of the timing in which they occurred. There were numerous instances of angelic visitations and communication both from and with them. On several occasions, financial needs were suddenly met in ways that clearly point to the Spirit's generous supply. Miraculous healings of all manner of disease took place. What an atheist, or even a Christian who doesn't give much consideration to the providential work of God, might consider mere coincidence turn out to be sovereignly orchestrated meetings and circumstances in fulfillment of a promise long ago made.

My point in saying this is simply to alert the reader to the fact that prophecy, strictly defined, is actually only a small part of the many incidents that transpired in Kansas City. And to be perfectly honest, some are so odd, dare I say weird, that your immediate reaction may well be to dismiss them out of hand. But stay glued to the narrative and observe how often God confirmed the truth of what happened in a way that no mere human could have conceived or duplicated.

There are some for whom this narrative will be especially challenging. They are, for want of a better way of putting it, functional deists. Deism is the view that God created the world and then largely withdrew from its normal operations. He rarely intervenes in the lives of his people, and only then on special occasions when a notable miracle is called for, such as the parting of the Red Sea or the resurrection of Christ from the dead. It isn't that such people deny that God exists or think that angels have no involvement in the daily lives of his people. But they live as if it were so. This is why even though they aren't deists as such, they are *functional* deists. They have little if any expectation that God might answer prayer in a supernatural and surprising way. They hardly give any thought to the possibility that a particular effect might have its cause in angelic activity. If this is you, consider yourself warned!

The Charge of Heresy

The charge of heresy is one that I've often heard lodged against Mike Bickle and the Kansas City prophets. Is there any basis to this accusation? Sadly, the word "heresy" is promiscuously and flippantly applied by some to just about anyone who differs with their personal beliefs on secondary and tertiary issues. It seems to matter little if one believes in the Trinity, the virgin conception, the sinless life, penal substitutionary death and bodily resurrection of Jesus. If one dare also believes in the continuation of all spiritual gifts, the charge of heresy is quickly forthcoming. If one should affirm that God still speaks through revelatory gifts such as word of knowledge and prophecy, many are immediately cast into outer darkness in the minds of some especially critical "discernment bloggers."

My appeal to everyone is that we exercise a measure of restraint when it comes to the use of this pejorative term. A "heretic" is a person who stands outside the pale of saving grace. This individual has not been born again and is not justified by faith alone in the finished work of Christ. That you may embrace an understanding of eschatology that does not align with a particular denomination's stance on the issue does not make you a heretic!

That you should encourage others to earnestly desire spiritual gifts, especially prophecy, does not put you on the outskirts of the New Jerusalem.

At times, among a small group of "heresy hunters," the charge is made that anyone who believes the spiritual gift of tongues is still operative in our day is outside the bounds of biblical orthodoxy. It gets even worse for those, like me, who actually pray in tongues every day. We are consigned to eternal damnation. No one who is truly born again, so they say, could possibly engage in a practice that died out in the first century when the apostles went to their eternal reward.

What are we to make of this? When are we justified in describing someone as a heretic? I do not lay claim to being the final word on this, but others have labored to identify those so-called "doctrines" that are impermissible to the saved. One thinks immediately of any denial of the incarnation of Christ. The apostle John in chapter four of his first epistle unashamedly declares that anyone who denies that Jesus is the Christ come in the flesh is operating by the spirit of antichrist. Jesus himself said that if you do not believe that "I am he," the one who is from above, not of this world, "you will die in your sins" (John 8:24).

To deny that Christ suffered in the stead of sinners and by doing so secured forgiveness of sins for all who believe is blatantly heretical. We should also include in this list of heresies the denial that Jesus is fully human, as well as fully divine. So, too, with the truth of the bodily resurrection of Christ and his personal, visible return to consummate his kingdom.

A heretic is one who denies that we are saved and justified before God by grace alone, through faith alone, by Christ alone. Any reliance on one's self-determined and fleshly rooted "good works" is a clear indication that such a person knows nothing of the saving grace of God in Christ. If you need even more detailed insight into the ideas and notions that in the history of the church have been identified as heretical, I recommend Justin Holcomb's excellent book *Know the Heretics*. But I must move on.

So, why did I take the time to address the issue of heresy and heretics? The reason is simple. On countless occasions Mike Bickle has been labelled a heretic. The critics justify this because of his belief in and practice of the spiritual gift of prophecy and his claim to speak in tongues. Some extend this accusation to all of the so-called Kansas City prophets. Where, then, does Bickle stand on the issues raised? I can speak with complete confidence on this matter as I have known Bickle for over thirty-five years and served as his associate pastor for seven. I also lived in Kansas City for eleven years and was privileged to know most of the prophets who ministered there at one time or another.

Bickle has been a firm and unwavering believer in the inspiration and inerrancy of Scripture. It is his final authority on truth and error, good and evil. He affirms the Trinity, that God is one being who subsists eternally in three coequal persons, Father, Son, and Holy Spirit. He defends the virgin conception of Jesus, his sinless life, his penal substitutionary atonement, his bodily resurrection, and his personal, visible return to consummate his kingdom. He preaches without hesitation the depravity and sinfulness of humanity and the absolute necessity of the new birth. He affirms that if we are to be saved it can only be by grace alone, through faith alone, by Christ Jesus alone.

This latter doctrine was very much in evidence when Bickle visited the Vatican and met Pope Francis. Bickle and the others present were given strict instructions not to ask the pope any questions. But Bickle, never an adherent to such protocol (!), boldly stepped forward and asked Francis: "Do you believe that a person must consciously believe in Jesus Christ in order to be saved?" The question was likely in response to rumors that Francis had endorsed some form of universalism. At least on this occasion, the pope answered in the affirmative.

When the emerging church movement burst on the scene, Bickle stood in opposition to it. He has consistently denounced the Word of Faith movement and the so-called "prosperity gospel." These convictions are not simply bullet points in his statement of faith. They are beliefs deeply rooted in his heart and form the basis of his entire Christian life. He affirms a biblical sexual ethic that contends marriage is for one woman and one man. He adamantly opposes abortion and has labored vigorously over the years for its abolition.[10]

So, why, then, do some insist on attaching to his name the label of heretic? It is largely because of Bickle's charismatic beliefs and practices, and more recently, his sexual sins. To their way of thinking, anyone who believes that the Holy Spirit continues to communicate with God's people beyond, even if never contrary to, the Scriptures is a heretic. Anyone who daily prays in tongues and prays expectantly for the sick to be healed and believes that signs and wonders are still the purpose of God in the present day, is a heretic. By this standard, I too am a heretic!

I have taken the time to address this issue because some of what you are about to read concerning supernatural events in Kansas City will tempt you to label the prophets as heretical. Such stories of angelic visitations, the audible voice of God, miraculous healing, and similar phenomena strike

---

10. One should not conclude that my description of Bickle's orthodox theology in any way justifies his sexual misconduct, as if the latter is minimized by the former.

many as so beyond the pale of biblical orthodoxy that any who embrace them as true must be so deluded as to remain outside the kingdom of God, looking in.

My plea is that you would cease using the label of "heretic" for those who differ with you on the subject of the Holy Spirit or the end times or the proper recipients of water baptism or the variety of beliefs on biblical church governance and reserve it for those who openly and defiantly deny the foundational and fundamental truths of Christianity outlined above. Call the prophets deluded, call them crazy, call them gullible if you must, but please cease calling them heretics.

Chapter Three

Who Is Mike Bickle?

The simple answer to that question is that he is the acknowledged leader of the Kansas City prophets that we are exploring in this book. But there is more about him that you should know.

Michael Leroy Bickle was born in 1955, the son of boxing champion, Robert Leroy Bickle. Mike's father was a highly gifted boxer who won several Golden Gloves titles and was scheduled to fight as a featherweight in the Helsinki Olympic games in 1952. He ended up fighting as a lightweight and won his first bout. Tragically, he got entangled in a bar fight later that night and broke his right hand. Although he knocked down his opponent, Italy's Aureliano Bolognesi, three times, he lost on a split decision. Bolognesi went on to win the gold medal. Bobby Bickle became a professional almost immediately after the Olympics and was victorious in his first seventeen fights. After six years of boxing professionally, compiling a record of forty wins, eleven losses, and two draws, he retired. But not before he knocked out Terry Lloyd in the fifth round to win the Kansas State lightweight title. Bickle also served briefly in the Korean War, but never saw combat.

Bobby Bickle led a somewhat tumultuous life, often taking Mike into bars where the latter would perform for the patrons by doing an uncanny number of pushups. Mike was not the only child in the family, as Bickle and his wife, Peggy, also gave birth to another son, Pat, and five daughters: Sherry, twin sisters Kelly and Shelly, Tracey, and Lisa. Sherry passed away on August 8, 2021,[1] while the others still live in the greater Kansas City metropolitan area.

---

1. Not only did I officiate at the memorial service for Pat Bickle, the Bickle family asked me to do the same at Sherry's. A scheduling conflict made it impossible for me to do so.

Who Is Mike Bickle?

I first met Mike Bickle in January of 1991, while at a conference hosted by John Wimber and the Vineyard. Some seven thousand people gathered at the Anaheim Convention Center to hear such men as Wimber, Leonard Ravenhill, Paul Cain, Omar Cabrera, and Roger Forster. But the highlight of the week for me came after an invitation from Jack Deere to join him and a few of his friends for dinner. When I arrived, I met Bickle for the first time, along with John Dawson of YWAM, and a lady from Hong Kong named Jackie Pullinger.[2]

It was Pat Bickle, however, who garnered most of the attention in the Bickle family. Pat played both offense and defense for the Center High School football team and, although not especially large (weighing in at 155 pounds), had a bright future in the sport. The third game of the season against the Vikings of Oak Park High School took place on September 29, 1973. At the time, Mike was living in St. Louis and playing football at Washburn University.

On the second play of the game, Pat tackled the running back from Oak Park, Tom Lancaster (who weighed 205 pounds). The hit crushed his spinal cord and dislocated the fourth and fifth vertebrae in his neck. He fell to the ground, motionless, and remained a quadriplegic, paralyzed from the neck down until his death some thirty-three years later. Being the son of the well-known boxer Bobby Bickle, Pat's story became front-page news in the local paper. It seemed as if the entire city united in prayer for the young Bickle, and the Kansas City Chiefs joined in the promotion of a high school doubleheader football game fundraiser at Arrowhead Stadium that drew thousands of well-wishers. The mayor of Kansas City proclaimed November 17, 1973, Pat Bickle Day.

Pat's quadriplegia was unlike that of most who suffer this sort of injury. I've known several quadriplegics who can at least, to some extent, move their arms and hands. But from that day in September of 1973 until he entered into glory on May 5, 2007, Pat could move nothing other than his head. Nothing. A close friend who worked for several years with victims of spinal cord injuries told me that those who suffer what Pat did have a maximum life expectancy of twelve to fifteen years. We were all amazed, and rightly so, when actor Christopher Reeve lived nine-and-one-half years following his injury. Pat lived over thirty-three years! He left behind his "wife" of seventeen years, Kim, and a son, Malachi.[3] On May 5, 2007, at the

---

2. I urge everyone to read her autobiography *Chasing the Dragon*.

3. Pat and his first wife, Cheryl, were married on August 29, 1980, but later divorced. Although Pat and Kim were never legally married, they lived as if they were husband and wife.

age of fifty, Pat Bickle died at 11:40 p.m. I had the honor of officiating at his memorial service on May 8, alongside former NFL star Todd Blackledge.

The death of Pat Bickle has played a significant role in assessing the accuracy of the Kansas City prophets. Virtually everyone believed that Pat would be healed and that this event would possibly be the spark that ignited the great end-time revival. Bob Jones repeatedly prophesied that Pat would be healed, as did Paul Cain and John Paul Jackson. Numerous others whose names are not widely known joined their voices with those of the more notable prophets. One exception to this was John Wimber, leader of the Association of Vineyard Churches. Jack Deere told me in a private conversation that Wimber did not believe Pat would be healed before his death.

In 1986, when Bickle first shared much of the prophetic history in a public venue, he said that Augustine Alcala, whom you'll meet later in this chapter, called him in October of 1984 with a promise from the Lord. He said that the Lord would personally visit Pat and tell him he would be healed. His precise words to Mike were: "The Son of God will personally come to Pat and heal him." On a Friday, at 4:03 a.m., Pat fell into a trance in which he claims to have seen the Lord in a vision. He spoke to Pat, saying, "I have come," words that Pat understood to mean the Lord had come to heal him. Needless to say, Augustine was wrong. At the same time, I think we can all be more lenient with Pat, whose passion to be restored to full health could easily have influenced his interpretation of the Lord's words. Mike was certainly on board with the belief that Pat would one day walk again. However, by the time I arrived in Kansas City in 1993, Mike's perspective had begun to change. He was no longer confident in the prophecies of Pat's healing and suspected that his transition from this life into the presence of Jesus would constitute the "healing" that everyone else thought would come before he died.

Many have scoffed at the prophets because of their inaccurate predictions of Pat's physical restoration. I've often read of some who believe this alone serves to discredit the entire prophetic ministry in Kansas City. But a simpler, and more biblical, interpretation of the death of Pat Bickle is that everyone missed it! It evidently was never God's will that Pat be healed in this life. Those who prophesied his healing were simply wrong. This does not make them false prophets, contrary to what many cessationists contend. Nor does it undermine the legitimacy of the prophetic gift in today's church. To prophesy inaccurately is common among God's people. No one is entirely spot on in the exercise of this spiritual gift. False prophets in the NT are always unregenerate unbelievers who typically deny the incarnation

Who Is Mike Bickle?

and deity of Christ (see 1 John 4:1–6). By all accounts, the two people who retained their hope that Pat would be healed were Pat himself and Kim.[4]

So, if God didn't reveal to these many prophetically gifted people that Pat Bickle would be healed, where did they come up with the notion and why did they declare it with such confidence? These are not easy questions to answer, but I believe what happened is often typical of prophetic ministry. But first, let me back up to the time when Bob Jones first met Bickle.

Early in their relationship, Mike did not fully trust Bob Jones. He often wondered in those days if Jones might be the false prophet mentioned by Augustine Alcala (more on this below).

On August 8, 1982, Jones claimed to have had a vision of a man lying on a wooden board on top of a white horse in the middle of a dry creek bed. The Holy Spirit then released water into the dry bed that rose to only about four inches. Rabid dogs were following the horse on both sides of the stream, barking and threatening it as they moved along. The "dogs," said Jones, are the critics of the prophetic movement together with otherwise well-intentioned friends of Bickle who would seek to deter him from the calling God had placed on his life.[5] Jones's personal role in this scenario was to keep the horse in the middle of the stream. He initially believed that Mike was the man on the board, but later came to realize it was Pat Bickle and that the white horse was symbolic of Bickle himself. In his vision, the Lord flipped over the board and the man fell into the stream of water. This, so said Bob Jones, was prophetic symbolism of both the eventual physical healing of Pat and the launch of what would become the great end-time revival and harvest of souls. Clearly, Pat was not healed physically, and no such harvest has yet been seen.

Countless individuals sincerely and passionately desired to see Pat raised. They had undoubtedly prayed ceaselessly for it to happen. They all reinforced in one another the same desire and increasingly grew in their confidence that this was God's will and purpose. In other words, desires and hopes for Pat's recovery intensified in their minds, which they in turn (mis)interpreted as a revelatory disclosure from the Holy Spirit. This frequently

---

4. More can be read about Pat's life and death and his impact on the church in Kansas City in the book by Falls: *The Life & Legacy of Pat Bickle.*

5. Allen Hood, who served in various leadership capacities at IHOPKC for more than eighteen years, wrote to me about this prophecy concerning the rabid or mad dogs who, according to Bob Jones, would attempt to dissuade Bickle and the young adult prayer and worship movement from going forward. "This prophecy," wrote Hood, "came to be used by IHOPKC leaders to resist legitimate criticism both internally and externally of IHOPKC's leadership practices. It was also used in an elitist way to discourage persons from leaving IHOPKC, warning them not to become one of the barking dogs out there."

happens, even with those who are not particularly gifted in the prophetic. We all too easily project our own goals, aspirations, beliefs, and desires into the forefront of our thinking, wrongly assuming that these promptings of our own making are actually the work of the Spirit.

Pat Bickle's death in 2007 has also given rise to criticism of Mike when he would later tell the prophetic history of the church. Up until Pat's death, whenever Mike would tell his brother's story, he would mention the board, the white horse, and the significance of his being flipped over and into the water. But after IHOPKC was formed, whenever Bickle told the story, he omitted any reference to Pat and his prophesied healing. Some have used this against Bickle, contending that he arbitrarily omitted facets of the event in order to enhance the credibility of the story.

I'll have more to say later about Pat, but for now I want to mention one incident that would prove instrumental in the emergence and ministry of the prophets. Not long after Pat's injury, his father Bobby and his brother Mike were visiting him. They walked out into the hall and Bobby spoke to Mike:

> "Mike, I need to ask a huge favor of you. I have a strong sense that I'm not going to live much longer,[6] and I don't think your sisters will be able to provide Pat with the care that he needs. Will you promise me that you will be there to take care of your brother?"
>
> Mike's instant response was, "Yes, of course I will."
>
> "I need you to promise me," his dad repeated.
>
> "Dad, I promise you that I will take care of Pat. After all, he ain't heavy, he's my brother, and I love him so."

If you recognize those closing lines, it probably means you are a child of the 1960s. The ballad "He Ain't Heavy, He's My Brother" was written by Bobby Scott and Bob Russell. Kelly Gordon first recorded it in 1969. When the British group the Hollies covered the song it became a massive hit. Neil Diamond subsequently recorded the song in 1970. Regardless of which version he had heard, the lyrics stuck in Mike Bickle's memory and spontaneously erupted in his heartfelt promise to his father. I urge you not to forget this moment, as it will come up again at a critical time in the story of the prophets.

---

6. Bobby Bickle died of a heart attack some six months later while visiting his brother in Fraser, Colorado.

Conversion!

Mike Bickle grew up in the Marlborough neighborhood, near 80th and Paseo in Kansas City. The most important transformation in his life came in the wake of his coach offering to pay his way to a Fellowship of Christian Athletes conference in Estes Park, Colorado. The speaker that year was Dallas Cowboys' quarterback Roger Staubach, whose message God used to capture the heart of the fifteen-year-old Bickle. Mike was converted to faith in Christ on June 9, 1971. In 1972 he attended a meeting at an Assembly of God church in Kansas City, named Evangel Temple. Remember that name, as it will play a significant role in the prophetic history later on. It was there that Bickle first spoke in tongues. He had no idea what had happened to him, and later concluded that he had been deceived. Numerous individuals had told him it was all a counterfeit experience.

Upon his return to Center High School, Mike was often seen carrying a large Bible and wearing a nine-inch wooden cross around his neck. There were several occasions when Bickle was taunted and challenged to a fist-fight. Each time he refused to respond in kind to those who assaulted him. While in high school Bickle attended Colonial Presbyterian Church where Ted Nissen was the pastor. He immersed himself in the writings of J. I. Packer, A. W. Tozer, John Stott, Stuart Briscoe, and British pastor Martyn Lloyd Jones. Upon graduation from high school in 1973, Mike enrolled at the University of Missouri, hoping to play football for the Tigers. He suspended his college education in early 1974 and moved to Denver to be with Pat, who had been admitted to Craig Rehabilitation Center. Mike sat faithfully with his brother for some sixteen hours a day. On March 11, 1974, Pat returned to Kansas City. Mike then resumed his education in the fall of 1975, but only briefly. One day he stood up in class and walked out. Mike had long aspired to attend Dallas Theological Seminary, but the Lord had different plans for him.

The First Pastoral Calling

Rosebud, Missouri, was a small community of five hundred people, approximately a hundred miles southwest of St. Louis. In 1976 several families in a Lutheran church in Rosebud were asked to leave because of their charismatic experience. Four couples decided to plant a new church, and gave it the name, The Upper Room Fellowship. Two of the men from Upper Room heard Bickle speak in May 1976. At that time the church had grown to some eighty people. Bickle soon became the lead pastor of this tiny fellowship of believers and preached his first sermon on June 6, 1976. Subsequently, he often preached against virtually all charismatic doctrines and experiences, unaware that the church where he ministered was charismatic! The commitment of the people and their obvious humility began to erode his confidence in cessationism.[7]

Mike left Upper Room Fellowship in 1977 and became the young adult pastor at New Covenant Fellowship in St. Louis, where he served for the next two years. It was also in August of 1977 that he met Diane, his future wife, at Store Front Fellowship (another small congregation). He proposed to her on the first date, and they were married two months later. Bryn Jones, pastor of New Covenant, urged Mike to consider planting a church, the result of which was the launch of South County Christian Fellowship in 1979. Bickle pastored the church for three years as it grew to over four hundred members.

Answering the Call to Kansas City

The Bickle's loved St. Louis and never gave a second thought to moving. That is, until a seemingly providential visit from a young Hispanic man named Augustine Alcala. Augustine was born on March 28, 1943, in Bakersfield, Kern, California. He died on August 8, 2002, in Pecos, San Miguel, New Mexico, at the age of fifty-nine.[8] Fast forward with me to 1985, when Mike answered a question raised by someone in the church, "Where is Augustine? Why hasn't he been back to Kansas City?" Mike responded by saying the team are in touch with him but that Augustine and Mike are not in agreement about "what the standard for a NT leader should be." Mike expressed his love and appreciation for Alcala but said that the two of them do not see eye to eye on the standard for NT living. Mike affirmed Alcala's prophetic gifting, but not the style or manner in which he ministered publicly. Mike may also have been referring to Augustine's purported struggle

---

7. There is some doubt about Bickle's claim to have been a cessationist at this time in his life. In a conversation with Jono Hall, an IHOPKC staff member and later one who served on the Advocate Group, Bickle reported that he and Diane actually attended the large charismatic gathering in 1977 in Kansas City. Then again, Bickle may only have attended in order to gain information about the miraculous gifts of the Spirit that he at that time did not believe were currently operative.

8. If you wish to see Alcala "prophesy" to both Mike and Diane Bickle, go to https://x.com/starcazm/status/1787961561140596895. This occurred in December of 1983.

with homosexuality.⁹ "He won't be back to Kansas City ministering until we come into agreement," said Mike.

As Alcala tells it, he was driving past the St. Louis church one day when he heard the audible voice of God. As I have noted on several occasions in previous chapters, this is the sort of alleged experience that each reader must decide either to believe or not or perhaps hold in abeyance any premature conclusion about whether or not God operates in this manner in the present day. Numerous other similar instances will be cited in the pages to come.

At the time, Alcala knew nothing about the church and had no knowledge that Bickle was its young pastor. He inquired of a friend in St. Louis, Rick Shelton, if he knew of the church and its pastor. "Yes," his friend replied. "The pastor is Mike Bickle." Augustine's friend then called Mike on the phone and informed him that a prophet of God had an important word for him. "Will you speak with him?" Mike's immediate reaction was, "That's all I need! A prophet. Thanks for the call, but no, I don't have time for that right now." Bickle wasn't aware that Augustine claimed to have heard the audible voice of God, but even if he knew of it, "I would not have believed him anyway," said Mike. Bickle was inexperienced at the time concerning the proper and biblical way of receiving and processing prophetic words. He wasn't even entirely certain about the legitimacy of prophetic ministry. He also was admittedly somewhat skeptical about a person hearing the audible voice of God.

Undeterred, Alcala decided to visit the church anyway. He entered the building and made his way to the front row. It happened to be a Sunday when Bickle arrived late, so he quietly slipped into the sound booth at the back of the auditorium. Another man was leading the service, at which some 350 people were present.

Augustine wasn't one for religious propriety, so he stood up and introduced himself. "Hello! My name is Augustine and the Lord uses me to speak prophetically." As he sat in the sound booth, Mike was rather put off by this bold declaration. But as Augustine continued, Mike was drawn to listen as the information he shared was quite accurate. "How could he know these things?" he asked himself repeatedly. As if that were not enough, Augustine then identified four people in the congregation, people Mike knew well, and spoke things about them that he could not have known through any natural means. It was then that Augustine directed his words at Mike, although he had no idea he was addressing the pastor of the church. He had assumed from the start that the older man on the platform was the senior leader,

---

9. I have been told by several more informed individuals that Alcala died of AIDS.

something that baffled him because his friend had said that Bickle was a young man.

"That young man at the back of the room," shouted Alcala.

"Me?" Mike responded.

"Yes, you," said the prophet pointing directly at him. The only one in the room who didn't know he was speaking to the pastor of the church was Augustine. It's an important lesson for us about the prophetic. Simply because a prophet receives considerable information from the Lord, he doesn't always know everything. In any case, Augustine continued: "Young man, the Lord is going to set you on a new path and brand-new direction. God will show you this immediately and confirm it supernaturally."

The "word" wasn't one that pleased everyone present. A few clapped, but even more muttered under their breath, "Who does this guy think he is? How dare he speak so disrespectfully of our pastor, calling him 'that young man.'" Bickle himself was uncertain of how to respond, and said he would have to listen to the tape recording of the service to discern if there was truth in what Augustine had spoken. When the service ended, and still unaware that Bickle was the pastor of the church, Augustine approached Mike and invited him to lunch. "The Lord has certainly got some powerful things in store for you to do. I'm trying to get to the pastor so that I can invite him out too." The older man whom Augustine had mistakenly thought was the pastor joined them. It was only after they arrived at the restaurant that the prophet realized who the pastor truly was.

"I heard the audible voice of the Lord," said Augustine. "This is a very serious word from God!" This was at a time when Bickle was still somewhat skeptical of all things charismatic. He wasn't about to be duped by someone he had never met. He wasn't even sure that God spoke audibly, outside of what we read in Scripture. The idea of a "prophet" speaking to him was equally strange. And he was perfectly content living in St. Louis. Moving was the farthest thing from his mind. Bickle wisely turned to the elders of his church and asked them to process and pray about this "word" to determine, as best they could, if it was really God.

When Mike processed the issue with Diane, she declared her belief that they would live in St. Louis for the rest of their lives. Mike was in agreement. "I love it here," he confidently declared. But that was all soon to change, for on the very next day the Lord confirmed in Mike's heart that he was to move to Kansas City. Still, he and Diane remained in St. Louis for another three months, praying about what God's will for them might prove to be. Finally, in September, Mike shared with the elders that he was sensing a clear call to Kansas City. They struggled, as did Mike, with Augustine's "word" but finally came to the conclusion that this was indeed God's call to move.

Who Is Mike Bickle?

The Grooming and Sexual Abuse of a Fourteen-Year-Old Girl

This is the point in our narrative where I feel compelled to introduce a profoundly disturbing component of Bickle's life. When Dwayne Roberts called me on August 2, 2023, to inform me of the information he had received regarding Mike's sexual conduct, he mentioned that there was a lady in St. Louis during the time of Mike's ministry in that city. He said her name was Tammy Woods (Woods is her maiden name). Several individuals suggested that there might have been a measure of inappropriate behavior between the two, but since Woods had never come forward with testimony to that effect, no further exploration of the issue could be undertaken. Of course, we were later to learn that Tammy Woods was now a fifty-nine-year-old mother and grandmother. After assuring Mike repeatedly that she would take his sexual abuse of her to the grave, never speaking a word of it to anyone, the pressure became more than she could bear. Those who may not be familiar with this scenario should visit www.JulieRoys.com where Tammy's story, first told to the *Kansas City Star*, is repeated in considerable detail.[10] Suffice it to say that she was only fourteen years old and serving as the babysitter for Luke and Paul Bickle when the grooming began. I mention this part of the story because it was during Bickle's pastoral tenure in St. Louis that this egregious sexual abuse of Woods began. It started shortly after Woods's fourteenth birthday in 1980 and continued through her college years until she got married in July of 1988.[11]

Woods also confirmed with me that during her junior year at the University of Missouri, Bickle visited her and was once again sexually abusive. This took place in 1988, some six years after the church in Kansas City was founded and some eleven years into Bickle's own marriage.

One additional element in Bickle's abuse of Woods is something that Bickle has persistently denied. According to Woods, as well as both of the women identified in this book as "Jane Doe," Bickle told her that his wife, Diane, would die and that he and Woods would be together. Initially Bickle insisted that he was referring to a partnership in ministry, not marriage. But Woods thinks otherwise. Bickle also said that Diane herself frequently told him early on in their relationship that she feared she would die young. It was to this that Bickle insists he was referring when he mentioned to Woods about Diane's death. However, the first "Jane Doe" (Deborah Perkins) with

---

10. You can read her story at Roys, "EXCLUSIVE." Additional information was provided to me by Woods in a text message on July 18, 2024.

11. Bickle's sexual involvement with Woods was actually criminal in nature. However, it appears that the statute of limitations has long since expired.

whom I spoke told me that Bickle made the identical statement to her at least fifty times over the course of four years and that she always understood him to be referring to their eventual marriage. The second "Jane Doe" (whom we now know was Terry Hartley) claims that Bickle said the same thing to her and that the reference to "being together" had marriage in view.[12] In fact, Bickle told her that Diane would die in an earthquake in St. Louis after which they could be married. I encourage you to read the timeline and disturbing details of Bickle's grooming of Woods in appendix B.

Very soon after, in obedience to this strange and strong call issued by Alcala (or by God, through Alcala, if you are inclined to believe his story), Mike and Diane, their friend Bob Scott, and a dozen or more families all sold their property and made the move to Kansas City with the intent of planting a new church. But before launching out on this venture, Bickle embarked on a trip that was to mark his ministry forever.

Encounter in Cairo

In September of 1982, just prior to moving to Kansas City, Bickle accepted an invitation to join several other pastors on a mission trip to India. Mike had no idea of what God had in store for him on the return trip. An encounter awaited him that would forever impact the spiritual genetic code of the soon-to-be-founded church in Kansas City. When the conference in India was concluded, the other pastors headed east to return home. Mike, however, headed west. He had long had a heart for the poor of the earth, but he wanted to see first-hand who they were and how they lived. In short, he wanted *God's* heart for the poor. He wanted to see them as God saw them. After making brief stops in four major cities, among which were Seoul, South Korea, and Calcutta, India, Bickle made his way to Cairo, Egypt. Upon his arrival there he did what had become his custom, strange as it was. He instructed the taxi driver to take him to the slums of the city. "I want to see the poor," Bickle told him. As he walked among the homeless and helpless, God touched him with the depths of their poverty, especially in comparison with the opulence of the Christian West. It was a shattering experience that forever changed Bickle's perspective on life and ministry. But that was only the beginning.

That night he checked into a dismal little hotel in Cairo. His room was approximately eight feet by eight feet. It had a bed, so to speak, a squeaky ceiling fan (no air conditioning), and primitive plumbing. Bickle even had

12. Hopkins and Roys, "EXCLUSIVE."

Who Is Mike Bickle?

company: numerous bugs of considerable size and boldness! But he was unfazed by his surroundings. His heart was fixed on God.

As he knelt beside his bed, interceding for the work in Kansas City that he was soon to begin, Bickle claims that the Lord visited him in a powerful and personal way. The presence of the Lord filled the room and Mike became frighteningly aware of the nearness of God. The Lord spoke (or so says Bickle). He didn't hear an audible voice. But he claims to have heard a voice, nonetheless. It was, to use his own words, the "internal audible" voice of God. "I could hear it inside me with absolute clarity," said Bickle. "I could hear in my spirit the enunciation of words and the intonation of God's voice. It was unmistakable and inescapable." He explains yet further:

> It came with such a feeling of cleanness, power, and authority. In some ways I felt I was being crushed by it. I wanted to leave, but I didn't want to leave. I wanted it to be over, but I didn't want it to be over.... The awe of God flooded my soul as I experienced a little bit of the terror of the Lord. I literally trembled and wept as God Himself communicated to me in a way I've never known before or since.[13]

What God is claimed to have said consisted of four things. First: "I am inviting you to become part of a movement that will touch the ends of the earth."

Bickle was overwhelmed by this "word" and began to weep as he repeatedly said, "Yes, Lord, yes!"

"You have only *said* 'Yes,'" the Lord replied, "but you have not yet *obeyed*. Many have said 'Yes,' but few have actually done my will."

The second thing God spoke concerned the foundational values on which this work would be built. There were four of them. This work would be characterized by night-and-day prayer, holiness of heart, extravagant giving to the poor, and unwavering faith. These are by no means the *only* values essential to the work that Bickle believed God was calling him to begin. There are numerous others, such as Bible study, evangelism, love of the brethren, worship, etc. But these four were to constitute the unique undergirding of what God intended to build. Bickle believes these four were singled out by God because in their practical outworking they have a tendency to incur a stigma of reproach.

The third thing the Lord said to Bickle came in the form of a warning. As he continued to weep, the Lord said,

---

13. Bickle, *Growing in the Prophetic*, 79.

> Guard your heart, for if you lose this vision, it will be your brothers who have stolen it from you—it will not be the world that does that. It will be the reasoning brothers who do not know my ways that will try to take this thing from your heart. Guard your heart lest your brothers steal this from you. If this standard is upheld, which I am inviting you and your people to follow, you will fulfill a purpose that will touch the ends of the earth.[14]

Over the years there have been several occasions when friends and well-meaning brothers in Christ tried to convince Bickle that he was building the church incorrectly. These individuals, so said Bob Jones, were the rabid dogs that he saw in his vision. They were not being malicious, but simply did not understand why Mike pursued the ministry in Kansas City in the way that he did. Mike never claimed that the way in which he applied the values given to him in Cairo was to be universally followed. He simply insisted that he and those who would join him in this work must embrace certain unique standards.

The fourth thing God is claimed to have communicated to Bickle was perhaps the most stunning of all. His voice was unmistakable: "*I am going to change the understanding and expression of Christianity in the whole earth in one generation.*" Many have misunderstood this phrase, and in an attempt to ridicule Bickle's experience have speculated wildly concerning its meaning and fulfillment. But there is really very little mystery here. During my years in Kansas City Bickle and I discussed this on multiple occasions. One may choose to dismiss his experience altogether, but we should at least give him the opportunity to explain it for himself.

The fundamental essence of the Christian faith was once for all established through the foundational ministry of the apostolic company (Eph 2:20) and is not subject to change in any way, shape, or form. Bickle has always insisted that this "word" from God has nothing to do with any alteration whatsoever in the biblically rooted and historically affirmed doctrines of the Christian faith. He is not suggesting that God told him that the latter would be transformed or reduced or expanded upon or in any way altered. Bickle has always affirmed his sincere belief in the creeds of the ancient church. He honors the contributions of such great men of faith as Augustine, Luther, Calvin, Edwards, Wesley, and numerous others. My point is simply that the "understanding" of Christianity referred to in the "word" Bickle received has nothing to do with what we Christians have believed and still do believe on the basis of an inerrant and inspired biblical text.

---

14. From personal conversation with the author.

The change in "understanding" concerns how the non-Christian world perceives the Christian world. It simply refers to how the unbelieving world sees and interprets the body of Christ. It also needs to be made perfectly clear that, contrary to numerous critics, Bickle never claimed that *he* would be the one to change the understanding and expression of Christianity. It was decidedly a work of *God alone*. The world generally considers the church irrelevant, if not laughable. But God intends to move in such power as to alter how the world sees the church. The power and purity of the early church will return in unprecedented proportions and the unbelieving world will no longer be able to ignore or mock the body of Christ. It is *their* understanding, not ours, that Bickle believes will undergo a massive transformation. Throughout history, and especially in our postmodern society, unbelievers have mocked the church. They have accused us (on occasion, rightly so) of hypocrisy, legalism, elitism, arrogance, and any number of other failures. Perhaps the most persistent perception on the part of unbelievers is that the church, and Christianity in general, is devoid of power. And it grieves me to admit that there is much truth in this accusation. This perception of powerlessness is what would undergo a major change, according to the "word" Bickle claims to have received. One may choose to reject altogether the experience Bickle claims to have had, but he at least deserves the courtesy of being interpreted on his own terms.

The phrase "the expression of Christianity," so said Bickle, simply refers to how the church goes about doing her business. It looks at what the church does and how it expresses its corporate life. God's intent is to shatter the complacency and apathy of the church and revitalize its mission and ministries. All through the past two thousand years the church has repeatedly undergone changes in the way it went about its ministries. Bickle clearly believes that as we approach the second coming of Christ the church will live out its calling in unprecedented purity and the power of the Holy Spirit. One may again choose to take issue with his eschatology, as I do. But if he is to be critiqued, we must all be certain that before we launch our response that we fully grasp what he means and avoid the sort of caricatures and misinterpretations that stifle healthy dialogue.

Following this encounter with the Lord, Bickle left his room and walked the streets of Cairo late into the night. He pondered over and over what God had said. He pondered over and over his own feelings of inadequacy, recognizing that his pledge of obedience could only be fulfilled with the energizing help of the Holy Spirit. The spiritual genetics of what was to become South Kansas City Fellowship and later Metro Christian Fellowship were forever established.

A Call for Discernment

Did this truly happen in the way Bickle has described it? Needless to say, no one was present to confirm or deny his experience. Although some have scoffed at his claims concerning this experience in Cairo, many are inclined to believe it happened just as he said. They appeal to subsequent events that appear to confirm Mike's testimony.

The most disconcerting fact about Bickle's alleged encounter with the Lord in Cairo is that it happened at the same time Bickle was grooming and sexually abusing Tammy Woods. We are being asked to believe that God would communicate to an active pedophile something as profound as Bickle claimed. For many, that is simply asking too much. I'm somewhat inclined to agree. Bickle's egregious sexual misconduct involving Woods makes it highly unlikely (in my opinion) that the abuser in this instance would be blessed with such a profound revelatory visitation from the Lord. The evil nature of Bickle's abuse of Woods is described by the latter in considerable and disturbing detail in appendix B.

Mike Bickle Meets Paul Cain

In 1984, Bickle flew to Phoenix and met up with Augustine Alcala. They had planned on driving from Phoenix to Anaheim, California, to attend a Vineyard conference. The drive from Phoenix to Anaheim took them through the Arizona desert and into Southern California. As they were making their way west, Augustine began telling Mike about a prophet named Paul Cain. Mike had never heard of him before. Augustine shared some stories with Mike about Paul and said it would be great if the two of them could meet.

Suddenly Bickle spoke, "I'm hungry. Can we stop at the next fast-food place and get something to eat?"

"Sure," said Augustine. Not long thereafter they came upon a McDonald's restaurant, near Blythe, California.

As they stood in line, waiting their turn, Augustine once again mentioned Paul Cain by name. When he did, a young man two or three people ahead of them in line turned around.

"Augustine," he shouted! "It's me, Reed Grafke."

"Reed," shouted Augustine in response. Augustine and Reed had known each other for a few years but hadn't seen one another in quite some time.

"What are you doing these days?," asked Augustine.

"I'm traveling with a prophet and serving as his administrative assistant. His name is Paul Cain."

"Reed," said Augustine, "there's someone I think you should meet. His name is Mike Bickle."

Let's pause and ponder the providence of God. What are the odds that Bickle and Augustine would be traveling by car to Anaheim on that day? What are the odds that they would suddenly be talking with each other about a man named Paul Cain? What are the odds that their hunger prompted them to stop at that precise location, in the precise fast-food joint where Reed Grafke would be standing in line? What are the odds that Reed would himself be present in that restaurant, in the California desert, on the precise day and hour when Mike and Augustine arrived? And what are the odds that a normal conversation would be overheard, leading to Bickle meeting the man who was serving as Paul Cain's administrative assistant? Well, God has never been hindered by the odds stacked against him. One more thing. As I mentioned earlier, this isn't so much a prophetic event as it is an expression of divine providence, in which God orchestrates a meeting that would seem to defy the odds of it being fabricated by any human.

Grafke proceeded to write down Cain's number on a card and gave it to Bickle. He encouraged him to contact Paul. When Bickle and Alcala got back in the car, they were breathless. "What just happened," Mike wondered aloud? At that moment, Mike took from his pocket the piece of paper on which Grafke had written the name of Paul and his address and phone number. He rolled down the window and threw it away. "This is a holy moment. If God has truly orchestrated this providential encounter, then he will orchestrate my connection with Paul without me taking the initiative and contacting him."

Three years later Bickle received a phone call from a man in Birmingham, Alabama, inviting him to a small prophetic conference. Mike agreed and flew to Birmingham with a few of his staff members. There were some fifty people present. At the beginning, the host said, "Stand up, turn around, and introduce yourself to the person behind you." Mike turned and found himself face to face with a grey-haired man: "Hi, I'm Mike."

"Hello," he responded. "I'm Paul Cain."

"Paul Cain, the healing evangelist?" Mike asked.

"Well, yes," replied Cain.[15]

---

15. The first encounter between Bickle and Cain is told in slightly different terms by Bill Jackson. If Jackson is to be believed, Bickle was booked as the main speaker at the conference. "Paul Cain had heard that Mike would be there and went to meet him. The conference host recognized Paul and at one point invited him to come forward to say a few words. Paul spoke prophetically to the team from Kansas City Fellowship, and by

Mike would often tell the story of how they later went to a restaurant to share their respective stories of life and ministry. About fifteen minutes into their conversation, Paul asked if they could move to a table in the corner of the restaurant.

"Why?" asked Mike.

"Well," said Paul, "I'm tired."

More than a little confused, Mike wondered aloud why sitting at this particular table in this place in the restaurant was unsuitable. Paul's response was Mike's first exposure to his prophetic gift.

"Well, all these people walking by are exhausting."

Still confused, Mike asked why.

"OK, I'll tell you. Our waitress has serious kidney problems. And that man over there is immersed in sexual sin. And the guy at the table next to him is contemplating divorcing his wife."

Mike was more than a little curious as to how Paul might know these things about people he had never met. Paul explained that these were expressions of his friendship with the Lord. "Friends talk to each other and share information," said Paul.

Mike, never one for social proprieties (!), turned to the waitress and asked her if she had kidney problems. She did not respond well, feeling that her privacy had been invaded.

"How did you know that? I don't even know you."

Mike tried to explain, but nothing seemed to satisfy her.

Bickle then walked over to one of the men and said, "Excuse me, sir, but are you contemplating divorcing your wife?"

Again, the stunned response and confirmation of Paul's word were unmistakable.

Mike declined to ask the other man if he was struggling with sexual sin in his life! Wise move.

This was Bickle's first exposure to Cain's prophetic gift. And the rest, as we say, is history.

---

the time he was done, they were all on the floor weeping" (Jackson, *Quest for the Radical Middle*, 199). What I have discovered on several occasions is that when Bickle tells these prophetic stories he often compresses events and provides a summary that omits numerous details. His concern seems to be with the one primary issue without regard for ancillary details. Sadly, it provides his critics with reasons to question his integrity in the communication of certain events.

Luke 4:18 at 4:18 on 4/18 (?)

The prophetic experience of Mike Bickle and the church in Kansas City cannot be fully understood without giving serious consideration to the influence of 4:18. That undoubtedly sounds strange to many of you, so let me briefly explain why. But before I do, please note that the event in question is perhaps, once again, less an example of the spiritual gift of prophecy and more an illustration of divine providence. The reason for this will become clear as we proceed. You should also understand that my research on this topic was undertaken without any prior assumption as to its truthfulness or falsity. I was determined to secure the facts and leave it at that.

Mike Bickle's expectation of a future, glorious expression of all spiritual gifts, especially prophecy and healing, plays a monumental role in the prophetic history of his church. Bob Jones, Paul Cain, and Bickle, among others, often spoke and prophesied the coming "last days ministry" in which a glorious and global revival would occur. This revival would entail a billion-soul harvest of saved men and women, together with the widespread operation of the prophetic and especially divine healing. My purpose is not to explore the purported biblical foundations of this belief but simply to draw our attention to its central role in Bickle's life and ministry. But what does this have to do with the numbers 4:18?[16]

I placed a question mark at the end of the title to this section because of the uncertainty surrounding this providential, and somewhat prophetic event in the experience of both Paul Cain and Mike Bickle. I say "alleged" because of the conflicting evidence pertaining to the death of Annie Cain, Paul Cain's mother. There are today only four people still alive who were present during the final days of her life, three of whom were in the room when she passed away. But before we dive into the conflicting accounts surrounding her death, we need to understand the context and timing of what happened.

The best place to begin is with Mike Bickle's recollection of the event. He and I discussed this on numerous occasions in past years, but I have not communicated with Mike since the scandal at IHOPKC erupted. Bickle never wavered in the details surrounding Annie Cain's death, always telling the story in identical terms each time it came up. Consequently, I myself told the story numerous times in conferences and churches and have written about it in past days. If Bickle's account is factual, I make no apologies for sharing it with others. However, if the story Bickle has repeatedly told me is false, whether in large or small part, I owe an apology to the Christian

---

16. The 4:18 scenario, said Bickle, is "a core promise for what is yet coming" (Mike Bickle, sermon of April 16, 2021).

community for having unintentionally misled them. So, let's begin with how both Bickle and Cain describe the significance of 4:18.

Paul Cain's mother, Annie Cain (1885–1990), lived to the remarkable age of 104. It is remarkable not only because of the sheer longevity of her life but also because in 1929 she had been diagnosed with three terminal diseases and was given little if any chance to live.[17] As if that were not enough, the diagnosis came while Annie was pregnant with Paul. As she lay dying at home, she reported that an angel appeared at the foot of her bed and said, "Do not fear. You shall live and not die. The child in your womb is a male. You will call his name Paul, for he will preach the gospel like the apostle Paul of old and bind up the sickness of my people, and shall stand before kings." Annie Cain was healed and lived another sixty years.

Is this oft-told account of Annie Cain's physical infirmities and healing accurate? I see no reason to doubt it. However, whether or not an angel actually appeared to her and told her that she would have a son and that she was to name him Paul, is something that each reader must answer for themselves. One major problem in this alleged angelic encounter is that, contrary to what the angel said, Paul Cain did *not* "preach the gospel like the apostle Paul of old," at least with any degree of consistency. Jack Deere, who probably knew Paul better than anyone else, including Mike Bickle, having traveled with Paul throughout the United States and around the world for some sixteen years, has written that he never heard Paul proclaim the gospel. Jack would often write out for Paul a simple gospel presentation, often based on John 3:16, but he typically failed to articulate it to the audience. I can testify to that myself, as I never heard a clear presentation of the gospel on Paul's lips. I was present at several dozen of Cain's speaking engagements and he never, as best I can recollect, articulated the Pauline gospel.

What are we to conclude from this? There appear to be only a handful of possible interpretations. One is that Annie Cain never experienced an angelic visitation and never heard this "angelic prophecy" concerning the ministry of her son. If that is true, the explanations for this event are greatly reduced. First, it is possible that Annie Cain hallucinated or for some other reason believed that the angel had told her of Paul's future ministry. It is not at all uncommon for people in such poor physical conditions to experience delusional episodes. Such are often the result of medication. Just as frequently, they can be explained due to the traumatic impact of perceived impending death. The bottom line is that it is possible this event only

---

17. No one, as far as I know, has had access to the medical records of Annie Cain's terminal diseases to either confirm or refute this claim.

occurred in Annie Cain's imagination, or perhaps in a dream, but not as a result of an angelic visitation.

A second option is that the supposed "prophetic" declaration by the angel was not unconditional. Like many prophecies in Scripture (think of Jonah's declaration that Nineveh would be destroyed in forty days), this one may have been dependent on Paul Cain's commitment to and faithful proclamation of the gospel. We must remember that many prophetic words are not unconditional guarantees but invitations that depend for their fulfillment on the obedience of the one to whom the prophecy is directed.

I suppose there is yet a third explanation of this event. Perhaps Paul Cain did, in point of fact, preach the Pauline gospel in the early stages of his ministry, during the healing campaigns he conducted in conjunction with the healing revival of the 1950s and early 1960s. But one thing is certain: by the time he met Mike and Jack, he had, by all appearances, ceased to do so.

One of the challenges we face in the telling of these events is that Paul Cain is no longer with us, and neither is his long-time assistant and aide Reed Grafke. Reed served Paul for eighteen years before leaving to get married. Reed was one of a handful of individuals present when Annie Cain died. If only I had taken advantage of my friendship with Reed when he was still alive to ask numerous questions of him about this event, I could be more confident in reporting the details. I had the privilege of officiating at Reed's wedding to Monette Mathews, something that severely damaged my relationship with Paul Cain. More on this later. In any case, perhaps others spoke with Reed about it prior to his passing.

The more I think about it, there may yet be a fourth explanation, one that I seriously doubt and am somewhat reluctant to mention. Could Annie Cain have simply fabricated the story? Could she be guilty of deliberately lying about the angelic visitation and the prophetic word about her son? I suppose that is possible, but not likely. Although I never met Annie, nothing in her life, of which I'm aware, would indicate that she would stoop so low as to willingly and consciously lie about something of such a profound spiritual nature. The people with whom I have spoken who knew her well insist on her humility and godliness. Well, now back to our story.

A few months before Annie Cain's passing, Paul alleges that the Lord told him he would receive a prophetic sign in his mother's death that would serve both to encourage him and to confirm the nature of God's calling on his life. As Annie's final days on this earth were passing, she began to lapse in and out of consciousness. As Paul Cain tells it, a few days before she was to die, Annie awakened and spoke a verse of Scripture to Paul, convinced that it was God's word for her son and his ministry. The text was Luke 4:18, in which Jesus quotes from the prophet Isaiah to describe his earthly ministry: "The Spirit of the Lord is upon me, because he has anointed me to proclaim the good news to the poor. He has sent me to proclaim liberty to the captives and recovering of sight to the blind, to set at liberty those who are oppressed, to proclaim the year of the Lord's favor."[18] She then lapsed back into unconsciousness, from which she never awakened.

We are once again dependent on the veracity of Paul Cain's personal word that this truly happened. I know of no one who was present when Annie allegedly spoke this word to her son. If there was an eyewitness to this event beyond Paul himself, I hope that they will come forward and either confirm or refute it. We face an additional problem, insofar as Mike Bickle said it was on the day she died, only moments before her passing, that she whispered to Paul this verse of Scripture. So, which is it?

Here we come to yet another question about the legitimacy of this entire scenario. As Paul Cain and others stood around Annie's bed, just prior to her passing, Cain was anxious and worried that she might die before having the opportunity to give him the "word" from God that had been promised. And yet, as Cain would later tell the story, she had already given him the Luke 4:18 promise. That Paul Cain was deeply concerned that he might not hear the word from his mother is based on the testimony of an eyewitness who never left Annie Cain's bedside. I spoke at length, face-to-face, with this lady. Does this mean that the story he regularly told of Annie awakening briefly and delivering to him the word concerning Luke 4:18 is false? Probably. Or it could also be that this happened precisely as Cain insists and that he was expecting yet another word from God through his mother. The bottom line is that we may never know with absolute certainty.

Being aware that his mother was near the end, Paul telephoned Mike Bickle and asked him to fly to Texas, to be at her bedside with Paul. Bickle arrived on April 18.[19] He insists that he was totally unaware of the Luke 4:18 word that Annie had previously given Paul. He claims that he did not hear of it nor grasp its significance until several weeks after her passing. According to Bickle's testimony, he just happened to look at the clock on her nightstand as she breathed her last. He also said that when the question was raised as to the time of her passing (information necessary to fill out the death certificate), he replied, "Yes. As a matter of fact. She died at 4:18."

You must understand that at the time this occurred Bickle insisted that this meant nothing to him. He was still unaware of anything prophetic in

---

18. The English Standard Version had not yet come into existence at this time; I use it here as it is my preferred translation.

19. On April 14, John and Carol Wimber flew in from Anaheim to pray for Annie Cain. On the next day, Jack Deere also flew in from Anaheim but had to depart for a conference in Nashville on the 17th, the day before Annie died.

Annie's death. A short time after this, Paul informed Mike of his mother's last words in which she prophesied Luke 4:18 over her son. A friend turned to Mike with a curious look on his face. "Mike, do we know when Annie Cain died?" "Yeah. In fact, I was looking at her bedside clock when she stopped breathing. Oh, my goodness! She died at 4:18 in the afternoon!" There was still more to come. "What day did she die," the questioner continued? Thinking for only a moment, Mike suddenly experienced another shock. "She died on April 18th!"

This is the point in our narrative that causes me to pause and question the veracity of the entire story. An article in the *Kansas City Star* newspaper, updated on May 15, 2024, written by Judy L. Thomas, reports that Annie M. Cain didn't die on April 18 but rather on April 19. The article also carries a photograph of her headstone that records the day of death as April 19, 1990.

At this stage I need to provide details that put most everything in a new light. The people who were present in the home that day were Paul Cain, Reed Grafke, Mike Bickle, Mildred (Paul Cain's sister), Jenny (Paul Cain's niece), and a nurse who wishes to remain anonymous. The latter individual kept a detailed record of everything done and said, both in the days preceding and including the time of Annie Cain's death. She also made a tape recording of every relevant event and spoken word by those who were present. She and her husband placed the cassette tape in their safety deposit box, where it remained for the next thirty-four years. They retrieved the tape, and I sat with both of them and listened to it while taking copious notes.

On the tape, and according to what this anonymous nurse shared with me, "In the time that I was able to be with her (April 2–18, 1990) she could follow some verbal commands in that time, but I never heard her utter a word. I was with Annie all afternoon on the day she died—up until the time that she passed and afterwards—and she was nonverbal and unresponsive (unable to eat, drink, follow commands to move, etc.) all that day. Annie never awoke that day, and I never witnessed her speaking to Paul or anyone at any time."

At approximately 4:00 p.m. on April 18, Annie Cain appeared to stop breathing, but her heart was still beating. At Paul Cain's urgent request, the anonymous nurse provided CPR in the hope that Annie would revive. By 4:15 her heart stopped and all present at her bed prayed fervently that she would remain alive until she could deliver to Paul the word from God that he believed had been promised to him.

Annie ceased breathing and her heart stopped sometime between 4:00 and 4:30. A considerable period of time, at least several hours, passed before her body was transported to the hospital morgue. The reason is that Cain insisted that a female be entrusted with her body. He did not want a man to see his naked mother's body. It took some time before Reed Grafke and the unnamed lady were able to locate a female who could be entrusted with Annie's body, in keeping with Paul's request.

Here we have a conflict in the details of precisely what occurred. Mike Bickle contends that Annie whispered Luke 4:18 to Paul just before she died. Said Bickle, Paul leaned over and pressed his ear close to her at which time she whispered the prophetic promise based on that text of Scripture. But as we have already noted, Cain himself often said that this "4:18" word uttered by his mother occurred several days, if not weeks, earlier. The nurse who was at Annie Cain's bedside told me that at no time did she speak or whisper anything to anyone, clearly contradicting Bickle's account of the event.

They chose not to call an ambulance because they didn't want life-saving measures to be applied. They called the funeral home around 6:30 or 7:00 p.m., who in turn called the police. This was required anytime someone died at home. The police arrived and determined that everything had been done in accordance with the law. The medical examiner instructed those present to transfer Annie's body to the hospital.

The anonymous nurse asked permission and was granted the opportunity to ride in the van that was transporting Annie's body. Upon arrival at the hospital a doctor came and checked her vital signs and determined that she had indeed died. Sometime between 10:30 and 11:00 p.m., Annie's body was taken to the funeral home. Annie Cain was officially pronounced dead at approximately 11:00 p.m. By the time all the paperwork had been filled out it was approaching midnight.

The article in the *Kansas City Star* displays the death certificate which says she died at 9:50 p.m. But the anonymous nurse—who was taking meticulous notes and whose tape recording from April 18, 1990, I listened to—disputes this and insists Annie died sometime between 4:00 and 4:30 p.m. I'm only speculating here, but this may well account for the discrepancy in the time of Annie's death. The unnamed nurse with whom I spoke told me that she remembers it vividly. If accurate, it would at least allow as accurate Bickle's narrative that she died at 4:18. But Annie's death certificate records the time of death as 9:50 p.m. on April 19. However, next to the listed time of death is a box that reads, "The date signed, 4/23/90." The word that I have here rendered "The" is somewhat hard to read. It may be different. But the date is quite clear. In other words, it was at least four days, perhaps five, subsequent to her passing that the death certificate was signed and dated. It is entirely within the realm of possibility that an inadvertent mistake was made, thus recording the day of death as the 19th rather than the 18th.

Bickle also said that medical personnel present asked everyone, "When did she die?" That is when he replied, "I was looking at the clock on her nightstand and it said 4:18." But the only medical personnel present was the unnamed nurse, who insists that she "never asked Mike that question." When the police arrived later that evening to release Annie's body to the medical examiner, they asked about the time of her death. The nurse had it written down that she died "a little after 4 p.m." But she nowhere wrote down 4:18, nor does she remember the precise time of Annie's death ever being mentioned. The bottom line is that, according to the eyewitness testimony of the nurse, neither she nor anyone else asked Bickle about the time of death or ever heard him speak the time as 4:18 in the afternoon.

But what about the headstone? The photograph published in the newspaper clearly says, Annie Matilda Cain, October 20, 1885/April 19, 1990. I don't know who was responsible for providing the information to the cemetery. Nor do I know when the information was supplied or when the headstone was carved. It seems reasonable to conclude that whoever provided the cemetery with the information that appears on the headstone did so based on the death certificate. But the time and day of death on the certificate are quite clearly incorrect. I say "quite clearly" because of the unshakable testimony of two eyewitnesses (the nurse and her husband) who not only wrote down the day and time of her passing but also recorded it on a cassette tape.

My best conclusion from the details I have shared is that both the written and recorded testimony of the anonymous nurse cannot be questioned. Bickle's story as to the time of Annie's death appears to be entirely within the realm of possibility. I again remind us all that the nurse who attended Annie Cain up until the time of her death insists it occurred somewhere between 4:00 and 4:30 on April 18. It is not beyond reason to conclude that Bickle may have noted that the precise time was 4:18. The discrepancy between the information on both the death certificate and the headstone, on the one hand, and the detailed written and recorded sequence provided by the unnamed nurse, on the other, may never be resolved. For me, I trust without hesitation the testimony of this nurse who was present every minute and hour of every day leading up to Annie Cain's death.

I can only draw the following conclusions about this entire scenario. First, there is a conflict in Paul Cain's testimony of when (or even if) he heard his mother deliver the prophetic promise based on Luke 4:18. Bickle said it was moments before her passing whereas the nurse insists that Annie spoke no words to anyone. Second, Paul often said he heard this a considerable period of time before she died, and yet was deeply concerned on the day of her death that she might pass away before having the opportunity to speak it. Both cannot be true. Third, contrary to Bickle's retelling of the event, Paul did not bend over close to Annie's ear at which time she spoke the 4:18 word. Fourth, again contrary to Bickle's testimony, no medical personnel were present other than the anonymous nurse. Fifth, the nurse never asked him when Annie died, and he never told her, "4:18." Sixth, it is entirely possible that Annie Cain did die sometime between 4:00 and 4:30 p.m. on the April 18. Seventh, the extended gap between her death (approximately 4:00–4:30 p.m.) and the time the death certificate was signed (approximately 11:00 p.m.) indicates that not even the medical examiner can be entirely trusted.

In the final analysis, Bickle's recollection that she died at 4:18 on April 18 is within the scope of reason. But given the other inconsistencies in how the story was communicated by Paul Cain and Mike Bickle, as well as the eyewitness testimony of the unnamed nurse, I am reluctant to endorse this as a legitimate supernatural or providential event.

Addendum A:
A Misconception Concerning the Theology of Mike Bickle

Mike Bickle has long been the target of so-called "discernment" bloggers who believe him to be a heretic. Although I have earlier addressed this charge, and affirmed Bickle's generally orthodox interpretation of Scripture, there are a few additional areas where he has been attacked. I have said this before, but I must reiterate once again, that *we must never allow Bickle's biblical orthodoxy to diminish the gravity of his moral failure.* Nor should the reader assume that my defense of Bickle's theology indicates that I believe he should at some time return to public ministry. I do *not*.

One aspect of Bickle's theology concerns his interpretation of the Song of Solomon and what he calls the "bridal paradigm." In the next chapter I'll describe how Bickle came to devote himself to the Song as a result of a revelatory word he claims to have received from Bob Jones. But here my concern is with the accusation that his view of the Song is overly erotic, romantic, and comes close to portraying the believer's relationship with Jesus in excessively familiar and even sexual tones. On the website of the now defunct IHOPKC (www.ihopkc.org), there are several affirmations and denials that typically reflect Bickle's own views. Here is what it says about this first charge.

> We affirm that the Bridegroom message is about Jesus' emotions for us, His beauty, His commitments to us (to share His

heart, home, throne, secrets, and beauty), and our response of wholehearted love and obedience to Him. This message starts with experiencing Jesus' heart, emotions, and affections for us, and understanding that He delights in us, enjoys us, values our work, and calls us to partner with Him in ministry.

We affirm that the bridal paradigm refers to having a bridal perspective of the kingdom. As Christians, we see the kingdom through the eyes of a bride, with wholehearted, loyal love for God. There are many paradigms of the kingdom of God in Scripture, including agricultural, military, and economic paradigms. The Spirit uses the bridal paradigm of the kingdom to transform our hearts, so that the first and great commandment to love God with all our heart, soul, and mind (Matt 22:37–38) might take first place in our lives.

We deny, we refuse, all sensual overtones in proclaiming Jesus as the Bridegroom. Jesus is not our lover or boyfriend. We do not go on "dates" with Jesus. Receiving the "kiss of God's Word" (Song 1:2) has nothing to do with physically kissing God. Neither the spiritual interpretation of the Song of Solomon nor references to "the romance of the gospel" have anything to do with sensuality, but with the adventuresome love that is filled with a spirit of abandonment that sacrificially loves and obeys Jesus. An example of this is seen when Paul and Silas sang songs of love to Jesus after being beaten and thrown into prison (Acts 16:22–26).

We affirm that spiritual intimacy with God refers to developing a deep personal relationship with God through the Spirit and the Word. In other words, it is based on a deep understanding and knowledge of what the Word of God says about God the Father, God the Son, and God the Holy Spirit.

We deny that spiritual intimacy is associated with anything related to human sensuality.

Explanation: For example, in Song of Songs 1:2, the phrase "kiss me with the kisses of his mouth" (NKJV) can be seen as an analogy, a divine metaphor referring to Jesus imparting revelation of the words of His mouth to our hearts. We speak of "the kisses of His Word," not of physical kisses from Jesus.[20]

Yet another allegation is that IHOPKC in general and Bickle in particular embrace and teach the doctrine within the Latter Rain movement

---

20. In private conversations with me, a handful of former IHOPKC staff members have argued that, notwithstanding Bickle's insistence that the Song has nothing to do with human sensuality, it was often manipulated to groom young women, making them more vulnerable to sexual advances.

known as "the manifest sons of God." I'll respond to this accusation later in the book.

The perspective known as "dominion theology" (or at times, "the seven mountain mandate") has also been laid at the feet of Bickle. Here again is Bickle's and IHOPKC's response.

> We affirm that God's purpose is for Jesus to come back to fully establish His kingdom rule over all the earth. After the second coming, the saints will rule the earth under the leadership of Jesus Christ when He sets up His government on earth in Jerusalem in the millennial kingdom (1 Cor 6:2; Rev 5:10; 20:3–6). We believe that believers in this age are called to serve Jesus in politics and to help establish righteousness and justice in legislation. We do not have the assurance that all laws and governments will be changed until after the second coming of Jesus when He establishes His millennial kingdom.
>
> We deny that the Church will take over all the governments of the earth before the return of Christ.
>
> Explanation: Some believe and teach that all governments on earth will be transformed by the Church before the second coming of Jesus.

One final misconception concerns what has often been referred to as "Joel's army." When Paul Cain visited Kansas City Fellowship for the first time in 1987, he paused before walking into the building and spoke to Bickle: "I saw a banner over this building which reads: Joel's army in training." Here is how Bickle understands this concept.

> We affirm that the army in Joel 2:1–11 was an ungodly Babylonian army that destroyed Jerusalem in 586 BC. We believe that this passage has a double fulfillment in that it also points to the Antichrist's army that will attack Israel at the end of the age. We affirm that Joel was prophesying about the lifestyle of godly believers in Joel 2:12–17.
>
> We deny that Joel 2:1–11 describes the end-time Church.
>
> Explanation: The term Joel's army has been used to signify the people who walk out the principles of prayer with fasting as taught in Joel 2:12–17. The term has been used much like "Joseph Company," "Gideon Band," or "David Company" to signify the people who embraced the godly qualities that Joel taught about prayer, fasting, and wholehearted obedience. Paul Cain had a prophetic word about a "Joel's army in training," referring to a group of people who would give themselves to prayer and fasting according to Joel 2:12–17. When used like this, "Joel's

army" does not refer specifically to the destroying army mentioned in Joel 2:1–11, but to people who walk out the lifestyle portrayed in Joel 2:12–17. The misunderstanding comes from giving the title "Joel's army" to both the destroying army (Joel 2:1–11) and the group of people who give themselves to fasting and prayer (Joel 2:12–17).

CHAPTER FOUR

Who Is Bob Jones?

ANYONE WHO KNEW OR encountered Bob Jones would not instinctively identify him as a highly educated and socially sophisticated prophet in the Christian church. His appearance, mannerisms, and speech patterns would more likely place him as a regular guest on the old TV show *Hee-Haw*. Jones, born in 1930, in Gravely, Arkansas, was the son of poor illiterate sharecroppers. His clothes rarely fit him well and he struggled to string together two coherent, grammatically correct sentences. And yet those who knew him marveled at his revelatory gifting.

I never knew Bob Jones to the extent that I did Paul Cain, but I will never forget my first meeting with him. Noel Alexander, who will appear later in this book, invited me to join him and Bob for lunch. We sat down at a relatively high-dollar restaurant in Kansas City and began our conversation. "Hold out your hand," said Bob, "with your palm facing me." I obliged, having been informed by others of one of Bob's gestures upon meeting a person for the first time. Bob placed his hand up against mine, all five of my fingers aligned with all five of his. I could feel his fingers beginning to move. All this mind you, with a dozen or so expensively dressed businessmen watching with differing degrees of horror or embarrassment.

"Do you feel that?" he asked me?

"I'm not sure. What am I supposed to feel?" Bob proceeded to tell me that each finger on his hand represented one of the five ministry gifts listed in Ephesians 4:11. Suddenly, his pinky finger began to twitch.

"Uh, huh. That's what I thought. You're a teacher, ain't you?" I replied in the affirmative, and Bob smiled at what he perceived to be the accuracy of his insight. I must say that although he appeared quite sincere, I find this method of identifying someone's spiritual gift or calling in ministry to be both weird and lacking in biblical support.

"Whoa," he almost shouted. "Did ya' see it?"

"See what?" I replied. I looked over at Noel and he was as bewildered as I was.

"Right up yonder, near that air vent. It's a big blue angel. Oh, he's gone now."

I tried my best not to acknowledge Bob's comment, but the look on his face as he gazed at the ceiling undoubtedly caught the attention of everyone sitting near us. Thankfully, Noel instantly changed the subject of our conversation, thereby preserving what little social dignity remained for both of us. Bob, on the other hand, quite honestly couldn't have cared less what these executives might have thought. To say he was lacking in social skills is a massive understatement. If anything, he did his best to consciously violate them in the name of the Lord!

Early Life and Claims of Supernatural Encounters

Much of what you are about to read is entirely dependent on Bob Jones himself. No one else was present to verify or refute what Bob claimed about his spiritual experiences.

Jones claims that his first supernatural encounter occurred when he was seven years old. He believes it happened in August under a scorching sun, as he was walking on a dirt road, barefooted. He "saw" a white horse descend out of heaven, together with an angel. The angel stood in front of Jones and blew a silver trumpet in his face. Jones is convinced the angel was Gabriel. He was so terrified by the encounter that he thought he would die. If you are wondering what the purpose for this angelic visitation might be (on the questionable assumption that it was real), I have no good answer. Neither did Jones.

His life, however, was minimally affected by this event, as Jones soon turned to excessive drinking and a life of violence. After marrying Viola in 1951, he joined the Marine Corps the following year and served briefly during the Korean War. He later suffered a nervous breakdown and was admitted to the Veteran's Hospital in Topeka, Kansas. After nine days in the hospital, a demon supposedly appeared to him in a dream and urged him to kill the twelve people responsible for him being there (other reports say there were only seven individuals). Jones somehow found the strength to resist the temptation to follow the demon's command.

There are multiple stories that Jones would tell of being assaulted in the night by demons who threatened him if he didn't stop speaking out against abortion and homosexuality. He worked as a tree trimmer for a considerable period of time. On one occasion he describes being struck with an unbearable pain in his abdomen. During his time of treatment, he had a dream in which a man in all white appeared and gave him the option of either entrance into heaven or continued ministry on earth. While greatly tempted to choose the former, he opted for the latter.

Jones also claimed that during a thunderstorm he was struck by lightning. His time in the hospital was short-lived as he emerged from this experience with only a few minor burns. In the aftermath of this event Jones began to experience vivid dreams and visions. He also started sensing things about people of whom he had no prior knowledge. Bob Scott believes Jones

> ended up with a form of "Acquired Savant Syndrome" when extraordinary skills emerge after a non-disabling, traumatic head injury. Others have been struck by lightning or received a head injury and suddenly have extraordinary talents they never had before, like art or music, or the ability to perform rapid mathematical calculations. It seems the extreme electrical shock and trauma rewire their brain. Unfortunately, this extraordinary gift was in the possession of a very broken, dysfunctional, and needy human being.[1]

I have no way of knowing if this diagnosis is accurate or if Jones's experience is what accounted for his facility in the spiritual gift of word of knowledge. Scripture clearly teaches that this gift is distributed by the Holy Spirit according to the latter's will (1 Cor 12:11). Might the Spirit have used this alleged lightning strike as the means for imparting a spiritual gift? I doubt if anyone will ever know.

Bob Jones's First Meeting with Mike Bickle

Mike Bickle was only twenty-seven years old when he and Diane moved to Kansas City in late 1982. He held the first official meeting of South Kansas City Fellowship on December 5th.

In January of 1983 an elderly and respected pastor in the city by the name of Oral McClain asked if Bickle would be willing to meet with a man named Bob Jones. "Who is he?" asked Bickle. "He's a true prophet of God," came the reply. "He's been telling people for quite some time that a

---

1. Scott, *Some Said They Blundered*, 59.

twenty-seven-year-old man would come to the south side of Kansas City, preaching on intercession and revival." Mike was not pleased with the request. "That's all I need, a prophet to deal with," said Mike, with more than a little cynicism. Besides that, as I'm sure you recall, Mike had been informed by Augustine Alcala that in the early days of his new church a false prophet would appear on the scene. Augustine was the man who entered Bickle's church in St. Louis in June of 1982 with the astounding declaration that God had spoken audibly, the essence of which eventually prompted Bickle to leave his beloved St. Louis and plant a church in Kansas City. It wasn't until the fourth month of the church's young life that Bickle finally agreed to a meeting with Bob Jones.

Just as a reminder to us all, Alcala also informed Bickle that the work in Kansas City would draw thousands of young people, that in due time there would be a full manifestation of the gifts of the Spirit (1 Cor 12:7–11) in power, and that there would be misunderstanding and opposition to the new work, even from well-meaning friends. After Mike agreed to meet with Bob Jones and saw him for the first time, he was convinced that at least one of Augustine's four "words" was true.

"This is the false prophet, for sure," Bickle said to himself.

Jones walked into his office on March 7, 1983, wearing a long, heavy winter coat, despite the fact that winter seemed to have passed with the temperature that day reaching into the mid-70s. He did this to symbolize that there would be a double winter in Kansas City.[2]

Looking at Mike, Jones said, "Uh, huh, I've seen you."

"Yeah, and I've seen you, too," Mike replied (thinking of Alcala's warning of a false prophet).[3]

"Yup, uh, huh, this is it. Yeah, you're the ones. God told me several years ago that a group of young people would be coming to south Kansas City, led by a pastor in his late twenties who would preach on intercession and revival."

---

2. There is a discrepancy here in Bickle's memory. According to all accounts that I have searched, the high temperature in Kansas City on March 7, 1983, was 51 degrees. To Mike's way of thinking, that may still have been sufficiently warm to justify his surprise by how Jones was dressed. I also heard Bickle on Jim Bakker's TV show (date unknown) stating that it was around 80 degrees on that day. This sort of "convenient exaggeration" is one reason why many are highly suspicious of the prophetic history in its totality.

3. Many are likely asking at this stage of our narrative: Who was the false prophet? While I was still at the church in Kansas City, I asked Mike if this individual was ever identified. He said yes and proceeded to give me his name. I can only regard it as the mercy of the Lord that for the life of me I can't remember who it was. Perhaps that is for the best.

Needless to say, this caught Bickle totally off guard. He later checked with Jones's former pastor and discovered that Jones had spoken often since 1974 about a group of young people coming to south Kansas City in the spring of 1983, led by a man in his twenties who preached on intercession and revival. It wasn't to be the last time that predictive words from Bob Jones would be confirmed by a third party.

In the next hour or so Bickle was treated to strange stories of angels and visions and demons and dreams and healings and divine judgment. "It was like something out of *Star Wars*," said Mike. When he returned home after their time together, he commented to Diane, "That was better than any $4 movie I've been to. The sad thing is, I actually like this guy. It's too bad he's the false prophet." Bickle's fears seemed to be confirmed when Jones proceeded to prophesy his own acceptance.

"The Lord says that 'on the first day of spring, when the snow melts, they will sit around the table and they will accept you.' And he gave me the words, *agape* and *koinonia*."

"Who are 'they'?" Mike asked. "What are you talking about?"

"'They' means 'you,'" said Jones. "You at this church will accept me and never reject me."

It all sounded suspicious to Mike. But he listened attentively. After their time together, Bob turned to walk away.

"Oh, by the way. The Lord told me to tell you four things about the movement, and that you would understand. First, the work will draw thousands of young people. Second, there will be a release in time of the gifts of the Spirit, people will misunderstand what you are doing and will oppose the work here, and there will be a false prophet in your midst from the beginning."

Bickle was more than a little stunned. He checked to see if Augustine knew Bob Jones. Perhaps they had conferred on this "prophecy" in order to worm their way into a position of influence in this new work. But no, they had never met. Mike was convinced. But he still suspected that Jones might be the false prophet.

"Write down my phone number," Bob said, almost as an afterthought. "You may want to call me later."

"Oh, that's OK," Mike said, trying not to sound too offensive.

"Please," Bob insisted, "write it down."

"OK," Mike hastily wrote it down and shoved the piece of paper in his wallet.

Before leaving this phase of the story I need to describe one specific prophetic word that Jones gave Bickle. He not only told him that a day was coming when thousands of young people would gather in Kansas City for worship and intercession, but that there would also be a spiritual awakening in China and the Far East. Jones told Bickle of a vision he had in which numerous people standing in rice paddies wore what appeared to be cordless or unplugged TVs on their wrists or carried them in their hand, watching the prayer and praise services in Kansas City. We must remember that this was in 1983, years before the cell phone was invented and well in advance of the internet. Regardless of what you may think of prophetic ministry, this scenario is difficult to explain apart from God having revealed it to Jones. Of course, I suppose some may insist that it was the product of an overly active imagination, or perhaps even a demon.

An Astounding Confirmation

Two weeks later a friend of Bickle's named Art Katz came to town to visit for the weekend. After the Sunday morning service, Art met Bob Jones and engaged him in a long conversation. Mike saw them talking and fully expected Art to pick up on the fact that Bob was a false prophet. But that's not what he heard from Art.

"Who is that white-haired man over there?" asked Art.

"I'm not real sure," said Bickle. "I only met him two weeks ago."

"I don't care what anyone says," Art quickly replied. "This man is a prophet of God. He told me things about my life that no one could know unless God told him!" One thing in particular stunned Katz, as Jones told him the details of a dream he, Art, had experienced the previous night. Needless to say, Mike was a bit confused by Art's assessment. How could Bob be a false prophet and still read the secrets of men's hearts?

Art was scheduled to fly out of Kansas City that same Sunday evening, but bad weather forced him to stay overnight.[4] He and Mike visited another church that evening and arranged to meet with the pastor following the service. But in the providence of God, the pastor informed them after his message that an emergency had arisen and he was forced to cancel their appointment.[5] Mike may have been disappointed, but Art surely wasn't! He wanted to take advantage of the opportunity so he asked Mike if there was any way they could get together with Bob Jones one more time before

---

4. Records reveal that there was 0.3 of an inch of snow that fell on March 20. Whether or not that was a sufficient amount of snow to delay Katz's departure, he was determined to meet Jones again and so delayed his departure until the following day. See also the article by Shepherd, "Gentlest of Winters."

5. The pastor was Ernie Gruen. His church was Full Faith Church of Love in Shawnee, Kansas.

he had to leave. By now it was almost 8:30 at night. Art was on the verge of weeping.

"I've got to see that white-haired man again," he spoke with a trembling voice.

"Sure," said Mike, "I'll see what I can do. But I don't know where he lives. I don't even have his phone number."

Suddenly Mike remembered Bob's insistence that he write down his number.

"Wait a minute; I do have his number after all. I'll give him a call."

When Jones answered the telephone he said, "I've been waiting all day for you to call. Actually, though, I thought it would be Art who would contact me. The burden was on him." That night Mike, Diane, Pat Bickle, Art, Bob Jones, and several others gathered at Mike's duplex for a time of fellowship. What Mike heard next would change his life forever.

"Mike," said Bob, "I was mistaken about something I told you. Do you remember when I shared with you about a vision I had of a white horse and a man lying on a board on the horse's back?"

"Yeah," Mike replied, "so what?"

"Well," Bob continued, "I thought it was you on the board on the back of the horse, but I was wrong. It was your brother Pat. When Pat first asked me if I'd ever seen him, I said no. But last night an angel appeared to me in a night vision and revealed to me that I hadn't told the truth when I said I'd never seen Pat. Now I realize it was Pat lying on the board on the horse's back."

Earlier I recounted the story about Pat Bickle, Mike's younger brother, who was paralyzed from the neck down in a high school football game in 1973. I also told you that Bobby Bickle had asked Mike to make a covenant with him and God to commit himself to caring for Pat. Mike's dad sensed that he wouldn't be around very long to do it himself, and he knew that it would be too difficult for any of Mike's five sisters to undertake the task. Bobby Bickle died only a few months later, at the age of forty-five, and Mike was faced with the task of caring for Pat.

It was October of 1973. Mike and his father were standing outside Pat's room.

"Sure dad," said Mike. "It will be an easy thing, because he's not heavy, he's my brother and I love him so."

So, there they sat ten years later, with Bob Jones apologizing to Mike and Pat for confusing them when he saw the white-horse vision.

"Not only that," Jones continued, "but when the angel told me that it was Pat on the board, I commented to you in the vision about the heavy responsibility you had in taking care of him. I heard you say, 'That's ok, he's not heavy, he's my brother and I love him so.' The Lord said you would understand that sentence."

Bickle crumpled to the ground, weeping. "You have no idea of what you have just said. You have just quoted the very words I pledged to my dad in 1973 when I promised to take care of Pat. No one but God knew about it. Surely, you are a prophet of God!"

At that moment, Bob asked Mike: "What is today?"

"It's Sunday night, why? As a matter of fact, it's about 1:00 a.m. on Monday. But what difference does it make?"

"No," said Bob, "I mean what day of the month is it?"

After thinking for a moment, Mike answered: "It's March 21st."

"I know," said Bob, "but what is March 21st?"

"It's the first day of spring," Mike replied, finally putting two and two together.

"And why did Art have to stay overnight?" Bob kept pressing his point.

"Because of the snow," said Mike.

"Look outside. What's happening?"

Mike looked and said, "Well, it's melting."

As if to bring it all together in one momentous declaration, Bob said: "Thus says the Lord, 'On the first day of spring, as the snow melts, they will sit around the table in love (*agape*) and fellowship (*koinonia*) and they will accept you.' This night has been ordained of the Lord." Bickle himself explains the significance of what happened that night:

> The unexpected snow on March 21 was precisely predicted by Bob to confirm the prophetic vision that God was raising up a prophetic young adult prayer movement of prophetic singers and musicians in Kansas City. The prediction of unexpected snow coming exactly on March 21, after several weeks of unseasonably warm weather was a small yet significant sign in the heavens or sky that confirmed Bob's prophecy to us.[6]

A consistent theme in Bickle's telling of the prophetic history is the reason why he came to invest so much trust in Bob Jones and his revelatory gift. Whenever Mike was tempted to dismiss Jones, he would recall the remarkable and very personal experience on the night of March 20 and the early morning hours of March 21. He would do the same with Jones's prophecy of an undetected comet that I will explain later in this book.

---

6. Bickle, *Growing in the Prophetic*, 14.

The Song of Solomon

The legitimacy of Bob Jones's prophetic gifting was confirmed by several events, one of which was to set the trajectory of Bickle's teaching ministry for years to come.

As you probably know, the Song of Solomon is typically understood today to be a love song about the sexual and romantic relationship between a husband and his wife. This has not always been the case. In fact, prior to the middle of the nineteenth century, virtually the entire church, both Roman Catholic and Protestant, had understood the Song to be a parable or type or poetic analogy that focused on the love relationship between Christ and the church. It may well be both.

Bickle had never enjoyed the Song. He found it to be a bit too romantic for his liking. But one day he was alone in his office and the Lord took him to Song of Solomon 8:6–7. Here is the text:

> Set me as a seal upon your heart, as a seal upon your arm, for love is strong as death, jealousy is fierce as the grave. Its flashes are flashes of fire, the very flame of the Lord. Many waters cannot quench love, neither can floods drown it. If a man offered for love all the wealth of his house, he would be utterly despised. (Song 8:6–7)

The traditional Christian view was that the Song of Solomon portrays in graphic terms the love that exists between Christ and his bride, the church, and the individual members of it. Such was the view of all the medieval mystics, virtually all in the Roman Catholic tradition, even the Protestant Reformers such as John Calvin. Jonathan Edwards preached on the Song and took it this way as well. Charles Spurgeon too, in the nineteenth century, preached on it in the same way.

As I said, Bickle didn't know quite what to make of the Song, until that day when the Spirit came on him in power and directed his attention to 8:6–7. Mike began to weep, as he felt the presence of God and the importance of this text. He spoke through the intercom and told his secretary that he was not to be interrupted; not by anyone! He then returned to his meditation on these two verses.

About five minutes later, the secretary spoke to him: "Mike, I'm so sorry, but it's Bob Jones, and he says it's really, really important that he speaks with you." Mike was more than a little perturbed. Reluctantly, he told her to put Bob through.

"Mike," said Bob, "I'm in a hurry. I was actually getting into the car and on my way to the airport. I'm already late for my flight. But as I did, the Lord reminded me that he spoke to me in an audible voice last night. I thought it was important enough to risk missing my flight to run back in and call you. Can I share it with you?"

"Sure," Mike responded with more than a little exasperation in his voice.

"Is there a book in the Bible called the Song of Solomon? I had never heard of it before."

"Uh, well, yes," said Mike, whose interest was now slightly increased.

"Well, the Lord spoke clearly and said to give you Song of Solomon 8:6–7. He said that this was to be the 'cargo' that you should take to the nations. Are there eight chapters in that book? Well, there you have it. Got to go." And he hung up the phone.

Bickle fell to his knees once again and began to weep uncontrollably. "Amazing," he thought to himself, "that God would speak to Jones about this odd biblical book and give him the very verses that I'm meditating on. And even more, that Jones would interrupt his trip to the airport at just the time I was deeply in thought and prayer over that very text of Scripture."

It was clearly a prophetic sign and confirmation that Bickle could hardly ignore.

This is one more incident that depends for its credibility on the personal testimony of Bickle alone. As Bob Jones is no longer with us, one must decide if Bickle's word is sufficient to justify our confidence that this event happened precisely as he described.

Prophetic Tokens

The following was somewhat typical of the interaction between Jones and Bickle. It was Easter Sunday, April 3. Mike woke up with a deep desire to see the lost saved. For quite some time that morning he labored in intercessory prayer for lost souls. Although he was excited and felt considerable energy to preach that Sunday morning, his sermon was dry and barren. People were obviously bored. At the close of the service Mike issued six altar calls, but no one responded. After the service a man approached Bickle and asked for prayer. After praying, Mike touched his forehead and the man fell to ground, crying out for salvation. Then a lady came forward. Mike prayed, with the same results. Then it happened yet again, a third time. As Bickle was leaving the auditorium he encountered Bob Jones. "I saw you in a vision last night," said Jones. "You were getting ready to throw a net, but the Lord stopped you. It wasn't the appointed time. Instead, he gave you a fishhook. With it you pierced through and grabbed three fish and brought them into the boat." Bickle was understandably astounded. And yet again the legitimacy of this story is dependent on the integrity of both Bickle and Jones. Did it truly happen as Bickle described, or was this a fabricated event, borne of deceit? We probably will never know with certainty, but I'm inclined to believe it happened precisely as Bickle described.

A similar scenario played out during the Solemn Assembly. Bickle was deep in meditation on Psalm 27:4—"One thing have I asked of the LORD, that will I seek after: that I may dwell in the house of the LORD all the days of my life, to gaze upon the beauty of the LORD and to inquire in his temple." Bickle had turned this text into a prayer back to God, but never said a word on the microphone nor shared it with anyone else. The next day Bob Jones came to him and said, "The Lord wanted you to know he says, Yes."

"Yes to what?" asked Bickle.

"Yes, to the prayer you prayed yesterday; Psalm 27:4!" Could Jones have picked up on this by natural means? Yes. Could he have made an educated guess, given the fact that this text is one of Bickle's favorites? Yes. But it is also just as possible that the Holy Spirit revealed this to him to encourage Bickle in his pursuit and praise of the Lord.[7]

Prophetic Poetry and the Kansas City Royals

If you are a football fan, you are obviously aware that in February 2024 the Kansas City Chiefs won their third Super Bowl in the last five years. I write this chapter only a few days after the Chiefs defeated the Buffalo Bills to earn their third straight visit to the Super Bowl. Quite a few people from Kansas City have insisted that Bob Jones prophesied that when the Chiefs won it would mark the beginning of a great revival and harvest of souls. Mike Bickle has repeatedly stated that he never heard Jones issue a prophecy of this sort. One thing, however, is certain. No such revival has yet broken out. Whether we will ever know for certain if Jones spoke this predictive word, we do know that he was quite accurate when it came to the Kansas City Royals, the city's major league baseball team.

Before I describe what happened, I want to suggest that our world is filled with the prophetic poetry of God. By *prophetic poetry* I'm referring to the countless ways in which God communicates and reveals himself to us even in the seemingly mundane affairs of life. I'm not suggesting that we go

---

7. Among the many odd claims made by Jones is the one concerning the Red Heifer. He told several friends that he had just returned from seeing the ashes of the Red Heifer in a cave in the Qumran region of Israel. I trust that we can simply write this off for what it is: prophetic silliness.

to such an extreme that we find in *everything* something of spiritual significance. But let's not forget that every blade of grass that grows (Ps 104:14) and every drop of rain that falls (Ps 104:10–13) and every flake of snow that drifts earthward (Ps 147:16) and every breeze that blows (Ps 147:18) is the handiwork of God! The God who turns the heart of the king to accomplish his purpose (Prov 21:1) and works all things according to the counsel of his will (Eph 1:11) is more than able to take both the small and great things of his world and use them to make known his heart and ways.

11!

One rather surprising example of this occurred in 1985. On a Sunday morning in June, Bob Jones came to Mike Bickle and said, "God is going to speak to us through the baseball game." Your reaction to that is probably much like that of most who were in church that day. It seemed strange, to say the least. Bickle especially struggled with it, in part because he knows so little about baseball: he's a football fan. But Jones wasn't finished. "The Lord said that he would speak to this church through the baseball game, and that for a time it would appear that Kansas City would lose, but suddenly they will win."

At least one thing was clear from this word: The experience of the Kansas City Royals major league baseball team was to be a prophetic parable for what would happen to the movement of God in Kansas City. In case you are wondering, Jones didn't deliver this word in private but in public so that the entire body of Christ that day can testify to its accuracy.

The season was well under way when this word was given. It was June and the Royals were struggling. By the time of the All-Star break in July they were seven games out of first place. When September arrived, it didn't appear as if the Royals would make the playoffs. But a sudden winning surge late in the month catapulted them into the playoffs. They faced the Toronto Blue Jays for the privilege of going to the World Series.

Just as had been predicted, it appeared as if Kansas City would lose, only to win suddenly. The Royals fell behind three games to one but staged a remarkable rally to win the best-of-seven series 4–3. Game Six looked to be the end of the road for Kansas City, but a two-run ninth inning pulled out a victory for the underdogs.

The Royals were matched in the World Series against their cross-state rival, the St. Louis Cardinals. The media referred to it as the I-70 Series because Kansas City and St. Louis are connected by Interstate 70 in Missouri.

No one gave the Royals much of a chance against the more talented Cardinals. The Series did not start well for the Royals. They began by losing the first two games at home. It may interest you to know that, at that time, no team in World Series history had *ever* lost the first two games at home and come back to win. It only got worse, as after four games they found themselves on the short end of a three-games-to-one deficit. Those of you who are baseball fans know that virtually no one recovers from a three-games-to-one deficit in a best-of-seven series. In fact, it had only been accomplished six times prior to 1985. In the sixth game the Cardinals should have won, but a controversial call at first base allowed the Royals to stay alive for the drama of a seventh and deciding game.

Those who witnessed that sixth game will never forget it. Although I had not yet moved to Kansas City, I saw the play on television, together with millions of other fans. It was the bottom of the ninth inning and the Royals trailed 1–0. Jorge Orta hit a ground ball to the right side of the infield, forcing the St. Louis pitcher, Todd Worrell, to cover first. Umpire Don Denkinger called Orta safe. However, the television replay clearly showed that he was out. If you want to see what happened, you can watch it on YouTube.[8] The fact that he was safe totally changed the complexion of the inning and catapulted Kansas City to a comeback victory, 3–2. One other interesting baseball fact is that this was the *only* time all year that the St. Louis Cardinals blew a lead in the ninth inning!

Game seven was scheduled for Sunday night, October 27. On Saturday, the 26th, Bob Jones came once again to Bickle and said, "The Lord is going to speak to us through the number 11 in the game tomorrow." No one knew exactly what this meant, but so far everything else seemed to be panning out just as Jones had prophesied. Certainly, the part about Kansas City on the verge of losing when suddenly they win seemed to be happening. Numerous people who heard the "11" word were anxious for Sunday night to arrive. In case you may have forgotten, unlike most final games of the World Series, this one was a rout. The Kansas City Royals won by a score of 11–0! The newspapers dubbed it the "Miracle Series." They had their reasons for calling it that, and the church in Kansas City had theirs!

The Sexual Sin and Discipline of Bob Jones

Over the next six or seven years, Bob Jones was integral to the life of the church, especially when it came to prophetic ministry. Later in this book

---

8. MLB, "WS1985 Gm6."

you will hear of several incidents in which Jones prophesied with astounding accuracy. But dark days were looming.

Paul Cain approached Bob Jones on July 17, 1991, with prophetic insight into Bob's struggle with lust. Cain had no objective validation to his insights and therefore no action was taken at that time. Bob admitted he struggled with lust and heeded Cain's counsel that he not minister to any woman alone or lay hands on them in prayer. Jones sought prayer from Cain, Mahesh Chavda, and Rick Joyner and believed he had experienced significant breakthrough in his battle with lust. Cain then reported to Bickle what he had sensed concerning Jones's struggle with lust and encouraged him to keep an eye out for any indications of moral failure.

Bickle learned in October of 1991 that Jones had been inappropriately involved with two women. He confronted Jones with this information and the latter provided a partial confession. Bickle then communicated this with John Wimber on November 1 and informed him on November 2 of all that he knew concerning Jones's sin. Wimber in turn enlisted the help of Ken Gullikson, North American director of the Association of Vineyard Churches. Gullikson flew to Kansas City on November 3 and met with Bickle and Tim Johns, another pastor on Bickle's staff.

I should interrupt the flow of this chapter and quickly describe one reason why John Wimber was so devastated upon discovering Jones's moral failure. Sean Wimber, John and Carol's son had drifted away from the family and became addicted to drugs. Carol Wimber says that when Paul Cain first visited the Anaheim Vineyard (a story I tell in the next chapter), he informed them "that if John did as the Lord instructed (became a real father to the church), as a 'token of appreciation' from the Lord, our son Sean would 'see a great light before his next birthday and before John addresses the Vineyard again.'"[9] The national conference that year was in July and Sean's birthday was in August. Both John and Carol Wimber were greatly encouraged by this word from Paul Cain, but understandably somewhat skeptical.

Just as Cain had prophesied, Sean returned home in June, just prior to the conference. According to Connie Dawson, "Out of the blue one day, Jones knocked on Wimber's door. He asked to speak to Sean, but Wimber said Sean neither lived there nor was expected to visit anytime soon. Then suddenly, Sean walked in! Jones spoke words to Sean that opened his heart and caused him to repent and become reconciled to his family. As far as John and Carol were concerned, this was a true miracle."[10] John's reserva-

9. Wimber, *John Wimber*, 178.
10. Dawson, *John Wimber*, 156–57. On January 27, 2024, while in Yorba Linda,

tions about prophetic ministry were instantly transformed in the wake of these life-changing words from both Paul Cain and Bob Jones.

I now return to the story of Jones's moral failure. Bob met with Gullikson and other leaders in the church on November 4 and provided a more complete confession. In addition to the sexual dimension of his failure, Jones confessed to bitterness, slander, and creating division in response to the discipline Wimber had imposed on Jones in the summer of 1990. Wimber composed a letter on November 7, outlining the nature of Jones's failure and the discipline to be implemented. Jones also wrote a letter to the church confessing his sin and declaring that he was repentant. It should be noted that Jones was contrite and seemingly sincere in his confession of sin. The text of his letter is found at the end of this chapter.

It was at this time that Jones confessed to using his prophetic gift to manipulate two women into undressing in his presence. The sexual manipulation occurred periodically from March of 1991 through July. Although Jones kissed and fondled them, he never engaged in sexual intercourse. That is not to suggest that his sin was something less than egregious and reprehensible. My aim is simply to be as accurate as possible in describing what happened.

Wimber's letter concerning Jones was released publicly on November 10, 1991, and restrictions on Jones's ministry were put in place. They involved removal from all public prophetic ministry. Jones was also prohibited from traveling or ministering at any conference or retreat and was not permitted to receive phone calls or visitors to his home. The church was instructed to contact the pastoral staff should they discover that Jones had violated any of these conditions.

Considerable pastoral care and extensive prayer for both Jones and his wife, Viola, was provided, the results of which were communicated monthly to Bickle who in turn shared the information on Bob's progress with Wimber. Ten couples from the church who knew Bob and Viola well were assigned the task of staying in constant touch with them, to encourage and to hold them accountable. The church committed to providing monthly financial support to Jones beginning in January of 1992 given the fact that he could not receive honoraria from a traveling ministry. The funding would continue as long as Bob submitted to the disciplinary process. The length of the restrictions on Jones's ministry was not determined at that time, but it was expected to be considerable.[11]

California, visiting family, Sean Wimber had a massive stroke and brain hemorrhage. He was admitted to the ICU at St. Jude's in Fullerton, California. He underwent emergency brain surgery on February 2, 2024.

11. Jones was entrusted to the pastoral oversight and counseling influence of a

Who Is Bob Jones?

Loving pastoral care was also provided for the victims of Jones's sin through prayer and counseling. Jones himself repented to both women and openly confessed his sin against them. Bickle and the pastors at MVF were constantly available to help the congregation process the pain of Bob's moral failure. For three successive Sunday nights, public meetings were convened during which anyone could ask whatever questions they might have. The pastors also visited the other congregations affiliated with Bickle's church as well as the many small groups of the church. The children and teenagers of the church were also the recipients of instruction and counseling as they sought to process what had happened.

In a letter of November 4 composed by Jones in the presence of church leaders, he confessed to resentment and slander against the members of the congregation. He admitted that he used his prophetic gifting to justify sexual misconduct, actions that he said he now deeply regretted. Jones acknowledged that he became resentful in the wake of restrictions placed on him by Wimber in July of 1990. He now agreed that the discipline by Wimber was entirely justified, and he wholeheartedly submitted to the more recent restraints placed upon his ministry. In a letter composed by Wimber and distributed to all in the Vineyard, it was clearly stated that the purpose of the discipline was not to restore Jones to ministry but to his relationship and fellowship with Christ.

In a public statement to the church, Bickle spoke of the emotional devastation he felt at Jones's failure. He credited the love and support of the entire church for making it possible for him to survive the pain and to minister effectively to all. He also expressed profound gratitude for John Wimber and the entire Vineyard family of churches for their prayerful support. Bickle answered the question of many as to why God didn't stop this from happening. He responded by saying, "God did stop it. That is what is happening right now. Had the Lord not brought this to our attention when he did, Bob's sins could have been much worse than they are." Bickle labored to explain that the most serious sin in all this was the abuse of spiritual power.

Bickle argued that it is possible, as in the case of Jones, that a person might operate in prophetic power at the same time he is committing egregious sin. There is an "overlap," noted Bickle in the time during which ministry occurs and the time when God finally brings to light the sin of an individual. Considerable theological insight is needed to account for how a person immersed in sin can still function effectively in his/her gifting.

---

pastor named Larry Alberts. Believing that Jones had repented and been restored to the Lord, Alberts released him into public ministry in 1994. The Vineyard board, however, was not in agreement and prohibited Jones from ministering at any of its churches.

I can't avoid bringing up a deeply troubling fact that at the time of Jones's sin *Bickle himself* had only a few years earlier engaged in a much more severe case of sexual misconduct. You will recall Tammy Woods, who at the age of fourteen was sexually molested by Bickle (this continued periodically for the next several years). Although I'm hesitant to compare sins as to which of several is more severe, there can be no quibbling about Bickle's grooming and sexual interaction with Woods. Given her young age, it was much worse than what Jones committed. Indeed, it was not merely sexually inappropriate, it was criminal. Had Bickle been discovered when his abuse of Woods first occurred, he could easily have ended up in prison. This observation in no way minimizes Jones's sin. It serves only to accentuate the gravity of Bickle's.

In the immediate days following the imposition of discipline, Jones began to minimize his sin and the gravity of its impact on the church in view of the supernatural power that continued in his life. He apparently believed that, since he was forgiven, healed, and freshly anointed by the Spirit, he should be permitted to continue in ministry. He misinterpreted the reality of anointing on his life as God's endorsement of him rather than seeing it as God's kindness designed to lead him to repentance (Rom 2:4).

Was Bob Jones a righteous man who simply succumbed to temptation and turned to evil, or was he evil from the beginning, an impostor who had now been exposed? Why is power often found in those with strange and quirky personalities? Bickle was careful not to impose discipline so harshly that it would crush and destroy Jones, or so lightly that it would enable him in his sin and cause trauma to his victims.

At the American Gospel Roundtable discussion on April 1, 2023, in which I dialogued with Justin Peters and Jim Osman, the subject of Bob Jones was raised. Peters began by saying that Jones was "sexually immoral." My objection to that statement is that Peters was suggesting, perhaps even asserting, that Jones had sexual intercourse with two women. Jones did not. What he did was unconscionable and reprehensible. But we need to be careful about how we describe any particular sin. When I voiced my concerns with Peters's statement, cessationist critics jumped all over me for seeming to minimize what Jones did and creating a two-fold category of sexual sin. I was in no way, shape, or form diminishing the gravity of Jones's sin. Nor was I providing an endorsement or defense of Jones as a prophet of God. I was simply asking for precision in the way it was communicated lest people draw the wrong conclusion. So let me say once again for the record, Jones committed an egregious and horrific sin for which he was properly disciplined. Nothing can excuse, justify, or minimize the gravity of what he did. Let's just be precise in describing both what he did and what he did not do.

Bob Jones's "Ministry" in His Final Days

James Goll communicated to me via personal email that Jones made considerable progress in regard to his struggle with sexual sin. He sought help from one devoted couple who moved to Florida with him. This couple prayed with Jones virtually every day for two years. Jones and his wife Viola reconciled and worked on their marriage with considerable success before she died in 2005.

Toward the end of his life Bob Jones was invited to minister at Bethel Church, Redding, California. One especially disturbing video shows him leading a large gathering of mostly young people in the steps they must take to enjoy a trip to heaven. Jones himself often spoke of a multitude of trips to heaven that he experienced, during which he would "sit on daddy's [God the Father] lap." From what I know of Jones, I suspect that he would have insisted that we take this literally, which, of course, is absurd. The Father, being spirit, does not have a "lap"!

Jones instructed those present to close their eyes and breathe deeply. He provided step-by-step guidance to facilitate their journey into heaven, an experience he insisted they can enjoy as often as they wish. Not only that, but they are also capable of helping induce a similar heavenly journey in the lives of others. I trust you understand that there is no biblical basis whatsoever for this practice. It is deceptive, dangerous, and trivializes our relationship with the Triune God. Does such a late-in-life theology of Bob Jones serve to discredit him entirely? Perhaps so. But not necessarily. At minimum, it reveals a serious deviation from biblical Christianity in Jones's life. Many will point to this development as hard evidence that Jones was from the beginning a false prophet. I do not feel justified in drawing that conclusion, although I must say that it gives me pause.

You may be wondering what, if anything, Mike Bickle had to say about this development in Jones's life. For one thing, as far as I can determine, Jones never ministered from the platform at IHOPKC. Although Bickle himself claims to have been transported into the third heaven on one particular occasion, I am convinced that he would in no way have endorsed Jones in this practice of self-facilitating trips to heaven. The sort of experience that the apostle Paul had, as described in 2 Corinthians 12, was unexpected, unsought, and unprovoked. It was clearly a sovereign act of God. Jones died on February 14, 2014.

Visitations to Heaven?

What are we to make of Bob Jones's numerous claims to have visited heaven? It is difficult to calculate how often he asserted that he found himself in the presence of the Lord, either by trance, vision, dream, or while wide awake. These became the focus of Ernie Gruen's critique, which we will examine in detail in chapter 13. As of the writing of this book, there are several individuals in the charismatic world who insist that they, too, have been caught up into the third heaven, or some such equivalent location. One thinks of Kat Kerr, who has built her "ministry" on the strength of having made thousands of trips to heaven. One would have to be seriously deranged or unimaginably gullible to believe her. Other, more reputable individuals have also asserted that they were recipients of similar heavenly transports. It almost appears as if this has become a calling card of sorts, or, better still, a badge of spiritual honor or heightened anointing indicative of one's importance in the kingdom of God.

That the apostle Paul experienced this one time in his life is beyond dispute (see 2 Corinthians 12). But unlike most, if not all, of the claims made by individuals today, Paul refused to describe what he heard and saw, "things that cannot be told, which man may not utter" (v. 4). In fact, he repeatedly describes this incident in the third person, as if to deflect attention away from himself: "I know a man in Christ" (v. 2); "and I know that this man" (v. 3); "he heard things that cannot be told" (v. 4); "on behalf of this man I will boast, but on my own behalf I will not boast" (v. 5).

Are we obligated to assess all claims to have experienced something similar by the standard of Paul's description? Does the fact that most, if not all, who insist that they have been translated either into the second or third heaven, or into paradise itself (v. 3), speak of it in detail and even at times appear to boast, discredit them entirely? Or is it unreasonable to demand that any and all claims to have visited heaven must be tested and evaluated against the apostle's experience? The answer to these questions would take us far off topic, but I will confess that I remain skeptical of anyone whose alleged visit to heaven does not align with the one explicit example of this that we have in the New Testament.[12]

---

12. There is one additional example of a legitimate heavenly visitation, that of John the apostle in Rev 4–5. But when trying to justify their own experience, people such as Jones typically cite Paul's third-heaven encounter in 2 Cor 12.

Addendum A:

Bob Jones's Letter of Confession and Repentance

What follows is the letter that Bob Jones dictated in the presence of several leaders of Kansas City Fellowship. It was released to the congregation on November 4, 1991.

> Dear Brothers,
>
> I have held resentment against you and have spoken slanderously against you, and I now repent for this.
>
> In recent months I have manipulated certain people for selfish reasons on the basis of my prophetic gifting. I have been guilty of sexual misconduct, and I deeply regret this (I have not committed adultery).
>
> I deeply resented the public restraints placed upon me in my ministry by John Wimber in July 1990 and this resentment created an imbalance in my reasoning ability. Now I believe that these restraints were right.
>
> I embrace the present disciplinary process given by John Wimber and you, and I'm thankful for it.
>
> I ask forgiveness for [*sic*; he presumably meant to say "from"] those I have hurt, for I love each and every one of you, and I wish you well.
>
> Sincerely,
>
> Signed, Bob Jones

Addendum B:

John Wimber's Letter to Leaders in the Vineyard Concerning the Sin and Discipline of Bob Jones

> Association of Vineyard Churches
>
> November 7, 1991
>
> Dear Brothers,
>
> When a leader falls into sin, the Word tells us that elders "who sin are to be rebuked publicly, so that the others may take warning" (1 Timothy 5:20). We, the national Vineyard leadership,

believe that the rebuke of a leader discovered sinning should be published at a level commensurate with his visibility and ministry. Therefore, with much sorrow, we are writing this letter to you.

It has been discovered, confirmed, and confessed to, that Bob Jones, a recent associate of the Vineyard, and with a nationally recognized prophetic ministry, has been involved in serious sin. His actions have necessitated his being removed from all ministry at this time. The sins for which Bob has been removed from ministry include using his gifts to manipulate people for his personal desires, sexual misconduct, rebelling against pastoral authority, slandering leaders, and the promotion of bitterness within the body of Christ.

Regarding our pastoral concerns, our goal at this time is not Bob's restoration to ministry, but his restoration to his walk with Christ. Presently, Bob is fully cooperating with honesty and humility, and we are choosing to believe that his repentance is sincere. We ask you to pray for Bob and his wife and for us as we work together with them. A second, just as significant, pastoral concern is for those who have been sinned against. They are receiving pastoral counseling and are being helped in every way possible.

With any moral failure—whether it's done by a home fellowship leader, pastor, evangelist, etc.—it's important to distinguish the ministry from the sin. In this instance, we encourage those of you who have been positively ministered to by Bob to hold on to those good things God has done in you.

We encourage you not to make judgments against the value of the prophetic based on this incident, but would rather ask you to rejoice with us as we obey the word of the apostle Paul. "Brothers if someone is caught in a sin, you who are spiritual should restore him gently. But watch yourselves or you also may be tempted. Carry each other's burdens, and in this way you will fulfill the law of Christ" (Galatians 6:1–2).

Sincerely in Christ,

John R. Wimber
For the National Board and Council
JRW/RM

CHAPTER FIVE

Who Is Paul Cain?

PAUL CAIN WAS BORN in Garland, Texas, in 1929. He died on February 12, 2019, just short of his ninetieth birthday. He is far and away the most famous (or perhaps infamous, after you read of his moral failures) of the so-called Kansas City prophets. I first met Paul in 1993 while attending a conference in Houston, Texas. It was there that I received from him one of the more profound and life-changing prophetic words that God has been gracious to supply. More on this later in the chapter.

According to his own testimony, he was converted at the age of seven and became aware of God's call on his life at the age of eight. What may have been his first truly supernatural experience came at the close of a worship service in the Baptist church he attended. After returning home he had a sense the Lord was going to speak to him, so he hid under his covers in bed. His fourteen-year-old sister, Mildred, claims that she heard the audible voice of God as he spoke to Cain and became one of his most devoted disciples.

When he reached the age of fourteen, he launched a radio ministry and conducted healing services in a small tent. Paul eventually became an active contributor to what was known as the Healing Revival that extended from the late 1940s into the early 1960s, ministering alongside William Branham, T. L. Osborne, Oral Roberts, Jack Coe, and A. A. Allen, just to mention a few. At one of his first meetings in Dallas, Cain became frightened as he stood up to speak and began to shake uncontrollably. Many mistakenly took this as a sign of the Spirit's presence with Paul and rushed to the stage, confessing their sins, and asking for healing.

Paul was largely raised by his mother and grandmother. His father, William Henry Cain, died when Paul was only twenty-three years old. After he moved to Garland, Texas, he worked for the railroad until launching a landscaping business. Paul's father attended one of his son's revival meetings and claimed to have seen two angels standing on either side of Paul. This prompted him to walk the aisle and give his life to Christ. He died two years later at the age of seventy-eight.

Cain's connection to William Branham (d. 1965) is now viewed with considerable concern. Although there is a measure of doubt if Cain ever shared the platform with Branham, he was asked by the latter to fill in for him whenever Branham was unable to maintain a rigorous schedule.

In 1957, Branham claims an angel instructed him not to attend a series of meetings scheduled for Europe. In his place, he sent Paul Cain. Cain not only conducted meetings in Switzerland but also in Karlsruhe, Germany. I don't remember what year it was, but in the mid 1990s I accompanied Paul, his assistant Reed Grafke, Mike Bickle, and Jack Deere to Karlsruhe where Paul had expectations of a repeat performance from 1957. It never happened. The meetings were successful, but not to the degree that Cain had anticipated. The meetings in 1957 were said to have been attended by more than 30,000 people each night for one week. Approximately a thousand people came each night from the Russian zone in East Germany. One secular newspaper reported that attendance for the week had been upwards of 180,000 people. Numerous people were reportedly saved and miracles of healing were commonplace.

Branham had a reputation for his accuracy in the exercise of word of knowledge, allegedly calling out people's names, addresses, birthdays, and extended family members. He supposedly was quite good at identifying the illnesses of those present at his meetings without having met them. But in recent years, Branham's life, ministry, and especially his theology have undergone serious scrutiny. The best resource on Branham's life is the book by John Collins, *Preacher Behind the White Hoods*, published in 2020. One should also consult the website www.william-branham.org for a plethora of material on this controversial man. I provide a brief overview of several of Branham's theological errors in appendix C.

I can testify that from at least 1993 until his death in 2019 Paul Cain never gave any indication of having embraced these many doctrinal errors in Branham's ministry. Contrary to what has oft been said, Cain repeatedly rejected the doctrine of "the manifest sons of God," which I also described briefly in chapter 2 of this book. We had numerous conversations during my time in Kansas City and I often asked Paul about this. His denials of ever having embraced the idea were consistent. Did Cain believe in the manifest sons of God prior to his connection with Bickle and the prophets in Kansas City, and even after? Possibly. Is it possible that Cain endorsed the *theology* of the manifest sons of God while rejecting the *label* or name due to its pejorative nature? Yes. That is possible. I'll have more to say about this later.

But I must also acknowledge that Cain's distancing himself from Branham during his years in Kansas City may well have been deceitful. In a YouTube video,[1] shortly before Cain's death, he is seen and heard praying for Chris Reed, formerly of Morningstar Ministries. In it he says, "Help us to see what brother Branham really was and not what they say he was and help us have a good memory of our precious brother." This disturbing inconsistency in Cain's beliefs about Branham will likely never be resolved to anyone's satisfaction. It became increasingly clear to me over the years that I knew Paul that he was less concerned with biblical and theological orthodoxy than he was with supernatural signs and wonders. As long as the latter were in evidence, the former was minimized, if not altogether ignored.

In 1952, Cain's "miracle" services were recorded and subsequently broadcast on secular TV stations. A wealthy businessman who admired Paul and believed in his healing gift purchased a tent for Paul from evangelist Jack Coe. The tent could seat eight thousand people but was later expanded to accommodate upwards of twelve thousand. The miracles at his many revival meetings are the stuff of which legends are made. Whether or not they actually occurred will continue to be the subject of debate.

After withdrawing from public ministry in the midst of the healing revival, Cain lived in a small two-bedroom home in Phoenix for some twenty-five years. His primary focus, so he says, was, with the help of his sister, to provide care for his mother. He claims that he spent the rest of his time meditating on Scripture and praying.

Perhaps the most well-known of all Cain's "prophetic" words came in the form of a vision that he claimed to have "seen" more than a hundred times. The time is the end of history, just preceding the return of Christ, and the scene is a sports stadium filled with tens of thousands of people. Healings and all manner of miracles are occurring, together with mass salvations. Cain said that secular news reporters were astounded, with one news anchor declaring, "There are no sporting events to report tonight because all the stadiums, ball parks, and arenas are being used for large revival meetings and are filled with people crying, 'Jesus is Lord, Jesus is Lord.'"

Cain said he saw, in the vision, people ministering for three days and three nights without food, water, or change of clothing. He claims to have seen a billboard with the words: "Joel's army now in training." Christians present "will have the mind of Christ. They will partake of the heavenly calling and be a new breed, God's dread champions."

---

1. Reise, "Paul Cain and Chris Reed."

I must have heard Cain describe this scenario a dozen times over the years. He may well have had an experience in which he envisioned such an event, but as much as I wish it were true, I seriously doubt that it was a revelation from God.

Miracle or Elaborate Fabrication?

Although at one time engaged to be married, Cain remained single his entire life. I recall numerous occasions when he was asked to tell the story of the Lord's visitation and his reception of the gift of celibacy. As Paul told it, he was driving to a retreat center near Santa Maria, California, when the Lord suddenly appeared next to him in the front seat. Jesus was wearing a monk's black habit and a skull cap! He told Paul that he was unhappy with his engagement, an expression, supposedly, of divine jealousy. The Lord then said, "If you really want the kind of power and intimate relationship with me you profess to want you must remember that I walked alone."[2]

It was then that Paul saw flashing lights in his rearview mirror. Evidently Paul had become so captivated by the Lord's presence that he unconsciously drove through several red lights and stop signs.

> "Where is he?" asked the policeman in a somewhat shaky voice.
> "Where's who?"
> "Where is that man who was sitting in the front seat next to you?"
> "Oh," Paul replied. "That was the Lord."
> Upon seeing Paul's Bible on the dashboard, he asked, "Are you a minister?"
> "Well yes, you could say that," Paul responded.

The policeman was stumped. He wanted to be faithful to his duty under the law, but the idea of issuing a ticket to Jesus was more than he could handle. He told Paul that if he would exit the road and go to a motel for the night, he would overlook the obvious traffic violations that Paul had committed.

I frequently heard Paul say that he turned to the Lord and asked him, "What do you think about my engagement? You don't seem very pleased." It was then that the Lord expressed his concern with Paul's decision. Paul replied that he was willing to do whatever the Lord wanted, but if he was to remain single something had to be done about his sexual desires. The

---

2. This suggests that singleness is preferable to being married. "Walking alone" is portrayed as leading to greater spiritual power, a notion that I find decidedly unbiblical.

Lord proceeded to extend his hand and place it on Paul's heart. The burning sensation was intense, and yet Paul knew that this was the removal of all sexual desires and perhaps the impartation of the gift of celibacy. Cain then said that from that day until the present he has never experienced any sexual desires.

Of course, the inconsistency in this story is that Paul was later revealed to have been a lifelong practicing homosexual. Although the magnitude of his sexual sin did not come to light until about 2004, when those who interrogated him both as a team and individually they discovered that he had yielded to his homosexual desires for many years. The notion that Paul ceased to have sexual desires and lived a celibate life is an outright fabrication. Given my Protestant orientation, I would also question whether it is feasible that Jesus would appear to Paul in the garb of a Roman Catholic monk.

Does this, by itself, discredit the entire experience? Must we then write it off as a deliberate lie by Paul designed to enhance his spiritual status in our eyes? Probably. You, the reader, must decide this for yourself. For my part, I have to confess that I'm increasingly skeptical of its veracity with each passing day. Jack Deere, who traveled and ministered with Paul for sixteen years and undoubtedly knew him better than anyone else, including Bickle, believes that Paul concocted this story to explain to others why he never got married. Most evangelists and ministers were married, and it may be that Paul created this bizarre story to hide the fact that he struggled with homosexual desires.

An Undeniable, Life-Changing Prophetic Word

Jack Deere and I were classmates together at Dallas Theological Seminary. Although he was two years ahead of me, we developed a good friendship, especially after he joined the faculty at DTS and taught Hebrew, Semitic languages, and Old Testament theology. But once he embraced the contemporary validity of all spiritual gifts and developed a close friendship with John Wimber, he was dismissed by the seminary, in spite of the fact that he was a tenured professor.

Jack was relentless in his determination to broaden my exposure to the gifts of the Spirit. So, he invited me to a conference in Houston, Texas, hosted by Calvary Community Church. It was there, in March of 1993, that I first met Paul Cain. Jack had invited me to join him and Paul for lunch on the final day of the conference. I spoke very little and gave no indication of anything going on in my life. Also at that lunch was Marvin Gorman, an

Assemblies of God pastor in New Orleans who was responsible for exposing the sexual misconduct of Jimmy Swaggart.

Later that night, Paul called me out of the audience and delivered a ten-minute prophetic word of encouragement. The text he used was from Isaiah 58, especially v. 11: "And the LORD will guide you continually and satisfy your desire in scorched places and make your bones strong; and you shall be like a watered garden, like a spring of water, whose waters do not fail."

In the course of his message, throughout which he had been speaking of my ministry and how God wanted to use me, he paused. He said, "Sam, I know you have thought, 'Who's going to take care of me? If I give my life to pastoral ministry, if I deny myself and take up my cross, who will watch over me?' Sam, the Lord says to you, 'I will guide *you* personally. I *will* guide you personally; I will take care of you. I will guide thee continually.'" This very pointed application of the first phrase in Isaiah 58:11 was then followed by Paul Cain quoting the rest of the verse.[3]

At the time, I didn't fully appreciate Paul's words. I thought it was nice. But I couldn't make much sense of its application. After all, this was March of 1993. I was committed to the ministry at my church in Ardmore, Oklahoma. I had no intention of leaving. Our family was happy and the church was prospering. Leaving for another church was the farthest thing from my mind. Immediately after the meeting, Jack came to me and said, "Sam, you may not understand fully what Paul said, but get a videotape of it and write it down. It will probably take on new meaning in about five months." As it turned out, Jack's advice was right on target, to the very day!

In the few months that followed Paul's word to me, it became increasingly evident that God was leading me to join Mike Bickle's staff at what was then Metro Vineyard Fellowship in Kansas City. But this "leading" of the Lord never once included a recollection of the "word" Paul Cain had given me. To put it bluntly, I had completely forgotten it. Let me jump forward to August of 1993. I want to tell you what happened on the day we moved.

Moving day was August 18, 1993. It was one of the most demanding and depressing days of my life. Making the decision to leave our church family in Ardmore was among the most difficult I had ever made. When the time finally arrived for us to say goodbye, it was almost more than I could bear. We had spent the day before helping the movers load our belongings and saying our farewells to family and friends. We were scheduled to meet

---

3. Yes, I'm very much aware of the context of this passage. The focus is God's appeal to Israel concerning the sort of fast that pleases him, as well as their responsibility to minister sacrificially to the hungry and homeless. But I also believe there is a principle underlying its original intent that applied to me in the present day.

the movers at our new residence in Kansas City at three in the afternoon. It was very early Wednesday morning, August 18. I was depressed and worried that I had made a terrible mistake. I was fearful of the new responsibilities, both financial and occupational, that I was to assume upon our arrival in Kansas City. Ann was tired and apprehensive. Our daughters were just tired.

Melanie, our first-born (she was fourteen at the time), was in the car with me. Ann and Joanna were following us in the minivan. As Melanie rubbed the sleep from her eyes, she opened a going-away gift she had received from the principal of her school. It was one of those verse-a-day calendars that people set on their kitchen counters or on their bed-stand. Needing more than a little encouragement, but with no expectation I'd receive any, I said, "Well, Melanie, this is as big a day as we've ever had. We're moving to Kansas City. What's our verse for today?" She opened the calendar and turned to August 18.

If you haven't figured it out yet, the verse for that day was . . . Isaiah 58:11! This was the precise verse the Lord had given Paul Cain as a special promise to me at the conference in Houston, virtually five months to the day (as Jack Deere had "unwittingly prophesied"). I felt like I had been hit with a bolt of lightning. Slamming on the brakes, I jumped out of the car and ran back on the shoulder of the highway to Ann who was probably thinking that I had changed my mind about the move. I shouted, "Ann, you'll never guess what has happened. Today is the day. We're moving. We're stepping out in faith. And look at what verse is for today!"

I've been told there are approximately thirty-one thousand verses in the Bible. I do know, of course, that there are 365 days in the year. You tell me: What are the odds of that *one* verse appearing on that *one* day? They are astronomical, no doubt. But to a God who controls the universe and speaks through his people whom he has gifted prophetically, it is a mere trifle. To me, it was stunning, supernatural confirmation that indeed we had heard the Lord correctly and were doing his will.

Isaiah 58:11 Again

Before I move on, I need to share one other incident involving this passage of Scripture and how God continued to use it in providential ways.

In 1997 Ann and I were struggling over a major decision related to her job. From the time of our move there in 1993, Ann had served as the receptionist at our church in Kansas City, Metro Christian Fellowship (we withdrew from the Association of Vineyard Churches in 1996 and changed the name accordingly). She loved her job and everyone was thrilled to know that she was, so to speak, the "gatekeeper" for the ministry of our local fellowship. But another opportunity had come along.

The headmaster at our church school, Dominion Christian, had approached Ann about a teaching position. The possibility of returning to the classroom was quite appealing. Ann had taught school for several years at Trinity Christian Academy when we lived in Dallas. This job would give her the summers free, a higher salary, and also make it possible for her to spend more time with our two daughters.

I can't begin to tell you how much turmoil and inner anguish this decision created for both of us. It may sound like a simple decision, but anyone who has faced a choice such as this in which both options appear equally rewarding knows how difficult it can be. We prayed for weeks and sought the advice of friends and family. We were about at our wit's end when the headmaster called and said he needed a final decision by Wednesday at 11:00 a.m. It was Tuesday evening.

Ann and I prayed yet again for some clear indication of God's will in the matter and then went to bed, hoping for an answer by the next morning. I decided to attend the prayer meeting that we regularly conducted on Wednesdays from 10:00 a.m. to 12:00 noon. It was about 10:15 and I was deeply immersed in prayer, pleading with God for clarity so that our decision at 11:00 would reflect his best for Ann and everyone concerned.

Suddenly I had what felt like a random thought race through my head. Perhaps you know what I mean. One of those "out of the blue" ideas that just seems to pop into your head without cause or warning.

"Go check your mail."

That's what I heard in my head. I don't know how else to explain it. What made it so odd is that not only had I not been thinking about the mail, but it typically didn't arrive until around 1:00 p.m. Still, it was so unexpected that I decided I should "obey." I walked into the office where Ann worked and the mailboxes were located.

"Hey," shouted Ann, "the mail came early today. That's weird." I could tell from the sound of her voice that she was as uptight as I, worrying about what we were going to tell the school in about forty-five minutes.

I looked into my box and there sat one item, and one item only. It was a letter from Jean Raborg.[4] For those of you who don't recognize that name, she experienced a remarkable healing through the ministry of Paul Cain. Jean had shared her testimony at one of our conferences just a few weeks

---

4. You can read about her experience in the first edition of Jack Deere's book *Surprised by the Voice of God*.

earlier, but I hadn't expected to hear from her. There was no special occasion to warrant her writing me. Yet, there it was.

I opened the envelope to find a brief word of encouragement from Jean written on what appeared to be a fairly typical greeting card. But pasted to the card was a short article she evidently had cut out from another publication. The title of it was "The Graciousness of Uncertainty." I can't begin to tell you what happened in my soul as I read the three paragraphs in the article. I gave it to Ann and she read it too. Nothing could have spoken more clearly to Ann and me about what decision we needed to make. It was as if a huge burden simultaneously lifted from our hearts. We looked at each other and said, "Well, that settles it."

Then I saw it. At the bottom of the card was a biblical text. Jean hadn't written it. It was printed as part of the card itself. You guessed it! "The LORD will guide you continually . . ." (Isa 58:11).

Incidents like this understandably don't have the impact on others that they do on the people for whom they are intended. I certainly don't expect you to respond as Ann and I did. But given the magnitude of the decision we were facing, the deadline that had been given us for making it, the prompting in my spirit to check the mail, the fact that Jean's letter came on *that* day rather than Tuesday or Thursday, its bizarre and almost unprecedented early arrival at 10:15 a.m., the singularly appropriate message it contained, and what I can only call the divine imprimatur of Isaiah 58:11 staring us in the face, nothing could have been clearer that God had once again spoken in a powerful and loving way.

An Unusual Power Surge

Mike Bickle often spoke of one night when Paul Cain was ministering in prophetic revelation. The power of God was almost tangible in the room. All those present could sense the manifest presence of the Lord. Paul proceeded to call out seven names in rapid succession together with other information about each individual. Several people were healed and many repented of their sins. When Paul finished, the solemn silence that descended on the room was shattered by the sound of sirens as two fire trucks came to a halt in the parking lot of the building. The door swung open and several firemen with hoses and axes entered.

To their amazement, Mike said, "Sorry, but there's no fire here." To which the firemen replied, "Oh, yes, there is. It's a big one somewhere in the building. The circuits at our station have blown and set off the alarm. There is clear evidence of a huge power surge."

The firemen, in accordance with standard policy, searched high and low throughout the building, looking for any signs of a flame or smoke. They found nothing, and made a somewhat embarrassing retreat back to their trucks.

After the meeting Paul turned quietly to Mike and apologized. "I am really sorry about the fire scare. I should have warned you that that does sometimes happen when there is a lot of divine power in the room!"

How should we respond to this story? There can be no question that a power surge, indicating a fire in the building, had occurred. A few hundred people were present who can testify to it. But must we necessarily believe that Paul Cain's ministry was responsible for it? Was this a manifestation of the Spirit's powerful presence? Or could it have been a simple mechanical glitch that is explicable in non-supernatural terms? And on what basis does one make a decision? This is the sort of phenomenon that calls for wisdom and discernment. Personally, I remain undecided and am not aware of any empirical test that could be applied to judge its legitimacy.

A Worship Leader Is Exposed

It was, I believe, early in the spring of 1999 when I was once again a witness to Paul Cain's revelatory gifting. Or was it? It was Sunday night at our church and a worship celebration was in progress. I was sitting at the back of the auditorium when Mike Bickle rushed in and came straight for me. "Paul Cain called and asked that we come to his apartment immediately." "What's up?" I asked. "I don't know," said Mike, "but it sounded urgent."

When we arrived at Paul's apartment, only Reed Grafke, his assistant, was present with Paul. He had us sit down and said, "The Lord has revealed to me that Kevin Prosch has been guilty of adultery." Prosch, for those not familiar with his name, was a world-renowned musician, composer, and worship leader. He would periodically stop in Kansas City and lead at our Sunday services. Many of the more well-known worship leaders in the charismatic movement attribute their skill, motivation, and success to Prosch's influence.

Cain proceeded to describe Prosch's infidelities, down to the dirty details of where more than one of them had taken place, and when they occurred. The leadership at the church immediately called on Kevin to suspend his itinerant ministry and submit to discipline and counseling. He agreed, confessed his sin, and for the next couple of years showed signs of genuine repentance. His marriage, however, ended in divorce. He subsequently married Shelly Bickle, one of Mike's five sisters. Sadly, their marriage also ended with a divorce.

How did Paul Cain come by this precise knowledge of Prosch's sin?[5] Was it by revelation? Might this be an example of the spiritual gift of the word of knowledge referred to in 1 Corinthians 12:8? Or could it be that someone who was aware of Prosch's behavior contacted Paul who in turn passed it off to us as if it came from the Holy Spirit? Again, we are presented with an experience that calls for discernment.

Paul Cain in Kansas City

There were numerous occasions when Paul Cain visited the church in Kansas City and ministered in what all believed was a genuine prophetic gift. He didn't live in Kansas City until 1997, after Metro Vineyard Church withdrew from the Vineyard and changed its name to Metro Christian Fellowship. On several occasions there were other, less spectacular but no less supernatural, prophetic words from Paul Cain. In November of 1988, Cain called Bickle and said, "The Lord wants to deal with some *staph* infection and make the *staff* as white as snow. On the day I come it will be dry in the morning and white as snow after the meeting."

Cain was obviously using a play on words to make his point clear. He then told Bickle, "You pick the date." Cain eventually arrived around Thanksgiving. The meeting with the church staff began at 6:00 p.m. Outside, the ground was completely dry. By the time the meeting ended, there was an inch of snow on the ground, prompting several staff members to repent of hidden sin.

I vividly recall one weekend when Cain spoke both on a Friday night and a Sunday night. He called out from the audience no fewer than a hundred people combined on those two nights. The details he disclosed were quite stunning. We recorded the event and typed out in detail the words he delivered. I have retained that document. A couple of illustrations from other meetings may help you grasp the nature of Cain's gifting.

---

5. See the Addendum for Prosch's public confession of sin. You should also read the article on The Roys Report, cited in the introduction, that describes Prosch's alleged sexual relationship with worship leader Misty Edwards.

An Amazing Life

My wife and I have been blessed by getting to know Nancy Heche and her daughter Abigail. You may recognize her last name, as she is the mother of actress Anne Heche, who perished in a fiery car crash on August 5, 2023. Nancy's husband was one of the first recorded victims of AIDS in New York City, having lived a secret, double life for many years. On June 4, 1983, a short time after her husband's death, Nancy's son, Nathan, died in a single car crash at the age of eighteen. While some speculated it was suicide, it is more likely that he fell asleep at the wheel. Another daughter, Cynthia, died at the age of two months from a heart defect. Nancy's second daughter, Susan, passed away from a brain tumor on January 1, 2006. Anne had years earlier turned her back on the family and engaged in a widely publicized lesbian relationship with Ellen DeGeneres. When Nancy remarried, I was blessed with the privilege of officiating the wedding. Sadly, though, her second husband died of a heart attack while on the golf course only a few years into their marriage. Susan's husband, Jud Bergman, had since remarried, only to die in a car accident with his wife while in San Francisco in 2019. And as I said above, Anne died in that horrible crash more recently. Abigail, her only living child, has walked faithfully with the Lord for the past several decades.

To say that Nancy has endured incredible suffering in her life is a massive understatement, and yet she remains strong in the Lord. Let what you just read sink in: she lost one child soon after birth, her husband died in 1983, her son also died in 1983, another daughter passed away in 2006, her son-in-law in 2019, yet another daughter in 2023, and her second husband early in their marriage. But even those who are strong need encouragement now and then. At a conference in 1998, I was sitting with Nancy when she received a prophetic "word" from Paul Cain that would prove to be incredibly encouraging and comforting. Although Cain had never met Nancy, he asked her to stand up: "Nancy, I saw the March winds blowing. March is a special month for you. The Lord is going to bless you and give you the spirit of Nathan."

This is an excellent example of how a revelation might come accurately to someone who is, however, uncertain of its interpretation. When he sensed the Spirit speaking the name *Nathan*, he thought it had something to do with the Old Testament prophet who confronted David. What he didn't know, until we informed him later that day, is that *Nathan* was the name of Nancy's son who had been killed in a tragic car accident.

The next day this man again called out Nancy yet again and asked her to stand. "I saw that precious young man that was taken from you. The Lord said, 'I gave him to her in the springtime of the year. And I took him in the middle of the year.' I got a glimpse of him [Nathan] standing before the Lord, and he looks like he's thirty-three years old. That's all he's ever going to look from now on. That's not a doctrine," he was careful to add, "but that's how old he looks at this time."

Here's the significance of what was said. March is indeed quite special to Nancy. Her birthday is March 10, and her husband passed away on March 4, 1983. The Lord had revealed that Nathan had been "given" to Nancy in the "spring" of the year. Nathan's birthday is April 21! "I took him in the middle of the year," said the Lord. Nathan died on June 4, 1983, only three months after Nancy's husband had died.

As would be true of any mother devastated by the loss of a child, Nancy often had wondered if Nathan truly knew Jesus before his death. This word of encouragement is that he did. As a way of confirming it, the Lord had indicated that on this day in 1998 Nathan looked "thirty-three years old." Do your math. If Nathan was eighteen in 1983, had he lived he would have been exactly thirty-three when this word was spoken!

How do we know Cain didn't investigate Nancy's past and find out information that he later passed off as revelation? Well, we don't. Jack Deere later discovered that Paul actually had a program on his computer that contained extensive genealogies and personal information from which he might have gleaned these details about Nancy. Could it be that the Holy Spirit revealed this information to him so that, in accordance with the purpose of prophecy, Nancy might be edified, encouraged, and consoled (1 Cor 14:3)? I'm left in somewhat of a quandary, praising God for the way Nancy and Abigail were encouraged but simultaneously suspicious of the origin of Cain's insight.

"202" and General Douglas MacArthur

A former student of mine was going through a difficult season in her life. God seemed far away. Her job was unfulfilling. She thought about quitting and pursuing a different line of work. She certainly didn't expect what happened next.

It was at a conference being sponsored by our church. Although Paul Cain had never met her before, he asked this student to stand. As he was giving her words of encouragement, together with some advice drawn from a biblical text he thought was relevant to her life, he paused and said: "I just saw the number 202 above your head. I believe that is where you work." He then resumed delivery of the word.

I closely watched this young lady while he was speaking. I noticed her initial confusion when he mentioned 202 and then, about thirty seconds later, her sudden realization of what he had said. I later asked her what happened. She said, "When he identified 202 as the place I worked, I mistakenly thought he was giving the street address. My first reaction was that he had missed it. But a few moments later it dawned on me that 202 is the number of my office suite in the downtown building where I work!"

A similar incident occurred in the same meeting a few moments later. Cain was speaking to a couple about their call to evangelism when he paused and said: "I just saw a picture of a young boy dressed up like General MacArthur. I'll just bet your son's name is Douglas." Sure enough, they have one child, a boy named Douglas. This may strike some of you as a bizarre way for God to communicate to someone. I can only suggest you read your Bible again and take note of how often God does incredibly bizarre and strange things, at least by Western standards. Of course, in the final analysis the issue isn't one of normal versus bizarre but whether the revelatory incident is consistent with Scripture and edifying to those involved.

Paul Cain Meets John Wimber

Late in 1988 Jack Deere arranged for Paul Cain to meet John Wimber for the first time. Jack had only recently joined the staff of the Anaheim Vineyard and was anxious for these two men to make acquaintance. Jack asked Paul if God would grant a prophetic sign to confirm his message to John Wimber and the Vineyard. Paul said, "Yes. On the day I arrive, there will be an earthquake in southern California. And after I leave, there will be a massive earthquake elsewhere in the world."[6] Predicting earthquakes in Southern California is like predicting rain showers in the Pacific Northwest. It doesn't take a prophetic gift to be fairly accurate on something as commonplace as that. However, that is not the whole story of what happened.

The following is taken from the unpublished version of chapter 13 in Jack's book *Why I'm Still Surprised by the Voice of God*.[7] There is a reason

---

6. It was initially believed that Cain prophesied the earthquake would occur on the day after he left Anaheim. It actually occurred on the evening of the day of his departure. According to Bill Jackson, when Deere realized the error, he then remembered that Cain had not said "*the day after* I leave" but only "*after* I leave," thus leaving the timing ambiguous. Jackson says that Deere "apologized for the misquote. It was these kinds of disclaimers that raised the ire of many toward the prophetic because it seemed like backpedaling" (Jackson, *Quest for the Radical Middle*, 189). From all I know of Jack Deere, I am certain he was not "backpedaling." Jack is a godly man of the utmost integrity.

7. Cited here with Jack's permission.

Who Is Paul Cain?

why it never made it into the final manuscript of Jack's book, and I will confess my complicity in this omission toward the end of this chapter. Jack writes,

> Paul asked me to introduce him to John Wimber. I told John about him and tried to schedule a meeting for them, but it just wasn't working out. Then, in the summer of 1988, we moved to Anaheim with our three children to be on John's staff. In September that year, I asked Paul when he was coming to Anaheim to meet John. He said, "I don't know yet. But the Lord shows that there will be an earthquake in Southern California on the day I arrive."
>
> "An earthquake! The big one?" I asked.
>
> "No. It won't be the big one. But on the day I leave Southern California, there will be a big one somewhere on the earth. The Lord hasn't shown me where," he said.
>
> I told John about Paul's earthquake prophecy. He smiled, sort of a "been there, done that, heard all this before" smile.
>
> Paul got on a flight to come to Anaheim on December 3, 1988. At 3:38 am on December 3, 1988, my English Pointer, Skipper, hurled himself against the glass patio doors trying to get into the house, and then a 5.0 earthquake, centered under Pasadena, rumbled down the coast to Orange County and shook our house. That morning John and I rode together to pick up Paul, and I reminded John of the earthquake prophecy Paul had shared with me. "What kind of guy is this?" John said. "An earthquake is his calling card!"
>
> Paul's visit to the Vineyard was so supernatural that he quickly came into John's inner circle and was invited to minister at all the major conferences. Paul returned to Dallas four days later, on December 7, and the big earthquake that he prophesied came to pass. On that day two earthquakes struck Armenia just minutes apart. The first was 6.9 and the second was 5.8. They killed at least sixty thousand people and destroyed almost half a million buildings. I had never heard of God authenticating a prophet like this. I thought to myself, he must be special, the godliest prophet on the earth. And it made sense to me: it would be just like God to put great power in the frailest of packages.
>
> It turned out, however, that the earthquakes were signs of the damage Paul would do to the ministries and to the people who gave themselves to him.

These few stories that I've told convince me that Paul Cain had a genuine and quite supernatural revelatory gifting.[8] But you are about to read more concerning Cain that is the cause, at least in my own experience, of severe cognitive dissonance. I don't know how to reconcile two seemingly incompatible truths in this man's life. Perhaps those wiser than I will have an answer.

Revival in England, or Only Tokens of Revival?

An especially controversial episode in Cain's ministry came when he supposedly prophesied on August 5, 1989, that "revival will probably find its starting point somewhere in October" in England.[9] When October of that year came and went without revival, many wondered if Cain simply missed it. At a meeting on July 14, 1990, Cain again prophesied that "revival will be released in England in October of 1990."[10] He went on to clarify that "tokens" of revival will come in October of 1990. The awakening was to begin in London at the Docklands where the meetings were held. From there it would spread across Britain, into Scotland, and sweep through the continent of Europe. John Wimber was so impressed with what he had seen of Cain that he took his entire family to the UK to participate in what he believed would happen. It didn't. When Cain was confronted about this, he responded by repeating that he only meant that "tokens" of revival would be seen. R. T. Kendall challenged Cain on this but was rebuffed. "I was amazed by the way Paul exercised prophetic ministry," writes Kendall, "but not by the way he avoided correction. This always worried me."[11]

One of the recurring struggles in the lives of many prophetically gifted people, like Paul Cain, is their fear of ever acknowledging that their prophetic words might be wrong, either in whole or in part. To their way of thinking, such an admission would threaten their reputations and bring prophetic ministry into disrepute. But of course, we know that when a person receives a revelation from the Holy Spirit, a revelation that is always

---

8. In his book *The Quest for the Radical Middle*, Bill Jackson relates that at the Vineyard pastors conference in 1989 Paul Cain called out him and his wife by their "given names (which no one ever uses)" and told them where they ministered and things that would supposedly happen there (208). While Cain remarkably knew their given names, the events he prophesied would come to pass never did.

9. Cited by Jackson, *Quest for the Radical Middle*, 208.

10. Jackson, *Quest for the Radical Middle*, 210.

11. Kendall, *Prophetic Integrity*, 9. On pages 6–22 Kendall describes several remarkable prophetic words from Paul Cain that he personally witnessed.

infallible, having come from God, our interpretation of it and the application to any particular individual can often be mistaken.

A Disastrous Moral Failure

Most of you are undoubtedly aware that in 2004 Paul Cain was exposed for his alcoholism and engagement in homosexual activity. Although rumors of Paul's sexual proclivities had swirled for years, there was never any concrete evidence that might confirm it. Or, if there was, I was never informed of it. In 2004, Mike Bickle, Jack Deere, and Rick Joyner confronted Paul and spent considerable time with him in North Carolina, praying and pleading with him to confess and repent. He did, or so we all thought. Here is Deere's report of what happened.[12]

> There were three of us, all pastors, who were considered Paul's spiritual sons. In February 2004, we agreed to have an intervention with Paul. We met with his assistant first, who told us a story of consistent abuse, dishonesty, and drunkenness. We learned that Paul taped every phone conversation he had so he could later use the tapes for blackmail if anyone ever tried to accuse him of sin. And we learned that Paul had a secret history of sexual immorality. All of this and more came out over several weeks of confrontation.

During the course of their time with Cain, other details of his life and ministry surfaced. Deere explains:

> Although Paul could move in genuine prophetic power, he also faked revelations. We learned that he had a genealogical program on his computer. One of the things he was famous for was getting the address of a person and the names of their relatives. He mixed this information in with genuine supernatural revelation about healing, and he admitted this deceit to us.[13]

12. What follows is taken from an unpublished chapter that was initially intended by Deere to be included in his book, *Why I'm Still Surprised by the Voice of God*, and is cited here with Jack's permission. The reason for its absence will be explained later.

13. Lee Grady describes his encounter with Paul Cain in 1989. "I watched charismatic prophet Paul Cain manipulate an audience in Texas in 1989. In front of 5,000 people, he pretended to know the street addresses of several individuals. I was familiar with the ministry that hosted the conference, and I had access to a phone list that contained names and addresses of all the pastors in the group. I got a sick feeling in my gut as I realized that Cain was using this same phone list to make his declarations. I was shocked that a man who was considered a powerful man of the Spirit would stoop so low as to make people think he got information from God" ("Beware the 'Facebook Prophet' Frauds").

> He threatened the three of us with the ruin of our marriages and ministries if we did not cease our attempts at confronting his sin. Our goal was to restore him, not to expose him. But Paul didn't want to be restored. He wanted to be left alone. He left our restoration process. We published a statement on the internet, but it was far too mild. Some interpreted it to mean that Paul only had a single sexual failure in a moment of weakness. He told people that we had lied about him because we wanted his money. But the truth was that we were his primary fund raisers. He even accused us of committing adultery and incest.
>
> He had previously told me that the ministers in the healing revival of the 1940s were sexually impure, only in ministry for the money and fame. He told me he had left the revival stage because he couldn't stand the corruption of the leaders, going into seclusion and waiting for God to show him the pure leaders of the "last day" ministry. But it turned out that the revival leaders he spoke of had made him leave the stage because of his own sexual impurity. No church would allow him to speak. All this came out *after* we made his sin public. I also listened to multiple allegations of sexual assault.

Deere's concluding words are those of a heartbroken former friend and disciple of Cain. He writes,

> He was the most abusive person I've ever known. He drew people to himself and not to God. I never heard him freely confess a sin, and he always blamed someone else for his sin. It took us days of confrontation to get him to confess to the obvious. He told the grossest lies about anyone who refused to proclaim his innocence. He threatened all of his former ministerial friends—not just the three of us—with ruin when they would not excuse his sin. He battered one person without mercy until the person was on the brink of a breakdown. I confronted him several times about this, and he always said the same thing, "What else could I do? I was like a caged animal. All I could do was scratch and claw." I never saw him show any sorrow over sin. I never saw him repent of any sin.
>
> The most damning charge against him is that he could never state the gospel, though he always insisted on giving the evangelistic message at the conferences. I even wrote out the gospel for him to read at the conclusion of his "evangelistic" messages:

Jesus Christ, the Son of God, died on the cross for your sins. If you will trust him to forgive you and give you a new life, he will come into your heart and never leave.

Somehow Paul would manage to misread and garble this simple statement. When theologians from another country heard Paul attempt to preach the gospel, they said to me, "The gospel is simply not native to the soil of his heart." I could not disagree with them.

For these reasons I [Jack] am agnostic about where Paul is spending eternity.[14]

Bickle's Request

In May of 2004, I had moved back to Kansas City after spending four years on the theological faculty of Wheaton College in Wheaton, Illinois. We had been in Kansas City for only two weeks when the phone rang. Mike Bickle's voice sounded deeply concerning. "Come over to my house immediately." I did.

There were present in Mike's house (i.e., duplex) several of the leaders from IHOPKC. Mike shared some rather broad and general information about Paul Cain's moral failures and his alcoholism. After they all left, Mike asked me to stay, at which time the numerous details of what had happened in Paul's life were made clear. The three men were probably Paul's closest friends who felt a deep burden of responsibility to labor for Paul's restoration. Bickle then made a request of me. I don't know if it was his alone or if Jack and Rick had agreed. In any case, Mike made it clear: "We [I?] would like you to come on board as Paul's accountability partner. Whatever counsel you can give him would also be appropriate. I've thought of every possible candidate for this, and you seem to be the right person. Paul trusts you, and so do we."

I was not flattered by this request. In fact, it frightened me. I had only resettled in Kansas City a couple of weeks prior to the disclosure of Paul's

---

14. R. T. Kendall spoke similarly, declaring that Paul Cain "went to heaven under a dark, dark cloud" (*Prophetic Integrity*, 30). Deere identifies three types of prophets in Scripture. "Spiritual prophets use their prophetic gift to lead believers to love God and to lead unbelievers to faith in the Lord. There are carnal prophets, true believers with a true gift of prophecy who use their gift to exalt themselves and who cause division in the body of Christ. And there are false prophets. There are two kinds of false prophets: unbelievers who use the devil's power and unbelievers who have learned to traffic in the Lord's power" (*Why I Am Still Surprised by the Voice of God*, 246–47). I continue to struggle with knowing into which category Paul Cain should be placed.

sins. I asked Mike for some time to pray about it and he agreed. But before I could come up with an answer, I heard that Paul had abandoned the three men and was not open to the discipline and accountability they had imposed. I have to admit that I was greatly relieved to be free of a burden that I don't believe I was capable of carrying.

There is yet another reason I was skeptical of Paul's commitment to submit to my oversight. Several years earlier, Paul's longtime assistant, Reed Grafke, had fallen in love with Monette Mathews, a very close friend of my wife. Bickle knew that he could not officiate the wedding without alienating Paul, so Reed approached me. I was honored and happy to conduct the service, but it infuriated Paul Cain. The wedding was beautiful. Reed and Monette were happily married for twenty years before she died of breast cancer. This, despite Paul Cain's horrid "prophetic" word regarding them. Only Bickle and I were present when Paul said, "Thus saith the Lord. In five years, they will divorce." This was an egregious violation of everything we knew and believed about prophetic ministry. In any case, it proved wholly false. Now, back to the story.

Paul fled to California and located a pastor to whom he decided to submit himself. Neither I, nor Mike, Jack, or Rick had any confidence that this pastor was capable of handling someone as deceitful as Paul. After a short time under this pastor's oversight, Paul was affirmed and released back into ministry. People have often asked me if I had any further contact with Paul after the disclosure of his sin. In late 2004 (or perhaps early 2005), after Paul had returned to Kansas City (he always kept his home there and traveled back and forth between Kansas City and California), my good friend Jack Taylor came to town and asked that I take him to Paul's home. Jack wanted to pray for him. Paul came to the door to greet Jack and said a polite hello to me. That was the last time I ever saw him. He visited Oklahoma City several years later and, through a friend, asked if I would be willing to have dinner with him. On Jack Deere's advice, I declined.

An Obvious Lack of Discernment

While I acknowledge that Cain operated in a revelatory gifting in his early years of ministry, after the disclosure of his alcoholism and homosexual activity he displayed a serious lack of spiritual discernment. When the so-called Lakeland "revival" emerged, under the leadership of Todd Bentley, Cain traveled there and was escorted onto the platform to pray for Bentley. He spoke with unmistakable clarity about his opinion of Bentley. He said, he is "a man without guile," comparing Bentley to Nathaniel in John 1. Said

Cain, "The Lord spoke as clearly as he ever did before" about this feature in Bentley's character. Again, "I have never met anyone that has the integrity and possibility of leading this worldwide revival" as does Bentley. Cain concluded his comments by supposedly imparting to Bentley his own "mantle" of supernatural ministry, and then said, "I've met the new breed tonight."

But, as we all now know, Bentley was at this very time engaged in an adulterous relationship with his administrative assistant. He later divorced his wife and married his mistress. Bentley was later found to have been engaged in sexting with several young men, drug use, and excessive drinking. On September 3, 2019, Michael Brown released a statement that a panel of leading charismatic figures had been formed to investigate the many charges against Bentley. Its findings were released on January 2, 2020. Here is the most relevant portion of that report:

> The opinion we have reached here is theological, answering the question: Does Todd Bentley, founder of Fresh Fire Ministries, live up to the high standards required of those who serve as representatives of Christ? Is he qualified, according to our understanding of biblical standards, to be a recognized leader in the Church?
>
> As part of this process we sought to hear Todd's side directly, but he declined to answer a list of 60 questions compiled by the investigator after initially agreeing to respond. (Todd required the investigator to submit the questions through his attorney, after which he ceased communicating with Dr. Brown or the investigator.)
>
> Based on our careful review of numerous first-hand reports, some of them dating back to 2004, we state our theological opinion and can say with one voice that, without a doubt, Todd is not qualified to serve in leadership or ministry today. There are credible accusations of a steady pattern of ungodly and immoral behavior, confirmed by an independent investigator's interviews dating from 2008 up through 2019, along with other testimonies dating back to 2004. And while we only took into account first-hand reports, there are many other second and third-hand reports repeating the same accusations, often from people in different parts of the country (or, world) who had no connection between them, other than their interaction with Todd . . .
>
> Sadly, we see no signs of true, lasting repentance. Instead, we see a steady pattern of compromised behavior, including credible accusations of adultery, sexting (including the

exchanging of nude pictures or videos), vulgar language, and substance abuse.

And, to repeat, these charges have been brought by numerous witnesses over a period of roughly 15 years, right until 2019. Even more importantly, many of these activities have involved people for whom Todd was spiritually responsible (interns, staff, team members, individuals he was ministering to), making these violations all the more serious.

In our view, this disqualifies Todd from public ministry until such time that he has demonstrated true, lasting fruits of repentance, which would include: the breaking of these long-term, sinful habits; public acknowledgment of his sin, without equivocation, including asking forgiveness of those he sinned against; and submission to local church leadership until trust had been rebuilt. This would likely take a period of years.[15]

I should point out that Cain was not the only charismatic leader who endorsed Bentley. Several other prominent individuals did likewise. But Cain's reputation as a prophet who could allegedly see the secrets of men's souls is to be especially noted. Despite numerous claims that Lakeland was the beginning of the prophesied "last days ministry" I never sense that what occurred there was of God. Todd Bentley never preached the gospel. Sadly, as Jack Deere also stated, neither did Paul Cain.

Paul Cain's "Confession"[16]

The word "confession" is in scare quotes due to the fact that there is some doubt as to its sincerity. Not long after releasing this statement, Paul would on occasion deny ever struggling with alcohol or homosexuality. In any case, here is the published confession of his sin.

> A Letter of Confession, by Paul Cain
>
> I must apologize to the body of Christ for my recent conduct. I want to correct the denials that I made earlier in reference to charges brought against me. I acknowledge the following:
>
> 1. I have struggled in two particular areas, homosexuality and alcoholism, for an extended period of time.
>
> 2. I apologize for denying these matters of truth, rather than readily admitting them. I especially apologize to Rick

---

15. The Line of Fire, "Official Statement."
16. Grady, "Prophetic Minister Paul Cain."

Joyner, Jack Deere, and Mike Bickle for my misunderstanding of their attempt to discipline me according to Matthew 18. I have come to appreciate their loving intent for me in this process.

3. I am ashamed of what I have done to hurt those close to me and the pain I have caused those who have believed in my ministry. Particularly, if I have hurt anyone by my actions of emotional or sexual misconduct, I am very sorry. I sincerely ask for your forgiveness.

I have submitted to a team of leaders in the body of Christ who are supervising every aspect of my restoration. This team is headed by Larry J. Alberts (Fathers and Families Together, Minneapolis, MN) and Dr. Daniel J. Kim (Destiny Training International, El Monte, CA). Larry has considerable experience in restoration ministry and has been requested by leaders such as John Wimber, Rick Joyner, and Francis Frangipane to help restore highly significant ministers in the body of Christ. Daniel directs a training center which emphasizes biblical spirituality and prophetic reformation. I have submitted to Larry and Daniel to develop an appropriate program, involving professional treatments, so that I may walk in moral purity, spiritual and physical health, and wholeness of life.

With hope in Christ,

Paul Cain 2005

Yet another tragic development is that subsequent to the release of this "confession" Cain denied being an alcoholic and homosexual. Then again, at a later time, he conceded that he was guilty of both sins.

Addendum A:
An Update on Jack Deere, Mike Bickle, and Paul Cain

Although my focus in this book is on the events dating from 1982 to the founding of IHOPKC in 2000, I think it's important to include a few comments about some more recent developments. Please understand that what I'm going to share below all took place prior to the exposure of Bickle's sexual sin and deceptive lifestyle.

I have referred on several occasions to the doubts regarding the truthfulness of the prophetic history in Kansas City that have emerged in the minds of many. This is largely related to the disclosure of sexual misconduct among several of the more prominent so-called "prophets" described in this book. Jack Deere, who was far closer to Paul Cain than anyone else, has confessed that he is now wrestling with doubts about the integrity of the many stories I've described herein. In an article on his son's Substack page, titled "From Support to Scrutiny: Jack Deere Reevaluates #IHOPKC Founder and Kansas City Prophets' Legacy," Deere now confesses that "given that we now know that three of its prominent contributors: Mike Bickle, Paul Cain, and Bob Jones, were involved in clergy sexual abuse, IHOPKC's entire prophetic history is questionable, in my opinion."

Deere also has written about his interaction with Bickle in a chapter in *Why I'm Still Surprised by the Voice of God*.[17] In the interests of total transparency, I need to admit that I am partly responsible for the editorial changes Deere agreed to make in his chapter on Paul Cain. In fact, the email from Bickle to Deere, dated June 10, 2022, where the former pleads with Deere to remove this chapter altogether from his book, or at minimum to revise it, was also sent to me.

When I obtained a copy of Jack's manuscript, I immediately turned to chapter 13 where he describes his evaluation of Paul Cain. It raised a few concerns in my mind, so I forwarded the chapter to Bickle, knowing that he too would likely express reservations about it to Jack. His long email response is included below, having been earlier published by Deere in the Substack article cited above.

I also contacted Jack's representative at Zondervan to see if it would be possible to delay publication of the book. The latter was only a week or two away from being sent to the printer for the final stage of preparation before its release. The Zondervan representative agreed, and Jack proceeded to rewrite the chapter in such a way that his portrayal of Paul Cain was considerably less critical. Jack now regrets agreeing to Bickle's request that his chapter on Cain be rewritten. And I must confess that I, too, regret sending the chapter to Bickle and encouraging Jack to agree with Mike's evaluation of his comments on Cain. I want to publicly apologize to Jack for my part in his revision of his comments on Cain. With the benefit of hindsight, I believe it would have been better and more beneficial to the Christian community that Jack's original chapter be retained. Jack has himself released publicly that chapter, much of which I cited above.

---

17. Deere's book is, in my opinion, the best book available on hearing the voice of God and the revelatory gifts of the Spirit.

Who Is Paul Cain?

In any case, here is Bickle's email to Deere (and to me) asking that he either delete altogether or at minimum revise his criticisms of Cain.[18]

> Jack:
>
> I may be wrong but I feel certain that your publisher would honor your request to remove that chapter if you insisted on it. When I say "that chapter" what I mean is the 70% of chapter 13 that is about Paul Cain. I really appreciated the first two pages of that chapter. There are many examples throughout history and in the Scripture itself to illustrate the realities about false prophets without vilifying Paul.
>
> I decided to write out a few of the reasons that I am deeply troubled by what you wrote about Paul.
>
> Yesterday morning when I read chapter 13, pain and grief hit my stomach and it stayed with me all day yesterday. I wrestled with it through the night, and woke up today with the same pain and grief. It feels similar to what I experienced in 1990 when Ernie Gruen wrote his expose of Bob Jones (yes, he hit me too, but most of his document was about Bob Jones). I was deeply pained for Bob and so was he.
>
> I see no redemptive value in defaming Paul Cain. I agree with exposing ministries that we believe are predators. We do that to protect innocent young people from being manipulated by them. I see that as redemptive. But a dead man is not a predator. People do not need to be protected from a dead man.
>
> I refused to publicly mention Paul's ministry even once for 15 years (2004 to 2019) when he was alive.[19] After he died I have referenced a few of his prophetic words that it [sic] believe are genuine and helpful to the body of Christ.
>
> Paul Cain is rarely ever mentioned in the conversation of the body of Christ at this time. He has all but been forgotten—but this chapter will energize many to talk about him. This puts Paul back in the conversation of the body of Christ in a big way. That seems so unnecessary to me, and even harmful.
>
> I am concerned about the trouble chapter 13 will bring to you, to me, and to many in the body of Christ.
>
> 1. Trouble for You—it becomes a defining narrative of your ministry.

---

18. As noted, all this first appeared on Stephen Deere's Substack page and is used here with permission.

19. Several individuals present at IHOPKC during these years dispute this statement by Bickle.

When I read chapter 13 my first thought was that "you are bitter." To me your chapter seemed vindictive.

I shared what you wrote with Diane and her first comment was "Jack [sounds] very hurt and bitter." Just this morning, one of my main leaders asked me "if I heard the Jack Deere interview about Paul Cain" that occurred about 2 months ago (?). I told him that I had not heard anything about it. His first comment was that "he was surprised to see how bitter Jack Deere is." I did not prompt or solicit that comment from him, nor from Diane.

I feel sure that the majority of the people (who love the prophetic) who read chapter 13 will conclude you are bitter and not really trying to help the body of Christ but that you are venting your pain and anger. That sincerely pains me.

Jack you have written some of the most helpful books on the prophetic but I believe this one chapter will be what you will be most known for in the coming years. I believe you will be remembered for this one chapter even more than your many years of really good teaching and your excellent books.

Ernie Gruen wrote 200 pages against Bob Jones and me 32 years ago. He led a mega church for 40 years but today (even in Kansas City) he is most known as "the guy who attacked Bob Jones with angry accusations and bitterness and jealousy." His one angry document is the most defining narrative of his ministry—after 40 years of ministry his thousands of helpful sermons and even his multiple affairs are rarely mentioned.

Because I love you, I would hate this to be one of the primary narratives about your life in the years to follow.

I regularly recommend your books to pastors who visit IHOP who are being stirred to embrace the gifts of the Holy Spirit. Your books are truly classics. I believe this one chapter will shift "the narrative" about your books. It will be the part of your writings that will be remembered most. That sincerely brings pain to my heart.

2. Trouble for Me—many wasted hours in answering for you and my silence about you

Because of Ernie Gruen's one document—for the last 32 years I have been asked over and over to comment on Ernie and what he wrote and why he wrote it. It is wearisome to me. It never goes away.

Many visiting pastors and the parents of the students of our ministry school want to know my views on Ernie—why did he say what he said and more. Of course, I do not speak negative

[sic] about Ernie. I see no redemptive purpose in it. I mostly say that "I have no comment."

If you publish chapter 13, I am sure I will be asked over and over for many years—"why did Jack Deere write what he wrote about Paul Cain?" I do not imagine that I will ever agree with you that you wrote this because of following the leading of the Spirit, nor that you were just trying to be helpful.

In other words, I will be forced to say "no comment." Of course, they will understand that I did not agree with you. I will not tell them that I thought you were motivated by bitterness, nor will I say that I disagreed with you, nor that I was grieved by what you wrote, nor that I strongly appealed to you to not write it.

I would never say anything negative about you but I am sure the main thing I will be asked is "Do you think Jack was bitter?" I will have to say "no comment" and they will get it. This conversation will happen many times in the years to come—this one chapter is far more damning than Ernie's document. Therefore, I know I will be asked over and over about this—in a similar fashion to how I have been asked about the Ernie Gruen document. UGH!

I am pained beyond measure on how this will play out in my world. I will waste so many hours collectively in conversations about this. I will try to avoid this but having walked through this for 32 years I am sure this will cause me much unnecessary trouble. I will not lose friends or supporters over this—but I will waste many hours and I will be silently making judgment on you by saying "no comment." I hate being put in that position for many years to come. I will not recommend your amazing book anymore, because of this one chapter. I do not say that as a threat.

(I would never threaten you ♥). I am sure this will not affect your sales at all but it will pain my heart to not promote your book anymore. I really do recommend it strongly to pastors with a sense of pride in how really good it is and how proud I am in being your friend. You really are a great man and I love you dearly. Your tenderness and humility has increased as the result of your humble responses to the Lord in context to Leesa—this brings tears to my eyes when I tell people about you. I am blown away by this grace operating in you over the last years.

3. Trouble for Others—the increase of the spirit of accusation

There are several ways that I believe that this chapter will harm the body of Christ.

1. This one chapter will be extracted from your book by "the Hank Hannegraf type" ministries. This one chapter will be "a gift" to them to validate their accusations against many prophetic ministries. And since it comes from YOU as the most educated and experienced man in the prophetic, they will more boldly accuse and broad-brush many other prophetic ministries with "the falsehood of Paul Cain" as exposed by Jack Deere.

    This one chapter will supply these type of ministries with fresh and potent fuel to accuse prophetic ministries in increased ways. The increase of the spirit of accusation will be harmful to the body of Christ in various ways.

2. I believe your example will embolden people to rail against other believers. The "woke culture" that has accelerated so dramatically over the last few years has given many believers license to accuse and expose other believers in the name of honesty, transparency, and justice. Jesus' command to follow the Matthew 18:15–18 process of going to your brother in private to win him is being set side almost entirely today by millions of believers as they attack one another viciously without even pretending to serve a redemptive purpose in winning their brother. The increased harm in the body of Christ of millions being embolden [sic] in recent years to vent their anger on other believers that have offended them is one of the most troubling trends accelerating in the body of Christ today. I believe this one chapter in your book will emboldened [sic] them—if Jack Deere does it, then why can't I do it? Since Jack knows the Bible so well and since he is so experienced in spiritual things, it must be okay to publicly expose others who offend you. Again, this will result in an increase of the spirit of accusation, which is so harmful to the body of Christ.

3. Multitudes of people who have received spiritual strength and hope by true words given to them by Paul will suddenly question the validity of the word they received. I know many who find real hope in prophetic words given by Paul. Their cessationist friends and family members who warned them about the prophetic will pounce on some of them with "I told you so" arguments that mock the prophetic. Again this

will result in an increase of the spirit of accusation, which is so harmful to the body of Christ.

As I wrote in my email yesterday, I emphasize that whatever you decide in this is between you and the Lord. It will not change my love and respect for you. And I do not presume that I would ever "win an argument" with you and so I would not even try ☺. So you really do not need to answer to me for any [sic] these points.

If you make sense of what I wrote in this email then I am blessed, if you do not then I leave it "between you and the Lord" but I will know that I wrote this out of love and respect for you and tried to be helpful.

Much love, Mike

Addendum B:

Kevin Prosch's Public Confession of Sin[20]

In the past few weeks, God in his mercy has called me to accountability by confronting me with the seriousness of the sin in my life. It has been an excruciatingly painful experience, not only for me but also for the people close to me. I realise that if I am every going to be free and if, by God's grace, I am ever able to minister again, I need to publicly acknowledge what I have done and apologise to those I have hurt. This letter is my open confession to the Christian community.

First, I take full responsibility for all the pain and shame I have caused others who have loved and trusted me. I did not listen to or heed the counsel of the men God placed around me. I fully deceived them and others by living a secret life. I trusted very few people and even the ones I trusted, I still lied to. I even used my gifting to manipulate those closest to me, and I did it without remorse or consideration of the pain it would cause them. I committed adultery and used my gifting to manipulate the women involved. I pursued women, not only sexually but also emotionally and always for my own selfish gain and personal pleasure. The very gift God gave me to bless others with, I used to manipulate and seduce these women. I want to say again and say it emphatically; I am personally responsible for all the deception. I am desperately in need of healing in my life,

---

20. Cross Rhythms, "Kevin Prosch Confesses Sin."

not only for my sexual problems but also for the way I deceive others. I plan on stepping away from the ministry and will not be ministering publicly in the near future. I also intend to find a local church body under whose leadership, counsel, and authority I plan to submit myself.

Secondly, I want to personally and publicly apologize to the people I have hurt and to ask for their forgiveness for my reckless, self-centred, and destructive behaviour that has been ongoing for many years. I apologize, first of all, to the women whose lives have been devastated by my sins against them. I apologize to each of you for the betrayal of your trust and for all the pain I have caused you.

To Jill, my ex-wife, I especially want to apologize. I have dishonoured you the most, even when we were still married. I am responsible for it all. I lied continually to you and did not listen to you when you knew what the end result would be. I walked in pride and did not consider you. I only hope that you will someday be able to forgive me for not being the husband and man I should have been to you and that the shame I have caused you will not continue to affect you in your new life.

Chapter Six

The Solemn Assembly and Signs in the Heavens

ONE OF THE PRIMARY purposes of this book, as stated on several occasions in previous chapters, is to discern as best we can whether the events described herein actually happened. I do not approach each scenario with a predetermined conclusion about their veracity. There was a time when I affirmed, without hesitation, that everything in the prophetic history of Kansas City was true. But recent events at IHOPKC involving Mike Bickle have caused me to hold in abeyance any premature conclusions about whether these stories are true or false.

A great many of the alleged supernatural phenomena are dependent entirely on the personal testimony of Bickle himself. I never had reason to doubt the accuracy of his claims until his character came under scrutiny with the disclosure of his sexual misconduct. I am deeply grieved at having to say this in light of the high regard in which I held Mike for the past thirty-five years. At the same time, we must acknowledge that several events have been verified by others. These are events that do not depend solely on Bickle's word. In this chapter we will examine a few of them. When prophetic statements are confirmed by empirical data or scientifically recorded facts, it is only a hardened and cynical cessationist mindset that would refuse to concede that they actually came to pass.

The importance of events associated with what has come to be known as the Solemn Assembly cannot be overemphasized. I am persuaded that Bickle and others cling to what they believe God has promised them in large part because of the verified prophetic phenomena that occurred during the Solemn Assembly and its aftermath. Whenever doubts would arise in Bickle's mind, he would fall back on the undeniable reality of certain prophesied occurrences on the part of Bob Jones.

The Solemn Assembly and a Surprising Comet

On Wednesday night, April 13, 1983, five months after Mike Bickle had established what was then known as South Kansas City Fellowship, and less than one month after the stunning events of March 21 described in an earlier chapter, the Lord supposedly spoke yet again to this twenty-seven-year-old pastor concerning his purposes for the city. Bickle claims to have heard what can only be called "the internal audible voice of God." It was not a sound heard by the physical ear, but it was not for that reason any less real. When God speaks this way, only the recipient can "hear" it, for the words are received internally, i.e., in the mind and spirit of the believer.

Bickle contends that the Lord directed his attention to Daniel 9 and the plight of Israel which had languished in captivity in Babylon for years. Having read in the book of Jeremiah that the captivity was to last seventy years, Daniel began to fast and pray to seek God's favor on behalf of the children of Israel. The story culminates in the visitation of the angel Gabriel, who informs Daniel of God's redemptive plan for his people. So, too, Mike was to fast and pray on behalf of God's people and his purposes in Kansas City. God's words, so said Bickle, were unmistakable: "This people in the heart of this nation will be like Daniel. There will be five hundred people in this city who will rise up before me as a corporate Daniel to pray for the deliverance of this nation. For it is in bondage just like Israel was."

Although the church was only five months old and Bickle was largely unknown in the city, he felt God calling him to invite other churches to join South Kansas City Fellowship in this endeavor. Although it seemed a bit presumptuous on his part to do so, Mike felt he had no option but to obey. As Diane, Mike's wife, put it, "We can always move back to St. Louis!"

Needing confirmation of this word, Bickle called Bob Jones on the phone the next morning and asked if he could visit him. He was careful, however, not to say so much as a syllable about the content of what God had revealed. The only way he could be absolutely certain that he had heard God correctly was to obtain a second witness in a way that could not be controlled or in any way manipulated by man.

Not only did Bob agree to see Mike, he told Mike on the phone that he already knew what it was about, for the Lord had revealed to him what he had just revealed to Mike. Wanting witnesses who could verify everything, Mike took with him two young men (Chris Burge and Brad Chick) whom

The Solemn Assembly and Signs in the Heavens

he repeatedly informed about his experience. When they arrived at Bob's home, Mike was determined not to give any hints. He had to be certain that it was truly God who had spoken.

I realize, of course, that the most skeptical of those reading this book would be inclined to believe that Bickle informed Jones of the emphasis on Daniel 9 and the call to a city-wide fast. I can't rule this out, but in light of what happened during and after the fast, it strikes me as something of a stretch. Now, back to our story.

"I saw him," said Bob with great confidence.

"Who did you see?"

"You know."

"Who?" Mike persisted.

"I saw the angel, Gabriel. He visited me early this morning and said, 'Give the young man Daniel 9 and he will understand.'"

Jones proceeded to explain that God had called Mike to proclaim a twenty-one-day period of prayer and fasting and that five hundred would respond. Mike's jaw dropped. "Unbelievable!" There was no way the two young men could have informed Bob in advance of their arrival, for Mike didn't tell them the content of his revelation until they were already in the car on the way to Bob's home. All of us have to make a decision: either (i) Mike Bickle was and is lying; or (ii) Bob Jones was demonically informed; or (iii) the two of them are the authors of a massive conspiracy of deceit in which Bickle informed Jones of everything in advance of his visit; or (iv) God revealed it to them both as they claim.

If you are struggling with this, let me add one more factor. Bob Jones then declared in the presence of all that God would supernaturally confirm that he was indeed the author of this revelation by sending a sign in the heavens that could not be the product of human engineering. Jones said, "God is going to send a comet in the heavens as yet unpredicted by scientists. It will prove beyond a shadow of a doubt that God has called this time of prayer and fasting and that he fully intends to bring revival to this city and country."

We should pause and catch our breath for a moment and think of the implications of this word. Regardless of what you may think about prophetic ministry, you have to admit that this was a pretty bold statement. Jones wasn't interpreting someone's dream or giving advice on how to know God's will or assuring a distraught believer that his non-Christian wife would soon come to faith. Here was an unequivocal, unabashed prediction of a comet unknown to the scientific community. There isn't much chance here for sleight of hand or religious trickery or other well-known tactics of palm-readers and psychics. Bob Jones was putting himself on the line. He reiterated,

> God is sending a comet that as of today no scientist or astronomer anywhere in the world has discovered. It will come as a complete surprise to them. It will serve to confirm that God's calling of the Solemn Assembly and his purpose for the church in Kansas City and in the nation as a whole will come to pass.

Bickle called for the fast to begin on May 7, 1983. He had informed Bob Jones of this on the morning of April 14. Bob prophesied the appearance of the comet on that same day.

I can hear the rumblings of the skeptic: "But what if Bob Jones secretly found out about this comet *before* Mike came on the 14th? He could then easily pass off this information as a prophetic word just to enhance his ministry and magnify his status in the church."

Yes, he *could* have. But there is one problem. *The comet wasn't discovered for another eleven days!* Comet IRAS-Araki-Alcock was first discovered in data relayed to earth on April 25 by the Infra-Red Astronomical Satellite (known as IRAS) and then independently confirmed by two amateur astronomers, a man named Genichi Araki in Japan and another named G. E. D. Alcock in England who saw it with binoculars from his window. Although it was not an extremely large comet, it came closer to earth than any comet in over two hundred years and remains the second closest encounter in history (Lexell's Comet in 1770 came within 1.5 million miles of earth).[1]

When May 7 arrived and the fast was to begin, numerous pastors from other churches in the city were present. Mike had each of them introduce themselves at the beginning of the meeting. But the most exciting moment of that day came when Bob Jones walked in with an edition of *The Independence (Missouri) Examiner*. The headline read: "Comet's Pass to Give Close View." The article went on to report that

> scientists will have a rare chance next week to study a recently discovered comet that is coming within the "extremely" close range of 3 million miles. . . . Dr. Gerry Neugebauer, principal U.S. investigator on the international Infrared Astronomical Satellite Project (IRAS) said, "It was sheer good luck we happened to be looking where the comet was passing."[2]

---

1. It may be that subsequent to this event another comet came even closer to earth, but at the time of Jones's prophecy the one he predicted was the closest on record.

2. Bickle always told this story by asserting that Jones walked in with the May 7, 1983, edition of the newspaper. But the article by Jane Goulding that announced the comet first appeared in the newspaper on May 4, not May 7.

In a book devoted to the Hale-Bopp comet that was visible for several weeks in March of 1996, author and astronomer Fred Schaff comments on "the suddenness of this object's arrival."[3] In virtually every other written account of the comet, reference is made to the sudden and unexpected nature of its coming. Phrases such as "newly discovered" and "surprise appearance" are repeatedly used.

Bickle's "word" from God concerning the fast had been confirmed by Jones's "word" that he received from the angel Gabriel, which in turn was confirmed by the appearance of the comet as predicted. But that was by no means the last time God would speak through heavenly events beyond human control or manipulation.[4]

The Rains of Revival

On the final day of the fast, Bob Jones delivered what had to have been a disconcerting word:

> The Lord spoke to me in a dream last night and said that revival will not begin immediately as we had thought. Just as the ark of the covenant was hidden in Obed-Edom's house for three months, and just as Moses was hidden from Pharaoh for three months, so too God will withhold his move upon this city until the appointed time and season. And when it comes it will not be a day late.[5]

This was not good news to those who had been fasting, many on water only, for the last twenty-one days. But Jones wasn't finished:

> God is going to send yet another sign. There will be a three-month drought in the natural over this city, even as there will be a three-month drought in the Spirit. But on August 23rd it will rain as a sign to you that in God's time he will send the rain of the Spirit even as he has promised.

---

3. Schaff, *Comet of the Century*, 16.

4. A detailed account of the reality of this comet can be found at Marsden and Green, "1983d."

5. I should point out that Jones was not comparing the promised revival with the ark of the covenant or with Moses being hidden. Nothing in either of these two events has anything to do with Jones's prophetic word. It is, instead, the time frame of "three months" that Jones found significant. Conceivably, any other biblical event in which "three months" is relevant could have been cited.

The drought began at the end of June and extended until October 11. The error wasn't in the prophecy but in the mistaken report of it three years after it was issued. The drought didn't begin on June 1, 1983, but on either June 30 or July 1. It didn't last precisely three months but rather three months and eleven days. It broke on October 11. In fact, those three months in 1983 proved to be the second driest summer in Kansas City in over a hundred years.

Information concerning the extent of the drought was obtained from the National Climatic Data Center in Asheville, North Carolina, and the Kansas City International Airport Weather Station. The only summer drier than that of 1983 was in 1976 when seven-one-hundredths of an inch (0.07) less rainfall was recorded for Kansas City. The US Department of Agriculture issued a summary of crop production with a review of the growing season and the weather. They described the summer of 1983 as a "record-breaking heat wave," one result of which was a drop of over 28 percent in the corn yield from the previous year.

But what about August 23?

The church was scheduled to have a meeting that night, even though the weather reports insisted that no rain was in sight. As of August 22, Kansas City had received only 0.21 of an inch of rain for the entire month. Normal rainfall for this same period was 2.36 inches. People's nerves were on edge. What if it didn't rain? It seemed like everything was on the line: the validity of prophetic ministry, the purpose of the May fast, the credibility of both Bickle and Jones.

By evening, however, rain clouds had formed. When the heavens burst open and a torrential rain (0.32 of an inch in less than an hour) fell upon that small group of believers, they knew that God had spoken. Many ran from the parking lot shouting with joy, drenched from head to foot. It was an event that only God could control. Was it merely a lucky guess by Bob Jones, or had he prophesied the event based on a revelation from God? I'll let you be the judge. But it was only a brief respite, as the drought resumed the next day and continued unabated until its appointed time was fulfilled.

By the way, you may find it interesting, as I did, that on the front page of the *Kansas City Star* newspaper on the morning of August 24 was a picture of a lady, taken on August 23, sitting beneath her umbrella with a fishing pole in hand. The caption reads, "Just fishing in the rain." The article goes on to describe how the rain showers of the 23rd provided only a temporary break from the brutally hot and dry weather.

During the controversy that I will describe later, the charge was leveled that this entire prophetic scenario was a fabrication designed to enhance the reputation of Kansas City Fellowship. This was a very serious charge that struck at the heart of Mike Bickle's personal integrity as well as that of prophetic ministry in general.

The fact of the matter is, the prophecy was perfectly accurate. The *initial report* of it, however, was not. Three years after these events in 1983, Bickle was recounting what had occurred based on information provided to him by two of his staff members. In doing so, he mistakenly said that the drought began on June 1 and ended on August 23 with rainfall of three to four inches. Thus, whereas the public retelling of the prophecy was based on inaccurate data, the prophecy itself was true.

Bob Jones had indeed prophesied in May that there would be a drought of three months. He also prophesied that it would rain on August 23 as a sign that just as the drought in the natural would be broken, so would the drought in the spiritual be broken. It did in fact rain on August 23.

Three years later, in preparation for telling the story, Bickle asked a staff member how much rain had fallen. He was erroneously informed that it was three to four inches and unwisely, yet innocently, included that figure in his message. The actual amount of rain was 0.32 of an inch, but because it came in a deluge it was strikingly in contrast to the weather conditions that had prevailed in Kansas City in the seven weeks preceding, giving rise to the exaggerated estimate of Bickle's associate. The man who accused Mike and the church of a deliberate fabrication based his charge on what he heard in the audiotape of the report of this prophetic event.

In a personal email to me, Steve Lambert, who, together with his wife Jane, had been involved in the Kansas City church from day one, confirmed the reality of the rain. He wrote,

> Despite what the "official" weather bureau records suggest, it absolutely DID RAIN fiercely on the very day Bob Jones has prophesied following the solemn assembly. We were there and everyone was wildly anticipating what might happen after a very long, dry summer. At or about 7 pm the heavens opened. I'm not sure I've EVER seen it rain that hard. We were all jumping and shouting and laughing and celebrating after the disappointing end to the solemn assembly itself 3 months earlier. I tell you this because it was THIS EVENT (and one other) that kept me participating for the next decade even when I had serious doubts about Mike's theology on the critical role "we" played in God's timetable for the second coming. I couldn't quite shake the supernatural nature of that torrential rain and was kept by the thought that I didn't want to stand before the Lord someday

and have Him say, "I invited you to be a part of something truly historic but you were too cynical and walked away."[6]

Bickle's Reputation

There is yet another dimension to this story that must be noted. In a message he delivered on April 17, 1983, some three weeks before the Solemn Assembly was convened, Bickle declared quite enthusiastically that the promise of God to him was that the revival would definitely break out at the end of the three-week assembly. May 28 was the day that God's power would break forth in the city, with signs and wonders and a multitude of salvations.

This statement by Bickle puts him at odds with Jones concerning when the revival would begin. Bickle is heard on the tape saying that "my entire future is based on this," the latter a reference to the outbreak of an unprecedented outpouring of the Spirit's power. "If I'm wrong," says Bickle, "I'm ruining my future." The fact is, Bickle was wrong. Whether or not this mistake ruined his future is a matter of debate, but the initial flurry of prophetic promises (from Jones, Bickle, and even Augustine Alcala) concerning what would come about at the end of the twenty-one-day gathering of prayer and fasting was in stark contrast to Jones's word on May 27 that the promised revival would not immediately begin. One can reasonably conclude that in the terms that Jones and Bickle described it, such a revival never began.

Placebo

Notwithstanding the remarkable events just described, the elation of the people in the church in Kansas City soon turned to doubt, and from doubt to unbelief. Bickle would later comment that he now understands a little better the mentality of the ancient Israelites who resumed their murmuring not long after witnessing some of the most incredible miracles ever performed.

Bickle and his congregation had experienced a visitation from the angel Gabriel and saw it confirmed in a way that could not be manipulated. Then there was the prediction of the comet, which appeared precisely as prophesied. If that were not enough, the drought had come, as had the

---

6. Personal email from Steve Lambert to Sam Storms, April 13, 2024, cited here with permission.

The Solemn Assembly and Signs in the Heavens

prophesied rain on August 23. What more could one ask for? Surely, such experiences would banish all doubt. Well, not quite.

As the days passed, their faith began to falter: "Where was the promised revival? Why hadn't God acted as he had promised? Must we wait forever? Who is Bob Jones anyway? Were the comet and May 7, 1983, just a fantasy or were they truly God's word concerning his purposes for this people?"

On November 7, 1983, Bob Jones delivered yet another powerful prophetic word to Mike Bickle that was designed to forever put to rest any doubts he might have about what God had birthed on May 7, the day on which the solemn assembly had begun.

> "The Lord will send you a message from heaven on November 15th that will cause you never to doubt him again. He will give you yet one more sign that this is indeed a sovereign movement that he has raised up to touch the ends of the earth."
>
> "A message from heaven?" Mike asked, somewhat bewildered. "What does that mean? Will I be going up or will something or someone be coming down?"
>
> "I don't know," said Jones. "But you never know with these prophecies."[7]

How do you prepare for a divine visitation? When November 15 finally arrived (it seemed to Bickle like it would *never* come), Mike thought he would try fasting. That lasted a few hours. He finally gave up and had a milk shake. He thought it would be good to meditate and pray, but there wasn't much happening with that either. He tried praying in tongues for thirty minutes but that didn't work either. The night passed slowly and nothing had happened: no phone calls, no visions, no dreams, no voice from heaven, no strangers knocking on his door, no nothing.

Mike was sitting at his desk in the basement of his duplex. It was 11:00 p.m. Only one hour to go. Bored and a bit frustrated, Mike thought it would be a good time to read his mail which had been sitting on his desk for most of the day. He shuffled through some letters until he came upon a package that had been mailed to him by a lady in town whom he'd never met. The package had arrived that very day. He opened it and discovered a funny looking booklet of only fifty-three pages entitled *Placebo*. Its author was a Baptist minister named Howard Pittman. Mike had nothing else to do, so he began reading.

Howard Pittman had been long involved in law enforcement and had also served as a Baptist pastor for thirty-five years. In August of 1979,

---

7. This is how Bickle reported the story to me.

however, he suffered a potentially fatal rupture of his stomach arteries. While in the ambulance being rushed to the hospital, all his vital signs ceased. What happened next will prove difficult for some to grasp, especially for those who are skeptical about the possibility of believers today experiencing what the apostle Paul describes in 2 Corinthians 12:1–10. There, Paul recounts his "visitation" to paradise, or the third heaven, in which he heard and saw marvelous things. It was such a stunning experience that Paul himself never knew whether he left his body or remained within it. In other words, he was unsure whether he was in some sense bodily "raptured" or "translated" into the third heaven or whether he had an "out-of-the-body" experience in which his spirit alone made the "journey."

Pittman claims that he, too, appeared before God in the third heaven. When his life came under review, he was shocked to discover that God regarded his efforts as an abomination. He had "ministered" for his own selfish gain and promotion rather than for the glory of God. Pittman was quick to repent and pleaded with God for an opportunity to devote what remained of his earthly life for the glory of Christ.

There was more. God revealed a number of things to Pittman, only three of which I will take the time to share. First of all, the Lord told Pittman that this was the Laodicean age. The church in this generation had become lukewarm and was nigh unto being spewed out of God's mouth. This isn't to say that no other generation in church history was lukewarm, but only that ours is especially so.

Second, a day is coming when the church would perform signs and wonders similar to those in the book of Acts. Pittman relates, with more than a little embarrassment, how he thought to himself at the precise moment he heard this word from the Lord, "But God, I am a Baptist; I don't believe in signs and wonders for today."

The God who knows the thoughts and intents of the heart, thundered in response: "You are greatly mistaken." Again, Pittman was quick to repent of his misguided thoughts.

Third, and most important of all, the Lord told Pittman that he was being commissioned for a three-year period, during which he was to proclaim this message to the churches where God would send him. At the end of the three years there would be an announcement "from the sky" (!)[8] which would signal the beginning of God's recruitment of a new "Gideon's army" that would be instrumental in the coming great revival.

---

8. Although Pittman didn't specify that the announcement from the sky was the comet predicted by Jones, most have concluded that he could hardly have had anything else in mind.

Note this well: Pittman's experience occurred in August of 1979. The edition of the book Bickle was reading on that November night, 1983, had been published in 1982. Thus, there can be no objection raised that Pittman concocted his story *after* the events of 1983 which I described earlier in this chapter.

So, what was the date on which Pittman's "commission" or ministry was to begin? This was the question Bickle was asking himself as he continued reading. The hour was fast approaching midnight on November 15. There it was! Mike couldn't believe his eyes. Pittman's three-year commission from the Lord, given to him in August of 1979, was to begin on May 7, 1980. It only took a second for Bickle to realize what this meant. *The end of the three-year period, the date on which God would send a heavenly sign to mark the beginning of his recruitment of an army of believers to help bring in the coming great revival, was May 7, 1983!*[9]

If what Bickle and Jones have said is true (and for many, it is a huge "if"), the Lord had told Mike to call the Solemn Assembly and that it was to begin on May 7, 1983. The Lord sent the angel Gabriel to Bob Jones to confirm that it was indeed God who had spoken to Mike. The comet, undetected by scientists, was prophesied as a witness to the reality of God's purpose for Kansas City. The newspaper of May 5 reports on the fulfillment of that word. In the midst of a prophesied three-month drought, rain is predicted on August 23 to confirm yet again God's promise that his purposes would come to pass. And on November 7, Bob Jones assured Mike that on November 15 he would receive a message from heaven that would testify to the truth of what Mike had been told would begin on May 7 of that year. And what was that message? Quite simply, and yet almost beyond belief, God had several years earlier brought Howard Pittman to heaven and revealed to him that the day on which he would begin recruitment of Gideon's army was none other than May 7, 1983.

Bickle was convinced, at least on this occasion, that Bob Jones was right. Never again would he doubt what God had promised. Never again would he waver in faith that God would fulfill it. But we still have a huge problem.

The Oft-Predicted Coming Great Revival?

It is all too easy for us to get caught up in the prophesied events that we just examined and fail to ask the most important question of all: *Did the prophesied great revival ever happen?* Personally speaking, I find it extremely

---

9. We should remember that the comet was discovered on April 25, not May 7.

difficult to doubt the reality of the prophesied comet, the drought, the rain, and the truth revealed in Howard Pittman's book. But each of these events was designed to confirm that the promised revival would come. Has it? Has the "nation" itself experienced the spiritual transformation that these remarkable incidents were designed to confirm?

Let me remind us all of what was said in the many prophetic words that were given. Please note in each citation the italicized words:

> This people in the heart of this nation will be like Daniel. There will be five hundred people in this city who will rise up before me as a corporate Daniel to pray for the *deliverance of this nation*. For it is in *bondage* just like Israel was.

Has the United States witnessed this "deliverance" from "bondage"? Not yet.

Again, it was declared that "this is indeed a sovereign movement that he has raised up *to touch the ends of the earth*." Has the ministry of Metro Christian Fellowship in Kansas City (at least up until Bickle's departure in 2000) and the emergence of IHOPKC (until its implosion in 2024) touched "the ends of the earth"? Perhaps. The reach of Bickle and IHOPKC has truly been global. Many will testify that its influence has been substantial and widespread. But what, then, are we to make of this prophesied global "touch" in the wake of Bickle's fall and the collapse of IHOPKC?

In Jones's prediction of the comet, he explicitly said that it "will prove beyond a shadow of a doubt" that God intends the fruit of the Solemn Assembly to be *"revival" in both Kansas City and the country as a whole*. Has this occurred? If not, might it still come to pass at some point in the future? As if that were not enough, recall that Jones prophesied that the comet "will serve to confirm" that God's "purpose for the church in Kansas City and in the nation as a whole *will come to pass*." What are we to make of this? I find it difficult to believe that a spiritual awakening has come to "the nation as a whole." Should we retain our expectation that this will yet occur at some point in the future? Or should we honestly acknowledge that this part of Jones's prophecy has simply failed to materialize? Perhaps the promise was conditional, dependent on the obedience and sustained commitment of the church. As noted earlier, many biblical prophecies are not guarantees but invitations that require the faithful contribution of those to whom they are given.

You may think that I'm being overly pedantic, but we cannot afford to be less than meticulously honest about alleged prophetic words. Consider what Jones said about the word that God would send Bickle from heaven on November 15. It would be "a sign that this is indeed a sovereign movement that *he has raised up to touch the ends of the earth*." It would also signal the beginning of God's recruitment of a new Gideon's army "that would be instrumental in *the coming great revival.*" Should we retain belief that "the great revival" is "coming"? Or has the window for its fulfillment been closed by the failures of certain individuals and the collapse of the church and 24/7 prayer movement in Kansas City? Or could it be that to suggest that God's promised purpose is somehow dependent on one body of believers in one city is the height of arrogance and elitism? Might not God make use of Christians and faithful churches around the world to usher in the promised awakening? These are important questions that cannot be avoided. The answers to them are, at least presently, quite elusive.

Chapter Seven

The Blueprints and the Black Horse

Toward the final days of Mike Bickle's tenure at IHOPKC, he often mentioned the "black horse" as a symbol of trouble, a demonic spirit that would oppose the prayer ministry and sow the seeds of accusation among Christians. When anyone asked about the attacks against IHOPKC or Bickle himself, the finger was pointed at the black horse. So, where did this imagery come from and why was it mentioned with such regularity? The answer is found in what may well be the most stunning of all alleged supernatural encounters. I suspect that many reading this book who are unfamiliar with the story will scoff and ridicule once they hear it. My aim in this chapter isn't to convince anyone, but simply to describe the events as they happened, or *allegedly* happened.

The Blueprint Prophecy

A stunning series of supernatural phenomena began to unfold in the spring of 1984. On Friday, March 23, Bob Jones called Mike Bickle on the telephone with the news that he had again heard the audible voice of the Lord. Let me pause here to address the uneasiness that statements like this evoke in many Christians. Bible-believing evangelicals do not deny or question the reality of God speaking to people audibly in redemptive history. From the time of the garden of Eden to the call of Abraham, to the experience of young Samuel who heard God's voice but thought it to be that of Eli, to the revelations communicated in this fashion to the many Old Testament prophets, the audible voice of God appears regularly throughout the Bible.

There are several such instances in the New Testament as well. We see this first of all at the baptism of Jesus in the Jordan. Not only did the Spirit of God descend upon him like a dove, but "a voice from heaven said, 'This is my beloved Son, with whom I am well pleased'" (Matt 3:17). Something similar occurred on the Mount of Transfiguration. Peter's statement was interrupted when "a bright cloud overshadowed them, and a voice from the cloud said, 'This is my beloved Son, with whom I am well pleased; listen to him'" (Matt 17:5). After Jesus acknowledged that he came to earth to glorify the Father and fulfill his purpose, "a voice came from heaven: 'I have glorified it, and I will glorify it again'" (John 12:28). That it was an audible voice is clearly seen from the reaction of those standing nearby. The crowd "said that it had thundered.[1] Others said, 'An angel has spoken to him'" (John 12:29).

We also read of the angel of the Lord speaking to Philip about sharing the gospel with the Ethiopian eunuch (Acts 8:26). But later in the narrative we read that "the Spirit said to Philip, 'Go over and join this chariot'" (Acts 8:29). Was this voice heard audibly? We can't be certain, but I think it was. Paul heard Christ's audible voice on the road to Damascus. We read in Acts 9 that "falling to the ground, he heard a voice saying to him, 'Saul, Saul, why are you persecuting me?'" (Acts 9:4). The men who accompanied Paul also heard the voice but saw no one (Acts 9:7). Ananias, who would minister to Paul days later, twice heard the voice of the Lord in a vision (Acts 9:10, 15). The narrative reads as if Ananias and the Lord carried on a personal conversation. Cornelius heard "an angel of God" instruct him to send for Peter, and yet in the next verse it is the Lord who speaks to him (Acts 10:3–4).

When "the voice" came to Peter with the news that all foods were now clean, it makes sense that he heard it with his ears and not merely in his heart (Acts 10:13, 15). Not long after, Peter again heard the voice of "the Spirit" say to him, "Behold three men are looking for you" (Acts 10:19). An angel spoke audibly to Peter when he was in prison, instructing him to make haste in his escape (Acts 12:7–8). During a worship service in the church at Antioch, "the Holy Spirit said" to those present, "Set apart for me Barnabas and Saul for the work to which I have called them" (Acts 13:2).

These few texts that I have cited are sufficient to make the point that it is not altogether unusual for the Holy Spirit to communicate audibly with a human. I'm not saying that this verifies the reality that God spoke audibly to Bob Jones and others in Kansas City, but in the absence of any text that says God no longer communicates with his people in this way, I'm inclined

---

1. This, of course, is the source of the title to David Pytches's book, *Some Said it Thundered*.

to concede the truth of what they claimed. I should go on record by saying that I have never personally heard the audible voice of God. But that isn't because I believe such a mode of communication is invalid in our day. Cessationists typically argue that once the final words of canonical Scripture were penned the Holy Spirit ceased to speak in this manner. The obvious problem with this perspective is that canonical Scripture itself nowhere says any such thing!

Let's return now to the story of what happened on March 23, 1984.

The message Bob Jones had for Mike Bickle seemed strange, which, as we have come to expect, was par for the course!

"On Monday," said Jones, "God will give you *blueprints* for the movement."

Bob himself didn't know the meaning of this word, but he had no doubts about its truth. He was so confident that he called Bickle again on Saturday and then brought it up yet one more time on Sunday morning.

Monday, March 26, began without fanfare. But while Mike was out of the office during the lunch break, a man walked in unannounced and left on his desk an unusual envelope. This man had driven in four hours from somewhere in rural Kansas. Bickle and he had never met before nor was Mike even aware of the man's name prior to this day. It was later discovered that his name was Carl Autry.

When Mike returned from lunch, he found a note on his desk that read, "Mike, you don't know me, but I want to get with you. The Spirit of the Lord came upon me at 2:00 a.m. last night and He gave me a word for your church in Kansas City. The Lord told me he was going to give me the blueprints for your church." This pastor never contacted Mike again. But what he left behind was profound. There on Mike's desk, underneath the introductory note, was a manila envelope with one word written on the front cover: "Blueprints"!

You might think Bickle's first reaction would be to yell, "Amazing!" Far from it. He was actually skeptical. "What if this is a setup?" he said to himself. "What if Bob Jones and this guy are collaborating in a massive hoax?" His first response was to find out if Bob Jones and this Kansas pastor had ever met. He took every step possible, leaving no stone unturned, including numerous phone calls to people close to both this pastor and Bob, and concluded that the two men knew nothing of each other.

It wasn't that Mike seriously doubted Jones's integrity. Far from it. He trusted him implicitly. He just had to be doubly sure so that in the years to come his faith wouldn't falter in times of trouble. After his investigation, the only option was to conclude that God had indeed spoken to Bob Jones about the blueprints for the movement appearing on Monday.

In the coming days Bickle shared this information with Pat, his brother, and only a few others. The somewhat cryptic contents of what is referred to as "The Blueprint Prophecy" were kept strictly confidential. One element in the prophecy concerned the emergence of five congregations in the Kansas City metropolitan area, all related to Kansas City Fellowship.

Mike decided that he would not tell Augustine Alcala about this. Rather, he prayed, "Lord, if the Blueprint prophecy is from you, let Augustine tell me about the five congregations in the city. Only then will I tell him about what has happened." In September of that year Bickle and Alcala were driving home following a conference in Tulsa, Oklahoma, when Augustine turned and said, "I have a word for you. The Lord said there will be five congregations in the city."

"Good," Mike replied, "because I have a prophecy about that but decided not to tell you until the Lord confirmed it by revealing it to you independently." The significance of all this will become evident momentarily, but first I must describe what happened at the conference in Tulsa.[2]

The White Horse Is Coming

It was Sunday morning and more than a thousand people were in attendance at the conference being hosted by Richard Exley's church in Tulsa. The meeting this day was being held in the school auditorium. Those present from the Kansas City church included Bickle, Jones, Augustine Alcala, Jerry Reardon, and Louie McGeorge. The crucial moment came while Augustine was standing on one end of the stage, praying for a gentleman, and Bob Jones on the other. Bob suddenly turned to Mike and, pointing to an elderly lady a few rows back, quietly whispered, "The Spirit of God is on that lady in the red dress."

Augustine had absolutely no way of knowing what Jones had said to Mike, yet, almost immediately, from the other side of the stage, he called out that very lady and said, "Mother, come forward and we will pray for you." Mike recalls thinking to himself, "This is important. Both Augustine and Bob, independently of each other, have seen something spiritually significant happening to this woman."

As she approached the stage, Augustine said, "I'm going to do something that I rarely if ever do." With that, he handed the microphone to the lady and encouraged her to prophesy. Suddenly, with great authority and

---

2. Since Bickle had shared the prophecy about "five congregations" with a select few individuals, it is possible that one of them communicated this to Alcala. If so, this would seriously undermine the legitimacy of Alcala's word to Bickle.

volume, this frail, elderly lady uttered the following words: "I had a vision last night of a white horse coming to Tulsa. I was told to come here tonight and touch it."

This immediately caught Bickle's attention, because from the early days of the church a white horse had consistently appeared in visions to a number of prophetic people as a symbol of Kansas City Fellowship and the movement of which it was a part. At other times the white horse pointed to Bickle himself as representative of the church as a whole. She then turned to Augustine and said,

> Young man, in the near future you are going to have a brand-new experience. You are a true prophet and have seen both good and evil, but you have never seen both good and evil together in an open vision. In a short amount of time, two things will happen. First, you will see good and evil in total conflict. And secondly, so that you will know it is real, it will show up in the natural, in the flesh. There will be a token of it in the human body.

As they drove back to Kansas City, Augustine told Mike about the five congregations, and Mike in turn told Augustine about the Blueprint Prophecy. After reading it, Augustine replied, "I think it is from the Lord. But I think the Lord is going to let me ask him directly about it." The Blueprint Prophecy is not one that had been available for public distribution. At that time, insofar as it pertained only to Kansas City Fellowship, Bickle thought it should remain private. Although it is written in somewhat cryptic prose, it contains unusual clarity and predictions about several aspects of the church's vision.

A few days after their arrival back home in Kansas City, following the Wednesday night prayer meeting, Mike took Augustine to the home where he was staying. They were compelled to spend the night in the home of one of the professional football players on the Kansas City Chiefs, who happened to be a faithful church member. The reason Mike and Augustine were forced to stay at this home is that when they went outside to drive away, Mike's car wouldn't start. The next morning, after the events about which you are getting ready to read, the car started perfectly!

The only room with two beds was in the basement. Mike, Augustine, and the Kansas City Chief's player went to bed that night totally unaware of what was about to take place.

War in the Heavenlies

At 5:00 a.m. on Thursday, September 13, Bickle was suddenly awakened by an indescribably sharp pain in his right knee. "It felt like a red-hot sledgehammer had bashed my knee-cap." The knee began to swell up, making it virtually impossible for Bickle to bend it and even less possible for him to sleep. The pain was agonizing. But perhaps the most bizarre thing was that Mike had done nothing to cause such pain. He had not suffered an injury or experienced anything of a physical nature that might explain this sudden, excruciating pain.

As Mike lay there in anguish, he heard Augustine crying aloud. He looked and saw him on his knees between his bed and the wall rocking back and forth, with a pillow over his head. He was crying out, over and over, "Michael, help me! Michael, help me!" Initially, Bickle thought Augustine was calling out for him, but he did nothing, choosing rather to watch and listen in silence. He soon realized that Augustine was experiencing some sort of spiritual trance. Although he had by now broken out in a sweat from the pain, Bickle said nothing, not wanting to bring Augustine out of his trance. "No, no, no, no!" cried Augustine. Fifteen minutes later he suddenly became silent.

Finally, after two torturous hours of pain, Mike gave up on falling back asleep and attempted to go upstairs. However, his knee was by now so swollen and stiff that he could only scoot up the stairs backwards, one step at a time. He put ice on his knee and sat alone in the kitchen for another hour until his host joined him.

"What happened to your knee?" he gasped in unbelief.

"I don't know," said Mike, "but I think I better go to the hospital and get some sort of painkiller."

A few minutes later Alcala woke up and joined them, to this point unaware of Mike's knee or the pain he was suffering.

"Wow, did I ever have a spiritual experience last night!," exclaimed Augustine.

"Yeah, I know," said Mike. "I heard it. You were really scared, too."

"No, I wasn't," Alcala protested.

You must understand that Alcala had always insisted, perhaps a bit pridefully, that he was never frightened when he received dreams and visions from the Lord. "My God wouldn't frighten me if he appeared," Alcala was often heard to say. Bickle was keenly aware of this, and pressed the point. "Come on Augustine. I *heard* you crying out in fear last night."

"You what?"

"I heard you having this experience, and there's no way you can tell me you weren't afraid." The fact that Alcala then acknowledged Bickle was right was strong confirmation that the experience was indeed real.

"OK. Yeah. I was afraid," said Augustine, "but don't tell the other prophets."

Alcala then began to describe what had happened. It was a terrifying vision in which there appeared a huge black horse, perhaps fifteen feet tall, wide across the chest with rippling muscles. It was snorting smoke through its nostrils as it marched with arrogance down the road, intimidating everyone and everything in its path.

Suddenly, a small white pony stood in its way. The pony was only three feet tall and had tiny wings, about seven or eight inches in length, projecting out on each side. Augustine knew instinctively that the black horse was representative of a high-level demonic principality and that the white pony was representative of Bickle and the movement of which he was the leader.

Suddenly the black horse rose up on its hind quarters and viciously struck the white pony on its right knee! Like a dog whose foot has just been stomped, the pony squealed in agony and was hurled into the ditch alongside the path. This was precisely the moment at which Mike was awakened with the shattering pain in *his* right knee. However, Mike had no idea whatsoever that anything of this nature had occurred. And Augustine was completely unaware that he was speaking aloud in his trance or that Mike was awake listening to him.

In case you hadn't put two and two together yet, Augustine was experiencing the fulfillment of the prophecy given to him by the lady in Tulsa concerning the mortal combat between good and evil. And the token of this word being played out in the natural body was being fulfilled with excruciating agony in Bickle's knee.

Augustine, fearful of the black horse, began to cry out repeatedly, "Michael, help me. Michael, help me." This was the point in his vision at which Bickle began to listen. Suddenly the archangel Michael appeared and stood between Augustine and the black horse. He was wielding a huge sword, drawn and ready for battle. Augustine then saw standing just behind the black horse a man known both to him and Bickle.

The archangel Michael then explained the intent of the black horse: "That man will strike this immature white pony with the rage of Satan when he [the pony] goes to the east."

Michael then touched the black horse and overpowered him. At this point, Augustine had the presence of mind, despite being in a trance, to ask Michael, "Is the Blueprint Prophecy from God or from man?" Amazingly, Bickle claims he heard Augustine ask this question. But remember,

Augustine was unaware either that he was speaking or that Mike was eavesdropping on the incident. Michael responded, "The prophecy will bring great light and much truth, but it isn't everything that God will say. However, my servant who delivered it is independent, has unsettled issues in his life, and has unbalanced doctrines."

The black horse and the man behind him slowly began to retreat, as if to withdraw in defeat. There was then a stirring noise coming from the ditch. It was the white horse, which had recovered from the blow to its knee and was itself now fifteen feet tall with rippling muscles across its chest. The former tiny wings were now nine feet across. The horse rose to obvious victory and then became airborne, soaring upward into the clouds. With this, the vision ended as Augustine fell back into a deep sleep.

Only then did Bickle tell Alcala about his knee, having hidden it from him under the kitchen table until now. Mike now understood why the pain had come and why it was so intense. Augustine was stunned. The pain in Mike's knee continued unabated for another six hours. It only subsided when Augustine walked into Mike's office and said, "Your knee is fine now, isn't it?" Suddenly the pain left. It later returned, but not nearly with the intensity it once had. During the next few days, as Bickle hobbled around in obvious discomfort, his response to those who asked him what had happened was, "I was kicked by a horse!" Most laughed, thinking that Mike was only joking. But he knew better.

In the past Bickle had been reluctant to identify the man standing next to the black horse. But as time passed, he felt freer to speak of him. The man whom Augustine saw standing behind the black horse, the man that the archangel Michael told him would attack the white horse with the rage of Satan, was Ernie Gruen. Gruen was the pastor of Full Faith Fellowship of Love in Shawnee Mission, Kansas. He was something of the charismatic "pope" of the region, with numerous churches associated with him. When Bickle and Kansas City Fellowship "went to the east," Gruen released a 233-page document that accused Bickle and his church of occultic practices, manipulation, and pride. The document went global. Even Pat Robertson on the 700 Club made reference to it. The story was picked up by *Christianity Today* magazine and *Charisma*. Needless to say, Bickle's reputation was destroyed. I should point out that Bickle has always been careful to say that this didn't mean Gruen was himself demonized, but only that he was an unwitting tool of Satan to bring disruption and disunity to Bickle's church.

This experience occurred in September of 1984. No one at that time had any idea of what "going to the east" might mean. More than five years later, in December of 1989, Bickle and Kansas City Fellowship planted their first congregation in the "east," in Lee's Summit, Missouri. One of the associate pastors, Noel Alexander, came to Mike and said, "Well, I wonder if 'going to the east' in Augustine's vision was a reference to our planting a congregation in Lee's Summit. Let's wait and see what happens." Exactly one month later, in January of 1990, the attack against Mike Bickle and Kansas City Fellowship was launched. Seven or eight seemingly unrelated individuals and ministries from across the nation joined in the accusations. This was the beginning of the controversy to which I alluded earlier and will discuss in great detail later in chapter 13.

Bickle appealed to John Wimber, leader of the Association of Vineyard Churches, to come to Kansas City and adjudicate the controversy. Mike refused to defend himself, having heard directly from God to keep quiet and let the Lord vindicate him in due time. Wimber assigned Jack Deere to investigate all the charges against Mike. He found very few of them to have any basis in fact. The only thing Wimber concluded was that Mike had acted in pride and had promoted certain prophets prematurely. Bickle agreed and publicly confessed and repented.

When It Seems Convenient to Change a Prophecy

This prophetic event in 1984 brings me to a disconcerting conclusion. In his last sermon at Forerunner Church in October of 2023, Bickle speaks of the accusation and attack that will come against him from the black horse (evidently, a symbol of Satan's rage). But in order to make this statement relevant, he changes the experience that I just described above. As you may recall, the black horse did not "stand right in front" of Bickle, as the latter claims in this sermon. Bickle was, in point of fact, wide awake when the black horse appeared to Augustine in his dream. Let me remind you again of what Michael said to Augustine (not to Bickle): "That man will strike this immature white pony with the rage of Satan when he [the pony, i.e., Bickle] goes to the east." "That man," as noted, was Ernie Gruen.

In the years that followed, no one knew quite what was intended by this warning. But when, in December of 1989, KCF planted a church in the "east" (i.e., in Lee's Summit, Missouri), Noel Alexander approached Bickle and suggested that this might be what was intended when Michael the archangel spoke. Bickle confirmed Alexander's interpretation.

As it turned out, only two months later, in January of 1990, Ernie Gruen preached his sermon, "Do We Keep on Smiling and Say Nothing?" A couple of months after that, he released to the public his 233-page *Documentation* of accusations against the prophets in Kansas City. Everyone who was aware of this event believed that the attack of the black horse was the rage of Satan by means of the charges that Gruen leveled against Bickle and the prophets.

But now, in October of 2023, the story has changed. It isn't Augustine to whom Michael spoke in a dream, but Bickle himself. And going to the "east" is no longer the expansion of KCF into Lee's Summit, Missouri, in 1989, but instead refers, rather conveniently, to Bickle's orchestration of intercessory prayer on behalf of Israel in May of 2023. I suppose Bickle might protest and insist that Michael actually appeared to him at some time subsequent to 1984 and spoke the same warning of what would happen when he went to the east. But in all my years at the church and in the countless hours of recordings that describe the prophetic history, Bickle never once claimed that Michael stood before him and said this. And no one that I know from KCF at that time ever spoke of Bickle being personally approached by Michael and given this word.

It would appear that Bickle has made several alterations to the story of what happened in 1984. In the new version, it isn't Alcala to whom Michael appeared, but Bickle himself. It isn't Ernie Gruen who will attack Bickle and KCF in 1990, but Satan whose attack will come in 2023. It isn't because of KCF's planting a church in the "east" of the city, Lee's Summit, that provokes the accusations, but Bickle's orchestration of five million gentiles praying for Israel. Since Israel can be conceived as "east" of Kansas City, this fulfills the prophetic word spoken by Michael. Yet again, in March of 2011 Bickle traveled to South Korea and found in this momentous trip yet another application of what going to "the east" meant.

I suppose Bickle might try to account for these discrepancies by appealing to a double or even triple fulfillment of the black horse prophecy. The first installment, as it were, of the warning issued by Michael was in Gruen's attack against KCF in 1990. The second installment, or fulfillment, of the warning was identified as Bickle's ministry trip to South Korea in 2011. The third is found in Satan's attack against Bickle's efforts to mobilize prayer for Israel in 2023. But many who were part of IHOPKC and Forerunner Church at the time are convinced that the attack of the black horse was Bickle's way in 2023 of preempting the accusatory strike that he knew was about to be launched against him. These changes or adaptations of the original experience of Augustine and Bickle in 1984 were, in all likelihood, a deliberate attempt to provide an explanation for what was about to transpire in 2023. This *may* have been Bickle's calculated attempt to undermine the truth of the accusations he had been forewarned were soon to come, and to short circuit the influence those charges might have on the minds of the people at the church and in the prayer movement. Sadly, it is this sort of manipulation that has led so many to question the entirety of the prophetic history.

Addendum:
The Blueprint Prophecy

[Before you read this document, a few words of caution are in order. It is largely incoherent. The prose is horrible and the grammar and punctuation even worse. It is also written in the King James English, but that shouldn't be a problem to anyone. It is highly cryptic, often symbolic, and sentences don't follow in logical relation to each other. Several words are misspelled but I have left them intact and noted with [*sic*]. I honestly don't think you will learn much about the Kansas City prophets from reading it, but there are a few isolated points that I want to draw to your attention. Before I do, please note that you can discard all the recent versions of the Blueprint Prophecy that are abundant on the internet. They are highly edited and do not convey many of the points that Autry wrote. I say this because I have a copy of the original prophecy as typed on Autry's own letterhead. It is dated March 26, 1984. As for the important points in the document, Autry mentions the emergence of five churches in the city and urges Bickle to "take the bride to the city," a theme prominent in Bickle's ministry for many years. He also mentions the development of a school of ministry, which eventually became Grace Training Center where I served as president for seven years. Autry calls it the Divine Institute of Higher Learning. He mentions the "forerunner" ministry like unto John the Baptist, another central feature of Bickle's theology. The house of prayer is noted several times, as is the emergence of the nine gifts of the Spirit. One more thing: When he finally released the Blueprint Prophecy to the public, Bickle had made several editorial changes and deleted certain words. I have no idea why, or what significance we should attach to this. I mention this to point out that what you have below is the full, unedited, and original version of Carl Autry's word to Mike Bickle.]

> God shall confirm in your spirit; and not to proceed until He does. Then upon the confirmation you should begin to act immediately to take the bride to the city; and to the city of Kansas City, rather than having it, the city, to come to Him.
>
> Therefore there should be another church on the north side and on the east side and on the west side, even as it is on the south side. Therefore there shall be the (4) four churches:

Therefore that shall be the outer circle. Therefore the center shall be the hub. Therefore this shall be the (5th) fifth church. This shall be the church of my grace. I have shown you My grace. My grace is sufficient. My grace is Me in thee and in this shall be the (5) five-fold ministry, and yea even in the (5) five-fold ministry, yea, even in the outreach one shall be even the branch. One shall be apostolic church of the center and that shall be the church is on the south shall become the center hub. It shall be the apostolic church and even the outreach of the borders of the circle shall be the evangelistic outreach church. It shall be the Pastor's-Preacher's church and there shall be the Teacher's church.

The people of the city will be able to travel and sojourn—even as all the ministries shall flow even unto all the churches. So shall the city and my people flow unto thee. And thou shall even as in the days past, as I have said unto thee—thou art the Garden Center Church of my choice saith the Lord. Even in my Garden Center Church, I shall raise up thee as a plant of renown. Thou shall be known and thy ways shall be renown and I will bring and place upon thee and in thee and round about thee those that will be the caretakers of my church.

Even as I placed Adam in the center of the Garden to dress it—even so I have placed and set thee in this city to dress it.

Thou shall be a dresser of my vineyard, saith the Lord and the vineyard shall be these people that I shall bring unto thee and out of these. Even out of the loins of the blood line of the flesh of Abraham—even as I said there would be many seeds and many nations, kindred, and tongues, even from thee. Thou shall be known as my Mother-church. Also and out of thy loins shall flow many. I shall raise up and there shall flow forth many sons and daughters. Yea, even they shall be known and renowned, even as the children of the renowned and they shall be.

These children shall flow out of thy loins of thy spirit and that out of my spirit. They shall be spiritual children and they shall inhabit the uttermost parts of the earth. They shall inhabit the place that I have called for thee to settle and to raise up other ministries and other churches.

Thou shall set in order the pastors, as I call the signals—thou shall only be acting as I send in the signals to you. As I give thee the word of my messenger, thou shall hear and it shall be confirmed of a truth in thine heart. And shall act upon it.

Upon the acting of this, I will place within you and within your hands the (5) five-fold ministry. The ministry shall flow and rotate from church to church—rather than people from church to church.

Thou shall set in as I will call and place in thine hands to anoint with the Holy Oil even as this is my significance of my acceptance of those whom I by my Holy Spirit shall confirm and set into my [b]ody—that I would have to prepare for me a bride in this area. There shall—the people flow then into the tabernacles of habitation.

They shall flow from the north, and from the east, and the south and from the west. They shall come and they shall be dandled [?] by thy sides and by thy ministers. Thou shall be ministers of light and ministers of truth of Me, saith the Lord.

Even this shall be a people that shall be known of me and I shall be their God and they shall be my people.

Their responsibility lies within me and their safety lies within drawing close together, yea, I would have them draw real close together.

I say unto you again, that their safety lies in drawing real close together. There shall be unity of the spirit and of the doctrine and thy doctrine shall be my doctrine of my Spirit. I will prepare a place for my people and ye shall go forth and lead my people to a place of habitation. I will show thee and I will guide thee. I will be thy purse bearer. I will hand the checks and the money as the time is prepared for this. There shall be a time and a season and a place for my people to go. Even as I shall call them forth before the cities become desolate. And therein ye shall raise up unto you other cities that shall be the permanent place.

There shall be schools of ministry and they shall flow out of the city into the country—into the country, into the City of Habitation; saith the Lord.

This load shall be too heavy for thee, you shall not be able to bear the burden alone. I shall raise up helpmates, yea, even many help-mates both male and female. I will set them and call them to stand by thy side, and thou shall go forth and lead a people even as Moses led a people and there shall be those that [lift] up thy hands. You shall designate—consecrate this people and anoint and assign to and delegate.

I would have you to delegate the authority, duty, and responsibility, because you cannot carry this load yourself. The burden is too heavy and the journey is too far.

I will send wise men even as I sent wise men to behold my Son's birth, so shall I send wise men to teach thee and help thee and guide thee and be a strength and a source of supply to thee.

The Blueprints and the Black Horse

I shall be thy purse bearer and to those that will hear my voice and obey and yield and become obedient and truly do as my word says and set the Kingdom first in their heart. I shall raise up ministers of finance in this area. I shall bless them. I shall cause them to prosper and they will be prospering because it is. They will remember and know that of a truth that it is their Lord and their God that giveth them power to get wealth. They shall prosper when there is no prosperity. They shall bear fruit when others are barren and even thy land and thy habitation shall be a place of a forerunner—thou shall go before hand. Even as I sent Joseph before hand, so shall ye, go before even thy Spirit. Thy mind and thy leadership—you shall send forth the Joseph out of my bride and my congregation to prepare—even to make ready a time and a place that I shall choose and I—it shall be of my choosing and of my calling, said the Lord.

For even now, even as I have sent my messenger to share my ministry unto thee, there shall be. I shall visit thee and there shall be many that shall raise up out of thee and thou shall be known in thy ministries. From out of thee shall come forth the five-fold ministry. This ministry shall be known and established as the Divine Institute of Higher Learning.—shall be a school. I shall move quickly. I will do a quick work in teaching and in bringing up these people that must be brought up.

Yea, I say again unto thee, this must be a do-work, and a new work and as I open my hand—even out of the clouds, even as I have shown thee and I shall show yet that—that as my hand opens and pulsates so shall the children grow. Even the children shall grow mightily and quickly. I shall bring them up and teach them and lead them by the right way, that they might go and prepare a city for habitation and they may plant their vineyards and sow their fields and their cattle shall give their increase saith the Lord.

For even as I have sent my messenger and many have heard the voice that I have, saith the Lord, shot the arrow of my deliverance for my people. The arrow is the flaming arrow of my deliverance of my gospel and of my power.

The out-pouring of the latter rain shall begin in this area and upon this city. It shall be noised abroad even world-wide. They will stand in awe and there will return unto the Holy reverence of my name and of my people and they shall flourish and the way of my teachings shall be by my Spirit and by my word.

But I will do a new thing. I will visit them in the night season with dreams and visions as I have said in the past in my word, yea, even this is of my word. I will even send My angels.

I will even take people in the Spirit and will catch them away in the Spirit, yea, even unto the Divine Institute of Higher Learning and it shall be by me and I shall teach them in new ways. I have said before my word shall not return unto me void but that thing which I have said is Absolute, my word is Absolute. My word is sovereign. My word is established. My word shall be—and if there be those that are stubborn and rebellious and obstinate, I shall even remove the Royal Diadem and the Crown of Glory and I shall give it to even prepared to another, saith the Lord.

This is the day of my visitation unto you. I shall call the recording angels of Heaven and earth to record to you, this day that it is sealed upon you and it cannot be removed, in Jesus' mighty name.

For thou shall not build unto me or unto thyself buildings of places to ingather. For as of now, thou shall continue with the plan as I have given thee in the beginning.

For it is my plan and it shall be by my design, and shall not be by groping as in the dark, for my people that have been sitting in the valley & shadow of darkness have seen the light. Even as Paul had seen the light, but his fellow-laborers saw not the light, but he became the reflection of that light even as John bear witness of that light. My light is understanding.

For it is given unto thee, to know and to see that just one. For I yet have my many people that must yet come to the light. For out of the center of the Hub shall grow forth from the House of Prayer for I have said my house shall be called "House of Prayer." For this is of me and the fifth shall be my grace.

For out of my grace shall flow forth my divine grace and favor to all that are willing and obedient. For have I not said the first shall be last and the last shall be first. Thus it shall be as the fifth place of ministry [sic] is to be readied—then it shall be built by my design.

For into this place shall flow the outreach ministries and from these in-gathering meetings shall flow the fullness of Christ. Even unto the workings of the fullness of the gifts of the Holy Ghost. For when you have the nine gifts, come together. Then shall be fulfilled the scripture, these works and even greater works shall you do.

For there are the many that shall be raised up at the appointed time, for the world to see, and this is a part of the ministry of the end-time church. For even as I have called John to make ready a people for the Lord, even so shall this church bear the forerunner spirit that was upon John. This shall be a spirit of preparation and of preparedness, for this is the separation work.

For I have called for my people to come out and be separate—even unto me. For I will not have a piece of a people: but it shall be all or none. For, I place in your hands the final decision and you shall go forth by faith. Faith is by my grace and in my grace is my tolerance and contingency for flesh.

For the government shall be by the voice of twelve. For disciples shall be sent out. They shall go as servants into the out-of-the-way places to compel them to come in to my house that it may be full. For this shall move to the outer borders of the city for the final phases of the building of my "House of Prayer."

Chapter Eight

The New Wine of the Spirit and the Toronto Blessing

The next event to be noted took place in the spring of 1984. The precise timing is significant, as we will shortly see. Our confidence in the reality of this particular occurrence is entirely dependent on our assessment of the credibility of Bob Jones and Mike Bickle. My narrative of the event is precisely as Bickle told it to me.

It was early one Saturday morning around 7:00 o'clock and Mike Bickle was awake, but still lying on his bed. Suddenly, and without warning, he claims to have heard what he calls "the thunderous audible voice of the Lord." Earlier I referred to the "internal audible voice" of God. But this day Bickle claims to have heard the "*external* audible voice" of God! It isn't easy for him to describe. It sounded like the voice of many waters, as John the apostle describes in Revelation. It was also like the sound of eighty thousand fans in Arrowhead stadium cheering in unison for the Kansas City Chiefs. On the one hand, it sounded as if it were coming from fifteen miles away in downtown Kansas City. On the other, it seemed as if the voice was coming from directly in front of him, as if God were speaking face to face with Mike. He felt as if the entire room was shaking and the fear of God filled the place.

The words the Lord spoke were simple, yet strange; not what one might expect.

"I have a revelation for you," said the Lord.
If those words had been spoken to you or me, we would undoubtedly have been waiting anxiously for ominous words to come forth. That was certainly

Bickle's expectation. But what the Lord said next seemed oddly inconsistent with the stunning excitement of the moment.

"Call Bob Jones."

What? That's the word of the Lord? But Bickle didn't hesitate. Although I have never heard the audible voice of God, I can well imagine that once it resounds in your ears and heart that you obey it, no matter what is spoken.

Mike called Bob Jones on the phone and said, "You're never going to believe what just happened to me. I heard the audible voice of God tell me to call you."

"I know," said Bob, "and I've had an incredible experience with the Lord." Bob then proceeded to relate what had happened.

As Jones sat in his chair, he entered into what he alleges was a "trance" state. He was taken to "Joseph's dungeon" as it is described in Genesis 40. You may remember the story from that passage concerning Pharaoh's baker and cupbearer who had been thrown into prison with Joseph. They had heard of Joseph's ability to interpret dreams, and thus went to him with their dreams hoping to gain insight into their meaning. In brief, Joseph told the baker that he would be released from prison only to be hung. The cupbearer, on the other hand, would be fully reinstated to his office and would once again "serve wine in the presence of the king."

Jones understood that the baker was a type or representative of those ministries in America that were putting poison into the bread of God's word and damaging God's people. These were ministries that were characterized by pride and greed, and it was God's intent to bring them down. Perhaps it is only coincidence, but Jones insisted that there was significance in the fact that the first ministry with national prominence to come crashing down in the years following that revelation was that of Jim and Tammy Faye *Bakker*.[1] It's not uncommon among many charismatics to make much of alleged connections between words, even if they aren't spelled the same. They often tend to find spiritual significance in such correspondence, something that I find ridiculous. The cupbearer, on the other hand, was representative of those ministries that were characterized by humility. Those ministries that were committed to nurturing humility in the people would be exalted at the proper time.

Then the Lord spoke something to Jones of profound importance. He said that just as the cupbearer was restored to Pharaoh's court to serve wine in the king's presence, so too, after a time in the dungeon, the church would rise up to serve wine in the King's presence. The exact words spoken were

---

1. Personally, I find the alleged connection between Jones's experience and the fall of the Bakkers to be quite tenuous.

these: "In ten years, I will begin to pour out the new wine of my Spirit, and my people will again serve wine in the King's presence."

Assuming you believe Bickle's report of the event, this was a hard word to receive. Envision yourself in April of 1984 being told that the new wine of the Spirit would not come for another ten years! Bickle confesses that he was more than a little discouraged at God's timing. He thought to himself, "I'm almost twenty-nine now; in ten years I'll almost be an old man of forty!" However, the truly significant thing is that it was almost exactly ten years later, in January of 1994, that the wine of God's Spirit began to flow in a tiny Vineyard church just off the runway of the international airport in Toronto, Canada.

This word in 1984 was not, however, the only prophetic declaration concerning the renewal in Toronto. In August of 1993, Marc Dupont, a gifted prophetic minister, was speaking with Wesley Campbell, pastor of New Life Vineyard Fellowship in Kelowna, British Columbia, and John Arnott, pastor of what was then the Toronto Airport Vineyard Christian Fellowship. As they walked across a parking lot, Marc suddenly began to prophesy. He told Wes and John that within seven months a move of the Holy Spirit would begin in Toronto and would eventually sweep across the globe. He told John Arnott that he would be traveling worldwide and speaking to thousands of people. He also said that within six to seven months, as many as one hundred thousand people would flock to Toronto. The "Blessing," as it has come to be called, broke out in the third week of January of 1994, exactly as Dupont had prophesied.

On New Year's Eve, 1993, Paul Cain prophesied concerning this coming renewal in the power of the Holy Spirit.[2] "There is coming a fresh release and visitation of the Spirit to John and Carol," said Paul. "And this new move of the Spirit will bless the whole Vineyard." However, contrary to what everyone present was thinking, it was not John and Carol *Wimber* that Paul had in mind. Within three weeks it became evident that God had sovereignly chosen John and Carol *Arnott* of Toronto to steward this divine visitation. The question of whether it "blessed" the whole Vineyard is a matter of opinion. While many pastors and churches experienced spiritual refreshing and renewed commitment to their calling, just as many churches were disrupted, divided, and confused by what happened in Toronto. In fact, as we'll shortly note, John Wimber felt compelled to release the Toronto church from its association with the Vineyard.

---

2. The following is cited in Jackson, *Quest for the Radical Middle*, 301–2. Also see Dawson, *John Wimber*, 175–76.

Finally, one day Bob Jones called Noel Alexander on the telephone.[3] "Noel, I've just had a remarkable vision. I saw Sarah nursing Isaac. The Lord said that in two-and-one-half years Isaac will be weaned and Ishmael will be kicked out." This was in July of 1991. And yes, two-and-one-half years later, to the very month, the renewal broke out in Toronto. One other thing, in case you missed it: "Isaac" means *laughter*! Those of you familiar with what happened in Toronto will understand why many referred to the blessing as the "laughing revival."

The Toronto Blessing?[4]

After hearing from Happy Leman, Midwest regional overseer of the Vineyard, that a powerful visitation from the Spirit occurred when Randy Clark spoke at the regional meeting in Wisconsin, John Arnott invited Clark to speak at his Toronto church on January 20–24, 1994. Those days turned into six weeks of meetings that eventually led to a revival that lasted several years and touched virtually every major nation on the earth.

Ian Stackhouse critiques the Toronto Blessing in his 2004 book *The Gospel-Driven Church*. He points specifically to the "blessing" as illustrative of problems endemic to many charismatics when it comes to the subject of sanctification.

He faults the Toronto phenomenon on several counts, only four of which I'll note. First, although it must be said that Stackhouse doesn't regard Toronto in entirely negative terms, he does suggest that it has a decidedly "romantic" slant that seeks to avoid the encumbrance of excessive concern for words and doctrines. Second, it has contributed to "the development of a pneumatology in which experiences of the Spirit, evidenced at the level of phenomenology, become the sole means of legitimising the truth claims of the gospel. The long-term repercussions of this is [*sic*] a renewal movement detached from the central doctrines of salvation in Christ, but also a revivalism that requires ever more outpourings of the Spirit to secure its place in the world."[5]

Third, "Toronto has severed the link between pneumatology, christology, and ecclesiology, and further undermined the confidence of the church

---

3. Noel Alexander will be introduced in a subsequent chapter.

4. See Poloma, "'Toronto Blessing' in Postmodern Society," and especially her book *Main Street Mystics*. A balanced assessment can be found in Hilborn, *"Toronto" in Perspective*.

5. Stackhouse, *Gospel-Driven Church*, 175.

in its essential rites."⁶ And fourth, "contrary to the Toronto notion of resting and soaking in the Spirit, holiness is not simply a matter of letting go or resting, but of active appropriation of the power of the indwelling Spirit, who conspires to effect radical and ethical change in the world of the ordinary and the mundane."⁷

I have problems with each of these criticisms. First, Stackhouse fails to see precisely *for whom*, in my opinion, the Blessing was intended. The people most powerfully impacted were those who had become burdened with the lifeless and divisive dogmatism of a ministry that was exclusively (or primarily) word-based. Again, this is not to suggest that *all* word-based ministries are lifeless and dogmatic. The leadership of Toronto was not opposed to propositional truth or Christian dogma or to reasoned dialogue on the elements of biblical faith, but only to an intellectual arrogance or doctrinal legalism that tends to measure one's spiritual maturity solely in terms of one's theological precision. That some reveled in the subjectivity associated with the renewal (and what renewal or revival in history has entirely escaped this problem?) is undoubtedly true. But that's not the same as saying that Toronto was designed to diminish the centrality or life-changing power of biblical truth.

There is perhaps more a measure of truth in Stackhouse's second criticism. I suppose my objection is with his use of the adjective "sole." Experiences with the Spirit, when grounded in and consistent with the written Word of God do have a measure of apologetic value. But I don't recall many (if any) claiming that Christianity is true based "solely" on what they experienced at Toronto. Perhaps we would be better served to say that such experiences "confirm" or "bear witness" to one's convictions concerning the gospel.

Third, I suppose what Stackhouse has in mind here is the focus in the renewal meetings on experiencing an encounter with the Spirit that *appeared* to be detached from the preaching of the cross or the corporate life of the church. But why should that necessarily undermine the "confidence of the church in its essential rites"? Most of those with whom I spoke during the heightened season of renewal testified to being refreshed and re-energized to return to their local churches with a new and exciting commitment to live out the truths of the gospel. People were drawn to the power of Toronto not as an excuse to ignore the routine responsibilities of church life (OK, perhaps some were) but to receive a fresh infilling of the Spirit and a new vision for how they can better and more joyfully fulfill them.

6. Stackhouse, *Gospel-Driven Church*, 180.
7. Stackhouse, *Gospel-Driven Church*, 180–81.

The New Wine of the Spirit and the Toronto Blessing

In regard to these last two points, it must be admitted, there are always people who rely solely or primarily on experience and who irresponsibly shirk the biblical mandate for community life in the body. But I think it's unfair to suggest that Toronto *consciously* intended to empower such folk in their sin (although it may have inadvertently contributed to this problem). People who are inclined in this way will find an excuse to justify their ill behavior irrespective of renewal or seasons of revival.

Fourth, and finally, no one of whom I know who was part of leadership in the Toronto phenomenon taught or teaches that "resting" in the Spirit is a substitute for "active appropriation" of his power or for commitment to the classical disciplines of the faith. Far from it. Resting or soaking was encouraged precisely for its capacity to renew and refresh and empower weak souls to get up off the floor and get back in the fight against the world, the flesh, and the devil.

Stackhouse here falls prey to the "either/or" syndrome, as if to suggest that a season of "soaking" under the power of the Spirit's work in the inner person negates or is inconsistent with a focused and energetic pursuit of holiness in the grace of God. I would suggest that this phenomenon of "resting" or "soaking" was perhaps Toronto's greatest contribution, not because it was being recommended as a new model of sanctification or an antidote to the rigors of Christian living, but precisely because it was used of the Spirit to heal, refresh, cleanse, empower, and reignite in countless weary souls a love for Jesus and his word and his church.

Could it be that this objection is again related to the suspicion many have concerning the value of "non-cognitive" or "transrational" experiences? Although not a cessationist, perhaps Stackhouse is reluctant to acknowledge that the Holy Spirit can produce significant and lasting change in a person in the absence of conscious cognitive engagement.

So, yes, Toronto had its flaws, some of them quite serious. The pressure to find biblical warrant for bizarre physical manifestations was more than its apologists could resist. One example of this took place in Kansas City a year or two after the blessing began. We were hosting a conference that met in one of the large arenas in downtown Kansas City. One of the speakers at the conference was John Arnott, pastor of the Toronto Airport Vineyard and principal leader of the blessing. Mike Bickle and I were sitting off to ourselves on the upper row of the arena as Arnott began trying to make biblical sense of the many physical manifestations associated with the renewal. John Arnott is a good and godly man who did his best to be a faithful steward of this outpouring of the Spirit. But his efforts to associate the many bizarre sounds and physical gyrations with texts of Scripture was unintentionally misguided.

I could tell that Bickle was growing increasingly uncomfortable with what Arnott was sharing from the platform. He turned to me and said, "Sam. Pray for me. I've got to do something about this." He got up and made his way down the stairs to the back of the platform and slowly walked up behind Arnott. In a loving and pastoral tone, Bickle gently challenged the way Arnott was justifying the physical manifestations that were happening all around the globe in the wake of the renewal at Toronto. To his credit, John Arnott responded with humility and received Bickle's correction. Bickle was mainly concerned that numerous individuals present at the conference would return to their local churches defending the physical and vocal manifestations, seeking to justify them by citing biblical texts. If this were to occur, he anticipated being inundated with emails, letters, and phone calls from pastors who blamed him and the conference he hosted for the chaos that erupted in their churches.

In August of 1994, some seven months after the Toronto phenomenon broke out, Bickle and I were in Anaheim visiting John Wimber and his team. We talked extensively about what was happening in Toronto, trying our best to make biblical sense of it all. On Sunday night, a special meeting was held at the Anaheim Vineyard during which considerable prayer was made available to people, obviously with the expectation that the Spirit would make his presence known in their lives. Indeed, there was an incredible outbreak of power, as people wept openly, fell to their knees, some lying prostrate on the ground, while others stood trembling in the fear of God. And yes, there was much laughter, mixed in with some animal noises, which soon became the target of numerous critics. As Wimber, Bickle, and I walked from room to room, observing all that happened, I recognized a man who was part of a group of some four individuals. It was Hank Hanegraaf, host of the Bible Answer Man, who went on in subsequent months to be one of the Vineyard's and Toronto's most vocal critics.

Many simply "overinterpreted" the significance of what was happening, not simply in Toronto but virtually all around the world. Others felt compelled to artificially prop up and perpetuate the renewal when it was obviously (and by God's design) on the wane. And critics are right in pointing out that the Scriptures did not play as central a role as they should have.

But I cannot easily dismiss the countless pastors who told me how the Spirit of God reversed ministry burnout and restored zeal for their calling and to the church while at Toronto. I cannot easily dismiss the hundreds, if not thousands, of people who testified to having their affection for Jesus intensified, their courage for evangelism built up, their wounds from past abuse healed, their capacity to feel God's love enlarged, their marriages restored and addictions shattered, and their worship enlivened. So, let's not fault Toronto, or better still, what the Spirit of God accomplished through Toronto, simply because it did not fulfill the expectations of what it never proposed to be.

Prophetic *déjà vu*

I think it best at this point to describe another event in Bickle's life somewhat associated with the Toronto Blessing.

God's purpose in speaking to his people through dreams is often hard to grasp. It may be that he is calling the individual to intercede on behalf of someone else who played a dominant role in the dream. At other times, it seems as if the purpose of the dream is to issue a warning. On still other occasions, the Lord will provide direction for a person in terms of important decisions relating to job, relationships, or the like. And then there are those dreams that portray in advance something God intends to bring to pass at some time in the future. Thus, when the event comes to pass, one can look back on the dream in which it was prophesied and know with certainty that God is the author of it all. This latter scenario is precisely what happened to Mike Bickle in 1993.

In the spring of 1993 Bickle dreamed he was on stage with Benny Hinn, a well-known and quite controversial minister who at that time was pastor of the Orlando Christian Center in Orlando, Florida. Bickle had never met Benny Hinn nor had any communication with him. In the dream Mike was standing on a platform with Hinn in front of fifteen to twenty thousand people. Hinn was standing to Mike's left, with his right hand on Mike's shoulder. Mike was holding a microphone as he prophesied to the audience. One additional odd element in the dream was that Mike was wearing a leather jacket, in spite of the fact that he didn't own one. In case you are wondering, yes, Bickle shared these details with several of us on the pastoral staff of the church.

As he spoke, Mike suddenly thought to himself, "I'm not on John Wimber's platform." It seemed strange that he was not in a meeting sponsored by Wimber, for a significant percentage of Mike's conference ministry was either directly or indirectly tied to his friendship with Wimber and our church's affiliation with the Association of Vineyard Churches. In addition to this, as far as Bickle knew, Wimber himself had little if any contact with Benny Hinn. All in all, it seemed strange to Mike that he was present where and with whom he was standing.

Perhaps the most significant aspect of this dream wasn't what Bickle was doing but what it signaled about the church in Kansas City. The Lord made it clear to Bickle in the midst of this dream that his presence on the platform with Benny Hinn marked a time of momentous transition for our church. Mike did not discern precisely what this transition would entail, but there was no mistaking the fact that the experience was a marker, so to speak, of what we believed was a significant leap forward in the purpose God had ordained for what was then known as Metro Vineyard Fellowship (later to be renamed Metro Christian Fellowship).

As the years passed, the dream gradually faded from Bickle's memory. Some three-and-one-half years later, in October of 1996, Bickle was a scheduled speaker for the Catch the Fire conference at the Toronto Airport Christian Fellowship, the church pastored by John Arnott. It was Friday morning of the conference when a man approached Mike and informed him that he was a friend of Benny Hinn's and that Benny was in Toronto that very week conducting meetings. "Benny would like to meet you," he said. "Do you think it is possible for you to break away from the conference and come with me?"

Hinn's interest in meeting Mike was prompted by two things. Benny's now ex-wife had heard Mike speak at a conference in Dallas, Texas, earlier that summer of 1996. She was deeply touched by what Mike said and had shared it with her husband. Furthermore, Benny was a great admirer of Paul Cain and wanted the opportunity to meet Paul's pastor. So, Mike quietly exited the auditorium without telling anyone where he was going.

On the way to the auditorium, Hinn's assistant offered Mike his leather jacket, as it was quite cold in Toronto that day in October. After a thirty-minute conversation with Benny, Mike was invited to join him for the meeting that was about to begin. Mike took his place on the front row where a seat had been saved for him and enjoyed the next two hours worshiping the Lord. Suddenly, and without any advance notice, Benny stopped speaking and pointed directly at Mike: "Mike Bickle, come up here." Needless to say, he was stunned. Hinn directed Mike to ascend the platform where he stood on Hinn's right. As he stood next to Benny, he was handed the microphone and asked to share what was on his heart. Benny stood immediately to Mike's left, placing his right hand on Mike's shoulder.

Bickle had not come to the meeting expecting to do anything other than enjoy the time of worship and ministry. He had prepared nothing in advance and was caught totally off-guard by Benny's invitation. He opened his mouth and said, "I have only one thing to say." As he spoke these words, he thought silently to himself, "And I wish I knew what it was!" His mind was totally blank. It was as if he were free-falling through space, as everything around him slowed to a snail's pace. Virtually without thinking, Bickle began to speak: "There is soon to come across North America an

The New Wine of the Spirit and the Toronto Blessing

unprecedented tidal wave of the Holy Spirit's power. A revival of massive proportions will soon break out in our land."

As these words came forth from Bickle's mouth, he suddenly recognized that he was prophesying. The declaration had not been planned or in any way thought about in advance. Immediately the crowd of approximately twenty thousand people erupted in loud applause and excited shouts of joy and praise. When they calmed down, Mike once again returned to his chair and was seated. As he sat down, it hit him. To use the oft-quoted words of Yogi Berra, "It's *déjà-vu* all over again!"

"Wait a minute," Mike thought to himself. "I've been here before. I've done this before."

Suddenly the dream of three years ago rushed with crystal clarity back into his mind. "Of course," said Mike, "this is what I dreamed back in 1993. It happened today precisely the way I dreamt it back then!" Mike then rehearsed in his head every detail of the dream and its fulfillment. First, I'm standing on a platform with Benny Hinn, prophesying in front of fifteen to twenty thousand people. Second, Benny is standing on my left with his right hand on my shoulder. Third, I'm wearing a leather jacket, although I never owned one. And fourth, our church had withdrawn from the Association of Vineyard Churches only two months prior to this event. In other words, Mike said to himself, "I am not standing on John Wimber's platform."

Bickle was stunned beyond words. "It happened just the way I dreamed, right down to the last detail." It was then that Mike remembered the most important thing of all, namely, that this event would mark the beginning of a transition time for the church in Kansas City. Bickle immediately began to pray that God would make it clear to him what this meant. He was oblivious to what was happening in the auditorium, as he focused all his energies on hearing what he anticipated God would say next. Upon returning to his hotel, he immediately tried to take a nap, thinking that perhaps God would speak to him in a dream. But to no avail. He couldn't fall asleep.

That very night, Bickle found himself back at the Catch the Fire conference, still wondering about the meaning of it all. After the speaker had concluded his message, Marc Dupont went to the platform to make an important announcement. "I have been speaking with John Arnott about this," said Marc, "and he agreed that it must be done. I have a word from the Lord that is burning inside me, and I must declare it."

Bickle was all ears, saying to himself, "This ought to be good. I wonder what the word is." Mike was also attentive because Marc Dupont had shown himself to be a man of great accuracy when he ministered prophetically.

"Mike Bickle. Come up here!"

The words caught Mike off-guard even more than did Benny Hinn's earlier that morning. As Mike made his way to the platform, Marc called for the conference speakers and other international leaders to come up and pray for Mike. To be brief, Marc said, "Mike, the Lord says that this is a time of transition for you and the church in Kansas City. The time is imminent for the promises given to Kansas City to be fulfilled."

Bickle didn't hear much more of the prophecy. When the word about *transition* was uttered, Mike very uncharacteristically found himself lying flat on his back on the floor. "Unbelievable!" he said to himself. "Marc just spoke the very words that I had been praying about all day, the very words that God had spoken to me in the dream of 1993, a dream that became literal, historical fact only this morning!"

It wasn't long before the meaning and application of these prophetic scenarios became clear. After returning to Kansas City following the conference, Mike shared with a few of us in private that he felt led of the Spirit to step down as senior pastor of the church and launch what would become the International House of Prayer, Kansas City.

About the same time as his return from Toronto, Bickle entered into a season of personal transformation. He began fasting every week, from noon on Sunday to noon on Wednesday. As best I can tell, and I observed him closely, he never deviated from this rigorous practice until the time he stepped out of his role as senior pastor of the church in 2000. Sadly, though, and much to the confusion of all of us who thought we knew Bickle well, it was during these same years, 1997 to 2000, that Mike began his illicit sexual encounters with then nineteen-year-old Deborah Perkins. It began with a trip to Paris where he first engaged with her in a physical way (but never sexual intercourse). Their relationship became more intense as time passed until such time as Deborah met her future husband and married him.[8]

Many have asked me how Bickle could have been so seemingly devoted to the pursuit of intimacy with Jesus while at the same time pursuing intimacy of another, illegitimate, sort with this young lady. I honestly have no answer. Some have insisted that the only explanation is that Bickle was never saved in the first place. I cannot bring myself to believe that. And yet somehow he was able to rationalize his sexual interaction with this precious young lady. As noted earlier, I knew her then and since the disclosure of this scandal I have spoken in detail with both her and her husband. I was truly shocked by the nature of their sexual relationship. Deborah and her husband both attested to the fact that it entailed everything short of

---

8. I asked Deborah if she could either confirm or deny that Bickle was truly fasting during those three years. She affirmed that it was true, and that he often encouraged her to do the same.

intercourse. I remain as baffled today as I was when I first heard this news. It is beyond explanation, but no less undeniable.

IHOPKC was birthed in May of 1999 at the same time this illicit affair was ongoing. We gathered on Friday night at midnight and prayed until 8:00 a.m. on Saturday morning. I was faithful to attend every one of these gatherings and later was placed on the Board of IHOPKC. This was only the beginning of what would eventually become a ministry that would touch the earth. No one had any expectations of the scandal that would break out in 2023 or the implosion of the ministry in the wake of numerous allegations of sexual misconduct.

The Disengagement of the Toronto Airport Vineyard from the Association of Vineyard Churches

The controversy stirred by the Toronto Blessing would eventually lead John Wimber to remove John Arnott's congregation from the Association of Vineyard Churches (hereafter AVC).[9] I bring this up because it bears directly on one of the primary reasons Metro Vineyard chose to voluntarily withdraw from the Vineyard in August of 1996. To say that Bickle was unsettled by Wimber's decision is an understatement. Following our annual Passion for Jesus conference in the summer, we proceeded to compose a letter to the Executive Council of the AVC that would ultimately precipitate our departure from the Vineyard. But first I will describe the process that resulted in the Toronto church separating from the AVC, making use of several written communications and letters that passed between the relevant parties.

John Wimber's initial discomfort with what was happening in Toronto can be seen in his September 1, 1994,[10] communication to Bishop David Pytches (the author of *Some Said it Thundered*). Wimber began by saying "that there is no biblical or theological framework" for the phenomenon known as "roaring." "I don't see anything in the New Testament where Jesus and/or the apostles encouraged such phenomena or encountered such phenomena." This leads Wimber to put these kinds of things in a "category of non-biblical and exotic." Without dismissing the phenomenon of certain "animal" sounds, Wimber does not find any explicit justification for them. He refuses to label them as either demonic or divine. "I put this in the

---

9. An excellent portrayal of these events is provided by Connie Dawson in her biography of Wimber: *John Wimber*, 175–207. See also, Beverley, "Vineyard Severs Ties."

10. Wimber, who passed away in November of 1997, was kind enough to share this communication with me.

category of 'pondering/I don't know.'" His primary concern is what spiritual fruit, or lack thereof, is produced in the life of a person who has this experience.[11]

It's important to remember that this communication to Pytches reveals Wimber's initial thoughts about the renewal in Toronto. His more settled view will become evident as we proceed. But he does draw this conclusion: "I cannot endorse or even encourage this experience in our movement and ministry, but at the same time I recognize that it is happening and I would just leave it in the same category as I have of people shaking, or falling, or having other kinds of exotic phenomena that may have some limited biblical representation." It is the "main and plain" of Scripture and Christian experience that Wimber champions. He says that he doesn't "want to make our meetings a focus on 'phenomena.' I would like to make our meetings focused on the Word and works of the Spirit."

The September/October 1995 Board Report of the AVC provided the framework within which Vineyard leadership would interpret and react to the renewal and the phenomena surrounding it. Here is a brief summary of its main points of emphasis:

1. "We are willing to allow 'experiences' to happen without endorsing, encouraging, or stimulating them; nor should we seek to 'explain' them by inappropriate 'proof-texting.' Biblical metaphors (similar to those concerning a lion or a dove, etc.) do not justify or provide a proof-text for animal behavior."

2. "The ultimate test of manifestations should be the long-term fruit produced in a person's life, and the edification of the body of Christ."

3. "Rather than promoting, displaying, or focusing on phenomena, we want to focus on the main/plain issues of Scripture. For instance, witnessing, healing, demon expulsion, ministering to the poor and widows, etc.... We do not want manifestations to be a mark of spirituality. Rather, the fruit and gifts of the Spirit and a godly character should attest to true spirituality."

4. "When extra-biblical or exotic phenomena do occur, we want to avoid theologizing from them. *No doctrine should be based on a prophetic interpretation of a particular manifestation.*"

On November 21, 1995, Don Williams[12] makes an important point in his communication with John Arnott. Although Williams was not speaking

---

11. See Dawson, *John Wimber*, 194.

12. Williams passed away in 2022 after a long and distinguished career as both a Vineyard pastor and biblical scholar.

on behalf of the AVC, he does address a crucial issue concerning the compatibility of the Toronto church with Vineyard values. "I would like to say to the Vineyard as a whole that many themes in John Wimber's ministry are exhibited in Toronto. This really is a Vineyard ministry." One of the primary reasons why Toronto was eventually disengaged from the Vineyard was the belief that it did not reflect the traditional values of the Vineyard. Yet, Williams argues otherwise, pointing to "Worship in high praise and intimacy.... Honoring, teaching and preaching the Word of God.... Loving and healing the whole church." Williams also points to the international flavor of the people and Arnott's heart for world evangelism. He also cites as characteristic of Toronto: evangelism, platform testimonies, lay ministry, power of the Spirit, healing and deliverance, ongoing training, and vision for kingdom of God. Williams also affirms Wimber's insistence that "the renewal needs to be offered through the Vineyard grid."

On December 5, 1995, John Wimber met with the leaders of the Toronto Airport Vineyard, along with Gary Best (the national director of the Vineyard in Canada), Bob Fulton (the international pastoral coordinator), and Todd Hunter (national coordinator in the United States). At this meeting, Wimber suggested to John Arnott that the Toronto church be released from being associated with the Vineyard.[13] Two hours later, in a letter to Wimber, John Arnott acknowledged "some of what is happening in Toronto is outside the Vineyard model. We agree that you and the Vineyard movement should not have to continue answering for the move of God's Spirit in Toronto." Arnott continues,

> We don't understand all of the Lord's plan, but we believe that we are called to help facilitate this particular move of His Spirit. We understand that the long-term implications of this move of God may diverge from what He is doing within the Vineyard movement. That is His prerogative. We are doing our best to be faithful stewards of what God has entrusted to us, as are you.
>
> John, we accept the Board's decision to have our church disengage from the Association of Vineyard Churches. Would you allow us to leave with your blessing?[14]

In a follow-up to the preceding notification, dated December 13, 1995,[15] Arnott sent "An Open Letter for General Distribution,"[16] designed

---

13. The entire text of the letter from Wimber to Arnott is found in Dawson, *John Wimber*, appendix G, along with Arnott's Open Letter of December 12, 1995.
14. Arnott, "Letter to John Wimber."
15. Dawson, *John Wimber*, 199, dates the letter as December 12, not 13.
16. John Arnott, "Open Letter for General Distribution."

for those who desired more information about Toronto's disengagement from the Vineyard. He said that his church "will be disengaging from the Association of Vineyard Churches" on January 20, 1996, at which time he will announce the church's new name. Arnott states that he and his team "were surprised at the finality of the decision" made by the AVC on December 5. "We had hoped to have some input into the process. We thought the Board was not getting an accurate picture of what was taking place at the renewal meetings and that any 'issues' could be explained and resolved. The Board, we are told, thought otherwise and we were offered no opportunity for discussion. We were removed without due process." The bottom line, wrote Arnott, is that we were told that our church renewal services "were not mirroring the Vineyard model."

Both Happy Leman[17] (regional overseer of the Vineyard Midwest [Iowa–Illinois–Missouri–Wisconsin–Minnesota]) and Gary Best[18] (national director of the AVC, Canada) released statements that shed considerable light on the process. According to Best, no one in AVC leadership questioned the divine source of the renewal. At the same time, there was a strong consensus among Vineyard leadership that "the Blessing" was being constructed upon a theological foundation that was significantly different from what the Vineyard had long believed God had set in place for their movement. Best appealed to Wimber and the AVC board to consider the shock that Toronto would experience upon hearing that they were being removed from the Vineyard. Wimber and the Board of the AVC assured Best that they had appealed to Arnott and his leaders on numerous occasions in which they called for change, all to no avail. Toronto's reluctance to respond to Wimber's guidance indicated that John Wimber was not viewed as their leader. Best labored to differentiate between what he called expulsion and a withdrawal of support, although it is doubtful if Arnott recognized the distinction.

Two important statements to all Vineyard pastors were both released on December 13, 1995, one from John Wimber[19] and the other from Todd Hunter.[20] Said Wimber: "I would like to inform you that the Association of Vineyard Churches is formally withdrawing our endorsement from those who have operated in visible leadership in the Toronto Airport Vineyard."

17. Leman, fax message, December 8, 1995.
18. Best, "AVC Canada Summarizes Disengagement Events."
19. Wimber, "Notice of Withdrawal of Endorsement," a letter sent to all Vineyard pastors, including myself.
20. Hunter, "Letter Addressed to Vineyard Pastors." Cited here with permission. The full text of Hunter's letter can be found in the Special Collections at Regent University, Virginia Beach, Virginia.

Among the reasons for this decision, Wimber specifically highlighted the many physical manifestations present in the renewal meetings at Toronto:

> But we cannot at any time endorse, encourage, offer theological justification or biblical proof-texting for any exotic practices that are extra-biblical—whether in Toronto or elsewhere. Neither can these practices be presented as criteria for true spirituality or as a mark of true renewal. Our position is that the renewing works of the Spirit are authenticated by that which is clearly stated in Scripture as works of the kingdom of God. Though we understand that when the kingdom is manifest among us there may be phenomena that we do not understand, it is our conviction that these manifestations should not be promoted, placed on stage, nor used as the basis for theologizing that leads to new teaching.

Wimber then references the Board report of September/October 1994 and says that "we believe the leaders at the TAV have repeatedly violated the guidelines in this report, both in practice and in print, in spite of many expressions of concern." He continues,

> Therefore, it is my determination to withdraw endorsement from the principle [sic] leaders of the TAV who have chosen not to minister within the framework of the values and ministry style of the Association of Vineyard Churches. These individuals are no longer representative of, accountable to, or under the authority of the Association of Vineyard Churches.

Todd Hunter echoes in his statement much of what Wimber asserts. He points out that the AVC board does not believe the many manifestations are "an essential part of renewal or of the work of the Holy Spirit." He also declares that "there seems to be a fundamental belief among some leaders at TAV that one can't and should not administrate or pastor renewal for fear of quenching the Holy Spirit. The Board believes that the scripture requires us to pastor and administrate renewal and manifestations of the Spirit of God." One additional observation that Hunter makes is that "there is a difference in understanding of eschatology. The leadership of TAV has tended to tie this current outpouring with an expectation of a final last days revival signified by signs and wonders, ecstatic experiences, and other manifestations of power that supersede the normal practices of evangelism, healing, missions, and church planting. The Vineyard does not agree that this viewpoint is biblical or helpful."

Kansas City Fellowship's Initial Connection with the AVC and Its Eventual Withdrawal

In the early days of Kansas City Fellowship there were, among others, two primary themes that the church believed it was to champion: the prophetic and intercession. There was also a collective sense that KCF would cross-pollinate with a movement known primarily for its emphasis on worship and compassion. The first Vineyard conference that Bickle and his team attended was in June of 1984 where Wimber emphasized worship, compassion, and the kingdom of God. Over the next three-and-one-half years the team at KCF prayed fervently for God to confirm that he desired the church to join the Vineyard.

In October of 1987 Bob Jones claimed to have heard the audible voice of God that John Wimber would call Bickle in three months. Wimber's call to Mike came in January of 1988, during which he invited Mike to minister to his entire staff at their annual retreat. Then six months passed without any communication between Bickle and Wimber. But on June 5, 1988, Jones once again said he had heard God's audible voice telling him that Wimber would call Bickle within a week. Jones said that the Lord wanted to open to Bickle a large door to the Vineyard so that the emphasis on prophetic and intercession could be heard by fifty thousand people in the Vineyard and a million worldwide.

Wimber called the next week. In the course of their conversation, Bickle asked him how large the Vineyard was and he said, approximately fifty thousand people. When Mike asked him how many people he had impacted around the world, Wimber estimated it to be close to a million. The accuracy of Bob Jones's word convinced Bickle that the cross-pollination between the two ministries was in process of being birthed.

Bickle and others on the leadership team identified four reasons why KCF chose to affiliate with the Vineyard:

> First, we felt a clear divine call reaching back to January of 1984 when Bob Jones first spoke about a movement called "Worship and Compassion." Second, we were excited about the greater effectiveness of these four banner themes being deeply integrated. Third, we recognized our need for accountability and covering as well as the benefits of being part of a spiritual family of like mind. Fourth, we felt joined to John Wimber personally. This joining was grounded in deep affection [and] respect, along with gratitude for all he was then doing for us in the prophetic controversy that began in January, 1990.

Contrary to widespread perception, we did not join the Vineyard to seek refuge in the midst of the prophetic controversy. It is true that we needed this spiritual covering. While visiting our church in February of 1990, John Wimber committed to us that he would provide spiritual covering and see the controversy to its end whether or not we ever joined the AVC. Our continued gratitude during the next four months undoubtedly influenced our decision to join in May of 1990. But it was gratitude for protection that was already in place as opposed to joining in order to secure that protection.[21]

The events that led to Metro Vineyard Fellowship (formerly KCF) leaving the Association of Vineyard Churches and renaming itself as Metro Christian Fellowship need to be addressed. For quite some time Mike Bickle and our team in Kansas City were growing increasingly concerned that we were losing focus on the standards and values on which the church had been built. The relationship between the church in Kansas City and Vineyard leadership was strained, as the latter at times hinted and at other times openly stated that the former was not aligned with Vineyard values and seemed to bristle at being under the authority of the AVC. We knew something was up when we arrived in Anaheim in the summer of 1995 for the national pastor's gathering. John Wimber made it quite clear in his talk that he regretted leading the Vineyard into the prophetic movement, which was his way of saying that the influence of Kansas City on the Vineyard was not a healthy one.

I turned to Bickle and could see the disappointment in his face. Afterwards, he insisted that Wimber was speaking under pressure from subordinate leaders in the AVC and that his recent cancer diagnosis had drained him of the emotional and spiritual energy needed to lead as he should. "I know for a fact that John Wimber loves the prophetic," said Mike, as we walked out of the auditorium.[22] "This was less Wimber speaking and more the voice of other board members who had grown both weary and suspicious of the influence exerted on the Vineyard by Kansas City."

Things came to a head in the summer of 1996. At our annual conference in July, we invited Tri Robinson, Rich Nathan, and Wimber himself, among others, to speak. It was during the course of the conference that Bickle came under conviction that he had yielded to the fear of man and

---

21. Letter from the leadership of Metro Vineyard Fellowship (MVF) to the Executive Council of the AVC, July 4, 1996. I was one of the pastors at MVF who helped compose this letter.

22. Wimber's love of the prophetic is confirmed by his widow, Carol Wimber, in her book, *John Wimber*, 181.

had not held high the banner of the prophetic and intercession, which were the primary themes on which the church had been built. His personal conviction was reinforced by several prophetic words from individuals in the church and by a strong rebuke from Paul Cain.

In addition, there were obvious struggles with how the Toronto church was disengaged from the Vineyard. While acknowledging that certain issues needed to be addressed and changes in the pastoral administration of the renewal were called for, our team at MVF remained uneasy with the way in which Toronto was released. Bickle specifically asked if the four banner themes of intercession, prophetic, worship, and compassion are of paramount and equal importance to the Vineyard. "Will the Vineyard unashamedly endorse and pursue these values, or merely tolerate those who do? . . . We would find it difficult to remain in the Vineyard if the leadership is not unified in its promotion of all these values and practices. We desperately want to stay in the Vineyard, but only if there is a consistent and unified voice coming from the leadership, both in private and public."[23]

At the conclusion of two weeks of hosting our conference in June of 1996, our pastoral staff, and the church at large, experienced a season of intense repentance. This led to our decision to communicate with the AVC Executive Council our concerns and intentions for the future. For several days, from 7:00 p.m. to midnight, Mike Bickle and I hid away in his office to compose a letter explaining our decision. Michael Sullivant, another pastor on our staff, joined us to help with the writing of the letter. We mailed our statement to the Executive Council on July 4, 1996. Although the letter is written in the first person, as if coming from Bickle alone, Michael Sullivant and I were equal contributors to its content. You can read the letter in its entirety in appendix A.

In the wake of their reception of the letter, several leaders of the Vineyard (not including John Wimber) requested a meeting with us. Mike Bickle, Don Steadman, Les Woller, and I joined them in a conference room at a hotel near the Kansas City airport on July 31, 1996. The meeting was long and intense, but cordial. Its tone and direction clearly communicated to us that the time had come for our withdrawal from the AVC. On August 7, 1996, we sent the following letter of resignation to the AVC Board:

> Dear AVC Board,
>
> Thank you for taking the time to meet with us last week [a reference to the meeting of July 31]. I also gratefully acknowledge the many hours you have taken over the years to process and work through some of our mutual differences. You have shown

23. Our letter from the leadership of Metro Vineyard Fellowship.

diligence in this. The leadership team of Metro Vineyard Fellowship is forever touched by the many wonderful relationships that the Lord has blessed us with in the Vineyard. We also are grateful for the covering, correction and direction that the Vineyard has given us during our membership in the Association of Vineyard Churches for the last six years. Our team is especially thankful for the lasting impact John Wimber's life and ministry have made on us. We greatly love and will always treasure the values, practices and friendships that we have gained from the Vineyard.

It is clear to our leadership team that we need to resign as a member of the Association of Vineyard Churches effective August 8, 1996. It is our conviction that there are substantial differences between the mandates that we are called to proclaim and the mandates that you feel the Vineyard is called to proclaim. These mandates were presented to you in detail in the fourteen-page letter that we sent to the AVC Executive Council, so it seems unnecessary to review them here. Because of these mandates and our inability to resolve our mutual differences, we feel a sense of calling to pursue the course God has outlined for us. I do not believe it will work best for either of us that we continue in an official relationship with the AVC in light of our differences.

As both of us labor to proclaim the gospel and Lordship of Jesus, we look forward to a continuing friendship with those in the Vineyard family. We honor you and will continue to pray for you and ask that you pray for us knowing that this is a very difficult process for us.

Sincerely,

Mike Bickle, On behalf of the MVF Pastoral Team

CHAPTER NINE

A Third-Heaven Experience (?) and Controversy over Restoration of the Apostolic

LARGELY DUE TO THE emergence of what is commonly referred to as the New Apostolic Reformation (NAR), the issue of apostles and their authority has taken center stage in the debate between cessationists and continuationists. In the 1960s through the 1980s, speaking in tongues was the focus of controversy. Since then, the spiritual gift of prophecy became the primary target of those who deny that miraculous gifts are still operative in the church. In point of fact, it remains a hot topic. But increasingly in the past few years the question of the apostolic, be it a gift or an office or both, has emerged as the focal point of often contentious debate.

Many have been unjustifiably lumped in with this *movement*. I italicized the word *movement* in view of the controversy over whether NAR is actually a thing, an organized entity of some sort. I won't dive into the controversy on this point, but none can deny that there is a theology that is often referred to as NAR.[1]

We must remember that there is a profound difference between affirming that the gift/office of apostle is still valid in our day, on the one hand, and endorsing NAR, on the other. The former I believe.[2] The latter I

---

1. For more information on NAR, see Weaver, *New Apostolic Reformation*; Wagner, *Churchquake!*; Wagner, *Apostles and Prophets*; Cartledge, *Apostolic Revolution*; Miller, *Reinventing American Protestantism*; Christerson and Flory, *Rise of Network Christianity*. For a rigorous critique of the movement, see the books by Geivett and Pivec: *New Apostolic Reformation?* and *God's Super-Apostles*.

2. See the two chapters on apostles in my book: Storms, *Understanding Spiritual Gifts*.

reject. Many refuse to keep these two things separate and thereby conclude that anyone who uses the language of apostle, apostolic, or prophetic must be part of NAR. I urge you not to fall prey to this misconception. So, what then is the NAR?

Although beliefs similar to those of NAR had existed in previous years, the terminology itself was likely first coined by C. Peter Wagner in the early days of the twenty-first century. Wagner believed that there had emerged a new form or expression of church governance. No longer are churches to be governed by or identified with a denomination, but rather by their alignment under the authority of an apostle, or perhaps several apostles (and in many cases, prophets too). The local church, said Wagner, is shifting from being led or governed by elders and pastors to being under the authority and oversight of an apostle. I won't take the time here to respond, other than to say that Wagner's proposal is profoundly unbiblical. Apostles may well still exist, but nowhere in the New Testament do we find any form of local church governance other than that of a plurality of elders. Nor is there the slightest hint in Scripture that God ever intended the prescribed model of local church governance to, at some time subsequent to the closing of the biblical canon, be changed or transformed into one in which apostles usurp the role of elders or exercise authority over them.

Here, then, is a brief summation of the most important tenets of the NAR:

- Apostles and prophets are to exercise ultimate authority over the governance of the local church instead of duly recognized male elders.
- Apostles and prophets are believed to have extraordinary spiritual power.
- Apostles and prophets are believed to be recipients of revelation that is unattainable by the ordinary Christian.
- Churches cannot be expected to thrive unless they have the five-fold ministry of Ephesians 4:11 as the governmental structure of their assemblies.
- Many, if not most, in the NAR believe in the Word of Faith, according to which our words have creative power to produce what one proclaims.
- Many, if not most, in the NAR also embrace the health and wealth or prosperity gospel.

- Those in the NAR also believe, in most cases, that it is always God's will to heal the sick, and if one is not healed it is not God's fault but due to the lack of faith or the presence of sin in the life of the afflicted.

- Those in the NAR embrace some form of dominion theology, otherwise referred to as "the seven mountain mandate," according to which the church will increasingly influence and lead to the spiritual transformation of government, business, education, the family, religion, media, arts, and entertainment.

- Those in the NAR often affirm what they refer to as the transfer of wealth from unbelieving people to the church.

- Those in the NAR regularly practice "declarative" prayer, or prayers of "decree."

- Those in the NAR typically believe that miracles are to be a normative phenomenon in the experience of Christians and local churches.

- Advocates of the NAR regularly engage in what is known as "spiritual mapping" and "strategic level spiritual warfare," according to which believers fast and pray to identify and then engage the demonic principalities that supposedly exert power over geopolitical regions.

It's important that we understand the various tenets of NAR for the simple fact that some critics of Bickle have insisted that he is, as it were, a card-carrying member and advocate of its basic beliefs. Aside from his belief in the present-day reality of the apostolic, Bickle would reject each of the tenets listed above. Whereas it is true that many of the beliefs of the Latter Rain movement sowed the seeds of what would emerge as NAR, to my knowledge Bickle himself never endorsed any of its doctrines.[3]

I bring this up simply to point out that neither Mike Bickle nor the prophets who ministered in his local church ever conceived themselves as possessing unique authority or greater access to revelatory insights from the Holy Spirit, at least during the time frame in which I served on staff at the church (1993–2000). No one, whether pastor or elder, ever remotely claimed to be an apostle (although, at times, people did refer to John Wimber as an apostle, a title that he rigorously rejected). Did Mike Bickle function in an "apostolic" manner of leadership? Perhaps. But he did not, on that

---

3. Some contend that what Bickle denied in public concerning NAR, he affirmed in private. Of all those we might describe as belonging to the Kansas City prophets, only James Goll has "at times" (his wording, in a personal email to me) been identified with NAR. James is a founding members of the Apostolic Council of Prophetic Elders but, like most, denies that he is a "member" of NAR insofar as no such formal organization even exists.

basis, claim to have special privileges or knowledge that was unavailable to other, non-apostolic leaders (such as myself). No one in our church ever addressed any of us in leadership as apostles. If they had, we would have brought immediate correction to their misguided belief.

Has Bickle enjoyed a close friendship with leaders of the NAR? Yes. Has he invited them to speak from his platform? Yes. But he never did so as a way of placing his stamp of approval on their beliefs concerning NAR. They ministered in Kansas City based on their gifting, character, and years of personal relationship with Bickle, not their beliefs about whether apostles do or do not exist today, nor their claims about how the local church should be governed. Some would question Bickle's wisdom on this matter, arguing that by platforming such people he was publicly endorsing everything they believed. There is a measure of validity in this charge. However, Mike Bickle is many things, but a fundamentalist who practices separation from the brethren based on differences regarding secondary issues he is not. In the final analysis, it matters little if you agree or disagree with Bickle's criteria for inviting people to minister at his conferences. What matters for us in the immediate context of this book is to clearly distance him from any affiliation or agreement with what is known as NAR.

Although my concern in this book is only tangentially related to IHOPKC, the latter made clear in their statement of Affirmations and Denials[4] where they (and Bickle) stand on Latter Rain theology. There we read the following:

The Manifest Sons of God Theology

We affirm that all born-again believers will be "manifest" as sons of God after the second coming of Christ.

We deny that we will experience the fullness of our inheritance as sons of God before Jesus returns.

Explanation: Some uphold the false teaching that in this age believers can have faith that will enable them to attain to qualities of life that are reserved only for believers in the resurrection.

The Latter Rain

We affirm that the Church will experience the greatest outpouring of the Spirit in history before Jesus returns (Joel 2:28–32). This outpouring will result in a great ingathering of souls and a renewing of the Church so that believers will walk in godliness as declared in the Sermon on the Mount (Mt. 5:1–7:28). We

---

4. www.ihopkc.org. The information has since been removed from the website.

affirm the presence of the fivefold ministry for the equipping of the saints (Eph. 4:11–13).

We deny the distinctive doctrines that go beyond Scripture that are often associated with the Latter Rain theology that was popularized in the 1950s.

Explanation: Some have wrongly identified our ministry today with the false teachings that were popularized by some in the Latter Rain movement. At no time in the past did we have any relationship with this movement.

There is yet another reason why Bickle has been so often associated with this movement. It is found in what is undoubtedly the most controversial experience that Bickle ever claimed.

A Third-Heaven Experience?

On July 3, 1984, Bob Jones claimed to have had a powerful vision of the Lord. The Lord's presence was atop the golden ark of the covenant, on the mercy seat. There were several young men bearing aloft the ark on their shoulders. The Lord identified these as apostles who would be raised up for the end-time ministry. They were carrying the ark down Blue Ridge Boulevard in Grandview, Missouri. This seemed strange at the time because when Jones claimed to have experienced this vision the church (then known as Kansas City Fellowship) was meeting in Overland Park, Kansas. Later the church purchased the building that is located at the intersection of Blue Ridge Boulevard and Grandview Road.

Following these men, of which Jones counted thirty-five, was a parade of thousands of people marching to the glory of God. Jones's interpretation of the vision was that the Lord intends to raise up thirty-five apostles from this movement in Kansas City. These are not the only end-time apostles, for there will be others raised up from other streams within the body of Christ. But thirty-five are ordained to be raised in Kansas City.

One of the intriguing things in this vision was the fact that Bob Jones himself was not in the parade. He was sitting in the grandstands, so to speak, watching as the parade of worshipers passed by. More puzzling still was the fact that he was in a hospital gown, as if in some way ill or debilitated and thus unable to participate. As if that were not enough, when he looked down at his feet, he noticed that they were crippled. The Lord then spoke and said, "Bob, you are like Mephibosheth in 2 Samuel 9."

For those of you unfamiliar with the story, Mephibosheth was the son of Jonathan whom David chose to bless as an expression of love for his

A Third-Heaven Experience (?) and Controversy over Restoration of the Apostolic

friend. When Mephibosheth was young his nurse accidentally dropped him and injured both his feet (2 Sam 4:4), leaving him crippled for life (2 Sam 9:13). Nevertheless, he was honored by David and regularly ate at the king's table.

> "Bob, you are a Mephibosheth," said the Lord. "You are injured in your walk. Your tutors dropped you when you were young in the Spirit and you have a limp. You don't walk in a healthy way. You will always have that limp. Nevertheless, you will still eat at David's table."

Jones was perplexed by this. "My tutors dropped me. What does that mean?" The Lord then revealed to Bob that there remained a number of unresolved issues from early in his life that were never honestly addressed or healed. Those who were over Bob never adequately dealt with some of these foundational matters. Like the nurse of Mephibosheth, they "dropped" him spiritually and injured his feet. It almost seems as if Jones was prophesying his own future moral failure and disqualification from participation in the revival that he had often predicted would come.

Although he was still struggling with the meaning of his "injury," Bob informed Mike Bickle of this vision the next day at the annual church picnic, July 4, 1984. He also told Bickle that the Lord said he intended to visit him face-to-face to confirm this same truth. He didn't give a date for this visitation, but it was certain to occur. A little more than a month later, on August 8, Mike received a phone call at 10:30 one evening as he walked in through the door after one of the regular prayer meetings of the church. On the phone was Augustine Alcala, who by now was living in Phoenix, Arizona.

"The Lord has promised you a visitation, hasn't he?"

"I don't think so. Why?"

"Because the Lord says it is tonight!"

"Tonight?"

"Yes, tonight."

After he hung up the phone, Mike turned to Diane, his wife, and said: "Honey, has someone said something to me about a divine visitation?"

"Yeah, don't you remember what Bob Jones told you back on the 4th of July?"

"That's right," as Mike suddenly remembered.

Mike was a bit unsure of how to prepare for this. Do you fast? Do you sit in your chair with your face turned towards heaven? Do you kneel humbly or prostrate yourself in anticipation of the Lord's visit? Finally, he went to bed, quite certain that he wouldn't be able to fall asleep. Within seconds after his head hit the pillow, Mike was sound asleep.

He awakened only to find himself in a room that seemed to be about thirty-feet wide and thirty-feet long. All along the floor, as well as on each wall and across the ceiling, were clouds or a mist of some sort. Mike knew he was awake. He kept pinching himself on the arm and repeating, "I'm not dreaming. This is real. I am really awake. I'm not dreaming."

This account of his visitation to the third heaven presents us with a problem. In 1986, when Bickle told the story as part of the first public narrative of the prophetic history, he described it as an out-of-body experience. But if he were not in his body, how could he have pinched himself to verify that he was actually awake? On more than one occasion, as he told the story to me and others, he also described how he would pull the hairs on his arm to make certain this wasn't a dream. Some may wish to push back and argue that I'm being overly pedantic in my concern with such minor details. But how else are we to determine the truthfulness of Bickle when he relates the incident if not by close examination of all the details? Now, back to the story.

Suddenly Bickle sensed the presence of the Lord just behind his right shoulder. He's not sure if he could have turned to look had he wanted to. He's only sure that *he didn't want to!* Then the Lord spoke: "Young man, if you are impatient, you will cause great turmoil and much trouble to many people." The voice was firm and overwhelmingly powerful. Mike is still surprised at his initial reaction to what God said.

At the same time that Mike said aloud, "Yes, sir," he began thinking to himself, silently of course, "I'm not impatient. Why am I being rebuked for being impatient?" But then he said to himself, "You had better agree; after all, you are talking to God."

Then the Lord spoke again, but this time with even greater intensity and power: "Young man, if you are impatient, you will cause great turmoil and much trouble to many people."

"Yes, sir! Yes, sir!" Mike replied.

A third time the voice thundered with a frightening and piercing tone: "Young man, if you are impatient, you will cause great turmoil and much trouble to many people."

Although he didn't understand it at the time, Bickle later discerned that the impatience was related to setting leadership into place prematurely without divine permission. He knew that God's word to him was that he was not to look upon men in the natural, that he was not to judge by the hearing of the ear, but only by divine revelation. This time Mike fell to the ground and repeated over and over again, in fear and trembling, "Yes, sir! Yes, sir! Yes, sir!"

A Third-Heaven Experience (?) and Controversy over Restoration of the Apostolic

Here again we have a slight discrepancy in how Bickle recalls the event. In 1986, he said that it was while he was still in the courtroom of heaven that God told him his impatience pertained to the issue of establishment of leadership. Yet, when the story was told yet again years later, he said it was only after he returned to his body and reflected on the experience that he realized what the Lord's reference to "impatience" actually meant. This is not uncommon in the way Bickle would describe a number of alleged supernatural experiences. In the excitement of sharing what happened he tended to compress details into one event which actually were separate when they occurred. Or he would combine several elements of what happened into one unified account when in fact they occurred sequentially. Bickle tended not to care about minor points as long as the major issue was made with clarity. I don't think he can be accused of intentional deception. He simply did not feel compelled to be as precise as we might have preferred. For example, in more recent years, as noted above, he said this event occurred on August 8.[5] But in the telling of the story in 1986 he said it happened in mid-August. Some may point to such obvious discrepancies as proof that the event actually never took place at all. Others are quick to grant Bickle latitude in the way he reported such phenomena, insisting that such comparatively minor points hardly discredit the larger truth of what he shared. We again pick up the story.

At this time the floor to the room suddenly opened up and Bickle found himself falling through space. It was both a thrilling and horrifying experience as he passed by stars and even the moon. As he came closer and closer to earth, he saw the top of his duplex near Troost Street in Kansas City where he lived. As he fast approached it, he began to tense up and screamed, as if prepared to crash into it: "Aaaahhhh!"

He passed through the roof and into his body, asleep on the bed. The experience of falling lasted about ten seconds. Mike looked around the room, taking note of his slacks, which were lying across the chair, his shoes, and the clock beside the bed, which indicated it was 2:15 a.m. Diane was lying next to him, sound asleep. She didn't move or make a sound.

Suddenly, perhaps five seconds after hitting his bed, Mike claims that he was taken back up into the heavenlies. In this experience of being

---

5. This alerts us to yet another feature of the alleged supernatural events that took place in Kansas City. Bickle often pointed to how God would do amazing things on the same day, although in different years. August 8 became a significant example of this. It was allegedly on August 8 that Bob Jones had his vision of the white horse and the rabid dogs. He contends that it was August 8 when Augustine called him regarding the promised visitation from the Lord. It was on August 8 that Augustine Alcala died. It was also on August 8 that Sherry (Bickle) Doyle died, and it was on August 8 that the church officially withdrew from the Vineyard.

transported into heaven he again passed the moon and stars. He found himself once again in the same room, with the presence of the Lord standing just behind his right shoulder.

At this time the room opened up on his left and Bickle beheld a strange sight. He saw a long line of golden chariots. As he watched, a chariot suddenly moved forward and its door swung open. Mike was intuitively aware that these chariots represented apostolic ministry. He didn't count them precisely, but later said he guessed their number to be somewhere between twenty and fifty. When Bob Jones was told of the experience he responded as you might expect: "You old unbeliever. I told you there were thirty-five!"

What Mike heard next was more than he could endure. "Get in," said the Lord. Suddenly Mike saw his own heart and the condition of his soul with greater clarity than ever before. The sin of his life was vividly before him, and he felt altogether dirty and unqualified. The impact of this encounter made it impossible for Mike to do what he had always planned if he ever were to have an encounter such as this with the Lord. His plan was to do what Elisha did and ask for a double anointing. But instead, he could only cry out, "No!"

"Get in," the Lord repeated. "It has been ordained for you."[6]

"No!" Mike cried with even greater energy.

Mike spoke aloud: "It isn't just! It isn't just!" Both at the time and on later reflection Mike thought it strange that he would use those words: "It isn't just." But that's the only thing that came out of his mouth. Feeling unqualified and overwhelmed, he fell on his face. Two angels then came to his side and lifted him up and led him into the chariot.

As the chariot began to move off into the sky, Mike was startled by the brilliant blue color ahead of him. He again intuitively knew that the blue was symbolic of the divine revelation that would come in conjunction with apostolic ministry. This isn't canonical revelation. We aren't talking about revelation that stands on a par with that in Scripture. This is prophetic revelation that comes via the gift of prophecy, in dreams, visions, trances, and other ways in which God talks to and communicates with his people.

As Bickle was riding in the chariot, he was aware that the experience he just went through with the Lord was being repeated with others. He

---

6. Many will ask a perfectly legitimate question: If God "ordained" for Bickle to serve in some sort of apostolic calling, how can we reconcile that with his moral failure and the implosion of his ministry? I suppose some might suggest that from the time of this experience in 1984 until 2024, that is precisely what Bickle did. It was only after forty years that his disqualifying sins were exposed, bringing his apostolic ministry to an end.

heard the same cry of reluctance echoing from their lips: "No!" He heard the same "swoosh" of the chariot, as others were led into it by angelic beings.

Bickle looked over his shoulder, and the next person was commanded to get in one of the chariots. He also screamed, "No! No!" Then he heard the same thing happen to the others after him. Each one represented a young person who would be anointed in the years to come. Bickle insists that he did not see any faces.

At this time, Bickle found himself once again falling through the heavens. He again passed by the stars and the moon and again hurtling with great speed toward his duplex. As he fell into his bed, he sat up and looked at the clock next to him. The time was the same: 2:15 a.m.

Through the early years of the Kansas City church Bickle was extremely reluctant to share this experience with the general public. In fact, he told no one about it, not even Diane, for several months. He realized all too well how self-serving it might sound. Many will be inclined to interpret it as a man who is prophesying his own promotion. But many of us who knew Bickle well (or at least thought that we did) and have ministered at his side for years, will testify that he always appeared to be one of the humbler men we have ever met. Nothing in Bickle's life or ministry to that point in time indicated that he had made any attempt to capitalize on this experience to enhance his own position or power or to gain glory or money for himself.

This alleged heavenly visitation is mocked by most of Bickle's critics. Even those who are practicing charismatics find it hard to believe. I make no claim as to its veracity, but leave it to you, the reader, as I have on numerous occasions in this book, to decide for yourself whether you believe it happened as Bickle portrayed it. Bickle said that during the trip God did not commission him as an apostle. But he understood the experience to mean that if he was faithful, he would have an opportunity in the grace of God to fill an apostolic calling.

One final comment is in order. In 1997 Mike and I were discussing this event when I suddenly felt led to ask him a question. "Did you ever think about the possible significance of the *time* of your experience? You said the clock by your bed indicated it was 2:15 a.m. both before you entered heaven and after you returned. Aside from the theological implications for whether or not there is 'time' in heaven, why 2:15?"

"I don't know," Mike replied. "In all the years since it happened it never crossed my mind to ask the question."

Some of you will conclude that my question is the product of an excessively mystical fascination with numerology or perhaps a sign that I have fallen into hyper-spirituality. I am sensitive to these concerns and I readily acknowledge that we must be careful not to go searching in every mundane event for spiritual meaning. But what allegedly happened to Bickle was anything but a *mundane* event. Furthermore, on previous occasions I have learned to be alert to what one might call "spiritual tokens" in which God alerts us to his presence or to some lesson that is important for us to learn. It isn't all that unusual for him to use time, dates, or numbers in various capacities to send a signal to his people.

Now, back to Bickle's visitation to heaven. "So, you've never thought about why it all happened at 2:15?" I asked yet again.

"No. Do you have any suggestions?" Mike asked.

I thought for only a moment, and suddenly it burst into my mind:

"*Joel 2:15*. Do you know what it says?"

"No," Mike replied. "Do you?"

"No. But I think it's worth looking at. I've got a strong impression that it's significant."

We quickly opened to Joel 2:15 and read the words: "*Blow a trumpet in Zion, consecrate a fast, proclaim a solemn assembly.*" These were the very words Mike felt led of God to use when he called the churches of Kansas City to fast for twenty-one days back in May of 1983. Indeed, that period of fasting has long been known in Kansas City as "*the Solemn Assembly*."

Again, is it mere coincidence? That greatly depends on whether this event occurred as Bickle described or was an elaborate hoax. If the former, it might just as easily be the handiwork of a sovereign God reminding us yet again that he is in control, directing all things to their ordained goal. If we will but keep our spiritual eyes and ears attuned to his ways, I strongly suspect we might see more of such "tokens" of his handiwork.

Doubts about the veracity of Bickle's experience have often been raised in light of what he has purportedly told others about their presence in one of the chariots. You will remember that Bickle had always said he did not recognize any of the faces of those who joined him in the thirty-five chariots. And yet, Bickle informed me many years later that he did know of one person who was present. I don't have the liberty of mentioning this individual's name, but others have reported that Bickle informed them that they, too, were invited into one of the chariots. I can't help but wonder why his story has changed so often during the subsequent years. For many, this alone will serve to discredit the truth of what he claims to have experienced. I remain undecided.

The Reason for My Doubts Concerning Bickle's Claim

One reason why we should question the validity of Bickle's claim to having been translated into the third heaven is his ongoing sexual abuse of Tammy Woods. Bickle says this event occurred in August (the 8th?) of 1984. Tammy Woods was born on June 30, 1966, and was fourteen years old in 1980 when the grooming process began. I strongly encourage you to read appendix B at the conclusion of this book. His treatment of this young girl was nothing short of diabolical. She first met Bickle at a church potluck dinner. During Christmas break of 1980 Bickle took her to a restaurant and served her alcohol (another crime).

Bickle moved to Kansas City in 1982, when Tammy was sixteen, having groomed and abused her sexually for the two years preceding. Bickle tried to persuade her to move to Kansas City during her senior year of high school, promising to secure for her an apartment where she would live alone and work as his personal secretary. He had been abusing her since the fall of 1980, so when he claimed to go to heaven in August of 1984, his sexual relationship with Tammy had been growing for nearly four years.

Tammy was about to begin her sophomore year at Covenant College when Bickle visited her. He spent the entire day with her, having taken her to dinner, and later that evening parked on a scenic site overlooking the night lights of Chattanooga. There he told her that after Diane had died, he would bring her to that same spot on Lookout Mountain and propose marriage.

Bickle visited Tammy again while she was at the University of Missouri in Columbia. Tammy told me that when he visited her during her junior year that he sexually abused her once more. This would have been around 1987. Bickle cut off contact with Tammy in 1996 (he had called her regularly during those intervening years and occasionally took advantage of his ministry trips to St. Louis to see her). There was a period of five years, from 1996 to 2001, when Tammy had no contact with Bickle. I find it interesting that this was the same time frame in which he was sexually abusing Deborah Perkins. He then renewed contact with her in October of 2023 when the scandal broke.

During all the years they were involved sexually, Bickle repeatedly said that if they were caught, she would have to take the blame for having initiated the relationship. After all, Mike was married and a pastor (so-called!). How incredibly abusive! How incredibly despicable! It was in October of 2023 that he tried to persuade her to keep silent about all that happened between them.

For many years I believed, without hesitation, Mike's account of having been translated into heaven. My confidence in his integrity would not let me doubt the accuracy of his claim. But with the revelation of his abuse of Tammy Woods, not to mention the sexually inappropriate relationship he began with Deborah Perkins, I am left wondering about the reality of what he claims to have experienced. I apologize to all who heard me tell his story. I apologize to those who read about it on my blog and in other contexts. I am left wondering if the entire story is a complete fabrication. Here is why.

Tammy has provided us with a timeline of the development of her relationship with Bickle. As noted, it began in St. Louis when she was only fourteen years old. The sinister nature of his grooming of her is nauseating to read (see appendix B). Bickle's claim that he was translated into heaven allegedly occurred in August of 1984, during the same period of time in which Bickle was still sexually involved with Tammy, then eighteen years old. Is it feasible for us to believe that God would have granted Bickle this profound experience at the very time he was violating this young teenaged girl? One then wonders why God would not have rebuked Bickle or in some way communicated to him his deep displeasure with the sexual sin in his life. Does it make biblical sense that God would have blessed Bickle and invited him into an apostolic ministry while he was continuing to abuse this young girl? Would not have God spoken words of conviction to him?

I struggle to believe that the thrice-holy God would not have called Bickle to repentance and suspended any call to ministry of any sort on his humble and heartfelt confession of sin and determination to turn from it. But not only does Bickle say nothing about God addressing this issue in his life, he goes on to claim that God proceeded to invite him into an apostolic calling.

Why would God rebuke Bickle about his impatience in regard to promoting leaders but seem utterly unconcerned about the gravity of Bickle's sexual compromise? Perhaps God did communicate to Mike about his sexual sin, and he simply chose not to include that part of his experience in the narrative retelling of what happened. In my conversation with Tammy, she graciously suggested that perhaps Bickle's feeling of being "unworthy" to stand in God's presence was in reference to his guilty conscience for having abused her. But I find it hard to believe that standing in the very presence of God Almighty and hearing his audible voice would not have resulted in decisive repentance and a change of behavior. After such a stunning spiritual experience, why would Bickle not have immediately terminated his relationship with Wood, repented to her, and asked forgiveness for the way he had abusively mistreated her?

A Third-Heaven Experience (?) and Controversy over Restoration of the Apostolic

I struggle to believe that God would bring a man into his presence in heaven and bless him with great revelation and an apostolic calling while that married man was unrepentant in his ongoing criminal sexual abuse of a teenaged girl. It strikes me as profoundly inconsistent with what I know from Scripture about the nature of God. That he would provide Bickle with such an astounding experience and fail to rebuke him for his egregious conduct is unthinkable. That he would challenge him regarding his impatience in elevating leadership prematurely but not say so much as a word of conviction about his criminal sexual grooming and abuse of Tammy Woods is beyond imagination.

If we should ask why would Bickle fabricate such an elaborate story, perhaps it was his way of easing his own conscience. To envision himself being blessed by God in this way would provide him with an escape of sorts from the emotional and spiritual pressure of his sin. The most generous interpretation is that Bickle may have had a dream about this experience that he thought was happening while he was awake. Bickle has always insisted he was fully awake when all this occurred. However, it's hard to believe that a man or woman wouldn't know whether or not he/she was sleeping or awake, no matter how intense the dream might be.

Or the answer may be simpler than that. It's possible that he concocted the story to enhance his own reputation. Perhaps he took the "dream," assuming he had one, as God's mercy and forgiveness. Perhaps he convinced himself that the experience was God's way of telling him he was forgiven and to proceed with ministry. Only Bickle knows the truth. But for me, I must withdraw my previous unqualified endorsement of his claim.

I can't begin to describe how painful it is to draw this conclusion. It means I led people astray by telling them it really happened. It means my friend lied to me and countless thousands of others. But the incongruity of such a profoundly supernatural event taking place in the life of an unrepentant sexual predator leaves me no other option. I seriously doubt if Bickle will ever own up to fabricating this story. His reputation would suffer considerable damage beyond what has already happened. It would serve to reinforce our conclusion that he should never be permitted to enter Christian ministry again. Perhaps he will reject my conclusion, thinking that I have reversed my opinion for personal gain. I can honestly say, I haven't gained anything by drawing this conclusion. I have suffered greatly by owning up to the fact that I was deceived.

So, my conclusion that this alleged episode may never have happened is based on placing the timeline of his abuse of Tammy alongside the timeline of his claim to having been translated into heaven. Of course, the reality of his unrepentant, egregious, and criminal abuse of Tammy also casts a dark shadow on his other claims of supernatural and prophetic events. Numerous elements in the prophetic history took place from December of 1982 through August of 1984. I'm finding it increasingly difficult to believe any of the stories that Bickle has told.

Am I being too harsh? After all, someone may argue that by providing Bickle with these supernatural and prophetic experiences the Lord showed him mercy, called him to repentance, and gave him ample time to make things right. But I seriously doubt it. Tammy wrote to me in a personal email,

> This is only conjecture, but I would gather that Mike would say that whether or not the Lord communicated to him at this time was irrelevant, because he WAS repentant. In fact, he would probably attest that he was not rebuked because the Lord knew he was remorseful and repentant.[7]

Perhaps, but I find it hard to believe that standing in the very presence of God Almighty and hearing his audible voice would not have resulted in a change of behavior. After such a stunning spiritual experience, why would Bickle not have immediately terminated his relationship with Woods? The following is from an email sent to me from Tammy. It is cited here with her permission.

> Let me try and share the process. When Mike called[8] to confess the *"five bad things I did with Deborah,"* he rambled first for an hour about the prophetic history, weaving in the significance of her birthday and a prophetic dream he had about her. When he called closer to my story breaking in the KC Star, he did so to let me know he was going to *"call Deborah a liar without calling her a liar."* Mike told me that Deborah had said that he said "God said" that he believed Diane was going to die and he would marry her. He said *"I never said GOD SAID! And if people believe that I would say GOD SAID about such an awful thing, then they could also doubt the truth of the prophetic history and all that God said."* He was very manic and frantic in this conversation. He said he and Diane made a video the night before upholding the truth of the prophetic history and its multigenerational significance. Luke was present and Paul filmed it. He sent me the script from the video and it was everything he

---

7 Email dated November 8, 2024. Cited with permission.

8. This call likely occurred sometime in late 2023, as Bickle was initially confronted with his abuse of Deborah Perkins by her husband sometime during the third week of October.

A Third-Heaven Experience (?) and Controversy over Restoration of the Apostolic

summarized. (This script was later included in TRR [The Roys Report] I believe.) While he said he was concerned about the staff and interns losing support, he seemed more like Gollum losing his ring.

I'm so very sorry for the pain and disillusionment of betrayal. Those of us who have such a long history with Mike have so much reframing of our lives before us. But it's in the truth of those reframes that we are and will be set free. Shalom.

With hope,

Tammy

Chapter Ten

The Promise of Healing

In Isaiah 35:5–6 we read that a day is coming when "the eyes of the blind shall be opened, and the ears of the deaf unstopped; then shall the lame man leap like a deer, and the tongue of the mute sing for joy." It is widely argued that this is descriptive of conditions that will prevail in the messianic age to come.

Premillennialists place the fulfillment of this text in the thousand-year reign of Christ upon the earth following his second coming. Amillennialists believe it will be fulfilled in the new heaven and new earth of Revelation 21–22. What is important to note, however, is that Jesus appealed to this passage as proof that he was the Messiah and that the kingdom of God had come in his ministry. In Matthew 11 we read about the doubt that entered the mind of John the Baptist following his arrest and imprisonment. He sent word to Jesus with one question: "Are you the one who is to come, or shall we look for another?" (v. 3). Jesus answered by appealing to both Isaiah 35 and 61. The fact that *now*, through the ministry of Jesus, the blind receive sight and the lame walk and lepers are cleansed and the deaf hear and the dead are raised is proof positive that Jesus is indeed the expected one.

I urge you not to miss this point: It is the *present* reality of these miraculous deeds that attests both to the identity of Jesus and the advent of his kingdom. Whereas these promises in Isaiah 35 may well await the consummation for their complete fulfillment, the powers of that future age have already broken into the present. Jesus' point is this: "My identity is established by the fact that those miracles traditionally associated with the *future* messianic age are characteristic of my ministry and kingdom in the *present* age." Thus, we need not wait for the consummation to experience its power. Whereas the *fullness* of healing and restoration are *not yet* ours, we may *already* enter into a measure of their *fulfillment* in the present age.

Jehovah Rapha

As I described in an earlier chapter, the Lord supposedly instructed Mike Bickle to call his church and the larger body of Christ in Kansas City to a time of prayer and fasting. It was to be a *Solemn Assembly*, to use the words of Joel 2:15. They were to fast for twenty-one days and to pray from 6:00 a.m. until 12:00 midnight during this three-week period. Several went on strict water fasts and were present for the duration of each prayer meeting. Others fasted as they were able and attended as many of the prayer meetings as their jobs and family responsibilities would allow.

During the Solemn Assembly, Bickle claims that God provided him with a profound prophetic promise concerning God's purpose to release power for healing to Mike individually and the church corporately. What made the word so important was that it was given not only to Bickle but was also supposedly confirmed to Bob Jones.

It was late on Saturday night, the fourteenth day of the fast, around 11:00 p.m., when Bickle claims he experienced a powerful visitation from the Holy Spirit. The time of prayer and fasting had been hard and dry. Like everyone else, he was tired and grumpy. On the day before, Bob Jones had told Mike that he should read Psalm 28 and that it was of crucial importance to Mike's personal life with God. But the psalm also applied to the entire movement. Amazingly, though, Mike went through the entire day without even thinking of the psalm. The same thing happened on Saturday until he remembered Bob's word at about 11:00 p.m. It suddenly dawned on Mike that it might be a good idea to take a look at the psalm.

He began reading but made it only through verse 1 when suddenly the Spirit of God began to touch him in the area of his stomach. It began to burn like fire and grew progressively stronger. Mike was kneeling down and buried his face in the pillow hoping to muffle the sounds of his groaning. He wept intensely and experienced what he had come to recognize as intercessory travail. He could feel the power of God moving upward, all the while burning. The Spirit rested on his lips, again with a strong burning sensation for five to ten minutes. He tried to read verse 2 of the psalm and it came again! The power of God rushed down again into his stomach and then back up again to his mouth. It did this at least three times. Bickle didn't know what to make of it at first. All he could say was, "Wow, what is going on?"

Then it came to him. God didn't say anything, but he knew intuitively that God was anointing him for *healing*. Bickle had recently read four or five biographies of men who had been powerfully anointed by God for healing and it seemed that all of them experienced something like this. The only thing is, it was often not until two or three years later that the healing gift was manifest in their ministries. Bickle also knew that this anointing was not just for him; it was for the entire church body in Kansas City.

When midnight came, the sensation of God's power lifted. Bickle looked around to see if anyone else might be experiencing something similar. There were about two hundred people still present at the meeting, most of them tired and frustrated. For them it seemed like just another long prayer meeting where nothing happened.

But it didn't faze him: "Glory to God," he shouted. "How's everyone doing?" They were hardly in the mood for his exuberance! However, Bickle was determined not to tell anyone what had happened. After all, if God doesn't show another person the same thing, it just might be that it was his imagination. But deep down inside he was confident it was for real. It was then that he asked the Lord to tell Bob Jones what had happened. "Lord, if you tell Bob what occurred then I will know for certain that it was from you."

On the way home in the car Bickle turned to his wife and said, "Diane, it happened!"

"What happened? Why are you so happy?" She was totally exhausted like the others and was even less impressed with his late-night zeal. So, he explained to her everything that had happened. Before going to bed that night, he asked the Lord to do two things. He asked him for a supernatural confirmation during the night, like a dream, and he asked him to do the same thing for Bob Jones as a confirmation that what he experienced was real.

That night Mike had a powerful dream in which God reaffirmed the reality of his earlier experience. At this point in his life Mike had only received a couple of dreams that he felt were from the Lord. But there was no mistaking this one. In the dream he and Diane were in a giant banquet hall that was filled with thousands of people who were celebrating the Lord's presence with joy and dancing. The place was filled with every imaginable kind of food and colorful banners hung from the ceiling and on the walls. The music was overwhelming and the atmosphere was heavy with faith and expectation. Bickle recalls being stunned by it all.

The Promise of Healing

Suddenly a prominent healing evangelist[1] approached Mike and said, "The Lord has anointed you for healing, hasn't he?"

"As a matter of fact, I think he has," Mike replied. The man then did something strange. In what was obviously a competitive spirit, he handed Bickle a pair of dice and said, "OK. Let's see where you come out." On three consecutive rolls, the dice turned up 5-6 for Mike.

"Well, I guess you win," said the evangelist. He then acknowledged to Mike that the healing anointing on this new movement would surpass that of the stream of ministry in which he himself moved. The dream ended when the alarm went off. It was 5:30 a.m. The prayer meeting would resume in thirty minutes. The only thing in Mike's mind was, "Oh God, please tell Bob Jones!"

As people began to arrive early that morning, they were understandably tired and barely able to drag themselves in. Bickle was excited, though, but no one could understand why. The prayer meeting began at 6:00 a.m. and Mike was running out of patience for Bob Jones to arrive. It was Sunday morning and the Lord had impressed on Mike's heart to preach from Matthew 10:8—"Heal the sick, raise the dead, cleanse lepers, cast out demons. You received without paying; give without pay." He also gave him 1 Corinthians 15:10 concerning the grace of God. The Lord made it clear that "it will all be of grace from A to Z." Those two texts, Matthew 10:8 and 1 Corinthians 15:10, healing and grace, were important.

Finally, at 8:00 a.m. Jones walked in. Bickle knew something was up, because normally Bob didn't come until just before the service started at 10:00 a.m. On this day, though, he walked in smiling and gave the thumbs up sign! He signaled for Mike to come into the office.

With a poker face he asked him, "What's up, Bob?"

He said, "It happened to you last night, didn't it?"

"What happened?" Mike replied, being careful not to let on that anything had occurred. Once again, he didn't want to give him the slightest hint. If you get excited and give a hint, two years down the road you will start wondering if it was real or not. Mike had to know from God if it was real.

"I saw him," said Bob.

"Who did you see?"

"You know. The Lord came to you and put a banner over you that spoke not just of you but of the whole movement." Mike is working hard not to appear too excited.

---

1. Bickle was always reluctant to mention his identity, but he later informed me that it was Kenneth Copeland. Whether or not Copeland ever witnessed considerable healings in his "ministry" is itself a matter of considerable dispute.

"What was the banner?"

He said, "Jehovah Rapha, I am the Lord that healeth thee."

Mike asked him what else the Lord showed him.

Bob said, "The Lord told me to extend my fingers and say the number five: Grace be unto you!"

Needless to say, he had Mike's attention, for the number 5 is the number of grace in the Bible and that is precisely the message the Lord had given him from 1 Corinthians 15:10.

Then Jones continued,

> The Lord also told me to speak to you the promise of Matthew 10:8 [which he proceeded to quote]. Furthermore, God said to tell you, "I will be to these people Jehovah Rapha, and I will give them a license to practice healing in my name, and no disease known to man will stand before this people."
>
> The Lord said, "If you do not get into malpractice as a people, if you don't get into sin, if you don't take the money, don't take the glory, and don't get involved in sensual sins, I will never take away this license from this people. They will have it forever!"

As if that weren't enough, Jones then proceeded to tell Bickle the dream he had about the dice and interpreted its prophetic symbolism based on the concept that five is the biblical number for grace and six for man. "Five-six, five-six, five-six. Grace to man. Grace to man. Grace to man." Bob then said that the Lord told him there would be no movement that would be superior to the healing power that comes forth from this movement.

That Sunday morning was a powerful time for ministry and healing. However, immediately the anointing lifted and the Lord indicated that it was yet for an appointed time.

> "What happened this morning," said the Lord, "was only a down-payment. The necessary structures are not yet in order. The leadership has not yet come in. The people and the leadership are not yet experiencing the friendship and affection that is required for them to stand in strength under the pressure that will come with the increase. All this has happened, however, so that in the days of waiting you will not grow weary."

Needless to say, the legitimacy of this scenario is again dependent on the truthfulness of both Bickle and Jones. Were they telling the truth? Or did they collaborate on an elaborate lie to deceive the people and elevate their spiritual status in the eyes of the people? I know that you are growing weary of me saying this, but I have no other choice: you decide! I will say that in the prophetic history of Kansas City there were numerous alleged instances when Bickle would have a dream only to have it confirmed and repeated to him by Bob Jones. Many will argue that Bickle and Jones conspired to present each scenario in this manner simply to promote themselves as highly favored of God and recipients of his revelatory work. I'm not persuaded that such was the case, but the recent allegations against Bickle have served to undermine people's trust in his integrity.

At the same time, there can be no denial that the ministry of physical healing in Bickle's life and ministry—as well as later, after the formation of IHOPKC—was to some extent successful, but certainly not to the degree that "no disease known to man" would fail to stand against it. One cannot conveniently ignore what Bickle claimed in 1986 regarding this promise of physical healing. He stated in that message that the Lord revealed to him that the healing anointing to be imparted to Kansas City Fellowship "would be second to no other movement" in the last days. To be entirely honest, we simply must acknowledge that this has not come to pass.

Dominus

The next prophetic promise related to healing is what is known as the *Dominus* vision. Bob Jones again claimed to have had a dream in which he appeared before what he believed was a mighty angel of God who was filled with glory and light and power. Across his forehead was written the word *Dominus*.

Jones said to the angel, "I don't know you."

The angel looked at Jones and said, almost casually, "How are you doing, Bob?" Bob was startled, for no angel had ever spoken to him in such a way. He said, "Have a seat, Bob." They sat down, and Bob immediately recognized that they were in the prayer room at the office building. In fact, they were sitting on the ledge that extends above the place where the lectern is located.

I need to mention one fact before we proceed any further with this story. I often hear of people who claim to have experienced an angelic visitation. More times than not, they describe it as if there was nothing in the angel's appearance that might evoke fear. It's not uncommon for them to speak of the angel and his interaction with the person in almost jocular terms. I'm not suggesting this is impossible. There are several accounts in the New Testament where the angelic visitation was at least calm and reassuring. An angel spoke to Joseph in a dream about Mary's conception of the Christ child (Matt 1:20). We see something of a repeat performance in Matthew 2:13 where the appearance to Joseph of the angel of the Lord seemed uneventful in terms of the reaction of Joseph. Of course, we can't build a case on what isn't stated in the text. And there may well be a different spiritual atmosphere and human reaction when the encounter takes place in a dream rather than when the person is awake. But the fact that no fear or trembling is mentioned may be significant.

On other occasions the angelic manifestation provokes fear and anxiety. When the angel appeared to Zechariah in the temple, he was "troubled when he saw him, and fear fell upon him" (Luke 1:12). The angel had to comfort Zechariah by telling him, "Do not be afraid" (Luke 1:13). From that point on Zechariah and the angel carried on what appears to be a normal conversation (Luke 1:18–20). Mary was "greatly troubled" when Gabriel appeared to announce the conception and birth of Jesus (Luke 1:29), forcing the angel to say, "Do not be afraid, Mary, for you have found favor with God" (Luke 1:30). When the angelic hosts appeared to the shepherds "they were filled with great fear" (Luke 2:9). The same thing happened when the "angel of God" spoke to Cornelius. The latter "stared at him in terror" (Acts 10:4). In Acts 12:7–9 an angel showed up in Peter's prison cell and told him to get dressed and to put on his sandals. Perhaps the reason Peter didn't react in fear is that he "thought he was seeing a vision" (Acts 12:9). We are told in Hebrews 13:2 that "some have entertained angels unawares" (Heb 13:2). The fact that these people didn't respond in fear is likely due to their failure to recognize that the visitors were actually angels. I could go on and mention the many angelic manifestations in the book of Revelation, but I trust you have discerned my point.

I must confess that I find the nature of the alleged interaction between Bob Jones and this angel to be somewhat unlikely. It simply doesn't reflect the way in which angels typically appeared to people in the Bible. Jones may still be telling the truth, but we need to be cautious before we affirm an event that does not readily correspond to what we find in Scripture. Now, back to the story.

The angel then told Jones that the Lord is going to bring about a reunion in Kansas City of those angels that ministered in the healing revival of the late 1940s and 1950s. God is going to have them visit Kansas City. There would also be in Kansas City the healing angels who were present at the Azusa Street revival.[2] Jones claims that the Lord said, "I'm going to call them forth and bring them here [to Kansas City]. And there is going to be

---

2. The notion that angels might be involved in healing the sick is tenuous at best. We know from Hebrews 1:14 that angels are "ministering spirits sent out to serve for the sake of those who are to inherit salvation." Whether or not this service entails physical healing is a matter of dispute.

a display of healing power in the days to come that many people will never understand. But I am going to do it." The angel then said, "Bob, I want you to go and tell them [the church in Kansas City] something. Go and tell them that *I have chosen to make myself a friend to this people.*"

Jones then woke up. He looked up the name *Dominus* and discovered that it means "the Lord, the Sovereign One." When he went back to bed, he immediately fell back into a trance in which Jesus stood before him. Jesus said,

> "Bob, do you understand that that was me who stood before you a little while ago?"
> "No," replied Bob.
> "If I had told you," said Jesus, "you would have become so emotional you wouldn't have listened to a word I said. But I gave you my message and I veiled who I was so that you would be able to hear me. Go tell the people that I have gathered them together and I will establish myself as the friend of this people. And I will show them all the things the Father is doing. I will no longer call you slaves; I will call you friends, for I will show you all things." (See John 15:15)

The Lord then told Jones to tell Bob Scott (Mike's brother-in-law) and Mike Bickle that "I, Dominus, am going to visit them and I am going to give them the same message so that you will know that it is from me."

Jones immediately called Mike and Bob Scott and told them that Jesus had promised to be a friend of this people and that he intends to visit the two of you.

> But don't be surprised because you will not know it is Jesus. Rather, it will be your friend "Don." The Lord is going to appear to you with a different face, but he's going to come and show you the power that he showed me. But he's going to be your friend. Be very careful in the next period of time, for "Don" will come and show you his glory, and it will be the Lord.

Bickle and Scott thought it was funny and soon forgot the whole thing. Three days later Bob Scott came to Mike and told him he just had an incredible dream that was from the Lord. In this dream the Lord showed him that he was going to bring forth his power out of his armory to unleash his arsenal (i.e., the gifts of the Spirit). The only major character in this dream, explained Bob, was a close friend of his from St. Louis named "Don." He was with Bob all through the dream, encouraging him and smiling.

Mike and Bob Scott drove over to Bob Jones's home and informed him of what happened.

"I told you so," said Bob. "I told you that the Lord would appear to you in a dream and confirm what he showed me."

"But that couldn't have been Jesus. That was my good friend Don." [It was, in fact, Don Flynn, one of Bob Scott's good friends from St. Louis whom Bickle knew as well.]

Bob Jones lovingly chided them both, "I told you that you wouldn't recognize him."

Bob Scott said, "But that couldn't have been Jesus. This guy is the nicest person in the world."

Bob explained how his image of Jesus was of someone stern and judging; but "Don" in the dream was kind and friendly. Jones explained that one of the reasons the Lord chose to reveal himself in the guise of Bob's friend "Don" was to reaffirm that he indeed is going to make himself a "friend" to this people.

A few days later Mike Bickle also had a dream in which he was a representative of the entire church in Kansas City. He was in a large auditorium filled with people who were engaged in worship. Mike, however, was standing at the back of the auditorium next to his good friend "Don," but it was Don Steadman. Don was smiling and acting quite friendly.

Suddenly Mike said, "Don, the power of God is about to break forth in the midst of this people. I have to go up there."

Don smiled and said, "Go ahead."

Mike began running down the aisle and around seventy-five people spontaneously jumped out of their chairs and began to run to the platform, even though no one had issued an altar call. Bickle felt the urgency of people to receive deliverance, so he extended his hand to a lady and the power of the Spirit came upon her and she fell down as if lifeless. Now about two or three hundred were up and running. Again, Mike placed his hand on three or four and they too fell down under the power of the Spirit. Soon the power of God had fallen upon hundreds. "The power of God descended mightily upon the people," said Mike.

Mike then returned to the back of the auditorium and said, "Wow, Don, that's the power of God. This is incredible!"

With a wry smile of understanding, "Don" said, "Yeah, it is, isn't it? It really is coming, isn't it?"

Suddenly Mike woke up. At the time these events unfolded, the church was meeting in the facilities of Shawnee Mission South High School. Soon after these dreams occurred, several people from the church were standing on the stage in the school auditorium, among whom were Bob Jones and Mike. Mike began to tell them all about this incredible dream he had in which Don Steadman played a key role.

"But that couldn't have been the Lord," said Mike. "That was 'Don' my good friend."

Bob Jones again chided Mike and Bob Scott for being so slow to believe.

> You both had a vision of your friend Don and the power of God and I told you it would take place. And I tell you surely the Lord is going to make himself the friend of this people. Surely he is going to bring healing power again, and it will burst forth from this body, and it will happen everywhere.

At that moment one of the men standing with them looked down and noticed something striking about where Mike happened to be positioned.

"Mike," he said, "look at what you're standing on."

Mike looked down and was shocked to discover that he was standing directly on top of a name written out several inches high in white adhesive tape: the name was *Don*! Evidently, the school was conducting a play or dramatic production of some sort, "Don" being the name of the person responsible for operating the lights and curtains. His name was taped to the floor to remind him where to stand.

Coincidence? Perhaps. Contrived? It's possible. But I have learned that often the God who controls and providentially oversees everything, even so-called "coincidences," will provide small tokens as a way of confirming yet again the prophetic word that he has delivered. Many believe that the odds are simply beyond computation that Bickle would be standing on the very name "Don" at that precise moment for it to be anything other than an act of God bearing witness to the fact that indeed this entire scenario was God's doing. Others will disregard it as little more than an inadvertent happenstance that has no spiritual significance at all.

A Prophetic "Promise" That Never Came to Pass?

Once again, I am drawn to evaluate the legitimacy of any alleged "promise" via prophetic ministry by the actual outcome, or lack thereof. I suppose the defenders of Jones and Bickle will again insist that these were not divine "promises" but invitations that depended for their fulfillment on the faithfulness and obedience of the individual(s) to whom they were given. Those not inclined to grant Jones and Bickle even the slightest measure of integrity will simply say that no such prophetic promises were ever given.

As a practicing charismatic who believes in the contemporary validity of all spiritual gifts, I have no hesitation in affirming the ministry of healing in today's church (and throughout church history, for that matter). That I do not see healing as often as I might wish does not undermine my confidence in what Scripture clearly teaches. I earlier referred the reader to the published works of Dr. Craig Keener in which he documents hundreds if not more than a thousand verified healings, not only in past history but in today's church as well. I am not suggesting that the documented miracles in Keener's books constitute the fulfillment of the prophecies of Jones and Bickle. But the reality of what Keener writes does give one pause.

CHAPTER ELEVEN

"Noel Is Coming!"

NOEL ALEXANDER[1] HAD EVERY reason to stay where he was. For twelve years he owned and operated a tremendously successful dental technician laboratory, had just witnessed the birth of his first child, a daughter named Amanda, and seemed to have the future well in hand. He and his wife seemed to be standing at the threshold of a limitless future in South Africa. Then in April of 1975 he became a Christian and his world turned topsy-turvy.

"Sell everything you have and go to America to study for the ministry." Noel was a new Christian, but he knew immediately that it was the voice of the Lord. Disobeying wasn't an option. It took almost a year for him to divest himself of his business and belongings, but in 1976 he was finally on his way to the United States without the slightest inkling of the bizarre prophetic events that would await him.

Sunflowers and Souls

Noel and his family arrived in Kansas City and purchased a car that would take them to Colorado Springs. There Noel would enter Bible college and begin his preparations for the ministry. He not only completed his degree

---

1. As previously noted, several individuals who figure prominently in the prophetic history of Kansas City were sexually compromised, to put it mildly. But one who has remained faithful to his wife and has displayed all the signs of biblical godliness is Noel Alexander. Unlike Bickle, Alcala, Jones, and Cain, whose testimonies are highly suspect in light of their moral compromise, Noel Alexander is a man whose word should be taken at face value. All that follows was communicated to me by Noel in a lengthy face-to-face conversation.

but later attended theological seminary, from which he was graduated with the Master of Divinity degree, typical of those who study for the ministry in America. But before he so much as took his first exam, he had a life-changing encounter with God.

Noel and his family were driving into Colorado Springs in late August when darkness forced them to check into a motel. At 4:30 a.m. Noel was suddenly awakened from a deep sleep. The prompting in his heart was one he recognized. It was the same voice he had heard in South Africa telling him to come to America: "Come outside. I want to tell you something."

Most of us expect the Lord to speak in King James English or to use words that require a dictionary to understand. But he spoke to Noel simply and with unmistakable clarity. Noel never suggested that he heard the audible voice of the Lord. It was rather the internal audible voice.

After walking about one hundred yards from the motel, the spirit of intercession fell upon Noel with irresistible power. He found himself weeping loudly as he cried out for lost souls. The burden weighed heavily on him, both spiritually and physically. He slumped to his knees, agonizing over the destiny of those who didn't know the Savior. Suddenly, the Lord spoke yet again, this time in words that sounded eerily familiar: "Take off your shoes, for the ground on which you are standing is holy ground."

It was holy ground because God was there, and God had business with his servant. Noel quickly removed his sneakers (Moses no doubt took off his sandals!) and stood quietly, yet trembling, not knowing what would happen next. The sense of the Lord's manifest presence was almost more than he could bear.

He was facing the east, and the sun was just beginning to creep above the edge of the horizon, when the Lord said, "Turn around."

Noel obediently spun around to the west.

"What do you see?" the Lord asked.

"I see a mountain," he replied. Indeed, he was now facing the famous Pike's Peak. "And I see sunflowers everywhere, thousands of them leading up to the base of the mountain."[2] It was a beautiful sight as the sun now began to cast its beams across the fields, accentuating the bright yellow of the Colorado sunflower.

What Noel heard next was almost beyond belief.

"These flowers represent the souls of those who will be led into the kingdom of God through your ministry."

Noel was speechless. God wasn't.

---

2. When Bickle told this story as part of the 1986 prophetic history, he referred to the flowers as lilies. I choose to dismiss this as a glitch in his memory, hardly grounds for questioning the truth of what happened.

"What do you say?" asked the Lord.

"You know, Lord," were the only words that he could muster. Noel later explained that he felt his words were similar to those of Ezekiel when asked of God, "Can these bones live?" (Ezek 37:3). Ezekiel responded, "O Lord God, you know."

"Where's your faith?" the Lord asked. "Look to the left. Now look to the right." Countless sunflowers. Countless blooms.

Again, the Lord said, "These flowers represent the souls of those who will be led into the kingdom of God through your ministry."

To say that Noel was overwhelmed would be the worst of understatements. He could only weep as he held fast in his heart to the word of the Lord. He knew he had heard the word of God.

Yet, three months later, Satan tried to steal this promise from Noel's heart. "It wasn't real," he sneered. "It was only a fantasy. Who do you think you are that God should talk to *you*?"

But Noel was prepared. Following the encounter on that day in August he had built a small memorial of stones on the place where he had stood. He quickly jumped into his car and drove to the sight. Much to his delight, the stones were still standing. "See," he shouted, pointing to the stones, "it *was* real. Satan, you're a liar!"

Something else happened in 1976 that would profoundly impact Noel's life. It was November, three months after Noel's encounter with God. At precisely 3:00 p.m. Bob Jones had a vision. He saw the name, "Major General Alexander." He instantly knew the Lord was saying that when "Major General Alexander" would come, the movement in Kansas City would take a significant leap forward. Jones wasn't satisfied, so he called his friends to see if anyone knew of such a person. They didn't. He even called the Pentagon in Washington, DC, wondering if there might be such a man in the military. Nothing. By the way, Noel Alexander and Bob Jones didn't know the other existed in 1976. They would meet for the first time eight years later.

Noel Is Coming!

In March of 1984, Bob Jones stood up at the Tuesday night prayer meeting of Kansas City Fellowship and made a curious announcement: "Noel is coming!" This was ten days before Bob ever met Noel. There was a chorus of inquiring voices that followed: "What or who is 'Noel'?" Would Christmas come early this year? Was it a man or a woman? Not even Jones knew the answer.

Ten days later, on Friday, Mike Bickle and others from the church were attending a city-wide pastor's meeting. As Mike walked in, he couldn't help but overhear the loud words of a man with a deep voice and an unmistakable South African accent. He was speaking about intercession and revival, themes dear to Mike's heart.

"Hi, I'm Mike Bickle. I don't believe we've met. What's your name?"
"Noel."
"Noel what?"
"Noel Alexander."

After graduation from seminary, Noel began pastoring a Nazarene church in Wyandotte County, Kansas. Until that Friday morning, he had never so much as heard of Mike Bickle, Bob Jones, or Kansas City Fellowship. But later that night Mike spent several hours narrating many of the same prophetic stories you read about in this book. Noel was hooked. Mike then shared with Noel the word delivered by Bob Jones ten days earlier: "Noel is coming."

"I think you're the man!" said Mike excitedly.

Before I go any further, I need to explain what happened the night before Mike and Noel first met. Noel had just returned from South Africa, where he had the opportunity to witness firsthand the ministry of evangelist Reinhard Bonnke. Noel's background and training were in the Nazarene church, so he was anything but familiar with the supernatural gifts of the Holy Spirit. But he was determined to learn about them, especially after seeing it with his own eyes in his native country.

Much like the people at Kansas City Fellowship, Noel had been leading his church in nightly prayer meetings where they sought the Lord for revival. But on this night Noel had something else in mind. He told his wife, "I'm going to visit a charismatic church and find out what it is they believe. I've got to know if what's going on is God." After making a few phone calls, Noel heard of a meeting being held in a Howard Johnson hotel. Following the service, Noel engaged the speaker in conversation, asking all sorts of questions about the gifts of the Spirit.

"The Lord wants me to pray for you," said the pastor.

They then withdrew into the privacy of the hotel kitchen where the pastor and two others laid hands on Noel and began to pray. Without warning, the young South African began to speak in tongues! If this were not enough, the man then began to prophesy: "In a short period of time, indeed, within hours, something profound is going to happen to you."

That night Noel refused to sleep. He returned to his church and paced the floor until the early morning, praying in the Spirit. It was that very morning that he decided to attend the pastor's meeting where he first Mike Bickle.

It's Friday night. Bickle has wrapped up his story. "I want you to come with me tomorrow to an 'Intercessors for Israel' march down at the Plaza."

"Sure. I'd love to," said Noel.

There were hundreds at the march, but it was Noel Alexander and Mike Bickle whose faces appeared in a picture in the *Kansas City Star* the next morning. There's one more "coincidence"(!): the man leading the march was none other than the man who had prayed for Noel in the kitchen of the Howard Johnson hotel two nights before!

"I want you to meet the man who said, 'Noel is coming,'" insisted Mike.

Noel was only too happy to comply.

"Bob," said Mike over the phone. "I've got Noel."

"Yeah, I know. His name is Major General Alexander," Bob replied, somewhat nonchalantly. "Bring him over."

On the way to Bob's home, Noel shared with Mike the vision he had in Colorado Springs. He told him about the fields of sunflowers and what the Lord had said. The car was suddenly filled with the manifest presence of God. Both Mike and Noel were weeping. They knew that something truly profound was about to occur. The intensity of the moment was overwhelming, forcing them to pull off to the side of the road to regain their composure.

As they walked through the front door of Bob Jones's home, their host stood up from the sofa and walked to Noel with one hand extended above his head and the other held low, as if he were carrying something rectangular.

"The Lord showed me a man this morning and said, 'Hold a six-foot mirror in front of him so he can see himself and never again doubt that it was I who stood with him in the field of flowers. They were the fields of heaven. They were souls who would come into the kingdom through his ministry.'"

"Unbelievable!" shouted Mike. "That's just what he told me in the car on the way over here!"

In the telling of this story in 1986, Bickle stated clearly that the flowers were symbolic of the "hundreds of thousands" of souls that would be saved through Noel's ministry. I don't recall Noel ever telling me the precise number that would come into the kingdom, but it is clear that Bickle has succumbed to exaggeration in order to make the story more powerful. I don't doubt that Noel had this experience precisely as he described it, but I find it almost impossible to believe that "hundreds of thousands" of people were to be saved. I suspect that Noel would agree with me.

That being said, Noel was beyond stunned at what Bob Jones shared. He thought to himself, "I've stepped into another realm. I've stepped into the prophetic."

Bob then retreated to his bedroom and returned with a box. From it he withdrew several crumpled pieces of paper, most of them old and stained. When he found the one he was looking for, he showed it to Noel and Mike. "This is to prove to you that God is behind this." On the well-worn piece of paper were written the following words: "November 2, 1976. 3:00 p.m. When Major General Alexander is released, it will be a new step in God's purpose for this move." Noel could only weep.

In fact, his weeping puzzled Bob Jones. "How can a man named 'Major General' weep so much?" God was about to make it clear and in doing so confirm to Bob that it was truly a divine appointment. The Lord had told Bob that the man he was sending would have a sword in his hand and that "he was a master of the martial arts and a master of the Master's arts." A few weeks later when Noel spoke at Kansas City Fellowship, he shared his personal testimony, in which he revealed for the first time that he was a black belt in karate. Indeed, he had competed for a South African team in the martial arts. But he later gave up the practice, believing it to be inconsistent with the fruit of the Spirit, specifically, kindness. When Jones heard this, it confirmed in his heart that he had heard the Lord accurately. This wasn't the first time that Bob Jones and Noel Alexander were united in a prophetic revelation.

The Bus and the Millionaire

Four years later, in 1988, Bob Jones called Noel Alexander early one morning. "I've got something you need to see. The Lord told me to give it to you." When Noel arrived at Bob's house, he noticed a strange looking object. It was about twenty inches long, seven to eight inches wide, and crusted over with mud and rust. Bob had scraped off just enough mud to see that underneath was a cast iron bus that they later discovered had been made in the 1930s.

"Yup, it's got seven windows. I knew it."

"What does that mean?" asked Noel, still in the dark about the point of it all.

Bob then described to Noel an incredible dream he had experienced earlier that morning. In the dream, Bob saw a bus with seven windows on each side. Sitting beside each window were the leaders of Kansas City Fellowship. Bob instantly recognized six of them, but the seventh was covered with a haze. The bus was itself being pushed up a steep hill by the people of the church. When it reached the peak, it suddenly began careening, seemingly out of control, down the hill. Jones heard himself say, "See, the leadership is out of control. There are no brakes on the bus."

As the bus reached the bottom of the hill, it turned a corner perfectly. In spite of its speed, it safely proceeded on to the next hill where everything was repeated. Once again, although traveling at a high rate of speed, the bus managed to navigate the corner with no problem. Jones was aware in the dream of commenting on how it must be a competent driver who could exercise such remarkable driving skills.

At that moment, the bus came to a stop on a grassy knoll. All the church members who had pushed it up that first hill ran down to meet it. The door opened and the driver and the seven leaders emerged. The driver was Jesus, who said, "I am in control of this leadership and I'm driving the bus."

Jesus then walked over to Noel Alexander and said, "I'm giving Noel $1,000 as a down payment on $1,000,000 that will go for missions, which will itself be a token of the salvation of a million souls."

As Jesus was walking away, he suddenly stopped and turned around. "Bob, a millionaire will call you today."

Yes, I know, it does sound strange! But imagine how strange it must have seemed to Bob Jones. After all, it was *his* dream. The next morning Jones was working in his garden when he made a startling discovery. He had been working this 20 x 30 foot piece of ground for thirteen years. He thought every stone had been removed. But as he began again to till the earth, his tool struck something solid. He knelt down and began to dig it out. That's right: it was the bus! How did it get there? God only knows.

"Bob," shouted Viola, his wife, "telephone!"

Bob set down the mud-encased bus and made his way back into the house, understandably overwhelmed. Before Viola could say a word, Bob said: "It's a millionaire." A millionaire indeed. It was John DeLorean, world-famous car designer. Perhaps you recall the movie *Back to the Future* starring Michael J. Fox. You may also remember his amazement when he discovered that his good friend "Doc" had made his "time machine" out of a DeLorean! Bob Jones had once ministered to John DeLorean, who now felt an urge to call and thank Bob for his help.

Three days later ministers from the area had gathered in Kansas City for a leadership conference. Having heard of Bob's dream, Mike Bickle asked him to share it with those in attendance. About half-way through the story, at the point in the dream where Jesus said he was going to give Noel Alexander $1,000, Noel's wife Mieke (pronounced "Mickey") nudged her husband: "Honey, don't you remember what came in the mail yesterday?"

Noel was a little embarrassed that he failed to make the connection. He slowly raised his hand and interrupted Bob's story.

"You all can believe this or not. I just wanted to let you know that yesterday in the mail I received a tax refund check from the U.S. government for exactly $1,000! Not $999. Not $1,001, but $1,000!"

Noel and Mieke were so deeply moved that they didn't feel right in keeping the money. Although they could certainly have used it. Noel later told me, "It didn't belong to me. It was holy unto the Lord. I believed the Lord wanted me to sow it back as a seed toward the $1,000,000 he promised would eventually go for missions."

Noel and Mieke proceeded to make their way to the tithe box, into which they placed that $1,000 check, confident that the Lord would use it as a token on a much larger gift to fund mission to the nations.

In 1990 Kansas City Fellowship hosted one of its largest conferences ever. More than seven thousand people attended in downtown Kansas City. Through an unusual sequence of events, Bickle was put in contact with Terry Law from Tulsa, Oklahoma, who believed the Lord had called him to raise $1,000,000 to be used to purchase Bibles for Russia.

When Bickle heard this, he turned to Noel and whispered, "I wonder if this is the $1,000,000 for missions in Bob's dream?" Mike was determined not to mention Bob's dream or anything else that might be viewed as manipulative. Indeed, when he announced the offering, he did it on Wednesday morning, when perhaps the fewest number of people would be in attendance. "If it's really the Lord," he thought to himself, "he'll do it no matter what."

The offering taken that night, together with pledges received in the days following, totaled $1,400,000! My good friend, Don Steadman, was responsible for collecting and counting the offering. Not only was there this considerable amount of cash, but Don also discovered that seventeen gold rings had been donated as well!

I should pause for a moment and let it all sink in. The dream. The bus with seven windows. Jesus promising Noel $1,000. The $1,000 being a down payment on $1,000,000 for missions. The promise to Bob that in confirmation of the dream's divine origin, a millionaire would call him. Bob digs up the bus with seven windows. The millionaire calls that very day. Noel receives $1,000. More than $1,000,000 is given for missions work in Russia. It does tend to take one's breath away, doesn't it?

Noel took the bus to an antique dealer who offered him $1,000 for it. Noel declined his offer. The dealer said he had wanted a bus like this for a very long time. The dealer cleaned it up and discovered that it was an Eagle Coastline, made in only one year: 1923.

"Noel Is Coming!"

Noel Alexander and the bus

Sunderland, Peterborough, and Colorado Springs

Noel traveled to England at the invitation of Ken Gott to speak at several conferences. The first was in Sunderland, on October 1, 1998, where Gott had established a flourishing ministry. At the close, Noel walked out to the parking lot where he was confronted by a total stranger who said, "Are you Noel Alexander? The Lord says you are to go back to Kansas City where you and Mike Bickle are to start a twenty-four-hours-a-day intercessory prayer ministry."

To say that Noel was caught by surprise is an understatement. He didn't quite know what to make of it. That is, until the next day when he traveled to Peterborough for yet another speaking engagement at yet another conference. Once again, after speaking, Noel made his way to the parking lot where he encountered another stranger.

"Are you Noel Alexander? The Lord says that you are to return to Kansas City and start a twenty-four-hours-a-day intercessory prayer ministry."

Same words. Same prophetic declaration, from two complete strangers.

Upon his return to Kansas City, Noel waited some six months before he called Bickle on the phone and told him what had happened. Mike asked him when this occurred. After discovering the day and time, Mike informed Noel that he had been at a conference in Colorado Springs where Kingsley Fletcher had prophesied precisely the same message to him. Noel and Mike didn't need further confirmation that God was calling them to launch the house of prayer.

CHAPTER TWELVE

The Search for a Home

WHEN MIKE BICKLE, HIS brother-in-law Bob Scott, and a handful of other committed believers decided to move to Kansas City in late 1982, they had no idea where the new church would meet. One thing they did know, however, was that God would not have called them to establish this work if he did not intend to provide a suitable building.

The search began four months before their arrival in Kansas City. Bickle believed the Lord had promised to give him instantly what he gave up in St. Louis. Since the church there had almost five hundred adults in attendance, Bickle was determined to find a building that would seat at least that many people. That may not sound like a formidable task, but with only a handful of people, virtually no money, and no credit history at all, it was a major hurdle to jump.

It should be noted that many of the stories you are about to read are less examples of prophetic ministry and more instances of what I would call sovereign, providential provision in response to prayer.

During that four-month span, they employed the services of four real estate companies and looked at almost thirty buildings. They were, quite literally, laughed out of one real estate office after another. No one, it seemed, would even consider renting a facility to a church of fewer than twelve members who had no visible resources. And from a purely human point of view, you can't really blame them.

Finally, one of the companies said, "We've got one final possibility. If this doesn't work, we give up!" It was the Fox–Hill office building at the intersection of 435 and Roe Boulevard. It seemed perfect to Bickle, so he quickly signed the contract on a Friday, in spite of the fact that it required a $21,000 deposit by the following Wednesday! Mike immediately thought of Bob Scott who was responsible for managing the financial affairs of the new church.

"Hey, Bob," Mike shouted with enthusiasm, "we found a building. It's perfect!"

"How much?" Bob asked.

"It's a great place. We're lucky to get it."

"How much?" Bob persisted.

"Well, the monthly rent is $8,000. But don't worry. I'm sure the Lord will provide everything we need," Mike responded with youthful confidence. "Oh, yeah, there is one other thing."

"Uh, huh. I was waiting for this."

"We need to raise $21,000 by next Wednesday," said Mike.

As an expression of their faith in God's call, the little group of believers had decided not to tell anyone of their financial needs. It was Hudson Taylor who once said something to the effect that "God's work done in God's way will never lack for God's supply." They were determined to put the principle into practice. After all, if God had truly spoken to Bickle about starting the church in Kansas City, God would not let a mere $21,000 stand in the way!

As Bickle explained, "We all felt that either the Lord was going to kill this thing from the start or sustain it supernaturally." It's important to remember, however, that it is not necessarily sinful or a lack of faith to let financial needs be known. It might even be a display of one's pride. If one is not careful, it can often be disastrous. But in this particular case, Bickle and the others believed they had heard from God: "Don't tell others of the need. I will provide."

Don't get the idea, however, that these were super-saints who never wrestled with doubt. Although Bickle never wavered in his belief that God had called him to Kansas City, he vacillated between faith and fear when it came to the money for this building. He had used up every dime they had to write an earnest check, and there didn't seem to be any quick solutions on the horizon. With Wednesday's deadline looming large, all they could do was pray and wait.

The first sign of an impending miracle appeared on Saturday when a lady came to them with an unsolicited offer of $7,000! "That's awesome," they thought, "but we're still $14,000 short." On the following Tuesday evening, Bickle drove back to St. Louis to speak at the church of a long-time friend. It was less than twenty-four hours until the deadline. Mike's faith was being stretched, almost to the point of breaking.

Before the service began, a man approached him and said, "I believe the Lord has called me to move to Kansas City and be a part of the church you're starting. I also feel he is calling me to make the same sacrifice you're making." At that point, he handed Mike a check for $13,000! Bickle is no mathematician, but he realized now how close they were to meeting their obligation. He was well-aware that the normal honorarium for a speaking engagement like this was around $150 to $200. But God had something else in mind. Following the meeting, the church treasurer approached Bickle and said, "Normally we wouldn't do this, but the Lord has impressed upon us to give you $1,000. I trust that it will prove helpful in your new work in Kansas City."

None of these individuals had any knowledge of the amount that was needed or the Wednesday deadline. As Bickle drove home that night, he rejoiced yet again in the faithfulness of a God who never ceases to provide for his people.

Before I continue this story, I need to mention something that occurred in July of 1984 that will shed light on the "building program" philosophy adopted by Bickle and the leaders of the church. Bickle withdrew for a week of intense prayer and fasting regarding a permanent facility for the church. During this time, the only thing he received from the Lord was Psalm 68:5 where God is portrayed as the "Father of the fatherless." In light of his alleged experience in Cairo in September of 1982, Bickle knew instantly that this was part of the call to touch the poor of the earth. God "told" him that if he would build a house for the fatherless, God would provide the church with a physical house to dwell in. "You build my house," said the Lord, "and I'll build yours."

Extravagant giving to the poor and the fatherless has been Bickle's "building program" for many years. He believed that if he would be faithful to respond to God's call with extravagant giving to the poor, God will be faithful to provide an adequate home in which the work of ministry can be fulfilled. But one should never take such an approach apart from divine initiative. This is not a rule for all churches, but a particular divine mandate for a particular fellowship of believers.

"I Know What You Dreamed Last Night"

It was March of 1984, when Bickle received a phone call from a man he'd never met. Kansas City Fellowship was still meeting in the Fox-Hill office complex in Overland Park, Kansas.

"Mike," came the voice on the phone, "you don't know me, but I and several other pastors would like to invite you to be a guest speaker at a series of tent meetings we are holding in Grandview."

The Search for a Home

Bickle didn't even know where Grandview was at that time. It wasn't until May of 1985 that the facility described later in this chapter came to his attention. After trying unsuccessfully to find a legitimate excuse not to accept this invitation, Bickle reluctantly agreed to join them for the meeting.

Upon his arrival in Grandview, the man who had phoned and his friends informed Mike that God had impressed upon each of them that God was going to give him and his church a certain building in the Grandview area. This was a building other than the one that Bickle and Forerunner Church would eventually occupy. For obvious reasons, I will not mention which building it is.

Bickle, however, was not overjoyed by this news. "I honestly don't want that building. We are more than happy where we are in Overland Park."

But this group of pastors would not take no for an answer. They insisted on walking around the building, with Bickle in tow, as they claimed the facility for Kansas City Fellowship and anointed its outer structure with oil in the name of the Lord.

Mike was not convinced, at least at first. The very next day a young prophetic minister named Charles Lynn was driving to Kansas City, bringing with him Howard Pittman. Mike had long wanted to meet Howard and the opportunity had finally presented itself. Mike had only met Charles Lynn once before, and then only briefly. Upon his arrival in Kansas City, and after having introduced Howard Pittman to Mike, Charles said, "Oh, by the way, as I was driving up highway 71 in Grandview, the Lord told me that he is going to give you a building there." The building that God indicated to Charles Lynn was the same one that the others had said God would give to Mike's church.

"This is getting really weird," Mike thought to himself. "I can't imagine what's coming next."

A week later Mike received a phone call from a man whom he had never met.

> Mike, you don't know me. In fact, I didn't know who you were until I saw your name on a flyer advertising those evangelistic meetings in Grandview. I wouldn't have paid any attention to it were it not for the fact that last night the Lord spoke your name to me in a dream. He told me to tell you that he is giving to your church a building in Grandview, Missouri.

Yes, you guessed correctly, it was the same building the group of pastors had claimed for Mike, the same building that had been identified by Charles Lynn. By now, Bickle was beginning to pay attention.

It wasn't too long after this that the wife of one of the church's pastors informed Mike that she had experienced a powerful visitation from the Lord in a dream. Without any knowledge whatsoever of these other men or their comments to Mike concerning the building, she said that the essence of the dream was that God was going to give the church a certain building in Grandview, Missouri, the very building spoken of by Charles Lynn and the others.

Bickle was careful to investigate to make certain that none of the individuals in this scenario either had prior knowledge of each other or had in any way shared information concerning this structure in Grandview. They hadn't. Furthermore, what could they possibly hope to gain by conspiring to deceive Mike about this matter?

Yet despite all these amazing indicators that God was wanting the church to occupy the building, it never came to pass. On the surface, as of the writing of this book, this would appear to be yet another failed prophecy.

There is yet another building that was brought to the attention of church leadership, wondering if it might also fit into what God had in store for the church. Since the beginning of South Kansas City Fellowship (KCF/MVF/MCF), one part of the vision has been what is called *The House of Prayer*, a place in which Bickle hoped to see twenty-four-hours-a-day prayer meetings. Of course, that ministry was to be the International House of Prayer, Kansas City.

In 1984 Bickle experienced a powerful dream in which he found himself in one particular church building. He was speaking from Zechariah 4:6, using this text as a basis on which to dedicate the building. There was a spirit of revival in the place and a feeling of great expectation. The next morning Mike was in the car with Augustine Alcala on his way to a staff meeting. It just so happened that they were approaching the very building Bickle had seen in his dream. Augustine, of course, knew nothing in the natural about what Mike had experienced the night before. In fact, Mike hadn't had time to tell anyone anything. Augustine suddenly turned to Mike and said, "I had a vision early this morning in which I saw what you dreamed last night."

"Oh, really," Mike responded, with more than a little incredulity.[1] "If you saw my dream, tell me what it was." The car was now about two hundred yards from the building. Mike was careful not to give any hints or indications about his dream. Augustine then began to roll down the window. He extended his arm out and pointed directly at the building in question. "The

---

1. Although God does occasionally reveal a person's dreams to someone else, as we have seen on several occasions, it is uncommon, and hence surprising, and it is always to be approached with caution and care. I recount the story as Mike Bickle told it to me.

The Search for a Home

Lord wants you to know your dream was truly from him. He said he is going to give you that building, right there."

Aside from nearly wrecking the car out of shock, how would you react to something like that? If Bickle had only experienced a dream, with no confirmation from someone else, there would always be room for doubt as to whether it was truly from God or simply a projection from his subconscious of deeply cherished hopes. But when someone else with a proven track-record in prophetic ministry tells you precisely what you saw in your dream the night before, it's time to sit up and take notice. But there was another confirmation yet to come.

Bickle shared these matters with Bob Jones, asking for his input and evaluation. A few days later Bob said to Mike, "The Lord told me that in eight days he would confirm to you that your dream was truly from him."

"How will he do it?" asked Mike.

"I don't know, but I assure you that exactly eight days from today, it will happen."

Some of you may be wondering if the number eight is significant. In the Bible eight is the number symbolic of new beginnings. Perhaps the word of confirmation was to come in eight days because when the fulfillment of this prophetic promise comes to pass it would mark a new beginning in the life of the church, in particular, the inauguration of the House of Prayer. But as you will shortly see, the "promise" failed to materialize.

Seven days came and went. Nothing had happened. On the eighth day, a Saturday, Mike found himself playing football with his two young sons, Luke and Paul, in the front yard of his duplex in Kansas City. The last thing on his mind was that this was the eighth day of Bob's prophecy, the day of fulfillment.

"Mike! Telephone!" shouted Diane, his wife.

"Hello."

"Hello, Mike? This is G. W. Hardcastle. I don't know if you remember me or not, but we met when you first moved to Kansas City a couple of years ago."

What is important for you to know is that G. W. Hardcastle was the individual who was responsible for building the facility that Mike had seen in his dream and had founded the ministry of the church that was meeting in it! Bickle's memory went into gear as he began to vaguely recall who G. W. Hardcastle was. He continued:

> Mike, I know this may sound strange, but I'm in a restaurant in Los Angeles, California, having breakfast with a couple of friends. During our conversation, I brought up your name and

began to tell these men about your church in Kansas City. As I was telling them about you, I suddenly remembered the first time we shook hands. The moment I shook your hand I sensed the Lord saying that in some way your work and my building would be connected. As I thought about that just a moment ago, I felt the Holy Spirit touch me and I began to weep. The Lord said to go call you immediately. I didn't have your number, so I called information there in Kansas City. I hope you don't mind that I called you at home.

Bickle didn't mind! He was understandably stunned. Just as Bob Jones had said, on the eighth day the confirmation had come. A man Mike hadn't talked to in two years, while sitting in a restaurant in California, gets the "urge" to call him in Kansas City. But not just any man; the man who was himself responsible for the building Bickle had dedicated in his dream, the building Alcala saw in a vision. With this double confirmation of Mike's dream, the church anxiously awaited the unfolding of this prophetic drama.

But we have here the same problem that has reared its head all through this book. On more than one occasion when I was on staff in Kansas City, we visited the facility and sat down to talk to the man who was serving as pastor of the church. However, nothing ever came of it. Today, with the implosion of IHOPKC and Bickle's removal from ministry, one would be justified in concluding that this was a false prophecy. No one can explain Bickle's dream or Alcala's vision in confirmation of it, but there appears to be little hope that it will come to pass.

"Two Businessmen in Suits"

A few months later in the fall of 1984, Alcala told Bickle of a vision he received from the Lord. He explained that the Lord was going to release the church a year early from its three-year contractual obligation to the building. "How will I know when?" asked Mike.

"The Lord said that when *every seat is filled*, he will indicate it's time to move." Mike was a little puzzled by this word, but he was open to its fulfillment.

It was Sunday morning, the first week of December in 1984. Just before the service was to begin, Dennis Brown, one of the ushers, came to Mike on the platform and handed him a note: "*Every seat is filled.* What do we do now? People are still coming in?" When Bickle saw those words, in his heart he sensed it was time. He told Bob Scott that the Lord may be about to give them a token that they will be released from the building contract a year early. None of them believed it was likely, but they had seen stranger things happen!

The very next day, Monday morning, Bickle received a telephone call from the real estate agent. With an apologetic tone in his voice, he asked if there were any way possible that the church would be willing to sell the final year of its lease to Yellow Freight, a business located across the street that was desperately in need of more office space in close proximity to their main headquarters. They want it immediately, tomorrow in fact, and will gladly buy out the lease as well as bless the church financially for the inconvenience.

"Unbelievable!" was the only thought that entered Bickle's head. After regaining his composure, he realized that a quick decision had to be made. There was no time to communicate with the church body or to get their feedback on the situation. Knowing full well that he was in for criticism, Mike signed the deal. The church had four weeks to vacate the premises.

After a time without a building, the church entered an agreement with the Shawnee Mission South High School to utilize their auditorium. They held their first service there on the first Sunday of February, 1985. It would prove to be a historic Sunday.

Although considerable prophetic activity had occurred during the church's first two years of existence, there was still uncertainty about how to process revelatory words, dreams, visions, and the like, especially in the context of the corporate meeting of the church. So it was somewhat upsetting to Bickle when Augustine Alcala abruptly took hold of the microphone on that Sunday in February and announced,

> In four months, two men in business suits will come and make us an offer on a building that we can't refuse. On that day the Lord will answer his promise that if we would give our money to the poor, he would give us a building. We will be in that building by June 1st.

Everyone applauded enthusiastically. Everyone except Bickle, that is. Mike was upset that Augustine had violated the policy on how prophetic words were to be delivered. To make matters worse, he wasn't sure he believed the word. Mike was struggling with his pastoral obligation at this point. What if he were to let it go without comment or correction and it didn't come to pass? What Augustine would endure couldn't compare with the backlash Mike was facing. So, he took the microphone and tried to qualify what had been said: "What Augustine means is that sometime within the next few months God will give us indications about our future and will provide us with wisdom through men in the business community, but we can't be sure what it will look like." After the meeting, many in the church, including Augustine, chastised Mike for being overly cautious and filled with unbelief.

Several months passed uneventfully. During the first week of May, the church heard news that was initially upsetting. The school board informed them that they would have to vacate the auditorium by May 27 because of an asbestos problem. Everyone was understandably alarmed and concerned. "Where will we go? Where will we meet?"

Two weeks later, on a Monday, Bickle and Noel Alexander were invited to lunch by two men, John Shore and Skip Kopp. As they sat down with Mike and Noel, who were casually dressed, they began with an apology: "We're sorry for wearing these suits. We never do. But today we had to attend a special business meeting that required we dress up. But we'd like to make you an offer you can't refuse."

Bickle and Alexander cast a knowing glance at each other, understandably stunned by what was happening. The two men continued: "We have a large indoor soccer facility that is closing down on Friday, May 31st. We are a little concerned about vandalism in the area and we don't want it to sit unoccupied even for one day. If you like, you can take possession of it on June 1st."

There it was! Exactly four months from the time of Alcala's prophecy. The precise date he had mentioned. Two men in business suits making Bickle an offer he couldn't refuse. Why was the offer so good? Shore continued:

> I will let you occupy the building based on a handshake, without any written contract. We'll sell it to you at our original cost, even though we've made a number of improvements over the years. We won't charge you any interest whatsoever. And if you're late in a payment, we'll work with you. We believe in what you're doing and want to help in any way we can.

One reason for their generosity was that their purpose for buying the structure had been to stage evangelistic sporting events in Grandview. They now believed that Kansas City Fellowship could best accomplish this goal.

Before anyone had seen this potential new facility, Bob Jones claimed to have experienced a vision from the Lord in which he saw what he believed was the building God would provide for them. Although Bickle had initially been skeptical of Alcala's word, Bob Jones was not. He saw what appeared to be an expansive area of green grass on which the building was sitting. They didn't know what to make of this, thinking that perhaps the building would be located on "Lawn St." or "Grassways" or "Meadow Lane" or some such

The Search for a Home

name. Jones also said the Lord had given him Psalm 124 which, he believed, had something to do with the location of the facility.

"It will also be near a Church of Christ," said Bob. The only problem with all this was that no one had any idea of any place in Kansas City that remotely met the description. As it turned out, the soccer facility that was to become the church's worship center is located just off 124th Street, opposite a Church of Christ! The actual address is *12416* Grandview Road. If that were not enough, the floor of the fifty thousand square foot building was covered with *green* astroturf!

In the meantime, another group heard of the deal and offered Shore and Kopp full price on the building, together with a guaranteed credit line at the bank. "How can you trust them to pay it off? They are a young church with no credible economic history." Despite the fact that it meant the loss of thousands of dollars, the two men stood their ground: "We're sorry. But we gave them our word and we shook on it. That's good enough for us."

But the problems weren't over yet. The building was a mess. For one thing, there was no air conditioning. During that first summer people often fainted from the heat during services, both on Sunday and during the week. Bathroom facilities were minimal. And then news came in September that the church had two weeks in which to install a $35,000 sprinkler system or be shut down. Once again Bickle felt led of the Lord not to tell anyone of the need nor to take an offering. And once again, the Lord was faithful. Two days before the contract with the sprinkler system company was due, a check for $35,000 arrived in the mail from a businessman in Texas.

There is an addendum to this story. The building just described was the home of what used to be Forerunner Church and is located in Grandview, Missouri.[2] Before the two men made their momentous offer, Bob Scott wanted to purchase an office building for the church that he believed the Lord told him would not be physically connected with the main church facility.

Bickle wasn't convinced. The building Scott had in mind was too far away. Mike wanted to stay in the area of Overland Park, Kansas. But Bob was persistent, and informed Mike that the cost was $123,000. Mike reluctantly agreed and this time felt free to take an offering. He secretly hoped that the offering would be pathetically low, giving them an excuse not to purchase the building. The offering was $123,500! Needless to say, Bickle was convinced. The amazing thing is that in May of 1985 when Bickle went to inspect the soccer facility that would soon become the worship center, it

---

2. Following the implosion of IHOPKC and the scandal in Bickle's life, Forerunner Church closed its doors. As of the writing of this book, the building sits empty.

was located on the same street, one mile from the office building they had obtained only months earlier.

CHAPTER THIRTEEN

The Great Prophetic Controversy

NOT LONG AFTER MIKE and Diane Bickle moved to Kansas City and launched South Kansas City Fellowship, Ernie Gruen, then pastor of Full Faith Church of Love in Shawnee, Kansas, "accepted Mike Bickle with open arms as a man of integrity who was trying to do something for the Lord."[1] As an expression of his acceptance of Bickle, Gruen put him on the steering committee of the citywide Charismatic Pastors Fellowship (later to be known as Midwest Ministers Fellowship). However, according to Gruen, the situation became increasingly serious, "as it included accounts of wounded people, unethical practices, false prophecies, and damaged churches. Families reported how their lives had been tragically affected by their association with Kansas City Fellowship (KCF). The conviction grew in my [Gruen's] spirit that something was very wrong."[2]

Gruen claims that he then met with Bickle privately, after which he met again with Mike and members of his leadership team, efforts that he says "proved fruitless."[3] On Saturday, January 20, 1990, Gruen says that God told him that he must preach the message "Do We Keep Smiling and Say Nothing?," a message he delivered to his church on Sunday, January 21. On January 29, some eight days after preaching the sermon, Bickle wrote a three-page letter to Gruen affirming him as a man of sincere intentions, stating that he believed he had provided Gruen with sufficient answers to the questions he raised.

---

1. Gruen, *Documentation*. This 233-page treatise was released to the public in May of 1990 and soon spread globally. Gruen died on June 1, 2009.
2. Gruen, *Documentation*, 1.
3. Gruen, *Documentation*, 2.

Gruen assured everyone that he held no personal animosity against Bickle or any of his staff and that he and his team carefully compiled evidence based on tapes of messages preached at KCF and personal, written testimonies of individuals and churches who have been harmed. Gruen proceeded with this document on the conviction that "a budding Charismatic heresy"[4] was threatening the vitality of others in the city, one that would be more damaging than the shepherding controversy.

On March 30, 1990, Gruen sent a letter to Bickle describing how he had contacted twelve leading figures of the Apostolic Presbyters of the Network of Christian Ministries to see if they would mediate the situation. Gruen contends that by the time the *Documentation* was released to the public, he had received no response from Bickle or MCF. In this letter, Gruen states that he is "now convinced that your group [KCF] does not represent orthodox Christianity; that many of your church's prophecies are from familiar spirits [i.e., demons] and are actually divination; and that you are very close to becoming a Charismatic heresy and cult group."[5]

Gruen also claimed that of the forty-five pastors in the Kansas City area who contacted him, forty-four applauded his courage in speaking up. Numerous letters from these pastors are included in the *Documentation*, including one from The Christian Broadcasting Network (sent on April 28, 1990). By this time Bickle had requested that John Wimber insert himself into the controversy and help bring resolution. On June 12–14, Jack Deere met with Gruen and his staff to evaluate their charges and seek reconciliation. Two weeks later, June 28, 1990, Paul Cain, John Wimber, and Deere presented a response to Gruen who then agreed to cease attacking KCF and to terminate distribution of the *Documentation* after July 31. On that same day in June, Wimber and Bickle repented publicly to the congregation of KCF.

You should know that many of the alleged prophetic events or supernatural phenomena described in this book, together with several that I have not listed, are challenged by Gruen in his document. The primary focus of Gruen's investigation are four men: Bickle, Bob Jones, Paul Cain, and John Paul Jackson, with some 75 percent of his accusations directed at Jones. Each of these men were labeled false prophets by Gruen, who insisted they operated by means of a demonic spirit. Kansas City Fellowship, he would say in several places, is not a biblical local church but a cult. A cursory

---

4. Gruen, *Documentation*, 5.

5. Letter from Ernie Gruen to Mike Bickle, 1990. The full text of the letter can be found at https://x.com/ThouArtTheMan/status/1739161250272067683/photo/1.

reading of the document reveals that it consists largely of citations of Bob Jones obtained from cassette tapes of services at KCF.

When John Wimber was called upon to adjudicate this controversy, he assigned the greatest portion of the work to Jack Deere. I am in possession of two documents drafted largely by Deere that identify the most significant of Gruen's allegations and the response to each by Deere. One is a twenty-one-page treatise titled "Evaluation of Ernie Gruen's Accusations Against the Kansas City Fellowship." The other is a sixty-three-page document titled "Evaluation, Analysis and Response Documentation of 'Documentation of the Aberrant Practices and Teachings of Kansas City Fellowship (Grace Ministries),' by Pastor Ernie Gruen and Members of His Staff." In addition, I have several pages of handwritten notes by Jack Deere. Jack has proven to be immensely helpful in answering my questions during the composition of this book.

I should also point out that in light of recent events at IHOPKC and the discovery of Bickle's sexual indiscretions, Jack Deere is slightly less confident today in the conclusions he reached in his evaluation of Gruen's document. According to Deere, writing in 2024,

> My journey with Mike began in the late 1980s, around the time I started at the Association of Vineyard Churches under John Wimber. Tasked with investigating allegations against Mike's church by Ernie Gruen, my friendship with Mike led me to overlook significant concerns. I still believe Gruen's report contained numerous inaccuracies, misleading information and was motivated by jealousy. But my bias towards Mike skewed my focus. I was more concerned about debunking the allegations in a deeply flawed report, than considering important questions about Mike's character, which I had erroneously deemed impeccable.[6]

That being said, in virtually every podcast, article, email, or sermon devoted to this debate, hardly a person ever even indicates a knowledge of the detailed response by Deere to the many allegations by Gruen. They simply refer to Gruen's alleged devastating critique without noting the equally devastating response by Deere.

---

6. Deere, "From Support to Scrutiny."

The Allegations and Their Answers

Gruen's infamous *Documentation* runs to 233 pages and contains what Deere insists are no fewer than fifty serious allegations against Bickle and KCF in general, many of which are misleading or entirely false. It is widely available on the internet for anyone who wishes to wade through the many charges he levels against Bickle, the prophets, and KCF. My purpose here is to articulate the response to these many allegations that are the fruit of extensive research and countless interviews by Jack Deere, Jeff Grisamore, and others from KCF. In order to keep this material in a readable format, I will list each allegation by number, together with Deere's response.

I should also point out that nowhere in the *Documentation* is the statement of faith of KCF mentioned, in spite of the fact that it is entirely within the boundaries of evangelical orthodoxy. And although I only arrived in Kansas City in 1993, the statement of faith that I was responsible for crafting (with the considerable help of Michael Kailus, a teacher at Grace Training Center) likewise is fully aligned with the historic Christian faith. Similarly, nowhere does the *Documentation* even allude to the heart standards that governed KCF or the numerous prayer meetings that occurred almost daily throughout KCF's entire history.

(1) One of the more widely known accusations is that Bickle and Bob Jones fabricated the prophecy of the drought in 1983 to enhance their reputation as prophetically gifted. The fact is, the drought and the prophesied rainfall truly occurred, but the report of it in 1986 was in error. To sum up, Bob Jones did prophesy in May of 1983 a drought of three months duration. It turned out to be three months and eleven days. As noted earlier, it was the second worst drought in the previous hundred years of Kansas City, prior to 1983. Jones also prophesied that it would rain on August 23 as a sign that not only the drought in the natural would be broken but also the spiritual drought that was about to befall the church. I have already described this prophetic scenario and confirmed its accuracy in chapter 7. I encourage you to return there and read it again. In sum, for Gruen to write that this story "was a total fabrication to promote 'the movement'" was a grievous slander.

(2) Gruen also pointed to a prophecy from Bob Jones made in 1976 at the Berean Baptist Church. Jones declared that seven young people under the age of thirty would die within a six-week period. As best as can be determined, five people died in eight months in 1976 and one or two more within the next two years. Only three of them were thirty or younger. Clearly, Jones's prophecy was accurate in terms of the impending deaths of several individuals, but was inaccurate when it came to the precise number

of those who passed away and the time of their deaths. It needs to be said that this sort of reckless approach to facts by Jones serves only to undermine the prophetic.

(3) In the *Documentation*, Gruen charged Bickle and KCF with unguarded declarations concerning their role in the last days ministry. This is largely true. Bickle and the prophets were also guilty of exalting mystical experiences and of issuing prophetic words that proved to be inaccurate. This is the appropriate place to list several related errors in the ministry of KCF that both they and the Vineyard had discovered and begun to address *before* Gruen ever published his *Documentation*. These would include:

- The lack of accountability for prophecies that did not come true
- The release of people to teach publicly who were not qualified or gifted as teachers
- The attempt by some to establish a doctrine or practice on the basis of revelation alone, without biblical support
- Dogmatic assertions in the delivery of prophetic words
- Revealing negative prophetic words in public without first confronting the individual(s)
- Prophecies concerning babies and marriages
- The conferring of governmental authority or staff positions to individuals without prior consultation with the appropriate levels of leadership
- Giving prophetic words that affect a movement or church without first consulting with appropriate levels of church authority
- Public predictions of natural disasters and economic events without first consulting with appropriate levels of authority in the local church
- The use of prophecy to control other individuals
- The appeal to types and allegories to establish doctrines that lack biblical support
- Teaching that KCF and the Vineyard are elite groups, soon to be revealed by God
- Calling John Wimber, Mike Bickle, and others, apostles and prophets.

(4) Gruen also accused Paul Cain of embracing and teaching the "manifested sons of God" heresy (based on a misguided interpretation of Romans 8:19–25). I addressed this charge in the chapter on Paul Cain and

pointed out that he repeatedly denied believing in this error. I personally had several conversations with Cain during my years in Kansas City and heard him clearly refute this particular error of the Latter Rain movement. I suppose one might push back and say that Cain was lying to protect himself against the charge of heresy. That is certainly possible, but I find it unlikely. It should also be noted that Gruen never attempted to contact Cain personally to determine if he actually taught this doctrine. On a related note, Gruen accused Cain of lying when the latter claimed to have traveled and ministered both alongside of and in the place of William Branham when the latter was unable to fulfill an invitation. There is both truth and error in this charge. It is true that Cain never ministered "alongside" of Branham or shared a platform with him. It is false to say that Cain never filled in for Branham when the latter was unable to attend a service. Although it must be said that this is hardly something that someone should claim as a badge of honor or discernment insofar as Branham proved late in his life to be a heretic.

It must also be admitted that Cain often spoke in terms that could easily be misconstrued as an endorsement of the manifest sons of God theory. That is to say, he rejected the name of this heresy while seemingly advocating for at least a portion of its truth. Specifically, Cain frequently spoke and prophesied of a "new breed" of Christians in the last days who would operate at extraordinarily high levels of supernatural ministry. But he never suggested that these believers would attain immortality in this life or supplant the need for a literal second coming of Christ.

(5) Paul Cain was also accused of engaging in necromancy, or communication with the dead. Two of Gruen's associates had listened to a tape of Cain's ministry to a man whose father had died. Paul claimed to have experienced a vision in which the man's mother (she was alive, not dead!) was feeling guilty for her husband's death. Cain also declared that the woman's name was Wanda, and that her middle name was Jean (both of which were accurate). He said he saw in a vision the man's dead father in heaven, face to face with Christ. At no time did he assert that he was talking with dead people. In fact, he issued a disclaimer at the beginning of his ministry to this man, clearly stating that what he was about to share was not necromancy. Gruen himself never listened to the tape. Even after meeting with Cain and hearing the facts, Gruen continued to send out his *Documentation* with this charge unchanged.

(6) Deere points out that in his meetings with the pastors at Full Faith Church of Love, two themes emerged as the primary cause of the offense they carried against Bickle and KCF. The pastors at Full Faith were

convinced that KCF believes they are a sovereign movement raised up by God to fulfill a special purpose in the last days, and that they used this as a way to draw people and other churches into their movement. The former is likely true, but little evidence suggests that this was designed to draw people into their movement.

The leaders at Full Faith also reject the notion of "the two orders," according to which the first is represented by Saul and the second by David. They believed that KCF accused them of being in the first order. Bickle did on occasion use Saul and David as representative of current Christian ministries, the former being more fleshly and self-aggrandizing than spiritual, and the latter being more Spirit-filled, humble, and in a more intimate relationship with God, thus leading to greater power in ministry. And yet Bickle also said that he regarded his church, at least in the present moment, more like Saul than David. He also on occasion likened the "two orders" to the pattern of Samuel, who replaced the old order of Eli.

It is true that both KCF and the Vineyard (at that time) believed there was biblical support for the notion that in the last days God would birth a "new order" or "new breed" of believers who would minister in the power of signs and wonders. This generation of Christians will display unprecedented Christlike character and power and will see the fulfillment of John 14:12. No one can deny that this terminology has the potential to breed and reinforce an elitist mindset, and there are indications that some people at KCF embraced such an identity. The language of "new order"/"new breed" is unfortunate and lacking biblical support. Whether or not there will be an unprecedented outpouring of spiritual power on those who constitute the final generation alive when Jesus returns largely depends on one's eschatology.

There is also a measure of triumphalism in their beliefs about a worldwide revival, in which a billion souls will come to faith, as they undoubtedly view themselves as central to this prophesied end-time movement of God. The grandiose nature of this belief recurs often in the form of claims that upwards of four hundred thousand people will be saved in a single meeting and that signs and wonders ten thousand times greater than those in the book of Acts will accompany this "new order" of ministry. One may choose to dismiss this latter claim as hyperbole, uttered in a moment of heightened excitement.

(7) Bickle is also accused of referring often to "Mike's movement" or "the movement" or "his movement." This is false. While it is true that while in Cairo God allegedly invited Bickle to be a part of "a" movement that would touch the ends of the earth, at no time did Bickle claim that this was

"his" or belonged exclusively to KCF. When Bickle did use the terminology of a "movement" he had three things in mind. On occasion it could refer to what God would do in the last days through the ministry of KCF. At other times Bickle used it to refer to the activity of God in the United States. Finally, he also used it to refer to what God will accomplish globally, in the nations of the earth. The point is, there is nothing dangerous or heretical or prideful in using the term in these ways.

(8) Gruen also objected to Bickle referring to certain individuals as "prophets." The fact is, early in 1983, Bickle did call Bob Jones "a true prophet of God," and you can read about that event in chapter 5. If Bickle were inclined to describe anyone as a "prophet" it would have been Paul Cain. But KCF consistently labored to make a distinction between people who are "prophetically gifted," on the one hand, and those who operate at a high level of accuracy in the exercise of the gift, on the other. The latter may well minister in the "office" of a prophet. However, it must be acknowledged that there were times when the label of "prophet" was applied to certain individuals at KCF, but these singular incidents do not reflect the settled theology of either Bickle or the church. I should also point out that numerous leaders in the charismatic movement frequently use the title of "prophet." I hardly think that this is grounds for accusation or a cause for bitter criticism.

We should also note that on several occasions in the New Testament certain individuals, both male and female, are explicitly referred to as "prophets" (Acts 11:27; 13:1; 15:32; 21:10; 1 Cor 12:28–29; 14:29, 32, 37; Eph 4:11). In addition are the numerous texts that speak of people "prophesying." The point is that even if Bickle and KCF at any time referred to an individual as a prophet, they had considerable biblical support for doing so.[7]

(9) Contrary to Gruen's charge, Bickle and KCF believe there is biblical evidence to support the possibility of an "out-of-body" experience and that such is not occultic. They would point to the apostle Paul's experience in 2 Corinthians 12 and perhaps the apostle John's experience as described in Revelation 4:1–2. Related to this is the charge by Gruen that "KCF has an overwhelming emphasis on out of body experiences, angelic visitations, conversations with demons, visits to heaven and hell, visitations from the dead, visions, prophecies, [and] prophets." This is true, to a degree, at least in the case of Bob Jones and the many stories he told of such. While Bickle and other leaders have taught on angels, dreams, and visions, the language of "overwhelming emphasis" is an unjustified exaggeration.

7. In a taped message in 1986, as Bickle told the story of Bob Jones, he clearly refers to him as a "prophet of God."

The Great Prophetic Controversy

I should also point out that a reference to "out-of-body" phenomena was extremely rare in the Scriptures themselves. When this is compared with the excessive number of times that Jones and others claim to have experienced such occurrences it gives a person pause. Simply put, while acknowledging the potential for an "out-of-body" experience, it strikes me as unlikely that people such as Jones could have been made the repeated recipients of this phenomenon.

(10) Gruen also accuses Augustine Alcala of making homosexual advances to one of his friends. Deere was unable to interview the alleged witness in this case, but points out that even if it were true, Bickle clearly excluded Alcala from any further ministry at KCF from 1984 on. For more on this, see chapter 3.

(11) Another egregious charge was that a couple had received prophetic instruction to deliver their baby at home, the result of which was the infant's death. In point of fact, in the history of KCF, up to this time, there had been only one baby who died during delivery at home. My wife and I happen to know the couple that Gruen referenced, as they lived only two doors down from us during our years in Kansas City. They were diligent about the impending birth, had a midwife present, and at the first sign of danger they rushed to the hospital. Upon arrival at the hospital, the baby's vital signs were stable. The obstetrician was delayed by more than forty-five minutes in getting to the hospital and was not present when the baby began to experience fetal distress. The parents who lost this child were still members of KCF when Gruen launched his attack and confessed to intense wounding because of Gruen's comments. This couple also stated that at no time did any pastor, staff person, home group leader, or prophetically gifted person, or any other individual at KCF encourage them to have the baby at home. In his response letter to Gruen, Bickle made it clear that "we resolutely stand against prophecy that controls people's lives, which is witchcraft, and are equally appalled at the idea of babies being born at home due to controlling prophetic words."

(12) In December of 1988, James Goll (at the time we knew him simply as "Jim") arranged a private meeting with Ernie Gruen and then another with Bickle. He told them that he had a vision of the two men standing at opposite ends of the street, guns in hand, preparing for a feud to break out. When they all met together,[8] Bickle was under the impression that Gruen's complaints against him had been addressed before and that he didn't

---

8. In addition to Bickle and Goll, present at the meeting from KCF were David Parker, Michael Sullivant, and Noel Alexander.

understand why Gruen continued to bring them up. When this was addressed by Goll in a subsequent, private meeting with Gruen, the latter said he would not bring up such matters again. Goll told Gruen that if he changed his mind, he should contact Bickle and KCF first, before going public, to which Gruen spoke his agreement.

Gruen also claimed that in this meeting, Mike Bickle delivered an ominous spiritual warning, threatening Gruen with harm. Bickle had an entirely different interpretation of that conversation. When he found out how Gruen had interpreted his words he immediately apologized. And yet, having accepted the apology, Gruen proceeded to include this story in the *Documentation* more than a year later.

Michael Sullivant, one of the pastors at KCF, was present at this meeting and said, in an interview with Jeff Grisamore, that "Ernie misconstrued a statement Mike made in love that he [Gruen] took as a death threat." According to Gruen, Bickle said, "You touch[ed] me illegally and people who touch me illegally, bad things happen to them, things like death; other people who touch me illegally have died." Sullivant insists that Bickle "never said anything like that. Mike was trying to explain out of . . . a spirit of real concern for Ernie that if the Lord was for us and for what we're doing and behind us, it's a dangerous thing to come against it as he was coming against us, and I know Mike wasn't thinking of death." Sullivant insists that Bickle never used the word "death." When Ernie asked Mike if he was making a death threat, Sullivant contends that Bickle clearly responded with a resounding no.

After a meeting in February of 1989 between Full Faith pastors and those from KCF, the latter received the distinct impression that, whatever differences existed between the two churches, a resolution had been reached. Each of the KCF pastors believed that Gruen had promised he would not make anything public without contacting them first. On October 17, 1989, in a letter to Ray Thompson, a man who attended KCF, Gruen stated,

> I certainly share your concern and desire for unity. As you may or may not know, several leaders from Kansas City Fellowship and from the four Full Faiths met and differences between us were resolved. Our emphasis or vision may be different, but I am sure you would agree that unity and uniformity are two different things. Uniformity would be a terrible thing for all of our churches; so for [sic] my perspective we have already come together in humility and brokenness (as far as leadership is concerned).

The Great Prophetic Controversy

Obviously, this letter is greatly at odds with Gruen's report of his reaction to that meeting in his January 21, 1990, sermon that sparked the controversy.

(13) In the *Documentation*, Gruen claims that a Christian psychologist in Kansas City reported that he had counseled over a hundred disillusioned members and former members of KCF. Deere counters by pointing out that

> it is not fair, nor objective to offer an unnuanced statement that a psychologist has seen over a hundred disillusioned members from a church of three thousand who are presently unhappy with the ministry of that church. It would be important to know if they were ever happy with the ministry of any church as well as what kind of emotional problems they were having at the time of counseling. As it turns out, the man who was reported to be a Christian psychologist was not yet a psychologist. He was, at the time, still working on his degree. His objectivity may reasonably be questioned since he was a member of one of the Full Faith churches [overseen by Gruen] and a close personal friend of the pastor.

(14) An objection was also raised against Bob Jones's use of the phrase "Shepherd's Rod," which he intended only as a metaphor for divine evaluation. Each year, on the Day of Atonement, Jones said that a believer should go under the Shepherd's Rod to be evaluated for growth or persistence in sin, resulting in either promotion or demotion in local church ministry. While it may strike some of us as odd, that Christians are often evaluated by the Lord is clearly biblical, as a quick reading of Revelation 2–3 will demonstrate.

(15) Gruen also objected to those who said that in their dreams the Holy Spirit would often appear as a faceless man. But if the Spirit's primary role is to glorify the Lord Jesus Christ, it makes sense that he would appear as faceless in order not to draw attention to himself. There's nothing explicitly biblical that affirms this possibility, nor is there anything in Scripture that would necessarily preclude it.

(16) In the fall of 1989, for a period of about six weeks, there was a powerful visitation of the Holy Spirit on the students at KCF's Dominion Christian School (DCS). This experience was felt not only by the students but also by members of the faculty and administration. The teachers at DCS were careful not to promote emotionalism or certain manifestations as definitive proof of the presence of the Spirit. I spoke with many of the adults who were present and in my view the visitation was real. However, Gruen cites it as one more example of charismatic excess, suggesting that it was all

self-induced and that the children were manipulated by the faculty. Gruen also suggests in his *Documentation* that the level of academic achievement at DCS was deficient, in spite of the fact that the results of their standardized tests placed the students in the upper 10 and 15 percent of the nation. The educational qualifications of the faculty at DCS are quite remarkable, as Deere clearly demonstrates in his response to Gruen.

(17) The charge that "there is a glaring lack of emphasis on Jesus" at MCF is utterly baseless. Although one may object to certain elements in the theology of Bickle, a cursory glance at his book *Passion for Jesus* will easily show the Christ-centered nature of his ministry and preaching. While the book was published several years after Gruen's charge, I'm persuaded that it reflects what Bickle believed and taught from the very onset of his ministry.

(18) Gruen also quotes a pastor who charged Bickle with failing to keep his promises about financial commitments and reneging on his assurance that no changes would be made in the staff or programs at Christian Life Center. The statement from Gary Crowder, former pastor of Christian Life Center (CLC), accuses Bickle of coming to his church to explain his interest in having CLC merge with KCF. The clear implication is that Bickle was the person who initiated contact with CLC when, in point of fact, two elders from CLC first approached Bickle with news that the church was in a serious financial crisis. Crowder had earlier approached Gruen and Full Faith to take over the church, but they did not feel God was telling them to do so. Crowder also appealed to Full Faith for financial assistance, but they were turned down.

Two elders at CLC then approached Bickle who proceeded to give the church $10,000 with no strings attached. Bickle was told that the church was three months behind in payments on a loan, which KCF soon covered and then refinanced the entire debt on the building. Bickle insisted that he made no promises that he would not change staff or programs at CLC. He told both the music minister and youth pastor that they could stay if they wished, although both subsequently sought out other ministry opportunities. Financial records at KCF also reveal that both staff members were given six weeks of salary and benefits once CLC merged with KCF. KCF also gave $10,000 to Gary Crowder to help him emerge from his personal financial struggles.

There were essentially three elders at CLC at the time, two of whom were interviewed by Jeff Grisamore, one of the staff members of KCF. Both of them denied that anything remotely similar to a "takeover" occurred. They applaud Bickle for his patience and wisdom in the eventual merging of CLC with KCF. One of them made it clear that the transition into

KCF was essential, as CLC was "on the precipice of financial disaster and disbandment."

KCF was also charged with changing the locks on CLC's building and not allowing personnel to retrieve their personal property. But two elders at CLC and KCF together stated that the locks were changed only after the church had come under KCF's authority. They made this change when it was discovered that items were disappearing from the church, most likely from burglary. One item left in the kitchen of the church building was initially thought to belong to KCF. When it was discovered that it was the property of a CLC member, the item was returned to its rightful owner.

(19) On a related note, KCF was accused of executing a takeover of two churches in Olathe, Kansas. The leaders of the churches in Olathe were Wes Adams and Larry Fry, who over a period of two to three years had prayed and processed whether to come under the leadership of Grace Ministries. They affirmed that this progression was entirely by their initiative and not Mike Bickle's or anyone associated with Grace Ministries. Bickle actually resisted involvement with these two churches in the early stages, not wanting to be overburdened or distracted from his present focus. In an extensive interview with Wes Adams,[9] Adams affirmed that it was he who made contact with Bickle, not the other way around.

Adams had participated in the Solemn Assembly in 1983 but did not approach Bickle about coming under his leadership until March of 1986. Not long thereafter, both Adams and Fry met with Bickle and concluded that God wanted to bring the three streams together as one. Says Adams: "Again, it was initiated by us and not by them" (i.e., not by KCF). Everything was finalized a year later in March of 1987. Again, quoting Adams: "This was not something [that] was orchestrated or manipulated in any way by Mike, or by prophets." Contrary to Gruen, Adams insists that there was never any kind of prophetic control, manipulation, or deceit. Adams proceeded to deny every accusation made either by Gruen or former members of the Olathe church. When asked if he felt the two churches were "manipulated or intimidated by the leadership of KCF," he said no. The interview with Larry Fry revealed that he agreed on every major point with Adams. Fry even said that as he and Adams pursued affiliation with KCF, Bickle's initial response was one of "reluctance."

9. Dr. Adams eventually joined the faculty of Grace Training Center, the full-time Bible school that Bickle launched in 1990, where I served as president during my seven years in Kansas City. Adams earned a Ph.D. from Baylor University in New Testament Studies. He was a good friend of mine, and despite being paralyzed at the age of sixteen and spending the majority of his life in a wheelchair, he was profoundly productive until his untimely death.

(20) Bickle and KCF were also charged with teaching "dominion" theology or some version of Christian reconstruction or theonomy. This is patently false, as Bickle has always identified as a premillennialist and has consistently rejected any form of postmillennialism. At the same time, Bickle's consistent affirmation of a massive, global harvest of souls in the last days could easily be misconstrued as an endorsement of dominion theology. Again, sadly, Gruen and his staff made no effort to approach Bickle or his staff to learn if this accusation was true.

(21) There was yet another accusation that KCF had edited many of its tapes to remove damaging comments or theologically questionable statements. JoAnne McFatter, whom I know personally, was the person whose job it was to edit tapes at the church. When asked about it, she said, "I have never been asked by anyone at KCF to edit the tapes in any way that could be construed as deceptive."

(22) Bickle was also accused of using deceptive tactics to lure two other churches under the mantle of KCF. But both pastors of these churches and the majority of their members are delighted to be part of KCF. Full Faith insinuated that Bickle portrayed KCF as a "sovereign movement" raised up by God, and that a special blessing would come to those who aligned themselves with his church. Deere points out that "the negative testimonies acquired from these two churches are simply a report of former members who are disgruntled with this change." The fact is, KCF had turned down approximately fifty churches that sought to come under Bickle's leadership.

(23) It is alleged that in the prophecy of the white horse, described earlier in this book, Bob Jones referred to pastors and Christian leaders who would try to bring correction to Bickle as "mad dogs" or "rabid dogs." But Jones was referring to well-meaning Christians and leaders who would attempt to persuade Bickle to dilute the standards that he believed God had given him. The use of such language is probably unwise, but it is neither unbiblical nor heretical.

(24) Gruen also points to KCF's claim that it will be one of "twelve streams" globally that will emerge in the last days as the primary expression of God's end-times purpose. But Bickle has issued numerous denials of the accusation that he claims there will only be twelve streams or movements. Certain other prophetic voices at KCF have indeed asserted this, but Bickle himself refused to endorse it. As noted earlier, it is true that Bickle would often refer to Saul and David (and at times, Ishmael and Isaac) as representative of two approaches to ministry, but contrary to Gruen, he never used

this teaching to compel people to leave their church and join KCF. In fact, Bickle regularly insisted that we are all still part of the "old order" of Saul.

On a related note, several people interviewed by Gruen insist that they were repeatedly told that KCF was the center of a "new thing" God was doing and that its ministry would be on the "cutting edge" of God's last-days work. They claim that this notion was often used to recruit people out of other churches and into KCF. As I said earlier, there is a measure of truth in this, as Bickle and KCF were prone to grandiose and triumphalistic perceptions of their own importance.

(25) In conjunction with his other comments about Bob Jones, Gruen believes that the doctrinal foundation of KCF was established on the basis of the aberrant revelations of Jones. And yet, of the more than 2,075 messages given at KCF services since its inception, Jones has shared during a service fewer than thirty times. Jones's messages have always been understood as either parables or prophetic testimonies, but certainly not exegetical teaching that shaped the theological position of KCF. That being said, no one can deny that Jones exerted a significant influence on KCF when it came to the importance and proper exercise of prophetic gifting.

(26) Gruen also makes much of Jones's life before he came to saving faith in Christ. That Jones lived in rampant sin, including drunkenness, physical violence, and sexual immorality *before* his conversion is hardly grounds for disqualification from ministry. One need only remember that the apostle Paul was complicit in the murder of Christians before his conversion.

(27) The *Documentation* from Full Faith also disputes the alleged claim by Jones that he has had more revelations, visions, and supernatural experiences than all the men of God in the Bible put together. If Jones in fact said this about himself, he should have been called out and rebuked for such a self-serving statement. But both he and Bickle deny that either of them ever made such a claim. Bickle did say that Jones would typically receive five or more revelations from the Spirit every night, and we know nothing of the number of such revelatory experiences men like Elijah and Elisha received. Bickle also denied the charge that he had been deceptive in his public presentation of Jones. He also denied that he has said one thing about Jones in private but something contrary to it in public.

(28) Earlier in this book I told the story of how Bob Jones claimed to have had a visitation in which the emissary from God bore the name "Dominus," who, it turned out, was the Lord himself. He then prophesied to Mike Bickle and Bob Scott that Jesus would make an appearance to each

of them but in the guise of one of their friends named "Don." Contrary to Gruen's charge, no one ever said that *everyone* named "Don" was supposedly Jesus. Gruen also exaggerates and misrepresents KCF by alluding to the "appearance" and "reappearance" to Bickle and Scott of Dominus, but always in the form of their friend "Don." Such language suggests something that happened continuously when in fact Bickle and Scott only had one dream each in which they felt a friend named "Don" symbolically represented the Lord.

(29) Bickle was also accused of trying to enforce an artificial form of Christian unity by urging that all should be in agreement. But this is hardly heretical or manipulative, as both Jesus (John 17:21–23) and the apostle Paul (Phil 2:1–5) called for believers to unite.

(30) KCF has regularly been criticized for the doctrine known as the "city church," in which there should be only one unified church in a city, with all congregations committed to the same vision and leadership. Lee Grady points out that "many pastors in Kansas City felt threatened by what they perceived to be an attempt to 'swallow' other churches under KCF's banner. He quotes Bickle as saying that 'the way we used terminology created fear, division, and suspicion.'"[10] Although at one time Bickle did embrace a form of the "city church" perspective, he has since abandoned that view. I can testify that during my seven years on Bickle's staff I heard him on numerous occasions repudiate that notion. His more mature view is that the idea should have emphasized "unity through friendship" rather than "unity through a church government structure."

(31) Gruen charged John Paul Jackson with urging people to practice instant obedience to the prophets in order to avoid financial ruin. But Jackson was saying that in the future prophets would be able to warn people about impending financial collapse. He did not insist on this in the present day, declaring that God has not yet given that level of credibility to prophetic ministry. It is true, however, that both Jackson and Jones prophesied that in 1988 America would experience a precipitous and drastic fall in the stock market. Jones went so far as to counsel people to divest their stock holdings in anticipation of this crisis. 1988 turned out to be a positive year for the stock market, nothing resembling the dire predictions of Jackson and Jones came to pass.

One more comment of clarification is in order. Although Bob Jones, Paul Cain, Kevin Prosch, and Mike Bickle were guilty in varying degrees of sexual sin, no such charge was ever leveled at John Paul Jackson or any

---

10. Grady, "Resolving the Kansas City Prophecy Controversy."

of the other "prophets" in Kansas City. I knew John Paul well before his untimely death on February 18, 2015, and can personally testify to his godly character. His prophetic gift, although not perfect, was among the most accurate I have ever witnessed.[11]

(32) One of the more serious charges levelled by Gruen concerns Bob Jones's prophecy about the "elected seed generation" that will emerge in the last days and minister in far more signs and wonders than we see in the book of Acts. The "seed" are literal children, born since 1973 to families in the "movement," who were handpicked by Jesus and the angels of heaven to walk in great power. They are the best of every bloodline, predestined to be part of the end-time generation who will facilitate the greatest outpouring of supernatural power since the apostles walked the earth. They will operate in so much power that missing arms and eyes will be restored, they will walk through walls, and be used to raise hundreds of dead people back to life.

I must admit that I find this prophecy to be highly improbable. Nothing in Scripture explicitly supports this notion, and the suggestion that Christians will restore severed limbs and walk through walls is totally devoid of any biblical precedent. Thus, I believe Jones was rightly rebuked for advancing this idea.

(33) There can be no denial that Bob Jones and John Paul Jackson on several occasions prophesied healings that did not happen, together with other declarations that failed to materialize. On the other hand, I can personally testify that John Paul's facility in the interpretations of dreams far surpassed anything I saw or heard from other prophetic voices. John Paul and I, together with Rita Springer, were invited to speak at a conference at what was then Shady Grove Church in the Dallas–Fort Worth area. For more than an hour John Paul interpreted upwards of twenty dreams that people described, each one affirming their belief that his insights were spot on and quite helpful.

(34) On p. 178 of the *Documentation*, Gruen cites the testimony of a man who said that a prophecy was given to the elders of a church "with the full blessing of Mike. It was a strong prophecy of judgment and that of people dying. It just so happened one elder was already terminally ill with cancer." When asked about this alleged prophecy and his endorsement of it, Bickle replied, "Absolutely not. That is absolutely ridiculous. I've never

---

11. Jack Deere has also said to me personally—and in his book *Why I am Still Surprised by the Voice of God*—that John Paul's prophetic gift was one of the most accurate and edifying that he has ever witnessed.

heard of such a thing. I've never heard of even a remote incident that resembles that incident. As far as I'm concerned, that was a fabricated story."[12]

(35) In several places in the *Documentation* Gruen charges Bickle and Jones with "fabricating" certain prophetic stories to allegedly promote KCF in the nation and to induce members of other churches to join KCF. In this way, allegedly, Bickle destroyed other churches by "stealing members." The accusation of "fabricating" is a serious example of slander, especially when it comes with no corroborating evidence.

The End of the Controversy

Although KCF made numerous changes to its practice of prophecy, the relationship between the two congregations was, according to Bickle, "very strained."[13] Gruen agreed, "adding that the dispute 'rent the body of Christ in this city into two isolated camps.'"[14]

Most people over the past several years with whom I've talked about this controversy had no idea of what was going on in the life of Ernie Gruen. But Mike Bickle did, although he never shared this information with anyone. Before the controversy erupted, and before the 233-page document was released to the public, a woman who had direct and undeniable knowledge that Gruen was involved in an adulterous affair approached Bickle and shared the details with him. Bickle could easily have exposed Gruen and put an end to the controversy. But God had told Mike to keep quiet, and that the Lord would vindicate him in due course.

Fast forward to the spring of 1993 (Ann and I moved to Kansas City and joined Bickle's staff in the summer of 1993). Mike and several of his pastors were having lunch at the Western Sizzl'n restaurant across the street from his church. They were meeting with a lady named Jill Austin who was planning on moving to Kansas City. Austin had her back to the front of the restaurant and couldn't see anything. She looked at Bickle and said, "The Lord revealed to me that he put 'Saul's cloak' in your hand, but that you refused to make use of it to vindicate yourself."

You may recall that when David was fleeing Saul he went into a cave. Saul later came in, not knowing that David was there. David could easily have killed Saul to protect himself, but chose not to. Instead, he cut a piece

---

12. Bickle's response was given in an interview conducted by Jeff Grisamore.

13. Bickle, from an interview with *Charisma*, as quoted in the article "Kansas City Churches Reconciled."

14. See Gruen's comments in "Kansas City Churches Reconciled."

of Saul's cloak to later prove to Saul that he could have killed him, but chose in mercy to spare his life (see 1 Sam 24).

Austin then said to Mike, "The Lord told me that he was going to put an end to this controversy today. Today!"

"Today?" Bickle asked.

"Yes," said Austin, "today."

At that very moment, utterly unknown to Austin (who had her back to the entrance to the restaurant), Ernie Gruen walked in! Mike saw him from a distance and froze. Gruen and his guest didn't see Mike until they walked up and actually sat down at the table across from Bickle and his staff. Ernie looked up and said, "Oh, Mike, I didn't know you were here. I'd like to talk to you."

He pulled Bickle aside and said, "We need to put an end to this controversy today. Let's write up a mutual expression of forgiveness and sign it and send it to *Charisma* and *Christianity Today* magazine."

Bickle agreed (much to the dismay of his staff, who believed Gruen needed to publicly repent for his lies; to them, Bickle was letting Gruen off too easily). The joint statement signed by both Gruen and Bickle is included below.

Jill Austin's prophetic word was spot on. "Today," she said, "God will put an end to the controversy." And on that day, seconds after uttering the word, in walked Gruen with his proposal. You need to understand that Gruen's church was on the other side of the city, some twenty miles away. For him to eat lunch at the restaurant directly across the street from Bickle's church was bizarre.

So, Austin had nailed it. She told Bickle that God had put Saul's cloak in his hand, but that he had chosen not to use it. It was an obvious reference to the information Mike received from the woman who had knowledge of Gruen's affair. And on that very day, God put an end to the controversy.[15]

What few people at that time knew was that within days after Mike and Gruen signed the document putting an end to the controversy, Gruen fled the city with his mistress, leaving his church (and his wife) in complete disarray. "A letter announcing his resignation [from his role as senior pastor of Full Faith Church of Love] which Gruen faxed from Georgia, arrived only days after he informed his parishioners that he had resolved a personal dispute with Vineyard leader Mike Bickle."[16] Gruen eventually returned to

---

15. I say this while at the same time noting that several individuals in the coming years quoted Gruen as saying that he stood by the information in the *Documentation*.

16. Editor, "Gruen Resigns After Announcement."

Kansas City, reconciled with his wife, but his ministry was effectively over. In his letter of resignation, Gruen said,

> I hereby judge myself disqualified to continue in my offices: pastor, elder and apostle of Full Faith Church of Love Ministries. My sin causing this resignation is not committing adultery, but committing divorce. By divorcing I am breaking no law, but I am violating Scripture. I simply confess to you, I am guilty! Please forgive me and grant me your forgiveness.[17]

The truly sad thing about all this is that very few people ever heard about Gruen's adulterous lifestyle. The only thing people remembered is that Gruen had published a 233-page document accusing Bickle and his congregation of all manner of sin. Bickle never said a word in his own defense. Even to this day, you will read or hear people speak of the "prophetic controversy" in Kansas City and how Gruen had exposed Bickle. As we've just seen, this is largely inaccurate. The only news report of Gruen's infidelity and departure from ministry was provided by *Charisma* magazine. No report of the investigation into his charges against KCF and their baseless nature was ever released to the media.

Asking for Forgiveness

One final point to make. In about 1994 or 1995 (my memory fails me), seven of Gruen's associate pastors and pastors of churches in his network called us and asked for a meeting. I don't remember everyone from our church who was present, but certainly it included Bickle, me, Michael Sullivant, and James Goll. We sat with them as they each, one after another, tearfully repented to Mike and asked his forgiveness for participating in the sham 233-page report. They each acknowledged that they were pressured into producing this document by Gruen. It was a powerful moment. I know because I was there.

As if to settle it forever, the lead pastor who took over from Gruen after his removal from ministry eventually joined Mike's staff at IHOPKC and served faithfully there for many years.

---

17. Editor, "Gruen Resigns After Announcement." That Gruen had in fact committed adultery was only disclosed later. In his email to Jack Deere, cited earlier in full, Bickle refers to Gruen's "multiple affairs." He filed for divorce before he returned to his wife. After a period of time, he returned to Kansas City and reconciled with her.

Addendum A

Letter from John Wimber to Jamie Buckingham

In a personal letter to Jamie Buckingham, dated 1990, John Wimber wrote:

> Both Mike Bickle and the prophetic ministries represented by these congregations have submitted themselves to my spiritual authority and oversight. I have made a careful investigation of abuses and errors, both in pastoral ministry and prophetic ministry. While I have not personally found any of Ernie Gruen's charges to be substantiated, I have found certain excesses and errors that required both discipline and correction. I have taken the necessary steps to institute both discipline and correction in this matter. Mike Bickle and the individual prophetic ministries have submitted to the discipline and correction, and I am satisfied that we will not see these problems arising again in the future. (*The Buckingham Report*, July–August, 1990)

Addendum B

Ernie Gruen and Mike Bickle's Joint Statement—May 16, 1993

> This is a joint statement from the leadership of Full Faith Church of Love Ministries and Metro Vineyard Fellowship of Kansas City.
> Now there are varieties of gifts, but the same Spirit. And there are varieties of ministries, and the same Lord. And there are varieties of effects, but the same God who works all things in all persons.... For even as the body is one and yet has many members, and all the members of the body, though they are many, are one body, so also is Christ.
> —1 Corinthians 12:4–6, 12 (NASB)

Ernie Gruen and Mike Bickle have forgiven each other of all offenses. Their senior leadership has come together in a spirit of forgiveness; we also ask the Body of Christ to forgive us of any offenses that we have caused the Church universal. We feel it is time to bring to a close the events of the past. We believe it is time to go on and to seek to heal past wounds. We want to publicly lay down any personal animosities, wounds, or misunderstandings between the two churches. Under the Lordship of Jesus Christ as one Body, we want to be joined and knit together in His love, "being diligent to preserve the unity of the Spirit in the bond of peace" (Eph. 4:3, NASV). We desire the Body of Christ represented by our churches to flow together in the love and mercy of God and begin to rebuild relationships and friendships.

Ernest J. Gruen
Mike Bickle

Subsequent to the release of this joint statement, another document was crafted.

"Declaration of Repentance & Unity"

The leadership of Metro Vineyard Fellowship, Full Faith Church of Love, and the Midwest Ministers Fellowship (formerly a part of Full Faith Ministries) began a process of reconciliation in May of 1993 that reaches its culmination in the release of this joint declaration.

In spite of considerable pain and confusion, God has graciously used this controversy to accomplish much good in our individual hearts and churches. Yet as His human instruments we acknowledge that we sinned against each other in the process and in doing so brought division to the body of Christ and the purposes of God in Kansas City. We have fully confessed and repented of these sins and have forgiven each other. We are grateful to God and His great mercy for having brought healing and cleansing to our relationship.

This reconciliation goes far beyond mere tolerance or even mutual respect. We have entered into spiritual unity and heartfelt affection one for another that will enable us to stand together in our city on behalf of the gospel of Jesus Christ and the advance of His kingdom.

As an expression of this unity, Metro Vineyard Fellowship has accepted an invitation to join the Midwest Ministers Fellowship, a local network of churches designed to nurture relationships and equip ministers to be more effective in their callings. This action in no way alters or affects MVF's affiliation with the Association of Vineyard Churches.

We encourage you to join with us in giving all glory, honor, and praise to God for graciously orchestrating this experience of repentance and unity.

[Signed]
Mike Bickle
On behalf of Metro Vineyard Fellowship

Hal Linhardt
On behalf of Full Faith Church of Love

Howard Cordell
[Leader of the Midwest Ministers Fellowship]

Addendum C

Derek Prince's Statement About Kansas City Fellowship

[What you are about to read is Derek Prince's evaluation of the doctrines and practices of Kansas City Fellowship based entirely on his reading of Ernie Gruen's *Documentation*. Prince wrote this before the evaluation of that *Documentation* was undertaken.[18] I am quite confident that if Prince had obtained access to the conclusions of Jack Deere, his opinion of Kansas City Fellowship would have been significantly different.]

To: Friends and Associates of Derek Prince Ministries

Our office has been receiving requests from inside the U.S.A. and from other parts of the world regarding our relationship to Kansas City Fellowship.

As a result, Derek Prince has prepared a statement in which he outlines the contacts he has had with Kansas City Fellowship and some of their leaders.

Derek also sums up his personal evaluation of some of the doctrines and practices of Kansas City Fellowship.

Derek's statement is being sent to you because of your personal connection with Derek and our ministry. It is not intended for mass distribution. However, if you receive requests for information from people who would benefit from it, you may communicate to them Derek's evaluation as summarized in the attached statement.

David Selby
Executive Director
Derek Prince Ministries International

---

18. The full text of Prince's letter can be found at https://x.com/Torncurtainorg/status/1790840909602373742.

"A Statement from Derek Prince"

From various sources in various countries—as far apart as Israel and New Zealand—I have been receiving requests to explain my position in regard to Kansas City Fellowship (recently renamed the Vineyard Fellowship) and their related organization, "Grace Ministries." When I first began receiving these requests, I did not have enough information to offer a valid opinion. Since then, however, I have had firsthand exposure to the situation in Kansas City. I therefore offer the following brief outline.

The only time I can recall actually preaching in Kansas City Fellowship was at a Sunday morning service in 1986. I spoke on the deceptive tactics of witchcraft and warned against coming under its influence. I thought no more about this at the time, but someone who was present commented later that my warning was needed, but went unheeded.

[The statement that his warning went unheeded is contradicted by the fact that Michael Sullivant, one of KCF's principal leaders, asked someone who knew Derek Prince to tell him that "KCF had fully received his word."]

In 1988 Derek Prince Ministries conducted a seminar in a hotel in Kansas City on the theme of the "Last Days." In connection with this we offered a book containing the prophetic messages given at various times by Lance Lambert, David Minor and Rick Joyner. The prophecy by Rick Joyner was quoted by permission of a newsletter of James Robison. All such prophetic utterances must always be judged. So far as I was able to discern, there was nothing contrary to Scripture in any of those messages. I have never had any direct personal contact with David Minor or Rick Joyner.

Then in March 1990 our ministry conducted a second seminar in the same hotel in Kansas City. At this time I was asked by Mike Bickle to counsel with him and some of his leaders. I spent nearly three hours in discussion with them. I told them that I felt they were receiving and propagating error. Our meeting was conducted in a friendly spirit, but there has been no indication that they took heed to my warning.

Subsequent to this encounter, I studied a lengthy, detailed report entitled "Documentation of the Aberrant Practices and Teachings of Kansas City Fellowship," published by Rev. Ernest Gruen, pastor of Full Faith Church of Love, Kansas City. It is carefully documented, being based mainly on material published by Grace Ministries, or on transcripts of tapes made in Kansas City Fellowship, which they themselves circulated.

Very briefly, I can sum up the conclusions I have reached:

1. The material circulated by Kansas City Fellowship contains many statements which have no basis in Scripture and are frequently contrary to Scripture. Some of the purported "revelations" could be described as absurd and even blasphemous.

2. Some of the accounts of events and situations put out by Kansas City Fellowship have been proved to be untrue, but have never been retracted.

3. The overall effect of the material is to divert attention away from Jesus Christ and the Scriptures and towards subjective experiences and human personalities.

4. The circulation of the material from Kansas City Fellowship will inevitably expose the Body of Christ to much error and confusion.

These errors are deep-rooted and longstanding, dating at least as far back as 1983. If there is to be any effective remedy, it will require full and open acknowledgement, involving confession, repentance and renunciation. A mere change of label or of leadership is not sufficient.

These conclusions of mine are based on an examination of various doctrines and practices of Kansas City Fellowship. It is not my responsibility to judge the persons involved. Like all the rest of us, they will have to answer directly to Jesus Christ.

In presenting these conclusions, I believe I am fulfilling my obligation to many people in the U.S.A. and other nations who respect my judgment on biblical issues and respect my opinion. We are living in a period when it is more important than ever for all of us to cultivate "the love of the truth." (See 2 Thessalonians 2:9–12).

Those who feel they need further information about particular aspects of the doctrines and practices of Kansas City Fellowship should write directly to Rev. Ernest Gruen, Full Faith Church of Love, 6824 Lackman Road, Shawnee, KS, 66217, and request a copy of the 233-page report referred to above. I would suggest that they enclose a minimal contribution of $12 to cover the cost.

Signed,
Derek Prince

Conclusion

People are ambivalent in their opinions of so-called "rise and fall" narratives. They have something of a love-hate relationship with them. Most are reluctant to admit that they enjoy reading or listening to the demise or downfall of some person or institution, lest they be accused of having a warped personality that revels in the misfortune of others. And yet, like that devastating crash on the highway, it's hard not to look. I'm reminded of the reaction of many to Mike Cosper's immensely successful podcast, "The Rise and Fall of Mars Hill." When I asked people if they'd listened to it, a few said they had no interest in the ugly details of that particular church's implosion. But most looked forward to the next installment, admitting, with something of a blush of embarrassment, that it was too tempting to resist its appeal.

I suppose this book may well evoke much the same response. I can honestly say that I took no great pleasure in writing a book that chronicles one of the more sensational debacles among charismatic Christians. The fact that its focus is largely on one man whose friendship I once cherished made it even harder. It prompts me to wonder, is there nothing about the church of Jesus Christ that can "rise" without eventually "falling"?

Yes, there is. The church itself has certainly had its ups and downs over the past two thousand years, but we must never forget the promise of our Lord Jesus Christ who assured us that the "gates of hell shall not prevail against it" (Matt 16:18). Notwithstanding local church implosions and sexual scandals among its more prominent leaders, not to mention the financial mismanagement and pastoral bullying that have been so much in the news of late, the church itself will never "fall." So, how should we respond to the rise and fall of the Kansas City prophets? What is there for us to learn from their sad saga?

For one thing, all was not lost in their demise. The reality of God's supernatural activity and revelatory giftings cannot be ignored. Countless

Conclusion

thousands were greatly blessed by the ministries of even those figures who were guilty of sexual immorality. And we should never overlook the men and women of Kansas City who remained faithful to the Lord and their calling as stewards of his power and grace. In other words, not all of the so-called Kansas City prophets wandered from the path of obedience. One thinks immediately of godly men such as Michael Sullivant, James Goll, Noel Alexander, John Paul Jackson, and Jack Deere, just to mention a few.

If there is anything of supreme importance that we can take away from this all-too-familiar story, it is that *character always takes primacy over gifting*. That's actually become something of a cliché, but that doesn't mean it isn't still true. All too often we stand in amazement at the spiritual power of certain individuals that can so easily blind us to the deficiencies of their moral character. What we need isn't fewer people who operate in the prophetic and other of God's supernatural giftings, but more godly, mature, humble servants of the living God who have proven themselves good stewards of the Lord's manifold grace.

I have written this book with various fears that have lingered just beneath the surface of everything that was said. They repeatedly tugged at my soul with every story that I told. One such concern is that some will point to the "fall" of certain Kansas City prophets (or those who minister prophetically in countless other cities around the globe) to justify their embrace of cessationism. I pray fervently that no one will turn the final page on this volume more skeptical of the reality of prophetic ministry than they were when they first began to read. Notwithstanding the obvious failures of so many high-profile prophetic voices, I remain a firm and unshakeable advocate for the contemporary validity not only of the gift of prophecy but all the *charismata* we see in Scripture. I hope my fear will be laid permanently to rest and that this book will not be used to justify suspicion of what the Holy Spirit has done and is doing in the church of Jesus Christ.

Some undoubtedly will respond by saying, "Ah ha! I told you so! These charismatics are the very wolves in sheep's clothing that Jesus and the apostles warned us about." In case you hadn't noticed, religious wolves don the clothing of sheep in every facet of church life, both charismatic and cessationist. Be it a mega church or a mini church, as well as every size and sort in between, there will, sadly, always be those whose pride and ambition corrupt the blessings of God for personal gain. But there are far more, praise God, who labor quietly and humbly without fanfare, devoted not to their own glory and promotion but only that of Jesus Christ.

Concluding Principles, Lessons Learned, and Guidelines for the Future

So, what are the practical takeaways from the story of the Kansas City prophets? Aside from what we learn about either the reality or fabrication of alleged supernatural activity, what are the lessons that their rise and fall might teach us that will help us in the days ahead to be more discerning? Here are a few suggestions.

No individual, regardless of how impressive their personality, irrespective of the plethora of spiritual gifts they display, without taking into consideration the massive impact for good they may have had on your life, I say, no individual should be above criticism, accountability, or treated as untouchable.

No individual, male or female, no matter how much they stand to bless you and promote you and elevate your status in the church or ministry, no individual, I say, should be exempt from the biblical and moral standards to which all other Christians are accountable.

No professing believer, regardless of their global impact for good on the body of Christ, regardless of the high regard in which they are held and praised by respected leaders, no professing believer, I say, should be given a free pass to engage in behavior that would be regarded as inappropriate for all other average Christian men or women.

We must diligently resist the temptation to think that spiritual power is always a mark of spiritual maturity. When the fruit of the Spirit are made subordinate to the gifts of the Spirit, danger is ahead. As Tammy Woods has said in her testimony of being groomed and abused, "An abusive leader's gifting, popularity, or success is not Heaven's endorsement."

We must diligently resist the temptation to recoil from speaking truth to a fellow believer for fear that they are in a position to demote us, hinder our ministry, or tarnish our reputation.

We must never allow a person's past spiritual accomplishments, great and glorifying to God though they be, to paralyze and prevent us from placing their lives under the microscope of biblical evaluation. This is not to say we are to go about sniffing out sin where it may not exist, but simply that we are all susceptible to closing our eyes to it because of the undeniable good that a person may have achieved through the power of the Spirit.

We must never allow our commitment to biblical truth be diminished solely on the grounds that another professing believer has so horribly and wickedly twisted the Bible to justify their sinful abuse of another.

Conclusion

We must never be blinded to the sinful behavior of a professing believer because of their extraordinary insight into the meaning and application of biblical texts. The tendency in our hearts is to conclude from the latter that they would never be guilty of the former.

We must be alert to the governmental structures of either a church or para-church ministry that make it easy for the leader(s) of said ministry to escape the standards by which all others are held accountable. There must be some mechanism in place by which every person in any ministry can speak truth to power, without repercussion, no matter how comparatively weak or insignificant or far down on the "organizational chart" that person is perceived to be.

We must ensure that any believer in any ministry has some recourse by which he/she can speak truthfully to those who are over them in the Lord. No voice in the body of Christ should ever be silenced or muted without explicit biblical warrant.

There are times when certain friendships are so deep and intimate that we are blinded to the shortcomings of another. But a believer must never let a friend get away with what he calls out in an enemy.

We must be diligent to remember that not even the most outwardly godly and gifted leader is immune to sexual temptation. It is far too easy for us to be duped into thinking that a powerful minister may be tempted by money, fame, and prestige, but that he is above being guilty of sexual misconduct.

We must be constantly observant of the conduct not only of ourselves but also our spiritual role models and leaders. If we should see anything suspicious in the way he surrounds himself with members of the opposite sex, especially when they are considerably younger than he is, don't remain silent.

We must be quick to notice when a leader/pastor/minister spends unaccountable hours away from his family and coworkers, especially when that time is spent in the presence of members of the opposite sex. During my years as a senior pastor I would meet with all female staff members, be they nursery workers or ministry leaders, and encourage them to report anything unseemly in the actions or words of any male in the church. I assured them they would be believed and that they should never hesitate to come forward out of fear of being rejected as a troublemaker. Moreover, if they were ever made to feel uncomfortable by a joke, a gesture, or offhanded comment by a male coworker, they were encouraged to report this to me.

The day has come that no pastor or ministry leader should drive alone with a female other than his wife or relative. Call Uber or Lyft for them and pay for it yourself. Medical emergencies are an obvious exception to this otherwise rigid rule.

I pray that the many lessons we have learned along the way will serve to encourage biblically based prophetic ministry in the church. My heart also longs for greater facility in spiritual discernment so that we might more readily see the difference between sheep and goats, between those who serve themselves and those whose only desire is to exalt the name of Christ and to bless his people. If this aim has been achieved, if only in part, I will consider this book a success.

Appendix A

The Letter from Metro Vineyard Fellowship to the Executive Council of the AVC
July 4, 1996[1]

DEAR BROTHERS OF THE Executive Council:

It was a privilege to have three members of the executive council speaking at our conference last week. We want to thank John Wimber, Rich Nathan, and Tri Robinson for their significant contribution to us. We continue to appreciate the rich fellowship and spiritual covering of the Vineyard family, and pray that we might fully pursue the Lord together with you for many years to come. Our respect and affection are genuine.

The Reason for This Letter

We are in a dilemma that may impact our long-term relationship with you and thus need your wise input. Please forgive the length and formal approach of this letter, but we so highly value our relationship with you that we would rather err on over communication than run the risk of being misunderstood.

We are writing this letter to the Association of Vineyard Churches (AVC) Executive Council rather than to John Wimber personally because John informed us of his intention to resign from the Executive Council in the fall of 1996. He has repeatedly insisted on the Council's final authority

---

1. This letter was composed through the joint efforts of Mike Bickle, Sam Storms, and Michael Sullivant.

Appendix A

on all matters concerning the AVC. In honoring his request we are appealing to those who have the authority to direct the future of the Vineyard.

Last week we concluded our two conferences that spanned a period of nine days. This proved to be a spiritually significant time for me and our leadership team. The Lord confronted us in a sudden, yet dramatic, way concerning an issue of compromise grounded in the fear of man. This was surprising, yet unmistakable in its clarity and the power of conviction. I want to share some of what occurred, both in this letter as well as through a tape of one of my conference messages entitled, *MVF's Response to a Divided Heart*.

MVF's Prophetic History with the Vineyard

The Lord first spoke to me about the Vineyard through Bob Jones in January of 1984. He prophetically described a church movement that was approximately 35 miles southeast of Los Angeles that emphasized the "elementary principles of the kingdom of God." He proceeded to give several descriptions of the Vineyard which proved to be accurate.

Perhaps the most significant description was of the Lord's banner over the Vineyard, naming it "Worship and Compassion." We understood this to refer to the two general themes of the Spirit's activity in the Vineyard, which represents in our minds all the historic values and practices to which the Vineyard has been committed since its inception (which includes healing, evangelism, church planting, equipping, etc.). We recognize that this may sound overly simplistic, as if we were reducing everything in the Vineyard to merely two themes. However, this is not our intent. We have done this merely to facilitate communication throughout this letter.

The Lord had already revealed to us that He also raised a banner over our church and spiritually named it, "Prophetic and Intercession." Again, we are using these two terms to embody the particular values which became identified with our church in its early years (which includes holiness, fasting, end-time revival, simplified life-styles, etc.).

We will refer throughout this letter to "Worship and Compassion" and "Prophetic and Intercession" as the four *banner themes*. John Wimber himself has commonly used these four terms in precisely this way. We are not suggesting that every church has some mystical name or "banner theme" that they must try to decipher, nor are we suggesting that this is an established New Testament doctrine. This was a new concept to us and we still do not fully understand it.

The Letter from Metro Vineyard Fellowship to the Executive Council of the AVC

From the inception of our church we have experienced an unusual grace and activity of the Holy Spirit with regard to these two themes of *prophetic and intercession*, as the Vineyard movement has in the areas of *worship and compassion*. For example, the Lord gave our leadership team grace to intercede for revival three hours every night during our first two years and then six hours daily for an additional five years. To this day, we continue to meet three times daily, three days a week.

The Lord spoke to our leadership team during these early years that we would one day cross-pollinate with a movement named "Worship and Compassion." We believed that God's purpose was to fully integrate the four banner themes of "Worship and Compassion" and "Prophetic and Intercession." The Lord spoke this to us in January of 1984. The first Vineyard conference we attended was six months later in June, where John Wimber emphasized *worship and compassion* and the theology of the Kingdom of God. The conference had a profound impact on our church.

Our leadership team acknowledged that this might in fact be the group that we were praying to meet. The Lord confirmed to us numerous times that this was indeed the movement with which we would one day cross-pollinate. We intermittently prayed for the Vineyard over the next three and a half years, believing that God had appointed a specific time when we would officially meet and join by divine orchestration.

In October of 1987 Bob Jones received a dramatic prophecy by the audible voice of the Lord, saying that John Wimber would call me three months later in January, 1988. This would begin a strategic joining of the two ministries. You can imagine how I felt in January when I received John's phone call (we had met once in 1985). John explained how the Lord spoke to him directly to invite me to speak to his entire staff the following week at their annual retreat. I spoke on subjects related to the *prophetic and intercession*.

Six months passed without any communication between John and myself. Then, on June 5th, 1988, Bob said he again had heard the audible voice of the Lord regarding our involvement with the Vineyard. The Lord told Bob that John would call me within the week because the Lord wanted to open to me a large door to the Vineyard so that our message of the "Prophetic and Intercession" could be heard by 50,000 people in the Vineyard and 1,000,000 people worldwide. These words were also heard by many of our leadership team at that time.

The next week, John called just as the Lord told Bob he would. When I asked John how large the Vineyard was, he said it was about 50,000 people. I then asked how many people he had impacted world-wide. He said he had no way of knowing for sure, but that several people had estimated it to be approximately 1,000,000. I had no doubt as to the accuracy of John's response, having heard Bob speak those precise numbers just one week earlier.

During that conversation, John invited me to be with him on several occasions, which was the beginning of the Lord's opening to me a large door to the Vineyard, even as Bob had prophesied the week before. Because of the way these two appointments (January and June of 1988) with John were divinely announced and arranged, I knew it was God's purpose that I proclaim the two banner themes of the *prophetic and intercession*. Of course, there are many sub-themes related to these two, all of which embody a variety of values and practices.

Six months later, in December, 1988, Paul Cain had his first visit with John Wimber. It was asked if there might be a sign that would attend Paul's visit. Paul prophesied two earthquakes, one local, to occur on the day of his arrival, and one international (Soviet Armenia), to occur on the day of his departure. This story has been well-documented in *Equipping the Saints*, January, 1990. These earthquakes were natural events that contained prophetic signs. This is admittedly rare, but such natural phenomena being used by God as prophetic signs is scriptural. The message we clearly understood (and spoke on several occasions) was that as there would be two earthquakes in the natural, one local and one international, so also there would be local and international earthquakes in the spiritual. We believed that when "Compassion and Worship" embraced (cross-pollinated with) "Prophetic and Intercession" that there would come some disruption, as in an earthquake, both locally and internationally among personalities and certain structures in the Kingdom of God. Because of the spiritual impact of these four banner themes merging, Satan would attack in an attempt to shake this union.

It is important now that we *not* continue to be shaken by the "spiritual earthquake" caused by the union of these four banner themes. I confess that I have been shaken and have drawn back to some degree due to these pressures (e.g., criticism, lies, miscommunication, broken relationships, financial loss, etc.). However, last week I repented of my fear and the compromise it had produced.

The Four Reasons We Joined the AVC

We joined the Vineyard for four reasons. First, we felt a clear divine call reaching back to January of 1984 when Bob Jones first spoke about a movement called "Worship and Compassion." Second, we were excited about the greater effectiveness of these four banner themes being deeply integrated. Third, we recognized our need for accountability and covering as well as the benefits of being part of a spiritual family of like mind. Fourth, we felt joined to John Wimber personally. This joining was grounded in deep affection, respect, along with gratitude for all he was then doing for us in the prophetic controversy that began in January, 1990.

Contrary to widespread perception, we did not join the Vineyard to seek refuge in the midst of the prophetic controversy. It is true that we needed this spiritual covering. While visiting our church in February of 1990, John Wimber committed to us that he would provide spiritual covering and see the controversy to its end whether or not we ever joined the AVC. Our continued gratitude during the next four months undoubtedly influenced our decision to join in May of 1990. But it was gratitude for protection that was already in place as opposed to joining in order to secure that protection. That gratitude extends to this very day.

We regularly attended Vineyard conferences from 1984–1988. During 1989–91 I traveled extensively with John Wimber and was continually instructed and impacted by the Vineyard values. During this season we rejoiced in the opportunity to grow more deeply in the values and practices related to the banner themes of *worship and compassion*. The Vineyard leadership also repeatedly spoke publicly their affirmation of the values and practices related to the banner themes of *prophetic and intercession*.

We perceived that we mutually impacted each other. For example, we grew to value the emphasis of equipping weak people "now" to do the work of the ministry. We deeply cherish seeing common people confidently doing the works of Jesus in spite of their on-going struggle with immaturity. I enjoy the focus on people in the pew instead of preachers on the platform. I love the stability of an evangelical approach to the interpretation of Scripture (the majority of our pastoral staff were trained in evangelical seminaries). We love the emphasis on intimacy in worship, church planting, and evangelism. I have personally planted nine churches and have influenced a number of other church plants by others through the years.

Whereas I believe such issues must be at the forefront of the Vineyard leadership, the prophetic and intercession help to create an atmosphere of wholeheartedness that enhances spiritual motivation. As you well know, the plan to obey the great commission is most effective in relation to a Spirit-empowered environment of passionate believers who are diligently seeking the Lord.

When I traveled with John in 1989–91, I was thrilled as I heard all four banner themes being proclaimed. There were numerous large conferences that focused on topics such as equipping the saints for healing ministry, revival fire, evangelism, holiness, the prophetic, worship, as well as church planting strategies. On several occasions I heard prominent Vineyard leaders proclaim both in public and private the call to revival and intercession, the necessity of the prophetic, and the importance of simplified lifestyles out of compassion for the poor.

In August, 1989, at the international Vineyard pastors conference in Denver, we understood John Wimber to say that "Vineyard I" was dead and that "Vineyard II" was now beginning. It was clear that "Vineyard II" represented the merging of all four banner themes. We rejoiced as we joined the AVC, believing that each of these themes would now be essential in the Vineyard as well as a basis of our on-going relationship with you. It was an exciting season of mutual impact and appreciation.

MVF Under Divine Discipline

The season changed suddenly in 1990 as the Lord began to discipline us for spiritual pride, correct our abuses in the prophetic ministry, and remove a residue of legalism that had crept into our foundation. This was a painful and humiliating time in our lives, for which we still feel a degree of embarrassment. However, we feel it is a necessary part of our testimony that must be shared. We believe that while under your spiritual authority you skillfully helped us to correct these errors. You provided a safe family for us in the midst of significant controversy and attack. We are deeply indebted to John Wimber personally and to others in the Vineyard leadership who bore significant reproach because of our inclusion in the Vineyard family. I could never do justice in expressing the gratitude and love I feel for the Vineyard family. We simply could not have made it without you.

We earnestly sought to accept the discipline of the Lord and to live under its restraints, no matter how sorrowful they were at the time. We knew they would yield the fruit of righteousness in due time. When John spoke at our church in the summer of 1994, he pronounced his blessing over us saying that the Vineyard leadership had given him good reports about the necessary changes that had occurred at MVF. John then added that, from his own observations, he was delighted with the spiritual changes in our leadership team and asserted that we were a Vineyard church of which he could be proud.

In our conference last week, John publicly reaffirmed that he saw no indications of a religious spirit anywhere in our midst. He has encouraged me that the Vineyard leadership has seen good fruit at MVF. John's oft repeated words both privately and publicly over the last two years have been a source of encouragement to us at MVF.

Our Dilemma

Having said all this, we must acknowledge that our leadership team is facing a growing dilemma. We seem to be hearing two differing voices coming from the leadership of the Vineyard. We are open to the suggestion that we have simply misunderstood. Nevertheless, it has created a dilemma for us that we want to resolve as soon as possible.

Both voices seem to be heard privately and publicly. One voice assures us that the Vineyard is seeking the fulness of the Spirit's activity, which would give expression to those values and practices represented by the complete merging of the banner themes of *worship, compassion, prophetic, and intercession*. The other voice highlights *worship and compassion* but minimizes, and sometimes even opposes, the values represented by the *prophetic and intercession*. When we joined the Vineyard in May of 1990 all four of these banner themes were being actively promoted. We have patiently watched the diminishing emphasis on the *prophetic and intercession*. But we are given just enough hope in both public and private statements by Vineyard leaders that eventually all the activities represented by the *prophetic and intercession* will one day be in place.

Our immediate response has been to turn this concern into prayer for God's intervention while we wait. The Vineyard that we joined seemed to be enthusiastic about all four of these truths. We believe the Vineyard is indeed called to trumpet all four. I have been content to wait patiently for God's perfect timing, especially since I was the one under divine discipline whom you so graciously embraced. I felt the only reasonable thing for me to do was to take my seat towards the back of the table. However, as a result of what transpired at our conference, I believe the time has come for me to speak. As I stated earlier, I now believe that what I thought was patience and humility in not responding to the two voices was in fact compromise rooted in the fear of man. This is a sudden, but I believe divinely orchestrated, turn of events for me and our leadership team.

Simply put, our immediate dilemma is this. The Lord will no longer allow me to ignore the absence of emphasis on the values and practices represented by the banner themes *prophetic and intercession* in our relationship to the Vineyard. We must be joined in a partnership to those who will passionately proclaim all four of these truths.

Appendix A

A Crucial Two-Fold Tension

We believe that perilous times are going to increase throughout the world. God's answer is Spirit-empowered prophetic churches that fearlessly speak the mind of the Lord with both compassion and conviction, confirmed with signs and wonders that release the oppressed. Satan's assault on the human race will never be effectively challenged by the church in its present condition. The body of Christ desperately needs a revival of unprecedented proportions. We must seek to fully embrace *all* the essential truths revealed in the New Testament church. To properly equip the saints for this revival, we must walk out a two-fold tension.

First, as weak vessels we must *now* proclaim with confidence the kingdom of God. We believe it is wrong to wait until we are specially qualified or spiritually mature before we begin to proclaim the kingdom to others. We are called and qualified to proclaim this message from the day we are born again. We must not despise the day of small beginnings. We must seek to fully obey the great commission *now*.

Secondly, and at the same time, we must be keenly aware that there is a much greater demonstration of the Spirit's power available to those who earnestly seek God's face. This calls for intensive intercession, regular fasting, together with grace empowered holiness and heartfelt repentance. There are certain dimensions of God's power that *He will not release apart from this kind of intensive, focused, wholehearted seeking of the Lord.*

I believe that a multitude of churches will embrace this tension as men and women begin to trumpet the call and model it in a practical way. I believe the Vineyard is one of many ministries that God has invited to issue this proclamation. This will require wise and mature leadership that is grateful for the present activity of the Spirit, yet is also desperate to seek for the fulness that is still to come. Such prophetic churches are vitally needed to meet the present crisis.

If as leaders we are content with the state of the church, we will be ineffective in equipping others to wholeheartedly seek God for His fulness. I do not claim to understand what the fulness of God looks like. I do know it is a church that will have greater power, purity, and unity than did the early church. There is a certain anger that is aroused in church leadership by such a message, for it boldly confronts the carnality and exposes the lack of fruitfulness in those who tell their flock, "all is well." It calls for men and women who admit their leadership is in need of personal reform that only greater empowerment from on high can produce. I must admit this need in my own life and ministry.

We as leaders have no other option but to embrace prayer with fasting as an essential part of our lifestyles. This is costly to each of us personally and often unsettling to certain members of our congregations. This will cause no small turbulence even if proclaimed with tenderness, meekness, and tears, in part because of the spirit of antichrist that powerfully opposes God's last days work which began on the day of Pentecost (1 Tim 4:1–3; 2 Tim 3:1–9).

What Are We to Trumpet?

We will continue to energetically emphasize the values and practices that we have learned in a greater way from our relationship in the Vineyard family. We are keenly aware of our debt to you in this regard.

We also feel equally compelled to trumpet aloud those values that have been an essential part of the foundation of this church from its inception. They are as follows:

(1) *Prophetic.* We believe the Vineyard should be a safe place for prophetic ministry. In calling for a renewed commitment to the prophetic, we are in no way ignoring our past mistakes. We hope and pray that we have learned from them. But we do not believe the answer to such mistakes is rejection or disuse of the prophetic. Rather, we must strive for proper use of the prophetic as we establish a biblical model for its exercise in the body of Christ. After all, Paul himself commanded the early church to earnestly desire the prophetic gift (1 Cor 12:31; 14:1, 31, 39).

(2) *Intercession.* It is our firm conviction that intercessory prayer and regular fasting are crucial to the greater success of God's purposes on earth. We believe this calls for intensive, corporate prayer meetings in which we seek God for revival and a great harvest of souls. Our desire is to pursue and proclaim, both locally and abroad, the necessity of persevering prayer. This commitment is fueled by our belief that although there is a measure of power released on our current endeavors to do the work of the kingdom, we believe there is a significantly greater demonstration of divine power that will *only* come with diligent prayer and fasting which were common among NT church leadership (Acts 13:2–3; 14:23; see also Matt 17:21; 2 Cor 6:5; 11:27; Isa 30:18).

This approach to diligent intercession will be difficult to sustain without the hope and strengthening of heart supplied by the prophetic ministry. When the prophetic is set in divine order it will prove to be an essential dimension for equipping the church in earnest intercession for the greater outpouring of the Spirit. When the prophetic voice is removed, hope and encouragement for the intercessors is significantly minimized. We believe that consistent intercession is substantially fueled by prophetic revelation.

We currently have plans to strengthen our intercession for revival that will include regular all night prayer watches with regularly scheduled days set aside for corporate fasting. We greatly value the prophetic activity which has convinced us to seek God intensely for an unprecedented revival in the church throughout the world in this generation.

We want to make it clear that we reject all the unorthodox extremes of what has come to be known as "The Latter Rain Movement." The abuses of that movement were ultimately damaging to God's larger purposes for the body of Christ. We repudiate all attempts to identify us with those abuses.

(3) *Grace-Empowered Holiness.* We must address the prevailing issues of compromise and carnality in the church today. This will require leaders who are prepared to pay the price of angry members who withdraw their financial support and assail the church for taking such a stand. We believe that wholehearted, costly obedience can be proclaimed as God's norm without leading people into spiritual pride and legalism.

True holiness is pre-eminently expressed in fulfillment of the first and great commandment to be whole-hearted lovers of God, which invariably overflows in compassionate love for people (Matt 22:36–40). This concept is what I mean by the oft-repeated phrase "Passion for Jesus." My first calling is to equip believers so that the first commandment might be restored to first place in their lives.

We reject the Pelagian heresy of sinless perfection which continues to resurface in church history in a variety of differing forms. We also reject the gnostic heresies that foster dualism and other forms of hyper-spirituality. We reject the idea that holiness consists solely of abstaining from evil. It also entails the aggressive pursuit in God's grace of what is good and right. True holiness is expressed not only in purity of heart but also in social justice, emotional wholeness, healthy inter-personal relationships, integrity of speech, the sanctity of marriage, financial honesty, zeal for good works energized by a spirit of servanthood, etc.

We recognize the vital distinction between immaturity and rebellion. We believe that God blesses and uses immature believers whose hearts are sincere for the Lord. However, we also believe that there is a sphere of power and blessing that is entrusted to those who walk in mature obedience. We reject the growing sentiment in the body of Christ that God does not manifest a greater measure of blessing to those who diligently seek Him (John 14:23; 15:14).

(4) *Sacrificial Giving.* Isaiah 58:6–12 makes it clear that the *only* context in which God's fulness (as described in this passage) can be confidently expected is that of sacrificial giving to the poor. This is a non-negotiable divine requirement for the full blessing of God. That we can have a measure of effectiveness without it is evidenced by the growth of the church in the western world. But God's heart is deeply satisfied with co-workers who seek unity with His purpose for the poor (Luke 4:18; Isa 61:1).

Merely giving occasional offerings to the poor in a way that never really costs us in a personal way is precisely the leadership issue that Jesus was addressing with the Pharisees in Luke 21:1–4. Jesus referred to the "surplus" of the Pharisees in this passage, the giving of which cost them nothing in reality. The widow, on the other hand, gave out of her deep compassion and commitment. We believe God will release a distinctively greater degree of power to impact people as we come into unity with God's heart for the poor. In most cases this genuine unity will be reflected in simplified lifestyles. How can we be in heartfelt unity with God in this matter without it significantly impacting how we live and spend money?

We believe that God's leaders must set the example for the church in this matter of *taking less to give more.* Of course, no man can tell others how to specifically administer this in their own lives. Any attempt to do so will undoubtedly result in control and legalism. Whereas the call to sacrificial giving is inescapably clear, the personal application must be left to each individual before the Lord. Not all of God's people are called to simple lifestyles (the word "simple" itself being relative in every culture). Nevertheless, Isa 58:6–12 issues a crucial call that we believe is relevant to the western church to simplify in some measure out of compassion for the poor of the earth. The only request the Jerusalem apostles made of Paul when they consulted with him was to remember the poor, something to which he had already committed himself (Gal 2:10).

Jesus said that one of the root problems among the Pharisees was their love of money (Luke 16:14–15). The love of money is often rooted in fear. To expose this fear, or even to gently and tenderly confront it, will undoubtedly cause substantial conflict in our day even as it did in His day. I do not have the wisdom necessary to proclaim this truth in the most effective way. I am only suggesting that we must at least begin to trumpet this call as we seek God's guidance on how to apply it to our own personal lives and ministries.

We do not believe that poverty is a virtue or blessing, but rather a curse. We are against the spirit of poverty. We are merely seeking to embrace the admonition that Paul gave Timothy to be well-content with food and clothing (1 Tim 6:8).

Our desire is to see a church that is equipping God's people for the work of ministry, led by men and women who have confronted in their own hearts the fears related to the loss of personal comfort and convenience that inevitably come with prayer, fasting, and sacrificial giving to the poor. We believe the Vineyard is filled with men and women who are touched by this principle. Indeed, we have much to learn from those who are doing it more effectively than we at MVF (we were both inspired and challenged by the recent extravagant offering for the poor at the Anaheim Vineyard). But we must lift our voice together with many other ministries to call the church in the western world to a lifestyle that is consistent with God's heart for the poor of the earth.

Our Intentions

We fully intend to continue emphasizing all that is encompassed by the historic banner themes of the Vineyard (*worship and compassion*). We are fully committed to teaching and preaching the Word of God from an evangelical perspective that is grounded in the historical-grammatical interpretation of the text.

But we are no less committed to proclaiming the values and practices represented by the banner themes of the *prophetic and intercession*. This includes proclaiming, promoting, and equipping the saints to seek God for an unprecedented harvest of souls and a victorious (though not perfect) end-time church. This further entails the necessity of devotion to corporate intercession, the value of fasting, prophetic ministry, and simplified lifestyles borne of a compassion for the lost and poor of the earth (something quite contrary to the American mindset of taking and keeping all one can get).

We also intend to affirm the importance of the five ascension-gift ministries of Ephesians 4:11 (apostles, prophets, evangelists, pastors, teachers) as essential to the church operating in divine order and fulness. We do not think it is of primary importance whether they are referred to as ministry offices or ministry functions as long as they are recognized, honored, valued, and reproduced in others.

The Need for Courage

We believe that the church today desperately needs leaders who fearlessly obey God regardless of the cost. Such commitment from leaders with public visibility will impact and embolden others to take a similar stand. Courage begets courage and fear begets fear. Whereas we need to be "wise as serpents," we must reject that form of caution which is rooted in the fear of losing respectability. This is a painful stigma for any of God's servants to bear. However, the manifestation of God's power and presence will always bring such a stigma, which God in turn uses to protect His servants from pride (2 Cor 12:1–10).

The voices arrayed against us will never subside. The stigma of the anointing may cost us the endorsement of respected leaders in the conservative evangelical community. But if obtaining their approval becomes of paramount importance to us, it will cloud our discernment and lead us to become hesitant or perhaps even disobey God's invitation to take the next step in His plan. In a time of transition, the Lord told Joshua to be strong and courageous, an exhortation found repeatedly in Scripture (Josh 1:6–9). As leaders we must fearlessly and courageously do all that God has commanded.

We do not believe that the Lord called the Vineyard to be just another conservative denomination (even should it have the added dimension of the Spirit's supernatural ministry). A large number of Vineyard pastors came out of just such a context and have no desire to build another one. The Lord has rebuked me personally in these past two weeks for yielding to the pressure of wanting the respectability that comes from being regarded as conservative and orthodox. I am deeply committed to being orthodox according to *scriptural* standards. But I have put too much value in appearing orthodox by *human* standards. I believe the church in the western world, including the Vineyard, is continually faced with the same temptation. *We must not yield to it.* The only hope for countless believers is a multitude of courageous prophetic churches filled with the power of God. We cut off the blessing of God to them when we seek for respectability in leadership.

I am a weak man who needs the grace and strength that come from mutual fellowship with others who are likewise committed to fearless obedience irrespective of personal cost. I need your help because I am not courageous by nature. Will you lead us and others by setting the example we so desperately need? I was sorely tempted last week to justify myself on each occasion that I was convicted by the prophetic word. My vested interests were being challenged by these corrections. I humbly ask you to resist the natural temptation to dismiss such exhortations.

I acknowledge that I have no official position within the AVC. Thus, I run the risk of appearing presumptuous in speaking so boldly. However, I feel compelled by my fear of the Lord and my love for the Vineyard to tenderly appeal to you as my spiritual authority and dear brothers. I in no way attribute to your leadership my previous silence. It was solely the result of my weakness and failure. I need your inspiration in order to be fearless and to seek God wholeheartedly for His fulness without regard for the reproach it will inevitably bring.

Toronto: Three Unresolved Issues

In order for our leadership team to be at peace regarding how the AVC Board relates to what God has done in Toronto, there are three issues that need to be addressed. We can only resolve these issues with assurance that you have sought the Lord diligently concerning each one of them. We have a conviction that they are of such grave importance to the Lord that they would obviously require perhaps several seasons set apart for prayer and fasting by the Board, if not the entire Vineyard movement. What issues can be of more importance to spiritual overseers than these? Surely the Executive Council has sought the Lord in this way. Please share even a few of the details with us.

The first issue on which we are unsettled is whether or not the Holy Spirit is fully satisfied with the way in which this divine visitation was governed by the AVC Board. God gave the Vineyard movement in its early years a sovereign visitation of the Holy Spirit through John Wimber's ministry. The impact was felt by many churches throughout the western world. What a great privilege for a movement to have this in its history. Beginning in Toronto in January, 1994, God gave the AVC spiritual government over what became another sovereign move of the Spirit which had significant global influence. We all understand how precious a stewardship such as this is to the Holy Spirit. We are also aware of how rare it is for one movement to have a second visitation of the Spirit in such a short period of time. Therefore, the question is whether or not the AVC leadership has been sufficiently diligent to discover if there are any remaining issues over which the Holy Spirit is grieved pertaining to the way you governed this holy move of God.

God is jealous that the Vineyard movement be led in a way that continually attracts the Third Person of the Trinity regardless of whom it may offend. Such courageous leadership has been a hallmark of the Vineyard throughout its history. We know that you were mindful of the gravity of relating governmentally to the Toronto Blessing. We all understand that we must be careful to avoid offending the Holy Spirit. It is a precious thing to have the assurance of the Holy Spirit's pleasure in how we received Him in our midst.

Second, is it possible that the Lord might have more to say to the Vineyard concerning the process in which Toronto was disengaged from the AVC? Rarely can such a complicated matter occur without some errors in due process on the part of everyone involved. We know that you have already acknowledged some errors in this regard. However, does the AVC board have sufficient information from the Lord concerning His evaluation of the manner in which this anointed servant was treated? We are very sympathetic to the complexities of fully discerning all the issues. This requires you to carefully and judiciously assess and gently correct any errors you may yet discover. I urge you not to close the books on this matter too hastily. It would be prudent to ask the Lord if there are any lingering issues that call for more specific repentance to the Arnotts.

Third, although we admit that wisdom is rare, courage is in even shorter supply and is no less precious in the sight of God. I acknowledge that there was undeniably a need for some adjustments to be made in the pastoral oversight of the renewal. Addressing the issues pertaining to pastoral wisdom is the inescapable burden and responsibility of those with spiritual authority. We honor you for accepting this task.

Whereas wisdom is essential, an equally crucial quality in times of renewal is the courage not to yield to the fear of man in order to avoid the "stigma" that the anointing invariably brings. Few people resist compromising under such pressure. We believe John and Carol Arnott displayed uncommon courage and genuine godliness in the face of significant public reproach.

During my repentance last week, the Lord alerted me to His grief over the appalling silence of many pastors in failing to lift their voice on John Arnott's behalf, largely from fear of what it might cost in terms of relationships and influence. My plan is to write John Arnott and confess to him my silence at a time when he needed public support. Whereas I made a number of appeals on John's behalf to several leaders in the Vineyard, for fear of the consequences I failed to speak loudly and clearly enough to the entire Vineyard leadership. I must now rectify this in the fear of God. Please hear my heart and feel my love for you.

I am not suggesting that all of the concerns on how to wisely administrate the renewal are invalid, but only that we must equally honor and protect such a man. Therefore, the final unresolved issue to us is the need to honor the Arnotts for their courage notwithstanding any mistakes they may have made in pastoring the renewal.

In summary, we believe it is possible that God would grant additional and specific information in all three of these areas. All such information that you would humbly receive from the Lord would surely result in greater cleansing and healing within the Vineyard movement. This is the best context for us to seek the Lord for yet a third visitation of the Holy Spirit, which is the very thing we desire to do together with you. But how could we with confidence ask for the Spirit's visitation without having the assurance that He is satisfied on these issues. If we would seek the Lord with prayer and fasting, He may well provide us with surprising answers to these questions that I believe are not yet fully resolved in the Spirit.

Our Request of You

(1) *A meeting.* We are asking for a face-to-face meeting with either the entire board or the executive council. We believe the issues are serious enough to warrant considerable discussion. We are open to adjustment in our style, as well as the application of anything we have said, but we will not in any way compromise on the mandate given us by the Lord in our early years. The timing and location of this meeting are in your hands. However, we do believe that this should be done sooner than later.

(2) *Assurance of full participation.* Our heartfelt conviction is that the agenda we have outlined in this letter is God's purpose not only for MVF in particular but for the entire Vineyard in general. We are not aware that we are asking you to accept anything that was not normative for NT leadership. If we are, we want understanding and invite your correction. This letter was not written with glibness but with a certain anguish and trembling in presenting this to men of your stature. Before undertaking this task, our entire pastoral team joined in

a time of prayer and fasting for God to grant us favor in your hearts. We realize that this letter will become a standard of judgment for our church before God and men all the days of our lives. Therefore, we endeavored to write it *very carefully as before the eyes of the Lord.*

We need to know if we can pursue this agenda and still be welcome in the Vineyard family. Is the Vineyard leadership wholeheartedly committed to the *prophetic and intercession*, no less than to *worship and compassion*? Did "Vineyard I" ever truly die, or has it been resuscitated? Or are we simply being impatient? If the "Vineyard II" exists, how is it to be defined and what may we expect of it?

Will the Vineyard unashamedly endorse and pursue these values, or merely tolerate those who do? We refuse to be rebellious or insubordinate. Therefore, we need a clear statement from you. Can we in full submission to your authority pursue all four of the banner themes (worship, compassion, prophetic, intercession) to which God has called the Vineyard? We would find it difficult to remain in the Vineyard if the leadership is not unified in its promotion of all these values and practices. We desperately want to stay in the Vineyard, but only if there is a consistent and unified voice coming from the leadership, both in private and public. To proclaim these themes without your full partnership would force us to do it in rebellion to our spiritual authority, something we would never do.

(3) *Blessing on a Personal Letter.* We will soon fax to Todd Hunter a copy of our personal statement of apology and repentance to John Arnott. We are asking for your blessing and approval before we send it to him, since it will have implications for you. We plan to honor you for the wisdom you contributed to him, but we want to acknowledge our error in not more boldly honoring him for his courage and godliness.

(4) *A unified communication.* In the event that you perceive the need to make any public statement about the relationship of AVC to Metro Vineyard, we believe it would be wise for that communique to be a joint effort. We love and honor the Vineyard leadership and would knowingly do nothing to undermine or harm this movement that is so precious to the Lord. If the Executive Council chooses not to embrace and endorse the values articulated in this letter, we would leave broken-hearted, yet peacefully and with tremendous love and gratitude for all that you have done for us through the years. You can be assured of our godly response and good will in the event that our ministries go in two different directions. We desire to bless every part

Appendix A

of the body of Christ that preaches Jesus regardless of whether or not they proclaim the banner themes discussed in this letter. We may not be able to work closely with them, but we love and bless them all.

Again, forgive us for the length of this letter. We have a great desire to avoid any misunderstanding or miscommunication that would harm relationships in the body of Christ. We desperately want to stay in the Vineyard if it would fearlessly proclaim all four banner themes of *worship, compassion, prophetic and intercession.*

With genuine affection and deepest respect,

Mike Bickle
On behalf of the MVF Pastoral Team

In the aftermath of the previous letter and our joint conference on July 31, we sent the following document to the Executive Council.

Dear Brothers:
I'm writing to clarify some of the things we sought to communicate during our arbitration meeting of July 31, 1996, and to give an explanation of the underlying issues behind our 14-page letter of July 4, 1996. The nature of that meeting made effective communication difficult for all of us involved. We also believe that you do not fully understand some of the fundamental reasons behind our 14-page letter.

We care deeply about our friendship with you and many others within the Vineyard family. Therefore we would like to clarify some of the things that we intended to say. We are not seeking an opportunity for ministry within the Vineyard nor your endorsement of any kind. We write simply because we care about what you think and value our relationship with you. In other words, we love you and want the opportunity for future relationship. We continue to maintain that Vineyard pastors are among God's choice men in the earth. We sincerely enjoy them and feel significant unity of vision and values with many of them.

We do not want to address all the issues discussed in the arbitration meeting, but will focus on the ones that have been distorted in the process of being re-communicated. We take some responsibility for not making ourselves more clear and we acknowledge how difficult it may have been for you to fully hear and understand our true intentions.

First, our intention in speaking our concerns to you in that meeting was to be genuinely helpful. We desired to be faithful in pointing out what we believed were "blind spots" in the context of our spiritual family. We continue to care deeply about the Vineyard family. Our desire has never been to make a "power move," as has been suggested by some. Neither was our intention to give some "railing judgment" or to vent our emotions as we left the Vineyard. We do not believe our actions were disloyal. Our desire was to express our true commitment to the spiritual family in which God had placed us.

We continue to believe that some of the things we said could be helpful to you. We committed not to make known our concerns in a widespread way. We still intend to keep this commitment. However, you have made public several of the things that we spoke to you in private. That in itself is not a problem, except that some of the Vineyard leadership have not accurately communicated our intentions. Even in regard to the 14-page letter, we refused to release it even among our own elders until it was circulated widely by the Vineyard.

The only issues from the arbitration meeting we will address in this letter are the "inaccuracies" being communicated by some in the Vineyard leadership. Again, we understand how easy it is to "sincerely misrepresent" the things we spoke due to our inability to adequately speak our intentions and your inability to adequately hear and re-tell them.

This is not an accusation but a clarification motivated by our desire to continue in friendship with you. Please forgive us for any confusion we may have created by our lack of clear communication during or after the July 31 meeting. Therefore, we ask you to patiently bear with us as we restate a few of the things originally intended by our team.

Spiritual Slumber

One of the main issues that the Lord confronted in our leadership team last summer was a spirit of slumber. We understand this to include such things as a lack of the spirit of prayer and urgency for a life of extravagant and careful obedience. Our team met on several occasions to discuss the implications of this for us personally. We understand that it may take an extended period of time to discern and correct the full scope of this problem in our local church leadership. We also feel that this spiritual slumber is a main problem in the larger body of Christ in our nation. We saw aspects of this also manifest in some of the Vineyard leadership. This was not meant as some special rebuke but was an appeal to take pains to fully discern and correct this problem that is widespread in the western church.

If we all work on this problem together, I think we can be more effective in overcoming it. Some of the Vineyard leaders have been offended by this appeal. This was never our intention. We sought to make as clear as possible that this is a common problem that we are also in need of correcting, even to this day.

The distortion that we ask you to correct is that this was a special rebuke aimed specifically at the Vineyard instead of a general evaluation of a common need in the larger church. A primary reason for us even bringing it up was to establish a context for the intensity of our 14-page letter in July. We do feel strongly that the "times" are such that the only appropriate response to God is one of intensive, wholehearted seeking of God's face. This will require significant personal sacrifice in areas relating to regular prayer and fasting, etc.

The Removal of the Lampstand

We tried to state clearly that we were appealing to a concept that may have been originally used in the scriptures in a slightly different way. This warning of losing "the lampstand" was originally given by Jesus to the church in Ephesus (Rev 2:5). I don't believe it refers to the church no longer existing, but rather speaks to the unique privilege of the church in Ephesus being a "genetic setting" ministry throughout all Asia in that generation. That was an extraordinary grace that rested on the church of Ephesus. The Vineyard, likewise, has been used of God in a special way in regard to setting the "spiritual genetics" of numerous churches. Many non-Vineyard churches in the western world have applied Vineyard values and practices in an earnest and effective way. In this sense, the Vineyard has been a "genetic setting" movement. This is a privilege that most ministries never enjoy.

I believe it is possible for this dimension of the grace of God to continue even in light of John Wimber's changing role. It is obvious to me that God has used John significantly in allowing the Vineyard to be a "genetic setting" ministry. However, this lampstand aspect of the Vineyard may well continue with the same intensity through others.

The question that has been raised by some is whether this will be true after John's resignation. I believe it is possible for God to continue to use the Vineyard in this way. However, in our opinion this will occur only if the Vineyard leadership wholeheartedly embraces the values and practices set forth in our 14-page letter. Is it reasonable to expect such a unique privilege in the grace of God to continue apart from great earnestness for God and much divine help?

The Letter from Metro Vineyard Fellowship to the Executive Council of the AVC

It was never our intent at the July meeting to suggest in any way that the Vineyard movement will cease to exist. I publicly bless and fervently ask God for a mighty blessing on the Vineyard in virtually every conference where I have ministered since last summer. I have much joy and desire in your blessing as a movement.

Lack of Wisdom

Some have written that we said the Vineyard lacked wisdom. Actually, we stressed exactly the opposite. We believe that some of the Vineyard leadership has excellent wisdom. I hope that is clear.

MVF's (MCF's) Sudden Change of Position

This has been greatly misunderstood and innocently miscommunicated. Over the last 7-8 years, I have clearly recognized four distinct groups within the overall governmental leadership of the Vineyard.

First, I think of John Wimber personally. Second, there is the U.S. national board. Third, I see the international leaders in places like Canada, U.K., Europe, South Africa etc. Fourth, there are the 2-3 voices that rise to the top of the U.S. board which unofficially steer many decisions. These unofficial voices seem to change every several years.

I have been enthusiastic about the first three groups from the beginning. I continue to believe in them and could easily follow their leadership even today. My many statements of personal commitment to the Vineyard have always referred to these first three groups. I have been aware of the fourth group and the fact that the people in it change somewhat regularly. On several occasions, I have been in silent disagreement with them. I would take my concern only to God and not to anyone else in the Vineyard nor even to my own leadership team in Kansas City. This is a vital spiritual principle.

I have taught this principle for years, that it is better first to talk to God about men BEFORE I talk to men about God. I consider this to be a posture of humility and forbearance. I have found this biblical principle to be effective in bringing needed change especially in leadership arenas. I still hold to this principle.

I suspect that some within the Vineyard board have issues with certain people and decisions that they are rightfully "taking to God." This is called forbearance. Without this principle, each man would be continually spewing out his opinions without any sense of getting God's permission before challenging the leadership. That would produce an atmosphere of confusion and strife.

Through the years I have watched the Lord orchestrate several significant changes among those "2–3 voices" that seem to direct many things in the Vineyard.

When I shared my opinion with Todd that 2–3 men lead the majority of the major trends within the A.V.C. in the U.S.A., he at first strongly disagreed. I told him that it was structurally impossible for thirty men in different cities to really make decisions, especially since they can only meet several times a year. He seemed to agree. The formation of the executive council of approximately ten men was an inevitable result. However, within that group there are those with the real influence, as well as those who are grateful just to be a part and can usually be counted on not to rock the boat when they see unity among the principal "2–3 voices." These 2–3 primary men are the ones I had in mind in the 14-page letter and in the challenges given in the July 31 meeting.

So it is true that I've been enthusiastic about the Vineyard, but it is also true that I have been troubled for some time about the 2–3 primary leaders. I was never in the slightest way dishonest about my respect for and commitment to the first three groups that I have described. Neither did I change my mind about any of them in June because of the prophetic revelation that came during our conference.

Rather, what changed is how I related to the primary "2–3 voices." I was content to wait in prayer for ten more years for God to make necessary changes among them. I had seen Him do it several times before, and this primary Vineyard leadership seems to regularly change anyway. I felt no anxiety about God's ability to have His way in the Vineyard. However, the Lord made it clear that He wanted me to speak directly to them. This created a dilemma for me. First, I am not sure exactly who these men are. If I knew, then I would have addressed only them. I really don't know which 2–3 men are really driving the Vineyard. I hear their voice clearly, and often do not agree with some of their general trends. I argued with the Lord intensely not to press me to appeal to them. I knew it would be a risk on several levels. I felt it was important to present my defense along with my appeal because history showed that I probably would never be given a chance to appeal once it was clear that I was in disagreement on things as fundamental as their neglect of spiritual courage in key decisions for the entire movement.

The Letter from Metro Vineyard Fellowship to the Executive Council of the AVC

MVF's (MCF's) Agenda

We feel it is a significant misunderstanding to refer to our appeal as an "agenda" instead of using terminology that is more accurate. We made a very sincere appeal that you would consider certain "convictions" or "values." Prayer, fasting, holiness, sacrificial giving to the poor, prophetic revelation, revival etc. are values and convictions.

We sought to stress that we did not care who proclaimed these convictions nor when or how they proclaimed and walked them out. We simply desired assurance that they would, in fact, be highly esteemed as they were when we first joined the Vineyard. The term "agenda" implies secret strategies, personal styles, and structures etc.

We didn't have opinions about specific application of these issues, but only a concern that these values be promoted.

I boldly proclaimed these issues at over 20 conferences that John Wimber invited me to. He boldly proclaimed them himself. I can only assume that he appreciated them since he continued to invite me to travel with him to teach them. Now these very teachings have been referred to as some "agenda" that I supposedly held in a somewhat secret way.

When Rick Olmstead and Bert Wagonner visited our team we discussed in a precise way the issues that needed to be corrected if we were to truly be Vineyard. That was a helpful and edifying time. I assured them that we wanted to be Vineyard. I was in NO WAY led to the conclusion that the things written in our 14-page letter were to be abandoned or minimized in our quest to be Vineyard. I widely and unequivocally proclaimed them on John Wimber's platform all across the globe. It was unthinkable to me that one day they would be written off as my personal agenda that was somehow secretive and manipulative.

When I spoke to Todd about the choice of the word "agenda" instead of "convictions" he assured me that the term was understood as a neutral term instead of one that suggested manipulation and secret ambition. How does one make an earnest appeal without it being written off as an agenda driven by ambition?

In August of 1996, Bob Fulton wrote a letter to the Vineyard International Consortium in which he said that John Wimber had asked me if I had any hidden agendas. I assured him that I had none. He now suggests, however, that I have confessed to having had one all along.

Seemingly the point of Bob's statement was that I was manipulative and secretive. This statement in his letter is significantly inaccurate. John never asked me if I had some hidden agenda that I was waiting to spring on the Vineyard and I never confessed to having had it all along.

I did admit that I have been troubled for some time with the lack of support for the convictions that we communicated in our 14-page letter. This is not at all the same as hiding some secret agenda.

Final Remarks

I request that you consider our appeals as coming from a sincere love for you and not a railing judgment. Please do not quickly dismiss them as coming from bitterness, dishonesty, or secret ambitions. Please consider that we do actually care about you. Also, we have absolutely NO judgments against the Vineyard in any way. We bless you privately and publicly at every opportunity possible. If anyone aligned with us fails to bless you, we intend to address the matter with them directly. My esteem for John Wimber has never been higher than it is now. I refer to him on a regular basis in my public ministry with great affection and honor. That same affection and honor are repeatedly extended to many of you that lead the Vineyard, a spiritual family that I will love dearly ALL my days.

Affectionately,

Mike Bickle and the M.C.F. Pastoral Team

Appendix B

The Grooming and Sexual Abuse of a Fourteen-Year-Old Girl

[THE FOLLOWING NARRATIVE FIRST appeared on the Substack page of Chloe Roberts, November 6, 2024, and is used here with the permission of both Roberts and Tammy Woods.]

Tammy's story turned a lot of our worlds upside down when she first came forward with her story of abuse at the hands of Mike Bickle in early 2024. Her bravery was inspiring as I read her story for the first time, even though her story broke my heart. I think this interview is honestly amazing. She is very articulate and sheds a lot of light on the manipulation that Bickle employed, while maintaining an open heart to the Lord and the process of healing.

Q: You shared your story with the world earlier this year, how has it been coming to terms with your abuse since then?

Coming to terms with clergy sexual abuse has been a journey of the heart for sure. Having never once framed myself as a victim of Mike, I had to initially just sit in the shock and horror of it all. At first, it was as if an internal detonator went off in my soul and everything went into slow motion. The stone-cold truth that I was a victim and a survivor of clergy sexual abuse crushed and crushes my soul. There have obviously been many feelings in coming to terms with this new life frame. Once the shock waves subsided, grief presented itself in all of its forms. Sometimes crashing over me like a tsunami of rage and sometimes rolling over me like a gentle tide of numbness or fatigue; often unexpectedly.

Appendix B

Facing and accepting this general new frame of clergy sexual abuse as a minor has not been the only truth with which I've had to come to terms. This last year has set me on a course of having to reframe 43 years of perceived friendship, camaraderie, trust, and redemption as it pertains specifically to Mike. I confess that this has been an anguishing reality. I am revisiting over four decades of encounters, conversations, experiences, and conclusions with Mike personally, but also those interactions that include the people I love most and the ministry passions of my heart. I am in the process of tediously applying new frames of abuse, deception, and manipulation to each context. It is both exhausting and liberating.

Apart from Mike in this scandal of abuse, I have also been coming to terms with the appalling culture of "silence" and vile "cover-up" in church leadership at IHOPKC and beyond. To date, I am incredulous, offended, heartbroken, and resolved to find my agency in all of these grievous plot twists. There are men whom I considered to be friends and co-laborers in Kingdom causes who have offered only their silence in response to my story coming forth, and I find this confusing, irresponsible, and the antithesis of "family." Likewise, there were men on the IHOPKC ELT (Executive Leadership Team) and ministry board to whom I referred as personal friends and have hosted in my personal home, who have engaged in ongoing lies, deceit, manipulation, and cover-ups, and their actions leave me speechless.

There are men whom I considered to be friends and co-laborers in Kingdom causes who have offered only their silence in response to my story coming forth, and I find this confusing, irresponsible, and the antithesis of "family."

The coming to terms has narrow application with regard to what Mike did to me personally as a minor and over the course of 43 years encompassing those I love and the passions of my heart before God. It also has broader application with regards to men in church leadership and the church in general. Suffice it to say, the emperor has no clothes and I am very much in the journey with the Lord in all of these matters of the heart.

Q: How has your life changed since you shared your story?

There have been numerous shifts in my life since last February; some painful, but probably all positive. The most obvious change has been in the area of ministry and employment. For the last several years I served as the Director of the Radiant City Center Prayer Room in Kalamazoo, Michigan. After a sabbatical in the wake of my story breaking, I decided to officially resign my position last May for the sake of soul rest and the labor of inner healing. While our finances have taken a significant hit in this season, my heart has been tended to just being Mimi to our three grand treasures.

In all the transition, I shifted from director, teacher, and leader to student and follower of those who have journeyed down this unfortunate path before me. I am reading books I never imagined I'd read by authors I never knew existed and I began weekly trauma therapy which I continue to this day. In it all I've gained new vocabulary and frames and with that, new understanding; and with that new understanding, new conviction; and with that new conviction, an emerging new voice.

The capsizing of life as I knew it has also brought shifts in relationships and rhythms of normal life. I'm learning for the first time how to really listen to and interpret rightly my own nervous system, and from that place of self-awareness, set boundaries and say "no." It doesn't sound like all that much, but for a 58-year-old #INFJ, it's a pretty significant accomplishment. I've intentionally shrunk former social circles sustained mostly out of obligation, where curiosity was disguised as compassion in all of this, and "family" was merely a hollow noun. My relationships are fewer and truer, and the genuine expression of family both natural and spiritual, has never been more desired or esteemed in my heart. We need each other, but we need each other authentically in every season of the soul. With regard to family, my 82-year-old mom and dad moved from Colorado to Michigan this summer and now live just seven minutes from me. I could not have asked for a sweeter kiss from Heaven for my wounded heart. You really never outgrow needing Mom and Dad.

While some relationships have been lost, others have been found. After 14 years of a cordial but distant relationship with my only sister because of all things IHOPKC and Mike, we have reconciled at last which has felt wonderful. How ironic that the very man and ministry that drove a wedge between us became the very thing that brought us back together again. Restoration is beautiful. In addition to gaining my sister this last year, I have also been gifted a new and treasured sisterhood with some of the fellow victims and advocates in the IHOPKC crisis. For these women, comrades in a cry for justice and new friends, I am forever grateful and by them continually strengthened.

In summary, the rhythms of my life this last year have become slower and simpler. I feel less guilty saying "no" to the machine of ministry, the culture of intensity, and the tyranny of the urgent. I'm quieter within and without. I'm less visionary and more conscious of being in the present-tense moments with the Lord and those I love most. I inhale and exhale gratitude on a regular basis as I reflect upon the kindness, goodness, and "never-letting-go-ness" of Jesus. I cry often in grief, and joy and am moved by beauty, and I hope that means I'm breaking tender instead of bitter.

Appendix B

Q: How connected were you with Mike and then later the IHOPKC world from your teen years to now?

This is an overwhelming question simply because it encompasses 43 years of my life, so rather than talking in overlapping circles, I'll try and speak into time frames as best as I am able. Suffice it to say, Mike connected and basically never let go.

The Beginning: Sophisticated Grooming—This began immediately after meeting Mike at a church potluck with my family in the wake of my 14th birthday. His on-ramp with me was babysitting and he made sure he was always the driver when picking me up and taking me home every Monday night. (side note: He never paid me for babysitting.) He pursued my parents aggressively the summer we met. They shared an August wedding anniversary with Mike and Diane, so they celebrated together each August. My family had a built-in pool, so Mike began arranging summer socials/dinners etc. with his family and others from the church centered around our pool. He bonded with my dad over football, playing in a weekly, city-league together with other men from the church; Mike was the quarterback, naturally. On occasion he would join my dad and uncle for Monday night football at our house. He acted naïve and spacey with my dad like a little brother, so my dad affectionately called him a "space cadet." He bonded with my mom over all things Bible study and her homemade desserts. He bonded with my Grandma, who lived in an apartment over our garage, over Clint Eastwood. He promoted our family as a pillar in the church and entwined our families. He came in fast and furious, large and in charge, charming and charismatic with an electric and contagious passion for Jesus. In a very short amount of time, he was like a trusted member of the family.

Summer 1980: I had just turned 14 years old at the end of June. I met Mike at a potluck dinner that summer and within days of that meeting, he picked me up from my uncle's veterinary clinic where I had spent the morning working the desk, and he took me to pizza supposedly to talk about babysitting. I was anxious and self-conscious and he did all of the talking. He shared Proverbs 31:30 with me "Charm is deceitful and beauty is vain, but a woman who fears the Lord shall be praised." Shortly after that pizza meeting, I began babysitting for his two boys every Monday night. Early on I would sometimes bring my best friend with me, and he would take us to Ted Drewes Frozen Custard for a dessert before taking us home. He called me to babysit at his house for other church-related events because the church was in a park within walking distance of his house. He became a frequent, unexpected visitor at our home that summer, and would spend much time engaging my parents in perceived friendship.

The Grooming and Sexual Abuse of a Fourteen-Year-Old Girl

Freshman Year: Just after I started my freshman year, Mike asked me a question as he drove me home from babysitting; that question would instantly turn my world upside down. Parked on an undeveloped lot near my home, he asked me if I felt for him as more than a friend. As a young teen, I had a crush on him, in the spirit of my young crush on the Hardy Boys. I felt embarrassed that he had discerned this and I was certain he was going to rebuke me. Instead, he asked me if I thought he felt the same about me. "Well, I do" was his reply. And from that infamous moment onward, I fell increasingly under his control. His pursuit of me multiplied. He would show up unexpectedly at my bus stop and pick me up and take me to school. Once or twice a week, he insisted I call him from a pay phone on my lunch hour for 30 minutes. When school was out, he would often surprise me and pick me up to take me home or to the racquetball courts. I tried cheerleading for the first semester of my freshman year and Mike would show up in the bleachers. My freshman locker was in the hallway next to the entrance of the freshman building. He asked me to show him the locker number and give him the combination and he would leave random gifts and notes in it for me to find. (That was long before the days when one had to go through security checks to gain admittance into a school.)

I played racquetball at a national level at that time, so I was on the court most everyday training. Mike regularly showed up at the club to watch me practice or play league and tournament games.

On Saturday mornings my sister participated in gymnastics, and because my dad worked on Saturday mornings as a veterinarian, Mike would often help my mom by driving my sister to and from her gymnastics class. He always had me ride shotgun in his Volkswagen Rabbit, and after dropping my sister off, he'd take me to a nearby park and hang out with me. If my mom drove my sister to gymnastics, he would come to our house and spend an hour or two alone with me. It was on such a Saturday morning that his advances became sexual in nature. On Saturday nights I had youth group meetings at the church and Mike would be there in his office preparing for Sunday morning. He would call me into his office before the meeting started, and often I never made it to youth group. When I did attend the actual youth group meetings, Mike would be sure to intercept me afterward and drive me home. Somewhere in this year Mike and Diane took my sister and me out to dinner and to the circus.

Christmas break of 1980, a number of people from our church took a ski trip to Colorado. Skiing in Colorado was something we did regularly for our family vacations, so my entire family signed up to go on this trip. Having arranged childcare for their boys, Mike and Diane also planned to accompany the group to Colorado. However, as the trip drew nearer, Mike told me to tell my parents that I wanted to stay home with my Grandma and that he would cancel last minute too. Mike was persuasive and the pressure was overwhelming. It was terribly out of character for me to do this because our family ski vacations were a highlight for me, but I did it, much to my parents' confusion and disappointment. Days before the group's departure, Mike found a reason to stay back alone, as well. With childcare already secured, he was free to spend hours every day with me, and he did. The first night after everyone left, he took me to an outdoor plaza where we walked around in the chilly night under sparkling holiday lights as Christmas carols filled the air. At one point, Mike decided we needed to warm up, so he ducked into a little Italian restaurant on the plaza and sat us down at one of the tables. There he proceeded to order two glasses of red wine, one for him and one for me.

Sophomore Year: My sophomore year Mike had me cut my hair and I was so sad about this. He continued to find all kinds of ways to spend hours with me at a time; sitting in parking lots, running errands, making copies of books at Covenant Theological Seminary library, teaching me to drive a stick shift in the Target parking lot, visiting my grandma in the hospital and afterward walking around the surrounding neighborhood, coming over on Saturday mornings when my mom drove my sister to gymnastics, arranging numerous family dinners and social gatherings at my house, Risk game-nights at his house etc. He'd have me be dropped off at the local library and then walk to the park by the church where he'd meet me for several hours. One afternoon he walked me all the way home in the rain from that park. He had endless ideas for how he could carve out hours at a time with me. It was in numerous such times alone with me that he sexually abused me. When he went to Africa for three weeks, he called me collect and talked for 15 minutes accruing a $50 phone call that I had to explain to my parents. That was a whopping phone bill back in the day! He brought me back a traditional African gown from that trip that I burned in my firepit this past spring. When he was on an extended fast, he'd come over to our pool and float on my mom's raft, while I read the Bible aloud to him; never quite slowly enough to his liking.

In summary of those teen years of high school when Mike was still in St. Louis, he found ways to have hours upon hours of connection with me via telephone calls and face-to-face interaction. He told me again and again that he believed Diane was going to die and that he would be free to marry me. And every hour with him left me more isolated from all of my other significant relationships.

Junior Year: Mike moved to Kansas City. This was a devastating year for me and one for which I have very few memories. Mike significantly influenced me to quit racquetball; something that had consumed my life for almost six years. At that time, I was sponsored by Ektelon, played the Women's Open, competed in the top ten in St. Louis, and was ranked fourth in the nation in my junior category. I was just shy of going professional, but he persuaded me to pursue "pure and undistracted devotion to the Lord." After he moved to Kansas City, Mike continued to call me, write me, and visit my house when they came to St. Louis to see their family members. This was an exceedingly burdensome year for me. I was gutted and alone.

Mike significantly influenced me to quit racquetball; something that had consumed my life for almost six years . . . I was just shy of going professional, but he persuaded me to pursue "pure and undistracted devotion to the Lord."

Senior Year: During my senior year of high school, Mike hatched a plan to get me to Kansas City with him. He said I should move to KC after my high school graduation, live alone in an apartment, and be his personal secretary. (Later he would actually carry out a very similar plan with the original Jane Doe.)

I needed to attend college in order to get my teaching degree. Mike told me I could enroll at a college in KC, still live alone in an apartment, and still be his part-time secretary. He told me to acquire secretarial skills, so I dropped my beloved French class, even though I had been recommended for participation in the foreign student exchange program, to pick up a year-long, two-hour secretarial practice course. I was deeply disappointed to let go of my French studies. The spring of my senior year, I auditioned for a lead role in the school musical on a dare and actually landed the part of Sarah Brown in Guys and Dolls. I learned that "theater" is synonymous to "therapy," and I remember my heart feeling like it was coming alive again for the first time in years. On opening night, however, Mike surprised me by showing up with my parents. He had been informed about the production by my mom and dad and had rerouted a flight through St. Louis overnight instead of going straight home to Kansas City. He was extremely upset that the script called for me to kiss the male lead.

College Years: I attended Covenant College in Tennessee for my first two years of college. During my sophomore year there, Mike drove three hours each way from a conference venue to see me. He took me out to dinner and sat with me on Lookout Mountain, overlooking the lights of Chattanooga after dinner. He said that when he could officially propose to me, he would bring me back to that spot. My junior year I transferred to the University of Missouri-Columbia where I would later graduate. That year Mike arranged to fly into a small airport in Columbia. He wanted to see my off-campus condominium, so we spent an afternoon together there before he flew back to KC. All this time, he continued to reiterate his belief that Diane was going to die and he was going to marry me. I had two visits from Mike at each of my colleges, several visits in St. Louis during holidays and summer breaks, and infrequent phone calls during my college years. During my years away at university, Mike made my parents' house in St. Louis a hub for the Kansas City prophets when they visited the city with him. However, after years of desperately crying out to the Lord for direction and confirmation, I told Mike in the fall of my senior year that I was going to marry my future husband.

Wedding Day: Mike told me he would not officiate or even attend my wedding because it would be too painful for him. Diane and the boys did attend. The morning of my wedding, Mike called from California to bless me. He didn't get far into the phone call when he broke down sobbing and cast a rain cloud of heaviness and confusion over my heart and my day.

During the years following, Mike would call me once or twice a year and maybe see me once every other year or so when he was in St. Louis. A few times he had me come to the airport, once with my toddler son, to visit with him on a layover. These exchanges were all centered on him and the grandiose things happening in Kansas City with the prophets. On a couple of occasions, he gave me a copy of a Christian magazine with his picture on the cover. I listened and was left feeling hollow and small.

1996 Cut Off: In the fall of 1996, Mike came and stayed at my house while helping the elders of our church (his former church) navigate some transitions. During this visit, Mike told me he was going to cut off all communication with me for good. It was sudden; it was unexpected; it was devastating. Though those one-sided conversations about how powerfully God was moving in Kansas City left me hollow in the wake of them, I still felt those crumbs somehow meant that I was still part of it; whatever "it" was. I felt I was still connected to something that REALLY mattered and carried more significance than my little life of diapers and Little Tykes, and now he concluded I wasn't even worthy or relevant enough for the crumbs. Turns out he was just beginning his abusive relationship with Jane Doe.

2001 Contact Resumed: For 5 years I had no connection whatsoever with Mike. That radio silence drove me deep into the Lord's tender embrace and His Word. I became anchored in my identity in Christ Jesus and confident in the Father's affection for me. Inner healing had begun. In 2001 Mike returned to St. Louis with a team from IHOPKC. After emptying the room of furniture, he held a meeting in my living room with about 40 pastors from the city to cast vision for the House of Prayer. In 2003 our small House of Prayer began and Mike returned on and off for various events at our ministry and at other churches in the city, usually staying at our home.

During these years, he bonded with my children and they affectionately called him "Uncle Mike."

We sent our three children and various youth from our House of Prayer to KC for camps and conferences, internships, and intensives. Our connection throughout those years was surrounding the House of Prayer. We hosted countless teams from IHOPKC in our home and House of Prayer; probably every former ELT member has sat around my kitchen table and eaten my chicken salad and homemade pies. Our second son was on staff at IHOPKC for two years before moving to Colorado. When my daughter was in KC for the summer Worship and Prayer Intensive, he took her out for Chinese lunch. When she got engaged, Mike and Misty took her and her then fiancé out to lunch in St. Louis, when he was ministering in the city. Mike added me to the IHOPKC staff emails for years, included us in "special meetings," sent me his notes for every weekly teaching, and promoted our family and especially my children publicly. We stayed in touch peripherally for decades this way.

Fall 2023: Mike called with increasing regularity after things began being exposed in Kansas City. He was desperately trying to control the narrative, align with me, and secure my silence. He grew increasingly manic in his phone calls until I blocked him permanently the day my story broke in the *Kansas City Star*.

Q: What are some of the emotions you remember feeling at the height of Mike's abuse as a teenager?

Once Mike began being romantically inappropriate and sexually abusive to me, he told me repeatedly that if we were caught and someone saw him that "I" would have to "own it." In other words, the guilt of initiative would have to be on me because he had a family and a ministry whereas I had geometry class. That threat of exposure and shame had me bound in persistent fear and anxiety as a little girl. Loneliness was another feeling that plagued me during those teen years. Mike isolated me from every other relationship and hobby, and when he wasn't with me, I was utterly alone. Confusion and more confusion; I was tormented by confusion. Did the prophetic foresight that Diane was going to die somehow allow for his premature relationship with me? He was my pastor, after all, and more knowledgeable about all things prophetic and God. Even as he told me he thought Diane was going to die and I could be Lukie's mom, he also sowed countless seeds about the high calling of celibacy. So when I was trying to seek the Lord about marrying my husband, I had the prophetic narrative of marrying Mike and the option of a life of celibacy before the Lord, on the table. It was a lot of pressure, confusion, and anxiety for one barely out of her teen years; all courtesy of her very convincing pastor. Finally, I wrestled with much insecurity during those years of abuse and beyond. Mike repeatedly told me that I was a "tool" used by God to humble and prepare him for his calling in ministry. Before I graduated from high school, I was left behind with a severe wound of abandonment in my heart. All of these emotions were too acute for an innocent heart and underdeveloped mind to process alone and they made for years of crying myself to sleep.

Mike isolated me from every other relationship and hobby, and when he wasn't with me, I was utterly alone. Confusion and more confusion; I was tormented by confusion.

Q: Looking back, what are some of the red flags you see in how Mike interacted with you and your family?

I think the age-old idiom "hindsight is 20/20" is applicable, as so many across the IHOPKC, prayer movement, and charismatic contexts have discovered and are now discovering. Mike masked, disguised, and hid so many red flags in plain sight for decades. To name a few in my personal context: hours of time alone with me, driving me places, showing up unexpectedly, leaving gifts in my locker, persuading my educational choices, driving my sister to gymnastics, asking me if I felt for him as "more than a friend," calling collect from Africa, prevailing upon me to cut my hair, attempting to persuade me to live alone in Kansas City after high school, visiting me in college, etc., etc., etc. When listed, especially with today's frames, they seem like obvious red flags; how on earth did we miss them?

Since coming forward with my story, I've had some backlash in this area especially concerning my parents. Based on these seemingly obvious red flags, my parents must have been naïve at best or negligent at worst. In reality, nothing could be further from the truth. This is where an understanding of the times and seasons in the early 1980s is important concerning these red flags. When I fell victim to Mike, there was no grid whatsoever for clergy sexual abuse. It doesn't mean that it wasn't happening, but it wasn't a documented, studied, and proclaimed actuality. Unlike today, pastors and preachers were the men you COULD trust, especially a charming, generous, passionate for Jesus, servant-hearted, family man like Mike Bickle. He tripped no alarms because, for the most part, there were no alarms in existence within church culture at that time. Leading experts in clergy sexual abuse and trauma therapy will attest to this timeline reality. And given that we were in the direct wake of the Jesus Movement and Charismatic Renewal, with "They Will Know We Are Christians By Our Love" on our lips, it was a season of excitement and joy, community and growing in the Lord for my family; we could never have imagined the sinister plot twist as it unfolded.

Q: *What was your initial response to hearing about Mike Bickle's sexual immorality in October of last year?*

Much like everyone else, I did not believe one word of the allegations against Mike as told to my husband and me by my supervisor at Radiant Church. I was surprised by my supervisor's grave sobriety especially because he was a former long-time IHOPer. But unlike everyone else, I thought I had a different frame altogether. I knew firsthand the mercy Mike had been afforded by the Lord and by myself, and I knew that he often referenced this with seeming gratitude. His sons did not grow up with an incarcerated father, and I was confident that he would never take such love and redemption for granted. After the conversation with my supervisor, I texted Mike three question marks (???) to which he immediately responded, "Some people are saying some false things about me." Convinced of his innocence, I dismissed the drama entirely.

Q: *What were some of the key factors that led to you waking up to the reality of the abuse and then deciding to share your story?*

Because of my altogether different frame from everyone around me (i.e. that Mike wasn't necessarily the holy man, but rather a forgiven-much man, and therefore a merciful man who loved God much via his obedience) I was the last one to ditch the "love bears all things, believes all things, hopes all things, endures all things" train of thought. All these years I had framed myself as his "greatest mistake," and because he was seemingly repentant and committed to bearing the fruit of repentance, I vowed to take his greatest mistake to the grave. I started to grow uneasy when Mike called to confess "five bad things" he did with Jane Doe, but before doing so, he prefaced his confession with an hour-long discourse on the prophetic history including Jane Doe's birthday and a dream he had of her. Not long after that phone call, more allegations came to light and Mike called again and confessed to kissing a well-known worship leader and being inappropriate with a former personal assistant. He grew more and more manic sounding with each interaction, and with a sinking heart, I knew he was lying and something was terribly wrong. Everything changed suddenly, however, when I was sitting alone before my fireplace on December 11, 2023, and I read Jane Doe's official victim statement. It felt as if an internal detonator went off in my chest cavity, as I realized with absolute horror that my life was a screenplay for her feature film. I lived some of the very words she spoke in her statement. He made ME feel like I was the center of his world.

He told ME he believed Diane was going to die and he would marry ME. He used secret codes of communication with ME. He called ME from another nation and bought ME alcohol when I was just 14 years old. He took ME to parks and he groomed MY family. The bottom line, I was treacherously duped and he was a predator, pedophile, and con artist. Though I didn't tell my family my story immediately, I did tell them that I no longer believed him.

Over the course of several weeks, three loved ones asked me direct questions concerning Mike; did he abuse me and did he ever tell me that he believed Diane was going to die and he would marry me? I panicked with each one and lied. It was during our church's annual 21-day fast and while re-reading Brene Brown's book Daring Greatly in January that I realized, with the help of the Lord's tender prodding, that I could not remain silent and just let the drama play out as it would in Kansas City, which is what I wanted to do to protect my own heart and the hearts of my loved ones. But I also realized that after 43 years, Mike was still controlling the narrative of my life and I could not live as a liar. By doing so, I would be complicit in all that he has done.

On January 30th, I wrote a would-be letter to Mike and Diane and for the first time, I put words to the story that had been buried in my heart's deepest vault for 43 years. After sharing that letter with my pastor and his wife, I was convinced by attorney Boz Tjividian to release my story in the *Kansas City Star*, which I did on February 7, 2024.

Q: The majority of your abuse took place when you were a teenager and you have woken up to it in your 50s. How do you think it affected your life?

Because my abuse did take place as a minor, I do believe there were long-term repercussions which I am just now beginning to see and accept via counseling and education. It is a journey of the heart.

Mike often referred to me as "a tool" in the hand of God to humble and prepare him for his ministry assignment. This lodged in my heart as an arrow. Tools are expendable. A tool is not cherished; a tool is something that is used and then cast aside. Therefore, I struggled with believing that I was enough just being me. My small life as a first-grade teacher and mom and homeschool teacher and later director of a small "Mom & Pop" house of prayer often felt "tool-ish" in comparison to his grandiose calling and existence. I felt like I was the weakest link in ministry, and when other male leaders from IHOPKC and in the prayer movement would avert my eyes and talk to my husband instead, it confirmed to me again and again that I was just a tool to further along other more important callings.

During the years of his abuse, Mike told me under no uncertain terms, that if he was caught, "I" would have to "own it." The burden of the initiative was always going to have to fall on me because he was a family man and a ministry leader. This constant threat and pressure not only created in me a fear and anxiety, but also a pressure to never fail. Never let down my guard. Always bring my "A-game." Failure to do so would result in shame and rejection. In my own strength, I became a people-pleaser on steroids, always believing that failure would result in rejection. I think I lived subconsciously with this fear of failure and subsequent fear of rejection for decades.

On a more positive note, I became a "mercy girl." I believed I was covering a "greatest mistake" and a "multitude of sins" like my Father. I believed that I was forgiving and offering a clean slate to a man who received such mercy from me and the Lord with a grateful heart and a man who went on to demonstrate the fruit of repentance. I believed I was part of a beautiful story of redemption, so I continued to posture my heart in the way of tenderness and mercy toward struggling and failed brothers and sisters throughout the decades. Mike was and is a con artist, but I became a safe haven for broken and failed people and remain so to this day.

Q: How has your relationship with the Lord changed in the last year?

My relationship with the Lord is only surer in the wake of all that has come to light. I see His fingerprints on every detail, I feel His gentle embrace of my heart, and I sense His nearness in my moments of stillness and chaos alike. From my family and therapist to my proven friends and newest sisterhood, I feel Heaven's persistent and healing hugs. I am not offended with the Lord; only grateful. Knowing that Jesus was there the moment my life intersected with Mike Bickle at that potluck dinner somehow makes it easier for me to surrender to the mystery of His sovereignty. I cannot answer the "whys" and probably will carry most of them across the threshold of eternity. What I am certain of, is that He carries me in every season of my soul and mile of this pilgrimage; "A-game" notwithstanding.

I am not offended with the Lord; only grateful. Knowing that Jesus was there the moment my life intersected with Mike Bickle at that potluck dinner somehow makes it easier for me to surrender to the mystery of His sovereignty.

That said, I must confess that in this mile, I do struggle with reading and sitting in His Word as I have for years, and in the corporate expression of worship be it in a church service or Prayer Room. I find solace in the Psalms, but so many of the passages in the Old and New Testaments, especially those taught so passionately by Mike and even myself, currently trigger my heart with grief. A daily devotional washes over my heart; a Psalm soothes my soul; a book gives revelation; a podcast validates and challenges me. I'm staying in what feels like a perpetual conversation with the Holy Spirit; the back of my head is just no longer visible in the front row of the Prayer Room.

As for church, my heart is limping. Often I feel like I've swallowed the "red pill" from the Matrix, and there's just no going forward in a "blue pill reality" any longer. The system is broken. The emperor has no clothes. We seem to be stuck somewhere between Hollywood and its polished celebrity culture and corporate America and its fixation on metrics. Mission, tradition, and metrics have taken precedence over people for whom Jesus died. There's a cry, yea wail, in my heart for depth and authenticity, rawness and realness, farm table and family. I think they call this koinonia; I call it simply "life-ing together." I have more reflections than words; more prayers than actions. I know He is found on the path of His flock, and so shall I be by His grace. I think my son Jojo distills it down pretty well in this chapter: "Love God. Love people. Don't take yourself too seriously."

Q: What are some tools, resources, and helpful anchors you've used to get through this past year?

These last eight months have been ones of rest, labor, and family. As previously mentioned, I began weekly trauma therapy in the wake of my story breaking. This has been enlightening, laborsome, and anchoring. Now including my parents, I am with my family multiple times every week, and this has been a strong anchor for my soul. "Sunday Fundays" are our altogether Sabbath days with one another, and our grandtreasures are the Balm of Gilead personified.

Books have always been my love language, and this last year, I have developed a voracious appetite for a new genre of books in the clergy sexual abuse and church abuse categories. Diane Langberg (mic drop). I've been in school and Dr. Langberg and Wade Mullen and Chuck Degroat and Scot McKnight etc. have all been incredible teachers in their books and podcasts. At my daughter's encouragement, I also began to include fictional books in my reading rotation this last year. Though I loved reading fiction books to my children during the homeschool years, it was a pleasure I never really allowed my grown-up self. After all, there were too many commentaries, end-times books, and prayer and fasting books that a responsible ministry leader needed to devour. This last year, however, I have engaged in the hard, emotional work of understanding clergy sexual abuse via Dr. Langberg's books, all the while mingling it with aliens from Andy Weir's "Project Hail Mary" and other fictional works.

I've cooked new recipes and filled our farm table with genuine fellowship. I've grown herbs and flowers and tamed the deer in my backyard with corn and Disney tunes. I've sat innumerable hours on my porch swing inhaling and exhaling grief and gratitude alike and worshiping in both song and stillness. In it all, I recognize that every movement forward and every steadying anchor are evidence of a tailor-made journey for my own personal heart from a good and faithful Father.

Q: What is something you want to say to others who have experienced abuse of any kind from people in the church?

I'm in no way in a position of expertise, having begun my own journey of understanding and healing from clergy sexual abuse just about nine months ago. However, for those who may just now be experiencing a dawning realization of a terrible past or present reality concerning sexual abuse within the context of the church, I think it's so important to remember that Jesus is not the church or its abusive leaders. Once that delineation is made, it's easier to lay down offense with God and run to Him instead of recoil from Him. An abusive leader's gifting, popularity, or success is not Heaven's endorsement. Jesus has seen and heard it all, and unlike the church with its cover-up culture and empowerment of predators, He will not be silent.

Secondly, silence protects and empowers the abusers. There is only one frame for pedophilia and clergy sexual abuse . . . CRIMINAL. All other abuse within the church be it emotional and/or spiritual is just that . . . ABUSE. Squeeze the Lord's hand, open your mouth, and tell your story. Like David's smooth stone in the forehead of the giant, your story is enough. Find that trusted someone and break the silence.

"I, the Lord, am your God, who brought you up from the land of Egypt; Open your mouth wide and I will fill it." (Psalm 81:10)

Finally, you're not alone. Listen to the truth whispers of the Lord and steep your soul in them over and over again.

I will never leave you nor forsake you
I am the Lord who heals you
I will strengthen you and help you
You are not alone
I will be with you
Don't be afraid, for I am with you.
I am with you always etc.

Appendix C

William Branham and the Latter Rain of the Holy Spirit

It is important for all to understand who William Branham was and his involvement in the emergence of the Latter Rain movement. Many have concluded that the church in Kansas City, largely through the influence of Paul Cain, was shaped to a certain degree by the theology of this movement.

In his biography of William Branham, John Collins contends that "Branham's tour through Canada in 1947 gave birth to the Latter Rain movement at the Sharon Orphanage in North Battleford, Saskatchewan."[1] Branham later distanced himself from the primary branch of the Latter Rain. Advocates argued that the outpouring of the Holy Spirit at Pentecost in the first century was interpreted as the "early rain" that was then followed by some two thousand years of relative drought and spiritual lethargy.[2] Those involved in this movement believed what they had received was the "latter rain" of the Spirit's work. Needless to say, this perspective largely ignores the many revivals that had preceded in church history as well as the experience of numerous godly Christian leaders.

A further brief word about William Branham (1909–65) is called for. He famously claimed to be guided by an angel who stood beside him and communicated otherwise unknown information about people in the audience. It was later revealed that his associates collected "prayer cards" with personal information from those who attended his meetings, providing him with information that he then passed along as divine revelation. He rejected

---

1. Collins, *Preacher Behind the White Hoods*, 297.

2. A few argued that the early rain was the revival at Azusa Street, not the outpouring at Pentecost.

Trinitarianism and denominationalism as demonic (the latter, he argued, was a warning sign of the mark of the Beast). He was misogynistic and, although not technically a member of the Ku Klux Klan, often endorsed their racist mentality. Branham's most notorious belief came to be known as the doctrine of "the serpent seed." Branham "believed that two seedlines had descended from Eve. According to the doctrine, the serpent in the garden had sex with Eve in the garden, producing Cain and the descendants of Cain's bloodline. Cain's bloodline, according to Branham, was filled with the 'intelligent' and 'educated' and were also 'builders and scientists.'"[3]

The movement emerged at the Sharon Orphanage and Schools in North Battleford, Saskatchewan, Canada, where about seventy students had gathered to fast, pray, and study the word of God in November of 1947. "What distinguished the Latter Rain revival from previous manifestations of Latter Rain thinking was the greater degree of control invested in the apostolic role, as well as the greater acceptance of spiritually elitist ideology, here exemplified by the Latter Rain's adoption of the idea of 'Manifest Sons of God' theology."[4]

The most controversial and disputed of all their points of emphasis was *the manifested sons of God*, according to which a new and elite kind of Christian with extraordinary spiritual power would be instrumental in subduing the earth. Some associated with the movement embraced the idea that the church on earth is itself the *ongoing incarnation* of Jesus. The church is becoming one in nature and essence with Jesus. As it takes shape it will eventually "manifest" the Son of God to such a high degree that there will be no need for a literal, personal second coming of Christ. The church will have become (or be "manifested" as) the Son of God on earth. There were even suggestions that some might reach a level of holiness that they could attain immortality in this life, escaping physical death altogether. I mention the Latter Rain movement only because some, over the years, have falsely accused Mike Bickle and the church in Kansas City of perpetuating these same doctrines and practices.[5]

---

3. Weaver, *New Apostolic Reformation*, 35–36.
4. Weaver, *New Apostolic Reformation*, 29.
5. See Weaver, *New Apostolic Reformation*, 34.

Bibliography

Alnor, William. "The Kansas City Prophets." Deception in the Church. http://www.deceptioninthechurch.com/kcp.html.

———. "Part Twelve: When Revival Doesn't Happen . . . Kansas City Prophets and Toronto @ HTB." Your Name Is Like Honey, November 29, 2021. https://yournameislikehoney.com/2021/11/29/part-twelve-when-revival-doesnt-happen-kansas-city-prophets-and-toronto-htb/.

Alnor, William M., and Robert Lyle. "Controversial Prophetic Movement Is Incorporated into the Vineyard." *Christian Research Journal*, Fall 1990. https://christian.net/pub/resources/text/cri/cri-jrnl/crj0044a.txt.

Armstrong, John. "A New Generation of Prophets?" *The Standard* (Baptist General Conference), March 1991.

Arnott, John. *The Father's Blessing*. Orlando, FL: Creation House, 1995.

———. "Letter to John Wimber." 1995. Special Collection, Regent University Library, Virginia Beach, Virginia.

———. "An Open Letter for General Distribution." 1995. Wimber Collection: Special Collections Regent University Library, Virginia Beach, Virginia.

Best, Gary. "AVC Canada Summarizes Disengagement Events." Letter sent to all Canadian Vineyard churches, December 15, 1995.

Beverley, James A. *Holy Laughter and the Toronto Blessing*. Grand Rapids: Zondervan, 1995.

———. "John Wimber, the Vineyard, and the Prophets: Listening for a Word from God." *The Canadian Baptist*, March/April, 1992.

———. "Vineyard Severs Ties with 'Toronto Blessing' Church." *Christianity Today*, January 8, 1996.

"Beware the 'Facebook Prophet' Frauds." *Charisma*, July 24, 2024. https://charismanews.com/culture/beware-the-facebook-prophet-frauds/.

Bickle, Mike. *Growing in the Prophetic*. Lake Marry, FL. Creation House, 2008.

———. *Passion for Jesus: Growing in Extravagant Love for God*. Lake Mary, FL: Creation House, 1996.

Campbell, Wesley. *Welcoming a Visitation of the Holy Spirit*. Lake Mary, Fl. Creation House, 1996.

Cannon, Steven F. "Old Wine in Old Wineskins: A Look at Kansas City Fellowship." *The Quarterly Journal* 10 (1990).

Bibliography

Cartledge, David. *The Apostolic Revolution: The Restoration of Apostles and Prophets in the Assemblies of God in Australia*. Chester Hill, NSW, Australia: Paraclete Institute, 2000.

Chevrau, Guy. *Catch the Fire: The Toronto Blessing. An Experience of Renewal and Revival*. London: Marshall Pickering, 1994.

Christerson, Brad, and Richard Flory. *The Rise of Network Christianity: How Independent Leaders Are Changing the Religious Landscape*. Oxford: Oxford University Press, 2017.

Collins, John. *Preacher Behind the White Hoods: A Critical Examination of William Branham and His Message*. Jeffersonville, IN: Dark Mystery, 2020.

Cross Rhythms. "Kevin Prosch Confesses Sin." June 1, 1999. https://www.crossrhythms.co.uk/articles/news/Kevin_Prosch_Confesses_Sin/31322/p1/.

Danielsen, Mary. *The Perfect Storm of Apostasy: An Introduction to the Kansas City Prophets and Other Latter-Day Prognosticators*. Roseburg, OR: Lighthouse Trails, n.d.

Dawson, Connie. *John Wimber: His Life and Ministry*. Lincoln, NE: The Wimber Project, 2020.

Dean, Robert, Jr. "Don't Be Caught by the Undertow of the Third Wave." *Biblical Perspectives* 3 (1990) 1–6.

Deere. Jack. *The Beginner's Guide to the Gift of Prophecy*. Grand Rapids: Baker, 2008.

———. "From Support to Scrutiny: Jack Deere Reevaluates #IHOPKC Founder and Kansas City Prophets' Legacy." Divine Detours, March 11, 2024. https://stephendeere.substack.com/p/from-support-to-scrutiny-jack-deere.

———. *Surprised by the Power of the Spirit: A Former Dallas Seminary Professor Discovers That God Speaks and Heals Today*. Grand Rapids: Zondervan, 1993.

———. *Surprised by the Voice of God: How God Speaks Today Through Prophecies, Dreams, and Visions*. Grand Rapids: Zondervan, 1996.

———. *Why I Am Still Surprised by the Power of the Spirit: Discovering How God Speaks and Heals Today*. Grand Rapids: Zondervan, 2020.

———. *Why I am Still Surprised by the Voice of God: How God Speaks Today Through Prophecies, Dreams, and Visions* Grand Rapids: Zondervan, 2022.

Editor. "Gruen Resigns After Announcement." *Charisma*, July 1993.

Falls, Daniel. *The Life & Legacy of Pat Bickle, and a History of the Kansas City Prophets*. Published by the author, 2020.

Firefly. *Investigation of Mike Bickle and the International House of Prayer Kansas City*. https://www.tikkunglobal.org/_files/ugd/c39fc4_0c894435ff7b456c83bd967bdf2f4ofc.pdf.

Geivett, R. Douglas, and Holly Pivec. *God's Super-Apostles: Encountering the Worldwide Prophets and Apostles Movement*. Wooster, OH: Weaver, 2014.

———. *A New Apostolic Reformation? A Biblical Response to a Worldwide Movement*. Wooster, OH: Weaver, 2014.

Gibson, Keith. *Wandering Stars: Contending for the Faith with the New Apostles and Prophets*. Vestavia Hills, AL: Solid Ground Christian, 2011.

Grady, Lee. "Charismatics at a Crossroads." *Ministries Today*, September/October 1990.

———. "Making Adjustments at the Metro Vineyard of Kansas City." *Equipping the Saints* (Fall 1990) 7.

———. "Prophetic Minister Paul Cain Issues Public Apology for Immoral Lifestyle." *Charisma*, March 2, 2005.

Bibliography

———. "Resolving the Kansas City Prophecy Controversy." *Ministries Today*, September/October, 1990.

Grudem, Wayne. *The Gift of Prophecy in the New Testament and Today*. Wheaton, IL: Crossway, 2000.

———. *Power & Truth: A Response to the Critiques of Vineyard Teaching and Practice by D. A. Carson, James Montgomery Boice, and John H. Armstrong* in Power Religion. Anaheim, CA: Association of Vineyard Churches, 1993.

Gruen, Ernie. *Documentation of the Aberrant Practices and Teachings of Kansas City Fellowship (Grace Ministries), Prepared by Pastor Ernie Gruen and Members of His Staff*. Published by the author, 1990.

Hill, Clifford. *Blessing the Church?* London: Eagle, 1997.

———. "Blessing the Church? XXVI." Prophecy Today, May 4, 2018. https://prophecytoday.uk/study/teaching-articles/item/1062-blessing-the-church-xxvi.html.

Hilborn, David, ed. *"Toronto" in Perspective: Papers on the New Charismatic Wave of the mid-1990s*. Carlisle, UK: Acute and Paternoster, 2001.

Holcomb, Justin. *Know the Heretics*. Grand Rapids: Zondervan, 2014.

Hopkins, Rebecca, and Julie Roys. "EXCLUSIVE: 3rd Woman Says Mike Bickle Groomed and Sexually Abused Her, Beginning at Age 15." The Roys Report, February 10, 2024. https://julieroys.com/third-woman-says-mike-bickle-groomed-sexually-abused-her-beginning-at-age-15/.

Hunter, Todd. "Letter Addressed to Vineyard Pastors." December 13, 1995.

Jackson, Bill. *The Quest for the Radical Middle: A History of the Vineyard*. Cape Town: Vineyard International, 1999.

"Kansas City Churches Reconciled." *Charisma*, July 1993.

Keener, Craig. *Miracles: The Credibility of the New Testament Accounts*. 2 vols. Grand Rapids: Baker, 2011.

———. *Miracles Today: The Supernatural Work of God in the Modern World*. Grand Rapids: Baker, 2021.

Kendall, R. T. *Prophetic Integrity: Aligning Our Words with God's Word*. Nashville: Thomas Nelson, 2022.

The Line of Fire. "Official Statement from the Leadership Panel on Todd Bentley, January 2, 2020." https://thelineoffire.org/article/official-statement-from-the-leadership-panel-on-todd.

Marsden, Brian G., and Daniel W. E. Green. "1983d: May's Surprise Comet." *Sky & Telescope* 66 (1983) 26–29.

Maudlin, Michael G. "Seers in the Heartland: Hot on the Trail of the Kansas City Prophets." *Christianity Today*, January 14, 1991, 18–22.

Miller, Donald E. *Reinventing American Protestantism: Christianity in the New Millennium*. Berkeley: University of California Press, 1996.

MLB. "WS1985 Gm6: Denkinger Calls Orta Save at First Base." Youtube, October 30, 2017. 1:16. https://www.youtube.com/watch?v=vyt1xEvqqow.

Pawson, David. *Is the Blessing Biblical? Thinking Through the Toronto Phenomenon*. London: Hodder & Stoughton, 1995.

Pittman, Howard. *Placebo*. Published by author, 1986.

Poloma, Margaret M. *Main Street Mystics: The Toronto Blessing and Reviving Pentecostalism*. Walnut Creek, CA: Altamira, 2003.

Bibliography

———. "The 'Toronto Blessing' in Postmodern Society: Manifestations, Metaphor and Myth." In *The Globalization of Pentecostalism: A Religion Made to Travel*, edited by Murray W. Dempster et al., 363–85. Regnum Books. Carlisle, UK: Paternoster, 1999.

Prince, Derek. "Derek Prince's Statement About Kansas City Fellowship." *End Time Evangelist*, May 11, 2024.

Pullinger, Jackie. *Chasing the Dragon: One Woman's Struggle Against the Darkness of Hong Kong's Drug Dens*. 1980. Reprint, Minneapolis: Chosen, 2014.

Pytches, David. *Some Said It Thundered*. Nashville: Thomas Nelson, 1991.

Reise, Dan. "Paul Cain and Chris Reed." YouTube, June 10, 2020. 3:10. https://www.youtube.com/watch?v=Xwl-GR2CbfE.

Roys, Julie. "EXCLUSIVE: Open Letter to Mike Bickle from Alleged Victim, Tammy Woods." The Roys Report, February 15, 2024. https://julieroys.com/exclusive-open-letter-to-mike-bickle-from-alleged-victim-tammy-woods/.

———. "International House of Prayer Founder Mike Bickle Confesses to 'Inappropriate Behavior' 20 Years Ago." The Roys Report, December 12, 2023. https://julieroys.com/breaking-international-house-of-prayer-founder-mike-bickle-confesses-to-inappropriate-behavior-20-years-ago/.

Schaff, Fred. *Comet of the Century: From Halley to Hale-Bopp*. New York City: Copernicus, 1997.

Scott, Bob. *Some Said They Blundered: Breaking My Decades of Silence on Mike Bickle, the Kansas City Prophets, and International House of Prayer-Kansas City*. Overland Park, KS: Joseph Company Global, 2024.

Shepherd, Josh. "Investigative Report Debunks Mike Bickle's Often-Told '4:18 Prophecy' as False." The Roys Report, May 16, 2024. https://julieroys.com/investigative-report-debunks-mike-bickles-often-told-418-prophecy-false/.

Shepherd, Marquis. "Gentlest of Winters Goes Out with a Blast of Snow, Cold." *Kansas City Times*, March 21, 1983.

Springer, Kevin. "Paul Cain Answers Some Tough Questions." *Equipping the Saints* (Fall 1990) 8–14.

Stackhouse, Ian. *The Gospel-Driven Church: Retrieving Classical Ministry for Contemporary Revivalism*. Carlisle, UK: Paternoster, 2004.

Storms, Sam. *The Beginner's Guide to Spiritual Gifts*. Minneapolis: Bethany House, 2012.

———. *Convergence: Spiritual Journeys of a Charismatic Calvinist*. Kansas City: Enjoying God Ministries, 2005.

———. "Revelatory Gifts of the Spirit and the Sufficiency of Scripture: Are They Compatible?" In *Scripture and the People of God: Essays in Honor of Wayne Grudem*, edited by John DelHousaye et al., 79–97. Wheaton, IL: Crossway, 2018.

———. *Understanding Spiritual Gifts: A Comprehensive Guide*. Grand Rapids: Zondervan, 2020.

———. *Understanding Spiritual Warfare: A Comprehensive Guide*. Grand Rapids: Zondervan, 2021.

Tillin, Tricia. "The 'Harp and Bowl.' 24-Hour Prayer Initiative and the 'Restoration of the Tabernacle of David.'" Birthpangs. http://www.birthpangs.org/articles/kcp/harp-bowl.htm.

———. "The Kansas City Prophets Exposed: The Roots of the Revival." The Cross and Word Archive. http://www.banner.org.uk/kcp/kcp-roots.html.

Bibliography

Wagner, C. Peter. *Apostles and Prophets: The Foundation of the Church.* Ventura, CA: Regal, 2000.

———. *Churchquake! How the New Apostolic Reformation Is Shaking Up the Church as We Know it.* Ventura, CA: Regal, 1996.

Weaver, John. *The New Apostolic Reformation: History of a Modern Charismatic Movement.* Jefferson, NC: McFarland, 2016.

Wimber, Carol. *John Wimber: The Way It Was.* London: Hodder & Stoughton, 1999.

Wimber, John. "Letter from John Wimber to Jamie Buckingham." *The Buckingham Report*, July-August, 1990.

———. "Notice of Withdrawal of Endorsement from the Toronto Airport Vineyard." Letter sent to all Vineyard churches, December 13, 1995.

———. *Power Healing.* San Francisco: Harper & Row, 1987.

———. "A Response to Pastor Ernie Gruen's Controversy with Kansas City Fellowship." *Equipping the Saints* (Fall 1990) 4–7.

———. "Unity and the Withdrawal of Endorsement from the Toronto Blessing." *Vineyard Reflections* (July 1996) 1–4.

Wright, Eric E. *Strange Fire? Assessing the Vineyard Movement and the Toronto Blessing.* Durham: Evangelical, 1996.

Wright, Nigel G. "The Kansas City Prophets: An Assessment." *Themelios* 17 (1991) 20–21.

www.ingramcontent.com/pod-product-compliance
Lightning Source LLC
Chambersburg PA
CBHW032051220426
43664CB00008B/956